MAKING SENSE OF DEVELOPMENT

MAKING SENSE OF DEVELOPMENT

An introduction to classical and contemporary theories of development and their application to Southeast Asia

P. W. Preston

Routledge & Kegan Paul
London and New York

First published in 1986 by
Routledge & Kegan Paul Ltd
11 New Fetter Lane, London EC4P 4EE

Published in the USA by
Routledge & Kegan Paul Inc.
in association with Methuen Inc.
29 West 35th Street, New York, NY 10001

Set in Linotron Times, 10 on 11pt
by Input Typesetting Ltd, London
and printed in Great Britain
by Redwood Burn Ltd
Trowbridge, Wiltshire

Library of Congress Cataloging in Publication Data

Preston, P. W. (Peter Wallace), 1949–
Making sense of development.
Bibliography: p.
Includes index.
1. Economic development. 2. Asia, Southeastern—Economic policy.
I. Title.
HD75.P735 1986 338.959 86-6670

British Library CIP Data also available

ISBN 0-7102-0813-8 (c)

For Rose and Beth

Contents

Preface

This text has the aim of introducing readers to the main contemporary theories of development in such a manner as to make clear the following: (1) that contemporary theories of development are constructed with reference to disciplinary traditions of enquiry that stretch back to the major social theorists of the nineteenth century; (2) that theorizing development is, intellectually, a creative, complex and problematical exercise rather than a narrowly technical one; and (3) that current interpretations of the Southeast Asian scene both draw on classical and contemporary theories and are themselves creative, complex and problematical.

The text is organized into four parts which deal, successively, with: the nature of social theory; the work of the classical theorists of the nineteenth century; contemporary theories and their application to Southeast Asia; and, finally, present debates upon both social theory and development theory. The stress throughout is on the active, creative and difficult business of theorizing; that is, of making sense.

Acknowledgments

I wrote this text, over a couple of years, whilst lecturing in the Department of Sociology of the National University of Singapore. I would like to offer my greetings and thanks to my colleagues and students of that time: most especially to my students whose questions and comments both prompted and helped shape this text.

A brief summary of the text

Part 1 The nature of social theorizing

Chapter 1 Social theory

There has been much dispute about the precise intellectual status of social science. In their discussions of the nature of knowledge in general philosophers have distinguished between two broad explanations: 'empiricism' and 'rationalism'. The former view saw knowledge as essentially a product of experience and the latter saw knowledge as essentially a product of thought. This distinction reappears in social science: there are those who think that social science is (or ought to be) like natural science and is thus essentially concerned with reporting how things are; and there are those who think social science is a variety of social philosophy and thus concerned with interpretive understanding. Both approaches make characteristic claims for the strengths of their views and each vigorously criticizes the other. This present text is constructed from a position of adherence to the latter tradition.

Gellner offers an example of a piece of work within the rationalist tradition, and is concerned to offer a general theory of modernization: the way he argues his case is of interest. Gellner reviews existing philosophical and sociological explanations of change and, having indicated their respective strengths and weaknesses, goes on to advocate a science – both natural and social-based politics of the transition to the modern world. The process of becoming modern can be understood as a species of scientific problem and can be ordered as a social-science-informed practical political task: for the industrializing nations of the Third World political power must rest with an industrializing elite.

Gellner's text opens up three further general matters: methods of change; morals of change; and models of change. All of these have been extensively discussed in the social scientific literature; and in the work of any one theorist these three elements will be present.

Part 2 Classical social theory and social change

Chapter 2 Marx and the dialectics of historical change

The arguments of Marx in respect of the dynamics of the capitalist system can be elucidated via: his ethic, his method and his discussions of capitalism.

The key to Marx's ethic can be found in the idea of alienation: the idea that humankind has become estranged from its true nature but might now overcome this condition. Human beings are taken to create themselves and their societies in and through their creative labour, and consequently a just and rational society is one that acknowledges this and is organized accordingly. A productive system that degrades human labour into mere work is a system of alienated labour.

Marx's method rests upon his 'materialist conception of history': it is an approach rather than an elaborated doctrine and its essence is the claim that people make their own lives in their productive activity. This productive activity is taken to be the central business of human social life and around it other more abstract concerns cluster. Marx uses the distinction between economic base and social superstructure. Any society can be analysed in terms of its characteristic economic base and associated superstructure.

Marx analyses bourgeois capitalism in line with this ethic and method: he looks to uncover the dynamic of the system and does so via a critical reconstruction of English political economy. Simplifying matters, there are two aspects to his analysis. (1) The economic dynamic: here Marx presents his analysis of capitalism characterized as centring on the private control of social production. Periodic economic crises serve to purge the system of unwanted production and capacity and they also have the effect of fostering unrest. (2) The social dynamic: here Marx presents his dichotomous model of class conflict such that class conflict between bourgeoisie and proletariat will serve to bring about those changes in society which the maturation of the economic base makes possible. The trend of history is towards the radical reconstruction of the capitalist system: the abolition of class society and the overcoming of the division of labour and thus of alienation.

Marx paid attention to the society of nineteenth-century Europe, and he had relatively little to say about the Third World. Subsequent theorists, however, have made use of his work to discuss development and underdevelopment, and the school of dependency theory is in direct line of descent from Marx.

Chapter 3 Durkheim and the evolution of the division of labour

Durkheim analyses nineteenth-century society in terms of the notion of the division of labour and he is concerned to argue that the moral order of contemporary society is changing: away from traditional ties of community towards the more informal ties of a society committed to notions of individualism. The normal state of affairs of a complex division of labour is one of organic solidarity secured by the new moral code of individualism. This ethic is to be reinforced via the establishment of guilds which will both regulate the behaviour of individuals and simultaneously make evident to them the nature of their contribution to the social whole. This is a corporatist strategy.

Durkheim's work, with its evolutionism and its concern for social life as a systemic phenomenon, has been influential within social science generally in the form of 'structural functionalism', and within development studies in particular in the form of modernization theory. It is modernization theory which is the most influential post-Second World War theory of development and it owes much to the work of Durkheim.

Chapter 4 Max Weber and the rationalization of the world

Throughout his life Weber was preoccupied with the nature of capitalism and with the development of capitalism in Germany, where he was concerned to argue for a political role for the German bourgeoisie. Weber's starting-point for enquiry was the individual: in this he opposed both Durkheim and Marx. In his early work on landed estates in Prussia he is at pains to elucidate the non-economic motives of the peasantry and to urge a course of action on the government which was politically rather than economically determined. Historically, Germany was constructed 'from the top down' by Bismarck and the key issue is whether the German bourgeoisie is mature enough to take control. Weber's 'ultimate value commitment' was to the future of Germany, for he was a committed nationalist.

Weber broadens his interest in the development of capitalism in his text *The Protestant Ethic*, where he argues against the mechanistic marxists for an effective, if restricted, role for ideas in history. Again there is a distinction being advanced between economic forces and politically willed action.

In his later systematic sociology the nature of human action is pursued and a series of ideal-types of action are sketched. Also presented is a more systematic political sociology and here Weber diagnoses capitalism as both tending to the bureaucratically conservative and thus in need of periodic injections of charismatic authority, and as symptomatic of the historical process of rationalization. Weber, in contrast to both Durkheim and Marx, sees no progressive trend in history.

Weber's work has subsequently been subject to various misunderstandings and the major one of these is that he refuted Marx by identifying a role for ideas in history. In post-Second World War development theorizing, Weber has been used to analyse the cultures of non-Western societies and his extensive studies of Eastern religions have been vulgarized into the claim that non-Western cultures are defective and needs must remake themselves on the model of the West.

Part 3 Contemporary theories of development

Bourgeois liberal theories

Chapter 5 Growth theory

Growth theory is constructed in the immediate period following the Second World War. The influence of Keynes on growth theory is extensive: he identifies and justifies the interventionist role of government and extensions to his work prepared by Harrod identify the possibility in theory of long-term growth. Political pressure flowing from the desire of the USA to order the post-war world, plus nationalist developmentalism and the influence of the example of the Marshall Plan, coincide to call forth a theory of growth applicable to the Third World. Its early formulations are the 1951 UN report and Lewis's 1955 text. Both are Keynesian in inspiration and focus on economics: matters of culture and society are included as 'social factors of growth'. The idea of development is conceived narrowly: it is evidenced in economic growth (and appropriate societal change) which is called forth by the application of the technical scientific knowledge of (Western) economic experts (and their co-workers). A relationship of super- and sub-ordination is thus legitimated and responsibility for the future reserved for the experts of the West.

Chapter 6 Modernization theory

Modernization theory replaces growth theory in the context of Cold War competition between superpowers for influence in the Third World: the USA offers 'modernization' to combat the USSR's offers of 'socialism'. The US theory is thus the ideological child of 'containment'.

Modernization theory rests upon a concern for economic growth. However, where Harrod was pessimistic, Solow's reworking of economic growth models generates an optimistic scheme: economic growth is relatively easily obtainable. Any radicalism in Keynes's work is now removed as neo-classicism is reasserted. But most importantly, the theory of modernization makes widespread use of the social sciences generally: sociology, psychology, anthropology, history, and so on.

Modernization theory rests on a definite theory of social change. It makes use of neo-evolutionist models of stable change: a manoeuvre which effectively removes change altogether. Ideas drawn from structural functionalist sociology are used to elaborate a distinction between 'traditional' and 'modern' societies. Modernization is the business of losing one set of attributes and gaining the other. The ethic of modernization theory is a naive liberal democracy, and the 'modern' is the image of the West in general and the USA in particular writ large.

Modernization theory reaches its apogee in Rostow's *The Stages of Economic Growth* in which he posits a five-stage shift from 'traditional' to 'modern' and simultaneously claims to have refuted Marx's theorems.

Chapter 7 Dissenting economics: neo-institutionalism

Within the broad body of the orthodox tradition of economics there can be identified a well-established and distinguished line of dissent. The form taken by dissenting economics varies from theorist to theorist but generally they have it in common that they reject the free-market assumptions of the orthodoxy and, instead, argue that any real appreciation of economic systems must pay considerable attention both to social and cultural circumstances and to the practical problems that confront societies.

Institutional economics, one version of dissenting economics, are associated with the early-twentieth-century European social theorist Thorstein Veblen who was a stern critic of liberal market societies. In the 1930s neo-institutionalism was closely associated with Roosevelt's New Deal programme to alleviate the effects of the Great Depression. Myrdal, the noted theorist of development, argues in a similar way.

Arguing out of the general background of the experience of European decolonization, Myrdal advances the idea of 'circular cumulative causation' – by which he means that social systems once set on a particular direction tend to adjust, automatically, so as to reinforce that tendency. It is a notion of social inertia. As regards the Third World, these societies are seen as lodged in a debilitating position in the world economy and as crippled by outmoded social forms. The remedy is state planning so as to shift the societies on to new upward tracks of change.

Chapter 8 After modernization

Modernization theory represented, for a period, something like a consensus within orthodox development studies. That consensus has now broken down. The present concerns of orthodox development studies can be grasped with the label 'international Keynesianism'. The key idea is of global interdependence and there are two major areas of concern: first, the 'rules of the game' with which we can associate calls for the New International Economic Order (NIEO); and, second, the transfer and use of resources with which we can associate the idea of basic needs.

The NIEO presented in the United Nations (UN) is a series of proposals for the reform of the world economic system. Around the idea of global interdependence the NIEO attempts to shift the balance of economic power towards the Third World. Trade reforms, monetary reforms, resource transfers, debt relief, technology transfer, and so on – all these concerned the proponents of the programme. At the present time, the programme is stymied.

The idea of basic needs derives from a utopian Latin American group concerned with arguing that a little more equality in the world would mean rather less poverty and a much easier development task. A 'basic needs' approach found favour with international agencies. Aid is to be channelled to 'those who most need it'. Basic needs are claimed to be obviously acceptable targets for help, urgent, and amenable to authoritative expert treatment. The fundamental strategy of orthodox interventionism is here repeated and, as might be expected, the approach has been seen by some as an excuse for First World interference in the affairs of Third World nation states.

Chapter 9 Monetarism

Monetarism can be understood as the economic doctrine of political conservatism in the West. Derived from the nineteenth-century 'Quantity Theory of Money', it has been the vehicle for a counter-attack upon Keynesianism. The approach has been much discussed in Latin America and dependency theory was constructed, at least in part, in opposition to monetarist views. The doctrine of monetarism is presently influential in the West: the position is pro-free market and anti-Keynesian-style intervention. The role of the state is reduced to providing the framework within which a laissez-faire market can operate. In those Third World countries where it has been official policy, there have been efforts to open up the economies to free trade and to encourage free enterprise. There have also been reductions in the social programmes of governments, plus the suppression of political movements of the left. The logic of monetarism is economically suspect and its political philosophy is a crude nineteenth-century liberalism.

Marxist theories

Chapter 10 Latin American dependency theory

Prior to the depression of the 1930s Latin America had played the role of primary-product exporter. However, government response to the depression, and subsequent war years, had the effect of encouraging import-substituting industrialization. After the end of the Second World War this situation was theorized by Prebisch and the social scientists of the Economic Commission for Latin America (ECLA). Ricardian ideas of international specialization and trade were rejected and industrialization was urged. Structuralist economics were produced and these aimed to model local disintegrated economies so that local governments could plan effectively. Structuralism fell out of favour as the drive to industrialization faltered and critics came to stress the radical political implications of the centre/periphery motif. Dependency theory emerged from this process of re-emphasis.

A noted theorist was Furtado, who advanced two general sets of reasons for underdevelopment in Latin America. First, external dependency – the legacy of history and colonialism. Second, internal political and social stasis – this too is seen as the legacy of the past. The upshot of this view is that Latin America has come to occupy a position of subordinate incorporation in the world economy and that development will require social reform as a prerequisite for the effective removal of external dependency.

Chapter 11 Neo-marxism and Paul Baran

Contemporary marxian enquiry into the issue of development has been heavily influenced by the particular context of the social scientific rediscovery of Marx in the late 1960s. This was a period of political and social conflict in the First World and it was an activist Marx who was represented.

This activist movement, when it came to theorize development, made reference to Paul Baran and thence to the intellectual tradition of marxism. Neo-marxism can be considered as the third major attempt within the marxian tradition to theorize development. First there was the work of Marx and Engels themselves, then the work of 'classic imperialism' – Lenin in particular – and finally neo-marxism.

The neo-marxian line revolves around the work of Baran, who speaks of monopoly capitalism which he analyses in terms of the idea of economic surplus. Monopoly capitalism, argues Baran, cannot realize the potential of modern economies and is, moreover, irrational and wasteful. Baran analyses the situation of the Third World in terms of how local economic surplus is realized and used: like the dependency theorists, he diagnoses subordinate and deforming incorporation within a world capitalist economy. The key to development is via socialist revolution and disengagement from the world capitalist economy. Baran's work has been much criticized by subsequent theorists who have tended to talk about 'left Keynesianism'.

Chapter 12 A. G. Frank

Frank's work is fashioned by the experience of Latin America in general and Cuba in particular, and he makes use of the work of Baran in order to fashion a quite distinct scheme.

Frank's work revolves around the idea that the capitalist system is beset by deepseated contradictions. Three contradictions relevant to analysing development are identified: expropriation/appropriation of economic surplus – the surplus of the many is seized by the few and this relationship extends in a chain-like fashion from the poorest landless peasant right up to the centres of metropolitan power; metropolis/satellite polarization – the immanent tendency of capitalism to centralization has issued in a division in the world between centres and peripheries; continuity in change – Latin America has been capitalist ever since the Conquistadors and it has only ever changed its surface form and not its real nature. Frank's vision is of a general world capitalist market with the peripheral areas locked into a position of debilitated subordination. The only hope he sees is through revolutionary socialism.

Frank has been heavily criticized by marxists and it has been suggested that the entire neo-marxian line can properly be regarded as having presented a 'mechanico-formal inversion' of the orthodoxy.

Chapter 13 Post-neo-marxism

There has been much debate within the marxian camp recently as to what is to count as a properly marxian analysis of development and underdevelopment. Roughly speaking, there are two tendencies: a deterministic and economistic line and a voluntaristic line which stresses political activity. These two tendencies can be associated with the ideas of, respectively, modes of production and specificity of enquiry.

The idea of mode of production comes from Althusser's reading of Marx: it is used to designate a particular sort of social production. Thus, the Third World is taken to comprise many modes of production: these can coexist with each other for long periods and the business of the transition from one pre-capitalist mode of production to the capitalist mode is typically a long-drawn-out and complex business. The idea of a sequence of modes of production discernible in Marx is thus revised and the question becomes how do differing modes interact. The value of this approach is much debated. The rather scientific notion of marxism affirmed issues in a tendency to produce elaborately detailed formal schemes.

The insistence upon specificity of enquiry is characteristic of the work of Cardoso and Faletto, who take from Marx the idea of political economic enquiry. They argue that this is a total approach to analysing society. In contrast to the orthodoxy with its many sub-divisions and distrust of ethics, political economy is concerned to make sense of the world in a thoroughgoing practical and political fashion.

Cardoso and Faletto analyse the present situation of Latin America in terms of the particular balances of class forces in history. At the present time, peripheral dependent capitalism is diagnosed and the authors proceed to analyse present-day balances of class forces: it is on the basis of such knowledge that alternatives to dependency can be identified. As with the mode of production approach, Cardoso and Faletto seek to go beyond the analytical schemes of Frank. Sensitivity to particular circumstances and to the legacy of Marx are stressed.

Orthodox and radical views of Southeast Asia

Chapter 14 Analysing Southeast Asia

The application of modernization theory to Southeast Asia is illustrated in four areas: political, economic, social and religious modernization. In each of these areas the concern for the shift from traditional to modern societies is displayed, as is the preoccupation of these theorists for scientificity of formulation. A series of 'summary judgments', in the modernization theory style, of the principal Southeast Asian nation states serves as a concluding note.

The application of the marxist view to Southeast Asia is illustrated in terms of discussions of the world-system context, the local economic base, and the local superstructure. The preoccupation of the marxists with the role of the state and local bourgeois as agents of international capitalism in the exploitation of local economies and societies is made clear. The chapter concludes with a series of 'summary judgments' similar to those offered on behalf of modernization theory.

Part 4 Making sense of development

Chapter 15 Lessons for the future?

The lessons of the post-Second World War career of development studies are considered in this final – rather more speculative – chapter. It is suggested that there are two sets of lessons. First, in respect of the nature of social theorizing itself, it is argued that this should be seen as a diversity of loosely related modes of enquiry with social scientific, scholarly, thought centred not on the familiar model of the natural sciences but, rather, upon the 'dispassionate pursuit of the truth' and (substantively) following traditions of thought established in their modern guise in the nineteenth century. Second, in respect of theorizing development, it is argued that the goal of provision of technical recipes for ordering change is now giving way to a richer appreciation of: (1) the complexity of the business of making sense of development; (2) the variety of particular interests in the matter; and (3) the linkages of present debates to the older, classical, tradition of social theorizing.

Part 1
The nature of social theorizing

Preamble

This study is concerned to argue that theorizing development in Southeast Asia is a complex business: it is appropriate to begin with some remarks on the nature of social theorizing *per se*. Accordingly, in Part 1 I will look at two broad conceptions of the nature of social theorizing: the natural-science-inspired pursuit of accurate descriptions (empiricism) and the philosophically inspired pursuit of plausible understanding (rationalism). The positive claims, typical problems and judgments of competitors of each approach will be noted.

A specimen text, that of Gellner, will be examined so as to open up the systematically debated social science concerns for models, morals and methods of change. At the conclusion of this brief enquiry into the philosophy of social science it will be clear that the author's preferences are for the 'rationalist' tradition – hence the title of the text.

1 Social theory

Approaches to theorizing: empiricism versus rationalism

The business of social theorizing encompasses a wide variety of activities. All these activities have it in common that they are attempts to make sense of the social world. Thus we can say that the term 'social theorizing' is a generic, or very general, one and that social theorizing is essentially about making sense of social situations. So we may instance, by way of examples, the following: literature and the arts; political and ethical schemes; the world of common sense; and the realm of formal social sciences, and so on.

Each of these, very diverse, ways of 'making sense' has its own procedures and goals;[1] and, inevitably, there has been dispute about precisely how these various strategies of making sense should proceed.

I will concentrate upon social science, our particular concern, and present two different views on the nature of academic social science theorizing: these two views each have different ideas about the nature, possibilities and problems of social science. Each view is informed by a particular philosophical theory about the nature of knowledge in general. These positions can be called 'empiricism' and 'rationalism' and in this chapter I will look at three points: first, the dispute as it appears within philosophy; second, the problems that typically associate with each position as they appear in social science; and, third, I look at the positive claims made for each position within the social sciences.

Within treatments of the history of philosophy authors sometimes find it convenient to identify two lines of thinking as to the *basis* of knowledge. On the one hand, there are those who argue that fundamentally knowledge comes primarily from experience, and that if we would be 'wise' then we had best go out and look at the world. On the other hand, there are those who argue that knowledge comes primarily from thought, and that if we would be 'wise' then we had better sit down to some serious thinking about the world. This is a bit of a caricature: usually in any one philosophical treatment of knowledge there is a mix of these elements. None the less, they have been used as general labels for particular dispositions: the one designating those who 'look to experience' (empiricism), the other those who 'look to thought' (rationalism).

With the 'invention' of social science through the nineteenth century these very general epistemological (theory of knowledge) views found expression, as one would expect, in the formulations of the new discipline. The presently identifiable divergent 'schools' within social science came into being at the same time as the discipline and reflect, in some small measure, the disputes within philosophy. For my purposes I present these two 'schools' of social science as follows: on the one hand, we have those who think that social science is, or ought to be, like natural science (where this is conceived in an empiricist way); and, on the other hand, we have those who think that social science is best read as a variety of social philosophy (where this is taken as tending to the rationalistic).[2]

Natural science as it is conceived by the proponents of the orthodoxy of social science, and in 'lay' or common-sense notions, presents itself as the collection of facts, the preparation of descriptive generalizations, and finally, the presentation of summary theoretical statements. Few theorists in social science would offer quite such a crude scheme today; none the less, it represents the unspoken common sense of social science. And it is this model that is invoked by those who would make social science like natural science.

Thus they confront the problem of collecting facts. In the natural sciences this seems to be straightforward; observation may require high technology but it is basically a matter of the measurement of the real world. Not so in social science: where are the equivalent 'facts' in the web of human relationships that is the subject-matter of social science? Taking measurements of the social world looks to be a difficult task even after you have decided that it is possible.

Similar problems confront the proponent of the orthodoxy when it comes to presenting the 'results' of observation. The detail of the social world does not lend itself, in the way detail of natural scientific enquiry does, to quantification and statistical analysis. People in groups typically inhabit a realm of meanings, hopes and fears, intentions, etc., whereas natural science deals with physical causes and effects. Translating the substance of social life into quantified and manipulable data is not just technically difficult: it is philosophically problematical. The orthodox either ignore all this, or resolve to try very hard to be 'objective'.

This brings us to a major related worry: that of the extirpation of value-seepage. The orthodox take natural science to be value-free, which is to say that the results of natural science are ethically and politically neutral. Clearly this is a plausible claim – even if it looks rather strained when one thinks of, say, research into weapons technology – but can the same claim be made in social science? The results of social science work evidently do have ethical and political relevance – so how can the social scientist be sure that values are not creeping into the research and biasing it this way or that? The orthodox worry about being 'objective' and value-neutral and they draw a clear distinction between science and ideology. It is ideology that lies at the foot of that slippery slope which opens up if the unwary social scientist becomes embroiled in value-laden work.

The issue which summarizes, for the orthodox, all these various insecurities in respect of their intellectual status, is that of the maturity/immaturity of social science. Taking note of the continuing argument within social science as to how it ought properly to proceed, the orthodox suggest that this squabble will subside when social science attains scientific maturity. This is a matter, it is said, of methodological, procedural and conceptual refinement. The continuing debate is evidence of immaturity, and in particular of a failure to off-load political and ethical concerns.

So much for the problems of those who would make social science like natural science. Let us now turn to those who would make social science a variety of social philosophy: they rather tend to affirm a rationalist epistemology. The active, creative contribution of thought to knowledge is stressed. Additionally, it is claimed that the advocates of the orthodoxy have a very restricted idea of science. It is suggested that they place far too much emphasis on scientific *experimental* procedure: their epistemology is swamped by considerations of a particular method. The 'rationalists' affirm a notion of science as *disciplined enquiry* and the split between science and ideology is denied. This creates the intellectual space for various disciplines, including social science, to lay claim to be producing knowledge without having to apologize for the manner of the production of their work – without, that is, feeling that the absence of an experimental procedure entails a reduced intellectual status.

In social science, conceived as a variety of social philosophy, the typical problems are these: starting-points, theoretical frameworks, criteria of truth and validity (relativism) and, in the background, the business of ranking competing schemes. Those who make social science a variety of social philosophy see the business of social theorizing as, centrally, *making sense* of the world so as to be able to act in it. The discipline aspires to an *interpretive* (and sometimes critical) knowledge rather than, as with orthodox schemes and natural science, a *descriptive* knowledge.

An initial problem for this (central) view concerns starting-points: what premisses are arguments which interpret the world to be based upon? Premisses have to be appropriate to given circumstances and problems. This seems to entail, generally, providing a set of premisses that are both coherent and explanatorily rich enough to accomplish interpretation. More particularly, this might involve: intelligible accommodation to the facts as they are ordinarily understood; and the illumination of the possibilities for the future in a way relevant to present practice.

A related problem concerns the matter of theoretical frameworks, ordered sets of premisses. In this 'school', theory is *not* a summary statement; it is, rather, the set of premisses deployed in order to make sense of the world. Theoretical frameworks tell us what sort of a world we have, what sort of explanations to provide, of which particular problems. Consequently, this 'school' is very concerned with theoretical frameworks, for once you accept the premisses of an argument you are bound, if it is valid in form, to accept the conclusions.

A central issue for those who affirm a notion of social philosophy is that of the use of the concept of ideology. The term can be used in a variety of ways: one of these is to designate those general, interpretive arguments designed to make politically relevant sense of the world. An issue that flows out of this area is that of rationally adjudicating between competing schemes.

In sum, for the orthodox the production of knowledge is essentially a matter of reporting how things are, and problems tend to cluster around accuracy of reports. For the social philosophers the production of knowledge is essentially a matter of generating interpretive understanding; the business has many guises, and problems cluster around the *making* of sense (by whom, how, when and what for?).

Turning to my final point it may be asked: what do the proponents of these two 'tendencies' claim as the *strengths* of their positions? Here the orthodoxy, those who invoke natural science, tell us that they produce a scientific-type knowledge that enables the social world to be organized in an authoritative way. Knowledge is the possession of the *expert*. In Western industrial societies much social scientific work, conceived in this fashion, feeds into the state planning machines, or corporations. And, on the other hand, the counter-tradition, who invoke social philosophy, see academic social theorizing as one activity amongst many which are concerned to make sense of the world. As academics, they are concerned to display the truth – and when they deal with society they often discover an interpretive role: making the actions of one group intelligible to themselves and to other groups.

These two approaches ('rationalism' and 'empiricism') and their associated social science approaches are not sharply exclusive approaches – they are 'tendencies' and both elements will be found in some proportion in the work of any one theorist. Most *do* lean clearly one way or the other – few inhabit the middle ground. In this text I will understand social science in this 'rationalist' or 'social philosophy' style. Academic social science is interpretive and concerned to display the truth disinterestedly. My view is that orthodox, 'empiricist' sociology is too narrow in conception. These sociologists' detailed descriptive work is valuable and useful; but the claim that was often made to the effect that empiricist sociology was the *only* legitimate sociology is false. However, let us now look at this business of social theorizing from another perspective.

Creative and prospective social theorizing: the example of Ernest Gellner

Gellner's book *Thought and Change* (1964) is an example of the social-philosophical-type social science that I have spoken of above. His work is interesting for a number of reasons, but, for the moment, I am interested not so much in what he says, but in how he says it.

Gellner's major concern, in *Thought and Change*, is to display the nature of a politics relevant to the industrializing/industrial present. Clearly this is an interpretive role and not just (as the orthodox empiricists would enjoin) descriptive: morals of change, models of change and methods of ordering change are all explicitly invoked and intermingled. This explicitness makes the total process 'self-conscious': *how* to theorize is a continuous concern. Gellner argues that sociology is, or should be regarded as, the heir of classical political philosophy because it now asks those questions central to both conceptualizing and legitimating modern society – sociology seeks to elucidate the nature of industrialism. Clearly this is a bold, and very interesting, claim and it is one that lodges him firmly within the European tradition. However, for our immediate purposes Gellner's text is of interest because: (1) he declares his goal, his intention, which is to rework political philosophy (which now embraces 'sociology') for the tasks of the present day; (2) he openly reviews and plunders the intellectual resources of his discipline – reworking available ideas to suit his declared intention; (3) he explicitly discusses how to theorize his problem once he has sketched its outline; (4) finally, he goes on to identify *some* of the more obvious consequences of his newly constructed position. In sum, Gellner's work is clearly that of an intellectual craftsman addressing complex and urgent practical problems. To put this another way – Gellner is in the business of making sense, he presents an argued case designed to interpret the world so as to guide action in it. (His addressees, those at whom his remarks are primarily aimed, are the intellectuals/planners/bureaucrats of complex modern industrial society.)

An outline of Gellner's argument might be useful at this point. Gellner reviews existing philosophical and sociological theories of change and, having indicated their respective strengths and weaknesses, goes on to advocate a science-based (natural and social) politics of 'the transition': the shift to the modern world. The process of industrializing can be understood as a species of scientific problem, and can be ordered as a species of social-science-informed practical (political) work. For the industrializing Third World nations political power must rest with an industrializing elite – Western-trained and/or Western-oriented. For the West, coming perhaps towards the later phases of 'the transition', this elitist, corporatist model of politics is muted (somewhat). Gellner's overall vision is revealed in his expectation of the future character of ideology (interpretive schemes) – there will be a dual system of explanation (of the social world): (1) broad, vague, legitimating slogans for the masses; (2) detailed scientific knowledge (natural and social) as the actual basis for ordering society – the property of the elite. Now we can turn to Gellner's argument – and concern ourselves with *how* he goes about assembling it.

Gellner is a political philosopher and sociologist. Writing in the mid-1960s, before the optimism of the period had declined, he attempts to redraw the boundaries of political philosophy. His desired goal in attempting this reorientation is to accommodate political philosophy to the requirements of the industrialism/convergence/modernization debate.

He aims to offer a general statement which presents the key ideas of this relatively new, and, at that time, very plausible, theoretical departure. His presentation also sketches out some of his proposals' main problem areas – he is a sophisticate and a scholar: he feels no need to offer routine condemnations of all things 'left', nor does he feel obliged to be overly enthusiastic about his own material.

Gellner begins (Chapter 1) with the claim that any society has, and inevitably needs, a scheme which will render that society's form and apparent historical direction both coherent and legitimate in the eyes of its inhabitants. An explanatory ideology, in other words.

In the Western world this has, since the Renaissance's reworking of mystical (religious) ideals of perfectability, typically been a notion of social progress. Often these matters have been discussed historically,[3] but Gellner presents another route through this material: he offers a schematic reconstruction. There are three forms of the idea of progress. Each has a philosophic and historical character, each has explanatory benefits and disbenefits. Gellner wants a scheme for the present. He identifies the following.

(1) *The episodic view*: there is, in world history, one move from a bad state of affairs to a good state. For example, the making of the 'social contract'. Sociologically, these schemes are unsophisticated. It is, historically, typically Enlightenment material.

(2) *The evolutionist view*: there is, in world history, an all-embracing and permanent process of cumulative progressive change. This is typically a nineteenth-century line. It tends to be associated with Darwin, but the extent to which Darwin both contributed to, and, less obviously remarked, borrowed from the social theorists is problematic. Gellner identifies three defects: (i) locating an event in a series does not explain it; (ii) a moral judgment has to be more than affirming the trend otherwise you run into the problem of the incoherence of affirming determinism; (iii) the scheme does not fit the experience of the Third World – this for Gellner is important as it is the experience of (debates on) the Third World that provides a learning method for everyone.

(3) *The neo-episodic view*: in Chapter 2, Gellner goes on to offer this, the outline of his new legitimating 'myth' of progress. It is constructed by selectively reworking the above-noted schemes. From the episodic theory he takes the idea of progress as an *event*, and from the evolutionist scheme the idea of progress as a *pervasive continuing process*. These two are run together in his neo-episodic stance which affirms that the politics of today must focus upon the *episode of progress* – that is, industrialism.

Gellner calls this a politics of 'the transition': the whole process is continuing. The episode of progress, this pervasive and continuing process, conceived in Gellner's particular fashion has for him the twin virtues of plausibility and manageability. The neo-episodic scheme posits an event in world history: it is empirically plausible and intellectually it does not expand to fill all available explanatory space.

Having thus far described the general character of the required new 'myth' – or legitimating theorem of modern, industrial society – Gellner proceeds to consider, over the next three chapters, the business of *how* to theorize this new scheme.

He begins, in Chapter 3, by reflecting upon the nature of a moral problem. It is characterized as being a dilemma where the appropriate rules of judgment, as well as judgments of detail, are problematic. We neither know what to think nor how to think. Gellner sees the business of theorizing 'the transition' as being a similar sort of task. 'The transition' will have to be grasped from the inside by the use of scientific thought. Scientific thought, for Gellner, is a qualitatively different sort of thinking from any other: in particular, it is *routinely self-critical*. 'The transition' is science-based and thus potentially self-conscious. It is science that is the key to grasping its character *and* the key to a new 'morality'.

Gellner reviews established, so to say, ethical theories and rejects them all. Thus, in Chapter 4, he looks at the following. (i) *Platonic*: concepts give standards as they classify the world; thus the notions 'gentleman', 'bride', 'court of law' both designate the character of phenomena and set limits of variation. (ii) *Hidden prince*: inside every man is a good man trying to get out: society is alienating. The young Marx is offering a version of this ethic. (iii) *Dream of the bureaucrat*: life is conceived as exemplifying rules; ethics are rules. (iv) *Way of residue*: a complementary ethic to (ii); here the goal is not specified but a series of obstacles are – so remove them. (v) *Supreme target*: behaviour is purposeful – therefore set a supreme purpose and rank intervening ones. Utilitarianism is an example. (vi) *The rail*: argument that freedom is the recognition of necessity. In history there is a fixed process – accept it. In this context, Gellner cites historicist schemes. Gellner then presents his ethic, industrialism: in the short term we *can* discern the future, it is an industrial society and a world free of want. He complements ethics (v) and (vi) taken *short term* – they seem to make his ethic of 'the transition'.

In Chapter 5, Gellner turns to matters of *method*. He looks to his philosophy of science. He starts by noting that social arrangements have often been legitimated in a dualistic fashion, by invoking parallel worlds. These are now out of fashion and there are now two favoured strategies: (1) centring explanatory theorems upon 'the totality'; and (2) centring theorems upon the individual.

Gellner rejects strategy (1) – it is liable to slide into general evolutionist nonsense – and affirms strategy (2). Here is the core of his Popperian liberalism: a celebration of the method of science. Enquiry is to proceed by the systematic elimination of error – the programme is limited in its formal claims, but hugely optimistic in respect of its possibilities. This 'science' encompasses both natural and social scientific concerns.[4]

In the wake of 'the transition', Gellner expects ideology to wither away. Why? Gellner points to: (1) fact of affluence, which reduces social tension; and (2) character of scientific thinking. Gellner sees a social system comprising (for presently relevant purposes) two sorts of thinking. There will be very general and vague legitimating ideas. The implication is that these ideas will virtually be mere noise. There will also be scientific thinking. Here the implication is that technical rationality will encompass not merely the natural sciences, but also social and, in particular, policy science. The model of Gellner's future industrial world is of rational order, functionally and hierarchically organized.

This all establishes the core of his stance: he now turns to some 'matters arising'. Gellner (in Chapter 6) acknowledges that there is one philosophy that actually does look at 'the transition' – marxism. The work of Marx, looking at the transition from capitalism to socialism, is undoubtedly the correct strategy. However, the particular concepts chosen are wrong – they should be replaced by those which centre upon the notion of industrialism. The *approach* taken in marxist analyses – the focus upon social structure and conflict in the process of change in the division of labour – is correct.

Then Gellner (in Chapter 7) looks at 'nationalism' and offers a straightforward reading of it. Nationalist sentiment is a functional requisite of the establishment of autonomous capitalisms within the world economy. Just as nationalism was needed 'first time around' to aid the bourgeoisie in establishing itself both internationally and domestically, so new nationalist industrialization elites find the doctrine of assistance. Nationalism is the culture of otherwise fragmented politics. So far as Gellner is concerned, it can be 'nice' or 'nasty' – it is the politics of philosopher kings, the modernizing elite.

Gellner's final chapter looks at the production of social knowledge. It is, he affirms, science that is 'the mode of cognition of industrial society, and industry is the ecology of science':[5] given this, it is the scientist who moves centre stage. The scientist displaces the 'man of letters'. Gellner sees a conflict between the 'sophisticated common sense' of humanist culture and the non-obvious conflicting science. Gellner takes this conflict to be quite profound – at base, there are conflicting views of man. Gellner confidently reports that the humanist image of mankind will be replaced by the scientific–industrial image of man (whatever that is).

In sum, Gellner reveals the essential nature of social scientific theorizing – he offers an interpretation (aimed at a particular group) which makes politically and morally relevant sense of the social world. Gellner's substantive position is that of an 'intelligent modernizer' – the modernization approach we will discuss in Chapters 10–13 of Part 3 of this text – and also close to the 'common sense' of political thinking in the West.

Gellner's work – like all prospective social scientific theorizing – involves morals of change, models of change and methods of ordering change all regarded 'self-consciously'. The elements of morals, models and methods have been extensively discussed in the literature and it will be useful for us to take note of some of these discussions.

Models of change, ethics of change and methods of change

The material presented below will overlap with Gellner's to a degree, but here we note more systematically the main positions on conceptualizing social change that have become familiar within social science. What I will offer, in effect, is a brief survey of the usual range of preoccupations theorists have in discussing 'change'. I will do this first for models of change, and add a note on evolutionism and marxism. Then I will look at morals of change and, finally, at methods of securing change.

Models of change

Many areas of concern within social science are made more difficult than they might otherwise be by the fact that the issues looked at are, at the same time, issues upon which societies' common sense, so to say, has a view. So in discussing change in society we immediately confront the common-sense view that change is all-pervasive and accelerating. This pervasive and accelerating rate of social change is often both (a) contrasted with a more stable past ('the good old days'), and (b) held to be responsible for many present social ills.

Smith[6] considers this type of common-sense view and (correctly) finds it unconvincing. He asks that we distinguish between significant social change and superficial changes in style. As I have said above, in social science we are concerned to grasp 'underlying' or 'significant' social change. Social theorists select amongst the variety of social phenomena according to sets of assumptions (theoretical frameworks): identifying crucial axes of social change can be done only within the context of a particular social *theory*. This, of course, was precisely the strategy adopted by the 'founding fathers'. Thus Marx saw significant social change flowing from class conflict within the progressive development of the mode of production generally. Weber saw significant social change evidenced in the 'disenchantment' of the world – increasing rationalization. Durkheim saw significant social change evidenced in the growing complexity of the division of labour.

Smith goes on to claim that people (including social scientists) are bemused by recent changes of a superficial kind *and*, he adds, by the undoubted major change of the coming of industrialism; furthermore, they are misled into thinking that change is essential to all social systems. If, he argues, we take a broad historical view, and if, he suggests, we recall that in language change is ascribed to a (pre-existent, stable) object, then we see that it is persistence or stability that is fundamental and not change.

However, (a) Smith's argument for the fundamental nature of persistence is unsatisfactory as the surface grammar of language cannot tell us about ontology and, in any case, (b) it is the recent major change to industrialism that is at the centre of social scientific concern. It is *the* key issue, as Gellner noted: theorizing 'the *transition*'. What this area of debate – change versus stability – does is to display some of the problems that attach to the choice of basic metaphors. The 'change versus stability' debate echoes: political radicalism versus political conservatism; optimism versus pessimism; the necessity of social scientific engagement versus the possibility of social scientific general description, etc. Ankie Hoogvelt,[7] dealing with approaches to theorizing development, remarks that what is crucial is the choice between the acceptance of historical change (marxist) and the pursuit of timeless ahistorical formulae (bourgeois).

Social theorizing – the business of making sense, as I have characterized it – is full of the use of metaphor. We inherit these metaphors from earlier generations of thinkers and often their thought comes to us as wholly unremarkable common sense, be it the common sense of society or the common sense of the discipline of learning we follow.

In talking about social change, Smith claims that there are two basic metaphors: *continuity* and *rupture*. Social change is seen as either cumulative, slow, ceaseless, etc., or as violent, discontinuous and periodic. In popular, or journalistic, parlance there is either evolution or revolution.

In respect of continuity we can note that in the nineteenth century evolutionary explanations of social change were frequently presented. It is often said that Darwin was the great influence here, but this is false – schemes of social evolution had been produced before Darwin's biological evolution. Indeed, it has been said recently that Darwin borrowed from the social theorists whilst thereafter lending them greater (superficial) credibility. For example, the social evolutionist Hebert Spencer (early twentieth century) was welcomed in the USA by business circles as they felt he legitimated their unrestrained pursuit of wealth – notions of natural selection and survival of the fittest sat easily with doctrines of economic laissez-faire.

Smith characterizes the logic of evolutionism with five points.[8] (1) *Holism*: the object of enquiry is the 'whole' not the parts, thus the broadest possible approach is taken – 'civilization' or 'culture'. (2) *Cumulative process*: there are no sharp discontinuities. (3) *Endogenous change*: the impetus for change arises from within the system. (4) *Increasing complexity*: there is a shift from simple social forms (traditional) to complex ones (modern). (5) *Unitary direction*: the whole process has a fixed direction. In another text Smith offers seven characteristics, but the gist of his analysis remains the same.[9]

Evolutionism fell into disrepute in the early years of the twentieth century. It was attacked by anthropologists of the 'diffusionist' and 'functionalist' schools: the former calling attention to external forces for change, and the latter pointing to the internal complexity and stability of societies.

Neo-evolutionary approaches were presented in the 1940s and 1950s – a revival of the evolutionist line. Elements of evolutionism, diffusionism and functionalism (especially) are run together into a general approach that claims to be able to explain *stable, ordered, change*. This is neo-evolutionism and it is the basis of theories of modernization.

The reason for Smith's interest in all this, and ours, is that evolutionist-type explanations of social change (and, by extension, development) have been very influential. They have claimed to explain change and identify an overall pattern: however, it seems more plausible to see much evolutionist-type argument of recent years as little more than a celebration of the history of the West (and the USA especially) as *the* model for all social change. The task of the 'underdeveloped' was to repeat the historical trajectory of the West. This is the argument we find in the cruder versions of modernization theory.

In respect of the notion of *rupture* we find a very different view. Here we have schemes of social change which stress the role of social tensions and group (inter and intra) conflict. Change is seen as discontinuous and periodic. Most importantly, we have the marxist school. In place of the pursuit of a theory of ordered and stable change, we have the presentation of a theory which postulates the existence of groups in society having conflicting interests. The interplay of these interests – the historical pattern of conflict – provides the motor for change. The historical world of 'industrialism' is seen as an expansionist capitalist system riven by class conflict.

The classical marxian expectations of the future of capitalism involved its gradual spread across the globe as capitalist entrepreneurs destroyed local ('historically outmoded') social forms and created in their place new centres of capitalist society. This optimistic scheme was modified around the turn of the century when the marxian notion of imperialism was presented. It came to be thought that the capitalist system might be longer-lived than originally anticipated and that peripheral areas might have their development hindered by the interests of the centres. In the post-Second World War period a new analysis of capitalism has been presented: the neo-marxists see an essentially static and stagnating capitalist heartland surrounded by a deformed and dependent periphery.

In summary it can be noted that when we consider social change it is not enough merely to aim to describe changes. The attempt to make sense of social change is central to social science, both now and in the work of the 'founding fathers'. Social change is grasped via a social theory which specifies the *crucial* elements of change.

Ethics of change[10]

Discussions of change within the literature of social science have been, in the main, couched in terms of approval. There are some social theorists who have regretted the rise of industrial society, but these figures are in a minority. The most familiar ethical term associated with discussions of change is 'progress'. This term can be elucidated by identifying the two principal eighteenth- and nineteenth-century versions of it, and from there we can turn to post-Second World War theories of development and identify a series of versions of the idea of progress. All the major theories of development are informed by Western ethics and this raises an obvious question. What have other ethical systems to say about development? I shall briefly consider Islam in the light of this question.

The idea of progress was given recognizably modern formulation in the eighteenth and nineteenth centuries. The term derives from Greek philosophy via Renaissance humanism, and I will not treat the history of the various formulations of the notion. It is the eighteenth- and nineteenth-century formulations that provide the reference-points for subsequent social theoretical uses.

There are two main positions: their political labels would be *liberal democratic* and *(radical) democratic*. The first position analyses society by invoking the specialist social sciences within a general evolutionary framework. The model of man invoked is 'man as consumer'. The ethic is thus not optimistic, the general scheme of historical change is implausible and the whole process is seen as only restrictedly intelligible. In contrast, the second position analyses society by invoking an historical materialist approach. The model of man invoked is 'man as doer'. The ethic is thus optimistic, the analysis of historical change plausible, and the whole process taken as amenable to 'interdisciplinary' enquiry and extensively intelligible.

These two positions form the background to post-Second World War theories of development. Three types of theories can be usefully identified at this point, each having a different idea of what actually counts as progress or development. These three can be labelled 'liberal market', 'social market' and 'radical democratic'.

The earliest group of theorists were those labelled 'liberal market' and their work falls into two parts: an early UK/UN line which was heavily influenced by economics; and a later line which was distinctly a US product and mixed in rather more sociology with the economics. Both versions, however, have it in common that *progress is equated with economic growth*. Development, or progress, is understood as a technical matter and taken as elicited by authoritative social-science-informed intervention and as presenting itself, primarily, in indices of economic growth.[11] The ideological function of this scheme is clear: a relationship of super- and sub-ordination is legitimated whereby the development of the presently underdeveloped is ordered by the experts of the developed countries and their agents.

The 'social market' theorists have it in common that they reject orthodox economics and substitute a 'sociologized economics'. Progress is no longer associated with economic growth, called forth by the application of the technical expertise of the economists, but is conceived more broadly: it becomes equated with planned, ordered, social reform. It is arguably the case that this position – *progress as ordered social reform* – represents the common sense of much of development studies: it is pragmatic, humane and plausible.

The third group, labelled the 'marxists', affirm a radical democratic ethic and a dialectical mode of analysis. The 'neo-marxists', within development studies, attempt to recover what is a rather submerged counter-tradition to the liberal democratic schemes noted above. The model of man affirmed is 'man as doer' and *progress is equated with the pursuit of (radical) democracy*.

Within social sciences the phenomenon of social change has been, in the main, viewed with approval and such approval has been expressed in terms taken from Western ethical schemes. Given that social science was constructed in the West during the period of the industrial revolution, this 'bias' should not surprise us. For our present interests in theorizing development there are two matters to take note of: one concerns the orthodox view of development, the other raises more general questions in respect of ethical systems.

The orthodox (liberal and social market) rather tend to take the whole business of development as being *technical or obvious* (and usually both). In the former case development is conceived as a matter of building appropriate physical, social and economic structures – largely a matter of accumulating a set of characteristics familiar in the experience of the developed nations. In the latter case development is taken to be the fundamentally uncontentious business of organizing decent lives for the presently disadvantaged Third World peoples. Both these views are products of particular episodes in the post-war career of development studies and both are wrongheaded. In opposition to these familiar views I would argue that the notion of development is not technical and certainly not obvious; it is an ethico-political notion and what is going to count as development, in a practical and engaged sense, will inevitably depend upon circumstance-sensitive and problem-specific analyses. What is going to count as development will have to be locally determined: such schemes can then be ranked against the criteria specified above.

This last remark introduces the general ethical question I mentioned above: it might reasonably be asked: must such ranking criteria be couched in terms of Western ethical systems? Indeed, in talking about development might we not make reference to non-Western ethics?

In the last few years one ethical, or religious, scheme has been proposed as a replacement for the Western ethics typically found in discussions of development: the Islamic revival has received much attention, and the notion of an 'Islamic state' has been advanced. Any detailed discussion of this ethic is, clearly, beyond the scope of this text. What I will do is look at the work of a noted Southeast Asian scholar, S. H. Alatas, in order to introduce the general matter of Islam, albeit very simply, and to raise an issue that has generated confusion and heat ever since Weber's seminal presentation of it: the matter of the impact (positive or negative) of religious doctrine upon processes of industrialization.

Alatas[12] addresses the issue of the relationship of religious ideas upon development directly by presenting, and refuting, what he calls the 'Weber thesis'. Alatas is careful to separate out the 'Weber thesis' from the general body of Weber's work. This thesis is then understood as arguing that the Calvinist ethic was the 'decisive and significant'[13] factor in the rise of capitalism. Alatas even speaks of a 'causative'[14] analysis. Weber's studies of oriental religions are noted – and taken as further evidence for the 'Weber thesis'. This straw man is then demolished: Alatas notes that the spirit of capitalism was present before Calvinism, so the 'strong' 'Weber thesis' fails. It is not at all clear whether Alatas would accept a 'weaker' thesis – either in respect of Weber's work or of religious doctrine generally. Thus he notes: 'The capitalist spirit is then viewed as the product of capitalism itself without any need for a religious initiation . . . Non-religious social and cultural factors can exert greater influence in the rise of an economic ethic.'[15]

Alatas then turns to Islam and notes its spread, along with traders, into Southeast Asia. Confusingly, he remarks: 'The point of interest to note is the mutual alliance between Islam and trade in the progress of expansion. This is not an accidental conjunction . . . *It issued forth from the very nature of the Islamic faith.*'[16] The 'Weber thesis' is rejected above – but now an Islamic version is seemingly affirmed. He goes on: 'The traits cited by Weber characterizing the Protestant ethic . . . are all strongly pronounced in the Islamic ethic. There is also the concept of the calling.'[17] At this point Alatas's argument becomes thoroughly confused: it seems that what he wants to say is that analysing Southeast Asia in terms informed by the 'Weber thesis' issues in an untenable pessimism about the chances of fostering development: better, thinks Alatas (if I have correctly diagnosed his thinking), to consider *specific clusters of historical circumstances* (economic, social, cultural, political, etc., factors). With this 'conclusion' I would concur: Alatas's confusion stems, it seems to me, from accepting a wrong view of Weber in the first place.

In a subsequent essay[18] this general theme is represented (with just as much confusion) – but the gist of his discussions is that Islamic ethics (nowhere actually spelt out) are not incompatible with modernization and that in any case it is other sets of circumstances that are really important. In Alatas's view, religious doctrine and industrialization are not incompatible; indeed, most of the time he seems to think they are not at all closely related.

The foregoing remarks have indicated that most social theorists regard change with approval, and that all post-war theories of development have been informed by Western ethics. My discussion of the question of 'other ethics' has been very brief and two general conclusions have been pointed to. First, that religious doctrines *per se* have no very obvious relationship (positive or negative) to the process of becoming industrial. In the literature of sociology it is, it seems to me, a misunderstood Weber that fuels debate on this point of doctrine/industrialization: this matter will be dealt with in Part 2. The second conclusion, which I think we can draw, is that social change is so very complex and religious doctrines so subtle (and amenable to further elaboration) that to suppose that a religious tradition can furnish an ethic amenable to deployment as a social-engineering strategy involves a double process of gross oversimplification.

Ethics are embedded in patterns of social life: and just as social change is a complex phenomenon, so too must be the interaction between formalized ethical notions and wider pressures for change (economic, political, historical, etc.) within any society.

Methods of Change

One of the major preoccupations of the Western tradition of social science has been with understanding mechanisms of social change. It is a fairly short step to a concern for methods of securing change. In a recent text, Giddens[19] has discussed the theoretical ground of any proposal for action to secure change: this centres on the extent to which social change is actively secured rather than experienced passively as the outcome of either structural change or chance events. Giddens talks about this in terms of the exchange between agency and structure.

So when we discuss change one major question is the extent to which identified changes, or desired changes, are to be conceived in terms of willed human actions (active) or social structural forces (passive). We could offer a narrowly pragmatic answer by invoking the notion of scale: thus as we shift from the macro-sociological to micro-sociological realm so we (arguably) tend to shift from passive to active explanations. In which case, studies of development would tend to be couched in terms of structural, passive, change. But this evasive strategy is not very helpful. Nor is the positing of an either/or dilemma as is sometimes found in crude 'Marx versus Weber' type discussions.

What is really at issue is how structure and agency mutually interact; and, in brief, the analysis of any particular set of circumstances will involve some mix of the two explanatory strategies. Thus, for example, we could discuss national development strategies in terms of effective action within the bounds of a particular colonial legacy.

So, in speaking of methods of change, we are obliged to take up a position on the matter of agency and structure. Any willed action will, inevitably, be context-dependent. Setting this issue to one side we can turn to look at the familiar patterns of active pursuit of change within the social world. We can also note, at the outset, that there is one method of securing change that is often discussed within development theory – that is, planned change.

First, though, we can look at group political action, the most obviously active mode of securing change. Such action can be pursued by formally constituted parties in a variety of contexts – some relatively open and some highly restricted. Other forms of 'political' action might include kin groups acting for mutual interest; pressure groups acting for some particular material interest. Also there are groups dissenting from the established order for a variety of reasons: such dissent can take the form of mild protest through to violent rebellion. Evidently, history is littered with examples of these active modes.

In addition to these familiar 'political' patterns development theory has seen a major preoccupation with planning: with deliberately engineered social change having specific goals in mind. The literature of development theory is suffused with the planning imperative – Gellner's text is one such presentation – and this should be noted at the outset as it is a theme that will recur throughout this text.

In sum, in respect of methods of change we must first establish the scope for active change and thereafter the particular social strategy for securing effective change, and these are highly context-specific considerations. However, in this text I will not be offering any recommendations; rather, I will be looking at the proposals of other theorists. And in this case we can usually pick out the method of change a theorist has in mind fairly easily because any theory must have an agent of theory-execution, otherwise there is no way the theory can be translated into practice. For example, Gellner, whom we have met above, offers his theory of 'the transition' – a massive social change that can be grasped scientifically – to the planners and bureaucrats, those in a position authoritatively to manipulate the social world to secure desired goals. This is one example: in the material that follows in Part 2 of this text – which deals with the trio of 'founding fathers' and their various theories of development – this trio of models, morals and methods of change recurs in many guises.

In sum, I have argued that social theorizing is an activity general to human life: it is the business of *making sense* and it presents itself in diverse guises. Concentrating upon social science (itself seen as diverse) I rejected the familiar invocation of the model of the natural sciences. Distinguishing between European 'social philosophical' and US 'empiricist positivist' approaches to understanding social science, I noted that it was the social philosophical line that acknowledged the claims for social theorizing I was making. The relationship between the two approaches is asymmetrical: the social philosophical line can understand empiricist positivism as a mode of engagement (manipulative policy science), whereas the empiricist positivist line can only reject the social philosophical line as non-science (nonsense).

The social philosophical line takes social theorizing to revolve around the theory-based interpretation of particular sets of social circumstances: the possibility of a natural science of the social is taken as illusory and its pursuit as ideological in the pejorative sense. An example of prospective interpretive theorizing was presented in the writings of Ernest Gellner, whose work involved the self-conscious mixing of models, morals and methods of change in pursuit of a politics relevant to the present 'transition' to the modern world.

The business of models, morals and methods of change was noted to reveal the typical ways in which these matters have been approached. Taking note of the 'Western ethics' built into theories of development, I introduced the matter of the relationship of religious doctrines to industrialization. I suggested that the relationship was not close and added that invoking particular ethics in a social-engineering fashion was a crudely manipulative procedure. I concluded by noting that the trio of models, morals and methods was present in many versions within theories of development, with schemes oriented to planning a particular favourite.

Part 2
Classical social theory and social change

Preamble

I am interested in presenting the work of the 'founding fathers' for a number of reasons. I shall present their work as being, in my sense, prospective and interpretive: thus my first interest in the material to appear in this section is as a series of illustrations of the claims about theorizing I have been making above. Each theorist makes use of specific intellectual resources, within particular historical circumstances, and each theorizes social change in a distinct way.

Gellner, as we have seen, suggests that *the* problem for social science is making sense of 'the transition' to the modern world. This was the concern of the 'founding fathers'; and their work has shaped subsequent enquiry. Thus when we turn to study the presently available theories of development, we will find that Durkheim and Weber have been used in various ways by theorists of 'modernization', whilst Marx has been represented in the 'dependency' school. It is necessary for a proper understanding of present theories of development that we be sensitive to the intellectual legacies of the 'founding fathers'.

When I treat the work of these theorists I will, following these interests, be concerned only with two general points: showing how the work of each theorist *argues a case*; and displaying the *theory of change* presented.

2 Marx and the dialectics of historical change

Marx, like any other major thinker, can be ‘read’ in more than one way. The obvious readings of Marx are those which centre their treatments on the following. (a) His political intentions (problems tackled): here it can be asked just what sort of analyses did he successively present? (b) His use of established intellectual resources: here the focus shifts to his use of Hegel, English political economy and French socialism. (c) The character and importance of the ‘finished product: here we find exegetical criticism. In these notes I will look at the way Marx argues a particular case in respect of change. I will follow strategies (a) and (b) – though it should be noted that the three listed approaches are not exclusive and most commentators combine them in some fashion or other. I will first look at Marx’s ethic, then his method, and finally his analysis of bourgeois capitalism.[1]

The key to understanding Marx’s ethic is to be found in his discussion of the notion of alienation. There are two ways in which this key idea can be approached; they are closely related but, arguably, one is easier than the other. The two are: (1) via Hegelian idealist philosophy; (2) via Marx’s criticisms of the assumptions of the English political economists.

Worsley[2] points out that in mid-nineteenth-century Germany, philosophy was a central academic discipline and it was the work of Hegel that was most influential. Hegel’s philosophy was idealist: ‘The centrality of thought – of the power of ideas, or as Hegel reified it, the Idea – was the centrepiece in this conception of the world.’[3] Human history was interpreted as the gradual extension of the power of reason: ‘The successive stages in the emergence and maturation of Mind – the human spirit – began with the perception of the immediate situation; then progressed to consciousness of the self; and finally, with the full flowering of

Reason, permitted understanding of the world as a whole, its laws of motion, and the place of humanity in that world.'[4] Hegel's idea of the dynamic self-development of the Idea is essentially progressive; but in his later years, as he became an establishment figure, he adjusted his views. The evolution of the Idea, the extension of reason, had reached its culmination, he argued, in his philosophy and in the Prussian rational state. To his philosophy is attached a political doctrine. The German state was seen as an embodiment of the Idea, or Mind, and from it order was taken to flow. That is, it is the state which pulls society into a coherent unit, and it is the state which identifies the general interest.

Marx thought that Hegel's notions of the dynamism and creativity of thinking (his 'dialectics') were correct; but he did not accept Hegel's idealism or his (eventual) political conservatism. We can trace Marx's reworkings of Hegel around two issues: religion and the denial of idealism; and the state and the denial of conservative authoritarianism.

Hegel's general philosophical system is essentially religious: if we substitute the word 'God' for the word 'Idea' then we have the following scheme. World history is the story of God's self-loss and subsequent rediscovery via the extension of reason. The Idea migrates into the material (the ideal becomes base): the internal dynamic of the material issues in the rediscovery of the Idea (human beings, *thinking* beings, extend rationality until it culminates in the rediscovery of the Idea). In German idealist terms the process can be formally characterized as follows: *reification* – thought becomes thing-like; *estrangement* – the original thought becomes lost; *alienation* – the original is now wholly other; *supersession of alienation* – alienation is overcome in rediscovery.

Hegel's remarkable general idealist system was attacked by a group, of which Marx was a member, called 'The Young Hegelians' (or 'Left Hegelians'). One line of attack focused upon religion – and thus idealism. The philosopher Feuerbach argued that far from the world and humankind having been created by God (or being emanations of the Idea) it was, in fact, humankind that made the gods: 'the gods, far from creating humanity and determining its fate, were themselves idealized creations of human thought, but of erroneous human thought.'[5] This same inversion of the true state of affairs is expressed, in Giddens's exegesis, thus: 'God is a fantasized being upon whom man has projected his own highest powers and faculties, who is thus seen as perfect and all-powerful, and in contrast to whom man himself appears as limited and imperfect.'[6] Feuerbach's critique was very influential: he substituted human beings for God, or the Idea, and he proposed that his philosophical system replace that of Hegel.

Marx found Feuerbach's strategy of 'inverting Hegel' fruitful, but he did not accept Feuerbach's solution: he went further. For Feuerbach all this loss of self, *alienation*, was the result of the operation of mind – the minds of men in general. In Feuerbach's scheme human beings were only thinking – but Marx points out that prior to thinking comes existing. Marx wants to start from the person, in all his/her complexity. It is the totality of 'human existence in society' that has to be looked at – alienation is a social and historical phenomenon.

At this point we can introduce the element of the discussion of the state. In Hegel's scheme the state was prior to, and ordered, society. This for Marx is an inversion of the truth: human beings, for Marx, are political animals as soon as ever they are social animals. Politics here is the routine negotiation of social meanings. Hegel's scheme extracts one aspect of human life and lodges that aspect, and its functions, in the state. For Marx, the modern state is 'an alienated form of political activity'.[7] In the political sphere radical democratization represents the overcoming of alienation. Later, Marx will argue that alienation in the *productive* sphere is the key to all forms of alienation and so democratization will have to begin in the productive sphere.

This sequence of revisions is complex: Marx rejects Hegelian idealism whilst affirming his dialectical strategy of enquiry. Feuerbach's materialism is critically appropriated: materialism is preferred to idealism, but Feuerbach's rather static (ideas as *reflections* of material world) understanding of materialism is rejected. Also rejected is Feuerbach's (and the other Young Hegelians') contentment with philosophical critique. At this point we should note the influence upon Marx of French socialist ideas and (in concert with Engels) his increasing concern for political economy which, in the ninteenth century, was *the* science of society.

In the period 1843–6 Marx (and Engels) wrote a series of texts which established the basis for all his subsequent work: chief amongst these are *The Economic and Philosophical Manuscripts* (1844) – sometimes also called *The Paris Manuscripts* – and *The German Ideology* (1846), which was written with Engels. In these texts all the complex movements alluded to above reached a 'first approximation' of the position Marx was to hold (and extensively develop) for the rest of his life. In the later text we find the first general outline of the idea of historical materialism and this we will look at later. It is in *The Economic and Philosophical Manuscripts* of 1844 that Marx discusses, in the context of a critique of political economy, the notion of alienation. This is, therefore, my second approach to the idea.

Marx's criticisms of the political economists rest on the charge that they take for granted the characteristics of the economic, social and political system – crucially, the existence of private property – of their day. Their work rests, in part, upon their treating human beings as essentially egotistical. The political economists in fact use English Utilitarianism to inform their analyses. The individual enters political economic theorizing as an abstract insatiable appetite in pursuit of satisfactions. Consumption is taken as the key to human character. Marx thinks this is a preposterous procedure, and the claims consequently absurd. The political economists are accused of merely abstracting and generalizing from the society they inhabited; and of failing to offer an explanation of labour in any fundamental sense. Human beings, for Marx, create themselves and their societies in social production. Bourgeois creeds of individualism are simply the ridiculous justifications for a historically progressive, yet humanly degrading, system. Marx then uses the notion of alienation to analyse the way in which modern industrial capitalism acts to distort this basic human characteristic: Marx analyses the degradation of creative human labour into mere work.

At this point we can introduce a familiar summary of Marx's discussions in *The Economic and Philosophical Manuscripts*.[8] Alienation presents itself in four ways. (1) The worker is alienated from the product of his labour: in capitalistic industrial society work is specialized, routinized and controlled by others. The worker's product exists apart from him: it confronts him as the wealth of the capitalist, or, abstractly, as capital. (2) The worker is alienated from the act of production: routinization, specialization, submission to external control and direction effectively destroy the typically human creativity of labour. In his work the worker denies his creativity and reduces himself to the status of an element in a wider process. Labour is not, in capitalist society, voluntary: it is coerced. (3) Human beings are alienated from their 'species being': capitalistic social relations degrade the collective human creation of self and society by reducing the social world to the vehicle for the satisfaction of private wants. Capitalistic social forms deny the social character of labour. (4) Human beings are alienated from their fellows: capitalistic social relations are typically fragmentary. Individual human beings do not confront each other; rather, role-incumbents do. Lives are fragmented.

This is thus the ethical core of Marx's work. Human beings, he argues, create themselves and their societies through their labour. A productive system that degrades labour into mere work is thus a deformed system inhabited by deformed people. The recovery of human creativity requires the reconstruction of the productive system. The fundamental contradiction of capitalist society is the *private* control of *social* production. The abolition of private property is the necessary condition of the establishment of a system of free, creative, labour. In *The German Ideology* Marx and Engels look forward to the effective overcoming of the present division of labour: human beings would not then be restricted to any particular sphere of activity.

Marx's method of analysis – historical materialism – was first presented in *The German Ideology*. There has been considerable debate in respect of precisely what Marx meant by this thesis: debate that has been coloured by the political (as well as intellectual) sensitivities of nearly 100 years' worth of commentators.

Historical materialism is best regarded as an *approach* to social scientific enquiry. It is not an elaborated evolutionist-type general theory. The key to the whole approach has been mentioned above: it is the claim that people make their own lives in their routine productive activity. This productive activity is taken to be the central business of human social life and around it more 'abstract' concerns – law, religion, art, etc. – cluster. Any existing or historical (or future *envisioned*) society should be analysed in terms of its pattern of economic activities and the associated cluster of 'cultural' factors. History, on this scheme, is regarded as the (largely unconscious) creation of human beings who are, in turn, subject to definite historically inherited constraints.

In the famous preface to *A Contribution to the Critique of Political Economy* (1859) we find the following summary formulation of the 'materialist conception of history':

> In the social production of their life, men enter into definite relations that are indispensable and independent of their will, relations of production which correspond to a definite stage of the development of their material productive forces. The sum total of these relations of production constitutes the economic structure of society, the real foundation, on which rises a legal and political superstructure and to which correspond definite forms of social consciousness. The mode of production of material life conditions the social, political and intellectual life process in general. It is not the consciousness of men that determines their being, but, on the contrary, their social being that determines their consciousness.[9]

In his formulation of the 'materialist conception' Marx made human productive activity the key to analysis of human life; he also made use of the *economic base/cultural superstructure* metaphor. This has been the focus of much of the subsequent debate: the metaphor can be read as revealing, in Marx, a latent economic determinism. Worsley[10] takes the view that Marx's work is indeed overly economic in tone and he proposes some revisions to the base/superstructure scheme. A similar view is advanced by Raymond Williams.[11] It seems to me that both commentators are addressing their remarks (with which I tend to agree) less to Marx than to subsequent misinterpreters (in particular, orthodox communists).

Worsley concludes by arguing that the use of economic determinist versions of the approach must be avoided. He also adds that grudging, or verbal, adjustments to determinist readings will not do either. He writes:

> It seems simpler and more scientific to conclude that Marx and Engels were right in insisting that it is necessary for people to produce, that social life cannot be sustained unless production is organized, and that both production and exchange entail crucial patterns of relationships. Other institutions, too, do have to be compatible with the economy. But the 'fit' can be quite loose; cultural forms, from art forms to forms of religion or family codes, can persist and be made compatible with quite different 'modes of production', and need only be slightly altered in the process, not totally reconstituted or replaced.[12]

It seems to me that this comment is reasonable whilst being overly apologetic. More interesting is the indirect point made by Worsley that the 'materialist thesis' is now widely and routinely accepted.

I want now to turn to the substance of Marx's work: his analyses of bourgeois capitalism. I will offer an introductory comment. Then I will consider in detail, first, the 'economic anatomy' of capitalism and, second, the 'social anatomy' of capitalism. (This distinction is mine and made for expository convenience only.)

The analysis of the capitalist mode of production begins from the position noted above: all societies must reproduce themselves from year to year and this requires that they engage in material production. We can posit a 'law' of social reproduction: production → consumption → production. This 'law' is the base of all economic systems. In capitalism this 'law' is hidden in a complex division of labour where the link between production and consumption is mediated by the mechanisms of the market. Supply and demand rather than production and consumption seem to be basic, but the market is actually secondary. Marx aims to uncover and display the underlying 'laws' of social production in capitalism.

Marx's economic analyses are complex. I will introduce them by presenting the ideas of: commodities; use value; exchange value; surplus value; labour power and the labour theory of value; exploitation; centralization and concentration; and contradiction. My exposition here will rest primarily on that provided by Giddens,[13] but there are many other useful summaries.[14]

Marx's 'economic anatomy' centres upon the analysis of *capitalist commodity production*. The capitalist system is historically novel in that production is oriented not to the satisfaction of social or human *needs*, but, rather, to the demands of *market exchange*: to the *production of commodities*.

Thus we may distinguish between *use value* and *exchange value*: each commodity has these – you can do something with the commodity or exchange it for something else. This latter element is pursued by Marx: it is what is novel to capitalism.

Marx tackles the problem of 'value' in a typically nineteenth-century fashion. He affirms the position adopted by political economists called the *labour theory of value*. Here the key claim is that all value is created by the expenditure of human labour. This notion of 'value' is further explicated in terms of the idea of the *socially necessary labour time* (which will depend on local circumstances) expended in creating the commodity and giving it its value.[15]

Products, or commodities, are exchanged in the market at their true values – according to the socially necessary labour time embodied in them. The capitalist buys labour and necessary inputs at their value and he sells the commodities at their true value. The system does not run on any sort of 'theft'. So how does the capitalist make any profit?

Marx explains that in capitalist society *labour power* is a commodity. Labour power can be bought and sold on the market just like any other commodity. Capitalism has 'free labourers' able to sell their labour power. Modern industry is very productive. In a day the labourer selling his labour power at the market price produces a surplus over his 'replacement needs' (the value of his labour power). Marx speaks of necessary labour – the time taken to provide the labourer's conditions of existence (food, housing, etc.) – and surplus labour – the time during which the labourer produces goods over and above his replacement needs: over and above the value of his labour power. Surplus labour is the source of *surplus value*. The ratio between necessary and surplus labour is called 'the rate of exploitation'.

The foregoing is a summary of the abstract model of the capitalist system: Marx went on to devote a considerable amount of effort in attempting to display how this fundamental logic manifested itself at the level of the market – in price movements, the point where orthodox economics begins. There has been much debate about these issues. The orthodox criticism centres on the difficulty of predicting prices using Marx's analyses but, as Giddens remarks, these criticisms are really rather beside the point as Marx wished to uncover the fundamentals of the system.[16]

Having established the mechanism of exploitation there remains the issue of the immanent dynamic of the system thus characterized: how will it tend to change over time?

The capitalist system is competitive and thus technically innovative.[17] Over time there is a shift to 'capital-intensive' industry: thus the organic composition of capital rises and, necessarily, the average rate of profit falls.[18] The economy as a whole may very well generate more profit – but the individual firms find that the rate declines. They respond by increasing the pressure of exploitation: longer hours, lower wages, an increased membership of the 'reserve army' of the unemployed. Each firm strives to cut costs and protect its own position. The system is thus anarchic: there is no overall regulation. The system is curiously able to contrive crises of overproduction. But it is overproduction of exchange values rather than use values. Crisis is endemic to the system: periodic crises serve to purge the system. Wages fall, factories close, production declines until, at the bottom of the 'business cycle', profitable investment opportunities are once again available to the capitalist. Crises thus serve a regulatory function for an anarchic and irrational system: they also serve to encourage centralization and concentration of firms (bankrupt firms are taken over, ailing firms merge).

Marx did *not* anticipate the disappearance of capitalism in one final revolution-triggering mega-crisis. Crises are regulatory; but they do cause misery for the proletariat and thus foster class consciousness.

Within the capitalist system production units become ever larger – in Marx's day, joint-stock companies appeared. The *individual* capitalist becomes redundant and the *social nature* of production is obviously displayed and increasingly acknowledged as firms become internally complex. The concentration of power, in giant firms, is similarly underscored.

The economic anatomy of capitalism tends in the direction of its replacement and, at the same time, engenders in the proletariat a consciousness of its position in the system which, in turn, is the basis of proletarian political insistence upon the realization of these immanent tendencies. The basic contradiction of the capitalist system is the private ownership/control of social production and it is the overcoming of this that ushers in socialism.

Turning now to the 'social anatomy' of the capitalist system we confront material which is both much more familiarly 'sociological' (and political), but which is also comparatively underdeveloped in Marx's formal writings. This last-noted point has meant that subsequent commentators (and political activists) have had to try to divine the outline of Marx's analysis of the 'social anatomy' of the system from scattered writings. None the less, the key *areas* of concern are fairly clear – even if the detail of analysis is not – and we have the following issues to tackle: class, ideology, base/superstructure, the state, the party and revolutionary change. Like the terms introduced above in the 'economic anatomy', these are closely associated with each other – and more generally, of course, with the terms of economics. They do not represent a list of discrete elements: they are separated out here for exegetical convenience.

Of all the social scientific terms associated with the work of Marx it is probably 'class' that is the best known. This is both reasonable – it is a powerful idea – and rather ironic, for Marx's *Capital* broke off, due to his death, where he had intended to analyse the concept.

It is a basic claim in Marx's general scheme – in his materialist approach to history – that what is crucial to comprehending human social life is the fact of productive activity. This involves two elements: (a) an exchange with the natural world upon which humankind works; (b) in the context of a related exchange between the people involved in this work. Human creative labour is social labour. Every productive system has this essential dual character – human being/nature and human being/social world. As Giddens puts it: 'Every kind of productive system entails a definite set of social relationships between individuals involved in the productive process'[19] – all this, of course, was a key element in the preface of 1859 cited above.

Productive activity: this is Marx's starting-point for examining industrial bourgeois capitalist society. He investigates this via a critique of its principal theorists, the classical political economists.[20] A key error, on their part, is their individualism: Marx calls them the 'Robinsonades' as their model saw human beings as isolated and non-social, like poor Robinson Crusoe.[21] The economics of the political economists reflected this assumption – contracts struck in the market place in pursuit of egocentric gratifications.

Marx insisted that production be regarded as a *social* practice. With the development of industrial productive enterprise, there grows up a complex division of labour and within this antagonistic classes can emerge as one group gains a privileged position. Class is *not* established by source of income, it is not an income group. Class is *not* a functional position within the division of labour.

The notion of class points to the existence of groups identified by the position occupied in relation to the social means of production. Specifically, in bourgeois society, class position is a matter of the ownership of private property in the means of production.[22]

Marx focused upon nineteenth-century bourgeois capitalist society: it is this specific historical period that comes closest to his abstract model of two antagonistic classes. Hence we have bourgeoisie and proletariat. In addition to these, we can identify other class groups.

Thus we may speak of *marginal groups*. These could be 'residues' from earlier social productive formations: for example, the 'free peasantry' of France and Germany in the nineteenth-century – leftovers from feudalism; similarly the English landed aristocracy.[23] We can also speak of marginal groups in a prospective fashion: we can try to identify newly forming classes. The following have, over recent years, been considered: youth, white-collar technocrats, a consumption-oriented working class (cf. the thesis of embourgeoisement) and the educational elite (a specific group of technocrats).[24]

We can also speak of 'functionally dependent strata': those groupings whose futures are intimately bound up with the fortunes of a particular class. Modern senior management would be such a grouping. (Clearly this would open up some interesting questions in respect of the locally recruited functionaries of multinational corporations located in the Third World. Profits versus development?)

Marx also spoke of the lumpen proletariat: the 'dregs' of society. In some recent theorizing some of these groups have been identified as progressive – students, hippies, and (more problematically as it is not at all clear that they count as *classes*) women and minority ethnic groups.

The key antagonistic class relations within capitalist society are, in Marx's scheme, those between bourgeoisie and proletariat. The extent to which, and the way in which, class engenders class consciousness will depend upon local circumstances. The result of class-conscious political action is similarly context-dependent. As Giddens remarks: 'Class relationships are the main axis around which political power is distributed, and upon which political organization depends.'[25] Thus when we look at modern industrialized societies we see that the existing pattern of relationships and state form will depend on the deals struck between bourgeoisie, landed aristocracy and proletariat in the various states. It is wrong to ascribe to Marx any scheme of mechanical movement (based on economic and class forces) of social forms through history: the specific concrete social formations have to be 'deciphered' and their historical conditions grasped. Thus may we understand their present dynamics.[26]

It is within the realm of political struggle that we most often encounter the notion of ideology. In a class-fissured society the ideas of the dominant group are presented in terms designed to legitimate the group's position. Social arrangements which are specific to times and places are explained (away) as natural and proper. Disadvantaged groups, on the other hand, attempt to propound alternative visions of society.

The notion of ideology has had a rather chequered career. It originated with the French philosopher Destutt de Tracy in the late eighteenth century and he intended the term to designate the 'science of ideas'. It was no less a historical figure than Napoleon who gave the term its familiar pejorative sense: he speaks of 'ideologues'. Thus ideology becomes the province of the dreamer or the charlatan.

There are a range of meanings given to the term in Marx. In *The German Ideology* Marx and Engels criticize The Left Hegelians for abstracting from history and focusing upon ideas. Failure to see the link between material relationships and ideal statements produces ideology – the world seen upside-down. Ideology in this sense flows from *errors of conceptualization and analysis*. Marx and Engels later extend this usage to include the products of apologists for particular social forms.

There is, however, another sense of ideology in Marx and Engels. Ideology is the way in which people became conscious of conflicts in their societies. In this sense ideology means the set of ideas which arise from a given set of material interests/circumstances. Ideology is thus 'making sense'[27] – the 'sense' reflecting circumstances. Here we have the notions of class ideologies: we do not have *error* (as above), rather we have particular cases argued from a particular point of view. But that point of view could be a restricted one, leading to misconception and error. Thus the two versions are rather tangled. Ideology has to be deciphered: explanations of the social world have to be set in their historical (political, social, economic, and group) location and, thereafter, investigated so as to disentangle sense and nonsense. This was Marx's approach to the *critique* of political economy.[28]

Closely related to the matter of the nature of ideology is the debate around the relationship of base and superstructure. If social productive activity is central to human life, just how does it fashion or shape cultural forms such as law, religion, art and political formulations (ideologies), and so on? We have touched upon this issue above and we saw then how complicated discussion of this issue had become. The marxist faces a dilemma. On the one hand, a strong determinism can be affirmed which is useful for political purposes – thus we can speak of, say, 'class law' (one law for the rich and another for the poor) – but intellectually difficult to sustain. Or, on the other hand, a looser, more subtly articulated, relationship can be affirmed which is more intellectually plausible but which also has its polemical edge dulled. And in mentioning 'polemic' we shift our attention into the realm of the political. To complete this sketch of Marx's analysis of the 'social anatomy' of bourgeois capitalism I will add a few brief remarks on marxian *politics*: state, party and revolution.

There is little systematic exegesis, in the work of Marx and Engels on the subject of politics. This apparent lacuna is discussed by Milliband,[29] who takes the view (to oversimplify) that the political was so pervasive in their work and lives that they simply took it entirely for granted.

Within marxian political thinking the state has occupied a fairly central position. The state is the key political institution of modern industrial society. In the *Manifesto of the Communist Party* Marx and Engels observe: 'the bourgeoisie has, at last, since the establishment of Modern Industry and of the world market, conquered for itself, in the modern representative state, exclusive political sway. The executive of the modern state is but a committee for managing the common affairs of the whole bourgeoisie.'[30] This represents the 'classic' marxian view, yet Marx himself did not pay a great deal of attention to analysing the state. This task, like others in respect of the 'social anatomy' of change, has fallen to subsequent marxist theorists.[31]

Much 'orthodox' communist thinking on this, and related matters, derives from Lenin's work, the experience of the Russian revolution and the subsequent struggles within the infant USSR to 'secure' the success of the revolution. Lenin's 1917 text, *The State and Revolution*,[32] argues for the inevitability of violent revolution and the necessity of destroying the state machine. To this familiar image is to be added Lenin's conception of the role of the Communist Party as the revolutionary vanguard of the proletariat. There is a shift from the comparative open-endedness of Marx and Engels on these issues towards a distinctly more specifically articulated view on the part of Lenin. However, the final (intellectual) descent into the rigid and mechanical formulations of official Marxism–Leninism was only effected in the period of Stalin's rule. In the 1930s in the USSR, Marxism–Leninism became an official state ideology – and marxist social theorists have been trying, with increasing success in recent years, to escape from this suffocating deformation of the work of Marx and Engels (and Lenin) ever since.

I have discussed Marx at some length so as to illustrate the claims I made about social theorizing in part 1. Like Gellner, I believe that social theorizing is, and has been since its inception in modern guise in the late eighteenth century with Adam Smith, centrally concerned with the attempt to render intelligible 'the transition' to the modern industrial world. This is not to say that all social theorists have operated at the broad scale of Gellner – clearly they have not. Much social scientific work has been addressed to particular elements of 'the transition': the task is so complex that any grasp of detail across a broad range of elements eludes all but the discipline's geniuses – and there aren't many of those! Again we could go on to note that much social scientific effort at the present time is less concerned with offering an ethically based, 'argued case' or with pursuing any intellectually pure (or academic) interpretation than with the provision of policy-scientific formulations: with servicing the information/interpretation needs of planners. This is true for First, Second and Third Worlds. Further than this, we could observe that social science is also at the disposal of the industrial–commercial 'economic base' of modern societies: the work of management, market research, opinion-testing, advertising, design work, the output of the media, and so on, is all informed to a greater or lesser degree by the work of the social sciences. Clearly in this realm we are far removed from the concerns of Marx or the mode of theorizing of Gellner. It is on the basis of these last two areas – 'applied social science' and 'policy science' – that claims are made for the technical scientificity of the social sciences. It is here that we find the naive celebration of the 'received model' of the natural sciences and the eschewal of concern for, and involvement with, ethical and political issues. It is here that we find Gellner's 'jejune official textbook definitions of sociology'.[33] The truth is both more exciting and distinctly more intimidating: the central tradition of social scientific enquiry has been with making sense of the transition to the modern industrial world. And it is Marx who offers the first well-grounded, richly elaborated, intellectually coherent and thoroughly engaged interpretation. The work of Marx is not merely a matter of intellectual discussion: the work of Marx spawned marxism – and this political application of Marx has its own very complex history. Marxism is thus both a body of social scientific ideas *and* a social movement. The social movement is obviously central to the history of the twentieth century. Intellectually, too, Marx is central to social science. Irving Zeitlin[34] prefaces a discussion of Weber and Durkheim with the subtitle *The Debate with Marx's Ghost*'[35] and he remarks that: 'in the twentieth century much of sociology (and social science generally) took shape in a critical encounter with the theories of Karl Marx.'[36]

I want now to add a final note to this treatment of Marx. I want to sketch the legacy of Marx in the particular areas of concern for development: this will let us see how present-day neo-marxian work follows on from the work of Marx. I can do this by making use of the work of Aidan Foster-Carter[37] and Gabriel Palma.[38]

Palma's article is concerned to argue that dependency is less a body of established truths and more an approach: one, he says, which recalls the style of classical political economy. Palma focuses upon the business of analysing the relations between centres and peripheries. This focus generates three principal analyses, and they, along with dependency, trace back to Marx and Engels.

The first of the attempts made within the marxian tradition to analyse the relations of centres and peripheries was that of Marx and Engels themselves. However, there is a problem in elucidating this early position as the discussion of the Third World is restricted to scattered remarks, both in scholarly texts and journalism. Marx and Engels seem to have supposed that the dynamism which they diagnosed as utterly essential to the capitalist system would manifest itself in both intensification within the established system and expansion of that system. Put simply – they expected the capitalist mode of production to spread geographically. Indeed, so confident was this early position in respect of the dynamic of capitalism that existing, non-Western and non-capitalist modes of production tended to be dismissed as moribund and unprogressive historically. This is a point which much subsequent debate has pursued and Marx's notion of the Asiatic mode of production has been widely rejected. However, in brief, Marx and Engels were optimistic about the future: they anticipated the spread of autonomous centres of capitalism wherever colonialism had broken down moribund social forms and introduced the seed of capitalistic change.

The second set of marxian attempts to grasp the relationship of centres and peripheries is to be found, argues Palma, in the classical statements of imperialism – Lenin, pre-eminently. These theorists were preoccupied by the situation in Russia and argued that, whilst capitalism was a progressive force, the situation of Russia as a 'late' industrializer made the whole process rather problematic. As regards the industrialization of the Third World, these theorists of classical imperialism began by taking up an optimistic position. The dynamism of the capitalist mode of production when implanted via colonial rule, as Marx and Engels argued, is granted. However, the rise of monopoly within the First World was seen as a potential brake on industrialization in the peripheries as new patterns of industrialization, fashioned to the interests of monopoly-capitalist enterprises, were established. Decolonization seemed to be a sufficient remedy: with the removal of monopoly-capitalist distortions, the local capitalist centre could proceed to industrialize (and, eventually, usher in a socialist system). In time, this optimistic position came to be revised: what was now stressed was the power of local elites to secure mutually beneficial alliances with monopoly capitalism, thus arresting the historical dynamic of the capitalist system in the Third World. And it is from this observation that contemporary theories of dependency usually start.

The third set of marxian analyses of the exchange of centres and peripheries is usually taken to have been generated by, in particular, the work of Paul Baran: his work has represented the notion of monopoly capitalism, such that the world capitalist economic system becomes split into a non-progressive capitalist core and a deformed periphery. Political action via 'disengagement' from this world system is, for Baran, the prerequisite of any progressive change. The well-known theorist A. G. Frank has followed this line. Other lines within this third marxian approach include a reformist position (associated with the Economic Commission for Latin America) and a line (Palma's favoured one) which stresses political economic analyses of the social and economic dynamics internal to the nations of the Third World. Palma is in this section of his text attempting to rescue dependency theory from the rather pessimistic and overstated position that the followers of Baran, and especially Frank, have adopted.

The work of this last-noted marxian approach to analysing relations of centres and peripheries has been massively influential within post-Second World War development theorizing. The line from Marx and Engels to the efforts of present-day theorists is, here, direct and clear.

Palma's paper neatly illustrates the way in which the work of Marx has been both 'handed down' *and* revised. This last issue is fairly central to Foster-Carter's analysis. Foster-Carter speaks not of dependency but of neo-marxism, and he has in mind the work of Baran and Frank. This work, and their notion of the active creation of underdevelopment, he characterizes by distinguishing 'neo-marxism' from both bourgeois theory *and* traditional marxism. Foster-Carter sees 'neo-marxism', like Palma, as a *contemporary version* of marxism. We will discover later that the matter of the application of Marx to development issues has become a contentious one: there is much debate as to what counts as a marxian analysis of development. And in this self-critical climate the work of Marx himself is of direct relevance and is explicitly treated. The influence of the other two 'founding fathers' is, arguably, rather less explicitly considered: none the less, with Durkheim's evolutionism and Weber's (misunderstood) idealism, this influence is extensive.

3 Durkheim and the evolution of the division of labour

The extent of my present interest in the work of the trio of the 'founding fathers' is restricted. I am concerned to show: (a) that they all argue cases; (b) that each has a clearly articulated *scheme of the logic of change* – and all focused on change to, and within, historically novel capitalist societies; and (c) that they are also important in that they have shaped subsequent social scientific work, including development studies.

Marx, we saw, made use of a radical democratic ethic (presented in terms of overcoming alienation); and a historical materialist analysis which, based on the idea of the historical self-creation of human society, analysed society in terms of the internal logic of the economic base and the subsequent adjustment to the cultural superstructure. The circumstances of the capitalist system were such that it would progressively abolish itself in favour of a more democratic (socialist) society.

In the same vein we can now look at Durkheim. I will look at the following points: (1) his ideas about sociological method, and social morality; (2) his text *The Division of Labour*; and (3) some of the subsequent debates about his work. I shall also consider how his work has fed into the bases of modernization theory.

Durkheim's general interest, like that of other nineteenth-century theorists, was with trying to comprehend the nature of capitalist industrial society. Ian Roxborough summarizes Durkheim thus:

> For Durkheim, the central fact of the transition from traditional to modern society was the dissolution of the old ties of mechanical solidarity which bound people to each other in the tightly knit communities of pre-industrial society. The interpersonal bonds had depended on spatial contiguity and

> personal acquaintance, and had broken down with the changes attendant on the emergence of modern society, particularly urbanization. These changes led to a progressive depersonalization of society and man could no longer turn to authoritative institutions such as the Church for spiritual guidance. The old sources of moral direction were in decay, and nothing had as yet replaced them. The soulless individualism of modern society could not cope with this problem of widespread anomie. Durkheim's prescription was the creation of new institutions to replace the old sources of moral authority with a new organic solidarity. He was one of the early corporatist theorists, and looked forward to a reintegration of human communities around the axis of corporatist guilds formed at the workplace. Anomie would give way to a new authoritative moral order.[1]

This would represent a widely accepted brief summary of Durkheim's interest in the shift from 'traditional' to 'modern' societies. For my purposes it serves to pick out the issue of *moral regulation*, and this is the matter to which we can now turn.

Durkheim's concern with the moral regulation of the social world is central to his work: it is a theme that is addressed in several of his major works. Here I will rely upon Giddens's text *Emile Durkheim: Selected Writings* (1972a) and offer notes on three relevant issues: social facts, moral science, and normality/pathology.[2]

As regards the development of sociology Durkheim (pp. 51–7) takes note of the newness of sociology and argues that it must be clear about its procedures and field of enquiry. This entails separating out of the complex real world a specified area: Durkheim wants to identify 'social facts' and take them as expressive of the 'social wholes' of which they are elements – here is an early allusion to the organic metaphor which is often invoked by Durkheim.

The nature of 'social facts' is pursued: a science, argues Durkheim (pp. 57–63), can exist only if it has a definite field to explore. The novelty of sociology is its treatment of its typical areas of concern – laws, customs, religion, etc. – as if they were things in nature. And just what is 'a thing'? It is, answers Durkheim, that which is refractory to introspective or ideational enquiry. It is that which demands empirical enquiry. Also – and this, let us note, is *not* the same thing at all – treating some social phenomena as 'things' is to assume a particular attitude towards them.

These matters are pursued further (pp. 63–7) and it is pointed out that law, duty, established social practices (all the concern of sociology), and so on, all exist externally to the actor. Moreover, patterns of action are not only externally given, but they are also imperative and coercive. This gives sociology its field: a social fact is to be recognized by its power of external coercion. External coercion, social constraint, is the key to identifying social facts and the crucial social facts for the sociologist centre upon the web of rules which social beings inhabit. Thus, says Durkheim (p. 71), sociology can be regarded as the science of social institutions.

To this characterization of field and 'style' of enquiry we can add a note on methods (procedures) and here Durkheim (pp. 73–82), anxious to separate sociology from other social sciences, speaks of *social causes, structure* and *function*. (So, generally, it is the character of the historically unfolding succession of social states of affairs that must be grasped.)

Turning now to the study of morality (pp. 89–96), Durkheim argues that ethical schemes tend to revolve around a few simple ideas which are then unpacked and applied to a variety of situations. The problem identified by Durkheim is that such moralists never study the social processes which create the rules the moralists speculate upon. A scientific study must look at actual social rules. These social, moral, rules are characterized by their being *obligatory*: and we can identify moral rules by the *sanctions* called forth by them. It is, he argues (p. 101), society that constitutes the moral world: 'morality consists in being solidary with a group and varies with this solidarity.'[3]

Finally, we can take note of Durkheim's ideas about normality and pathology. Durkheim declares (pp. 102–7) that his definitions will be based on observable phenomena. The normal will be the average; the pathological that which deviates from it. This formulation is refined somewhat by lodging normality/pathology within a group and historical context: the terms are context-dependent. Normality will be that which is *necessary* to *that* society. In the case of societies in transition the normal may be difficult to identify: Durkheim concludes at this point by noting that it is the business of 'every science of life . . . to define and explain the normal state and to distinguish it from its opposite'.[4]

In sum, these brief notes serve to illustrate the remarks made by Roxborough and indicate – in a very cursory fashion – how Durkheim understood his enquiries into capitalism. As Giddens puts it: 'Durkheim was . . . concerned with . . . the problem of the "*changing* nature of order" in the context of a definite conception of social development.'[5] This enquiry was itself subject to definite conceptions of scientificity. We can now turn to the influences upon Durkheim's early work and to the key early text,

The Division of Labour: an attempt to characterize the nature of changing forms of social solidarity and to distinguish normality/pathology in novel patterns of behaviour.

The Division of Labour, published in 1893, is usually taken to have introduced Durkheim's central concern with the *moral* nature of the social world. This focus of concern recurs in all his major writings. Now, as we saw in the discussion of Marx, the process of intellectual/political crystallization of a novel theoretical perspective upon society is very complex. This was true of the emergence of Marx's position and it is also true of Durkheim's views. I will attempt to sketch the major aspects of this process of 'crystallization' and then go on to offer a résumé of the main position presented in *The Division of Labour*.

The general intellectual milieu of the turn of the century included the widespread popularity of sociology. This claim is made by Lukes,[6] who goes on to say that a major reason for this was the work of the English philosopher and social theorist Herbert Spencer. The scheme proposed by Spencer was an evolutionist one: societies move from simple (and savage) social forms to complex (and civilized) forms. The mechanism of change is a sort of cultural Lamarckianism: a social struggle and survival of the culturally fittest.[7]

Spencer was not the only sociologist writing at that time: in Germany, Georg Simmel was working at Berlin, Ferdinand Tönnies was at Kiel. In the USA, too, there was a widespread development of sociology departments in the universities.[8] None the less, Durkheim saw France as the place where social science had received its most important elaboration: for Durkheim, sociology was virtually a French science and sociology was the premier social science.

Against this milieu we can identify two major areas of intellectual debt: Saint-Simon (via Compte) and a group of German social theorists. To this we can, following Zeitlin,[9] add the major negative influence of socialism in general and marxism in particular.

The German thinkers are discussed by Giddens,[10] who argues that two areas of their concerns were congenial to Durkheim: the first is their 'organicism' and the second their concern for the 'moral regulation' of society. The former point entails the use of an organic metaphor to characterize society. The social whole is made up of functionally interdependent parts. This metaphor, used this way, reflects, again, the pervasive influence of Darwin whose thought had, reports Giddens, an 'extraordinary impact . . . upon social thought, in the concluding decades of the nineteenth century'.[11] The second point relates to the stress these theorists place upon the idea of society as a *moral* community – and a moral community that can be studied scientifically. These views are reflected in the commentary upon Durkheim's work presented above.

The second positive contributory source used by Durkheim is to be found in Saint-Simon mediated by the work of Compte. Both are French theorists: Saint-Simon is said, by Zeitlin, to have 'straddled two epochs: the Revolution, on the one hand, and the conservative Reaction on the other'.[12] Durkheim follows Compte in developing the conservative aspects.[13] And, crucially, what we find is the idea that the modern world is an *industrial system*: it has evolved out of earlier social forms and it is to be understood as a system of functionally interdependent elements. Conflict within the system is either irrational or temporary: integration will be enhanced by the fostering of appropriate moral ideals and these are amenable to identification by positive social *science*.[14] The extent of requisite 'integration enhancement' and the vehicle of such interventions are matters upon which, as we shall see, Compte and Durkheim diverge.

Turning now to the third contributory element to Durkheim's position, we confront the *negative* influence of socialism and marxism. Here we can see how Durkheim's characterizations and proposals, in *The Division of Labour*, differed sharply from those of contemporary socialists. Where the latter saw social conflict and the necessity of social reconstruction before the benefits of industrial production could be enjoyed by the majority, Durkheim urged the necessity of acknowledging the social harmony engendered by the new, higher, social form with its new integrative pattern of solidarity. Any social science predicated upon the assumption of inevitable conflict was wrong, and social action based upon it futile – or worse.

The main claim of *The Division of Labour* is that the social system – post-industrial revolution Western Europe is the specific system in Durkheim's mind – is *not*, despite the decline of 'traditional society' (and despite the presence of social conflict), tending to disintegrate. On the contrary, a new pattern of interdependent social relations and appropriate moral rules has emerged such that it can be said that the *normal* state of a complex division of labour is one of organic stability.

The argument has three elements: To begin with, Durkheim follows what was a familiar nineteenth-century strategy of attempting to grasp the nature of the present by comparing it with the past. Thus we have a 'before and after' characterization. These could then be slotted into a series of such characterizations which expanded upon the basic dichotomy. Durkheim identifies the two 'ideal-types' of mechanical solidarity and organic solidarity by considering the nature of the moral order in traditional and modern societies. The enquiry continues by positing a mechanism to account for the shift from 'before' (traditional society) to 'after' (modern society): thus Durkheim speaks of increases in the moral density of society underpinning the evident increase in complexity of the division of labour. Finally, having offered his interpretive scheme Durkheim adds a tailpiece by way of a discussion of normal and pathological forms of the modern division of labour. The strategy of enquiry is thus, in essence, straightforward: an elucidation of the evolution of the division of labour. This strategy can be compared with Marx's focus on the dialectics of historical change and with Weber's focus upon the various manifestations of the broad trend of rationalization. I will have more to say about the logic of evolutionism in Chapters 10–13 of Part 3, where the critique of evolutionism which we met within Gellner will be further spelt out.

The first part of Durkheim's project attempts to grasp the nature of the present by noting (and taking as being of salient importance) the increase in social differentiation. This way of grasping the present is informed by organicist ideas: the social organism, like the natural organism, becomes more complex as it becomes more highly evolved. The nature of the present can be elucidated in a comparative fashion focusing upon the nature of moral order in traditional and modern societies. These are 'ideal-types' and are constructed with reference to types of legal codes. A legal code is an 'index'[15] of the moral character of a society. (In a legal code, Durkheimian-style 'social facts' have indeed become 'things' so it is an apposite starting-point for ideal-typification.) Durkheim distinguishes between repressive and restitutive legal codes: the former is characteristic of traditional society and the latter of modern society (and these 'ideal-types' are characterized in familiar terms: the former, small scale, rural, intimate, close knit; the latter, large scale, urban, anonymous, diffuse, etc.).[16]

Repressive law is penal law and its presence in society presupposes a strong collective conscience. The moral web binds people tightly and punishment is expiatory. All this is typical of the mechanical solidarity of traditional societies. It is to be contrasted to restitutive law.

Restitutive law presupposes a complex division of labour and functional interdependence. The law is concerned to compensate for broken contracts. The type of social solidarity is organic. The collective conscience declines in terms of its pervasive insistence upon adherence to general rules. The moral web is no longer tightly binding – it cannot be when individuals are engaged not in roughly similar tasks (as in traditional society), but in dissimilar tasks. Social solidarity is organic and is expressed in the doctrines of individualism associated with the complex division of labour.[17]

The *growth* of the division of labour is the second issue dealt with by Durkheim. This growth is a function of the *dynamic density of society* – the extent/character of social interaction. This increasing dynamic density is in turn underpinned by two general sets of reasons: population growth and technological progress. The shift from traditional (medieval European) society to modern (industrial Western European) is a matter of population growth, technological advance and the rise of the power/importance of the cities. Lukes[18] pushes this explanation back one more stage: why did this increase in dynamic density produce an increasingly complex division in social labour? Why not some other social form? At base, Lukes identifies in Durkheim an appeal to Darwin's notions of competition and survival. Darwin's mechanism of evolutionary change is once again invoked and (mis)applied. As we will see later, this invocation of a general-type evolutionary 'logic' (recall what Gellner had to say about these schemes!) is typical of modernization theory: 'differentiation', 'reintegration' and 'adaptation' are the terms used by Smith[19] to characterize their 'logic'.

If we now recall Durkheim's original concern – the nature of the moral regulation of industrial society – we can see an interpretation proffered that identifies a progressive evolutionary shift. Movement is away from tight-knit communities whose web of moral rules are 'religious' in character and tightly bind the individual into society, and towards loosely ordered social interaction in the increasingly differentiated division of labour with its reintegrative ethic of individualism. The image presented is of essentially smooth change and of a harmonious self-regulating system. And this creates a problem for Durkheim.

This brings us to the third element in Durkheim's argument: Zeitlin notes, of the image presented, 'Durkheim felt a certain uneasiness . . . for, after all, it was quite evident that the division of labour was not *in fact* engendering the solidarity he predicted.'[20] Durkheim's problem was that his scheme did not allow for the conflict that was clearly discernible in society. Durkheim responds with an *ad hoc* adjustment to his theory so as to make it at least minimally plausible: thus he grants that there is conflict, but argues that it is temporary.

Giddens presents a simple reading of Durkheim's discussion of existing (i.e. when Durkheim was writing) class conflict. The present state of social affairs is *pathological*: growth in complexity of the division of labour has been so rapid that moral regulatory codes have been out-stripped – they have not adjusted quickly enough. In a *normal* situation the social world would be as proposed above. Durkheim argues that the present division of labour is *anomic* – that is, the present situation of society approximates to the model of the English political economists. A direct way of tackling this problem would be via the introduction of workplace associations: these would offer support to the workers and identify to them – and to managers – their crucial, functional, roles. In short, Durkheim here proposes a corporatist and managerialist strategy. However, Durkheim also notes that society is rapidly changing and a programme of social reform can also be used to tackle this problem of conflict. The removal of systematic inequality, of inherited wealth in particular, will permit individuals to discover and occupy positions within the division of labour appropriate to their skills. The diminution of inequality tends towards the dissolution of the anomic division of labour but, for the present, Durkheim acknowledges that there is a forced division of labour.

In contrast to the, perhaps rather non-committal, exposition presented by Giddens, Irving Zeitlin offers a distinctly hostile critique of Durkheim's views. Having introduced the notions of 'anomie' and 'forced division of labour', Zeitlin comments: 'The problem of *anomie*, not the forced division of labour, is the first and more important order of business.'[21] Zeitlin argues that, having acknowledged the gross facts of conflict, Durkheim's work could have moved in 'two possible directions'.[22] The one choice would have focused on the *forced* division of labour: characterizations of inequality and strategies of alleviation would have been in order – i.e. Durkheim would have moved in the direction of Marx. The other choice, the one Durkheim in fact made, was to look at anomie: problems of social integration came to the fore – the workplace organizations are increasingly central to his prescriptions. Zeitlin remarks that: 'Justice was important but social unity even more so.'[23] Zeitlin continues:

> Here we clearly see the theme that was to remain central in all of Durkheim's work: social order at all costs. Society with a capital 'S' is, and must be, the sole arbiter of conflicting interests, and it is for 'It's' sake that conflicting interests must be settled . . . 'Society' becomes for him, as for conservatives generally, a polemical concept with which to counter critical-revolutionary theses.[24]

So much for *The Division of Labour*. It is appropriate to note, however, that Durkheim's interests in the nature of moral phenomena and the role of a properly constituted sociology in displaying, for practical purposes, the character of moral rules, both generally and in the context of modern societies, are pursued in his other works: *The Rules of Sociological Method* (1895); *Suicide* (1887); and *The Elementary Forms of Religious Life* (1912).[25]

I have presented Durkheim in the same style as I presented Marx and in line with my illustrative intentions declared at the outset of this chapter. It should now be clear that Durkheim's scheme is both interpretive and prospective: his scheme is compatible with the claims I made in Chapter 1 about social theorizing *per se*.

Durkheim's work is also of considerable significance for my later concerns. The links that can be drawn between Durkheim's work and that of post-Second World War studies of development are quite clear and distinct, although they are not as prominent as those links from present debate back to Marx. The crucial legacy of Durkheim has been his evolutionary conception of change coupled with his functionalist strategy of analysing systems. It is the Durkheimian interpretation of change (especially the ideas of differentiation, reintegration and the dichotomous characterizations, even though these did not originate with Durkheim – and, indeed, nor did the general evolutionism) that has come to underpin neo-evolutionary conceptions of change, and they in turn form the bases of theories of modernization. Durkheim is thus a significant intellectual contributor to what has been the single most influential theory of development produced in the post-Second World War period.

These links from Durkheim down to present-day 'structural functionalism', and thence to modernization theory, have been mediated by the influential work of Talcott Parsons. The work of Parsons and his followers dominated US – and thus First World – sociology up until the 1960s.[26] They are often accused of presenting an essentially static and conservative model of society.

Contemporary theories of 'modernization' follow Durkheim in stressing the stable evolutionary change of social systems conceived as essentially harmonious and self-regulating. Thus the contemporary theorists first define 'traditional society' (much as Durkheim would do) and then 'modern society' (again, much as Durkheim would): modernization is then introduced as the process whereby societies make the designated 'before–after' move. This scheme was presented in one very influential form by W. W. Rostow who, in his text *The Stages of Economic Growth* (1960), took the basic dichotomy of 'traditional' and 'modern' and expanded it to a five-element stage theory. There were, argued Rostow, five stages in the shift to the modern world from the traditional one which every country has to pass through. At the present time both Rostow and modernization theory are not well regarded by development theorists and, indeed, the broader intellectual movement these thinkers inhabit has been criticized as being scientistic and authoritarian.

One contemporary social theorist, Zygmunt Bauman, has coined the word 'Durksonian' to characterize one major tradition within social science. In his book *Towards a Critical Sociology* (1976), Bauman reviews the field of sociological thinking around the fundamental distinction between 'positive–constructive' and 'negative–critical' strategies of enquiry. These typifications are familiar in nineteenth-century social theorizing and they represent, roughly speaking, the empiricist–scientific and rationalist–philosophical views of knowledge which I introduced in Part 1, above. These typifications were familiar to Marx and to Durkheim.

The first-noted strategy, which Bauman identifies as that of Durkheim and subsequently Parsons, seeks to prepare descriptive and general explanations of a determinist, causal character. Society – 'a reality in itself' – is taken to admit of ordered enquiry upon the analogy of natural science. The heart of this explanatory mode is the equation of *explanation* with *prediction*.[27] The model of political activity this strategy of enquiry affirms is what has been called technical–rational, or instrumental–rational, action – that is, politics is reduced to rational administration where the administrators lay claim to specialist, expert knowledge. Put directly, what we have here is the ideology of the (authoritarian) planner – of a corporatist political system.

The second mode of enquiry – 'negative–critical' – follows the tradition of the French Enlightenment and, pre-eminently, Marx. In the presentation made by Bauman, critical theory (as the present-day version of this tradition is labelled) is taken to be the inheritor of the 'humanist' side of Marx's thought. The Marx of the early *Economic and Philosophical Manuscripts* is preferred to the, arguably, scientistic elaborations of his later work.[28] The contemporary theorist whom Bauman has in mind is Jürgen Habermas.[29] Habermas has been at pains to rescue the notion of social scientific enquiry from the narrow and restricted vision of the 'positive–constructive' theorists, with their associated 'politics of the expert': social science can, *rationally* (i.e. legitimately and defensibly), offer interpretive schemes. Thus does Bauman operate and, following Habermas's central affirmation of 'radical democracy', offers sociology a particular role: the critique of common-sense patterns of thinking where this task is taken as a prerequisite of social change. Social theorizing, for this school, is inevitably engaged – it does *not* aspire to the production of technical–rational descriptions of the social world and *nor* does it accept self-legitimations of the orthodoxy. These sociologists' material is not value-neutral; rather, it is oriented to servicing the needs of a technocratic politics of the expert. The critical theorists seek – after the example of Marx – to fracture the common sense of society and display the possibilities for the future lodged in the present. Bauman argues that when set against this schema of two distinct modes of social scientific enquiry, the 'Durksonian' approach presents itself as a science of unfreedom.

And if it seems that at this point we have altogether left the realm of studies of development, then I would point out that throughout the post-Second World War career of development studies the ideas of *expert* knowledge and the necessity of *planning* have been central – and modern corporatist schemes find an important antecedent in the work of Durkheim. These issues will be pursued at various points in this text; for the moment, what I hope is clear is the way in which the 'founding fathers' – in this case, Durkheim – continue to be important in contemporary debates.

4 Max Weber and the rationalization of the world

Max Weber is the third of the trio who are often dubbed the 'founding fathers' and, in some ways, his work is the most awkward to grasp. It has often been remarked that there are a whole series of Max Webers and, moreover, that the most familiar versions actually bear little resemblance to the original. I will take note of some of these various (mis)uses of Weber in the final part of my discussion. For the present we can note that *my* Max Weber is constructed so as to present his work with its concerns for grasping the nature of capitalism accentuated. I do not believe that this treatment, or 'reading', is unwarranted – on the contrary, I find it the most plausible of the various 'readings' on offer – but it should be noted that it is a quite distinct one: I find this 'reading' helpful as it lets us place in an intellectual biographical context the remarkable spread of Weber's interests. As Zeitlin characterizes his work there is a progressive 'broadening' of focus:

> His main interest, a lifelong preoccupation, was the origin and nature of modern capitalism, which eventually led him not only to a fastidious examination of the economic system of the West but all its major social and cultural institutions. Ultimately, this became a matter of understanding the peculiar nature of Western Civilization and the important contrasts with the civilizations of the East.[1]

I will follow, in a general way, this process of 'broadening out' which is evident in Weber's work in these notes. I will begin with a few remarks upon the intellectual and social circumstances of his early work and then take note of that early material directly. I will depart from Zeitlin's reading in one crucial respect in that I will stress that Weber was interested in capitalism *in Germany*.

When we consider the work of Max Weber we are dealing with

an approach to social theorizing which is quite distinct from that of Marx or Durkheim. Quite how Weber actually does differ from these two theorists has been a matter of some debate. However, simplifying matters, we can offer the following summary contrasts – and in doing so we note that it is in respect of Durkheimian-type material that there is the sharpest distinction.

Thus Weber's thought is to be *contrasted* with the positivist tradition inhabited by Durkheim. French sociology of this time (and as a result of Durkheim's influence) conceptualized society as an 'organic whole', a system-in-itself, morally and logically prior to the individual. Subsequent commentators have spoken of Durkheim's deification of society.[2] Weber stands in complete opposition to this view: it is the individual who is the starting-point of sociological theory-building. This claim is pursued in his 'systematic sociology', which I consider below. The major methodological novelty associated with Weber – the 'ideal-type' – is similarly non-positivist and has been presented as the key to an 'interpretive' sociology.

Turning to the vexed issue of the relationship of Marx and Weber we actually find a rather closer agreement on strategies of enquiry than is usually supposed. Once we set aside the vulgar idea that Weber 'refuted' Marx by identifying the role of ideas in history[3] we open up the more fruitful viewpoint which suggests that the whole of Weber's work can be seen as a sustained 'debate' with Marx. There is, however, the complication of the question of the 'real' Marx: the young, 'humanistic' Marx of *The Economic and Philosophical Manuscripts* (1844) or the later Marx of *Capital*. This matter arises simply because the work of the young Marx was not rediscovered until the 1930s – after Weber's death. There was no young Marx for Weber. The strictures which Weber makes of the work Marx, and marxist schemes generally, are focused upon the positivistic readings of Marx then current. In the generations after Marx's death the 'keepers' of his work – the Social Democratic Party (SPD) – became increasingly cautious and reformist. A mechanistic marxism suited their needs. And as regards subsequent claims that Weber refuted Marx, it is the material of 'official' versions of Marxism–Leninism that adherents of Weber have in mind. Zeitlin offers a modest conclusion on these matters: 'Weber's work must not be read as a repudiation of Marx's methodological principles but rather as a "rounding out" and supplementing of his method.'[4] My own feeling is that this formulation, with its tone of compromise, grants too much to the vulgar critics of Marx (who are, simultaneously, as we shall see in the case of some development studies work, vulgar celebrants of Weber). Weber's criticisms were based on a false reading of Marx (even if he could not have acquired a true reading) and his own positive proposals in respect of the nature of sociological analysis have been widely described as unsatisfactory.[5] However, for present purposes Zeitlin's characterization will suffice.

Returning to the contrast between Durkheim's and Weber's approaches to social analysis we can take further note of the intellectual climate within which Weber operated. Weber's opposition to 'positivism' reflected a widespread reaction: Stuart Hughes[6] speaks of the 'generation of 1890–1920' as effecting a 'revolt against positivism'. In this period a number of major intellectual figures – historians, sociologists, philosophers, psychologists – embarked upon studies of the social world which had it in common that they denied the possibility of any simple methodological borrowings from the natural sciences. The social world was human (and thus meaningful and intentional), historical (and thus constituted by specifics rather than 'laws'), and had to be analysed in appropriate terms (and what these terms were was not obvious). A final complexity derived from the recent 'discovery' of the power of the unconscious. This constitutes the bare bones of the 'revolt against positivism', but there is one other point to note: these thinkers *accepted* positivistic interpretations of natural science. Their revolt was thus partial and contemporary thinkers have suggested that this was an error of some magnitude.[7] Not only did Weber inhabit this intellectual milieu, but he moved in the same circles as those presenting these complex reworkings of social analysis. He was a friend of Simmel and Tönnies and he knew Georg Lukács (whose work is often characterized as a reconstruction of the young Marx before the rediscovery of the relevant texts). Weber also contributed to this reworking. Hughes characterizes this contribution in terms of an inspiring, if ambiguous, attempt at synthesis; thus he says:

> He [Weber] stands at more decisive meeting points than any other thinker. To begin to list these confrontations is to suggest his range and the ambiguous nature of his achievement: idealism and scientific method; economics and religion; Marxism and nationalism; political commitment and an insistence on 'objectivity' in social science . . . Even in his contributions to the terminology of social science his contradictions and ambivalences are mirrored'.[8]

This breadth of concerns is reflected in the intellectual biography of the man: an economic historian, a historian of culture, student of law and then a sociologist. Hughes writes as a historian of culture/ideas and thus his version of Weber is distinct from mine.

None the less, he does usefully and accurately display the complexity of the figure.

To this complexity, intellectual, personal and exegetical, we must also add his political controversiality: at the time and since. Weber was always interested in politics but save for a brief involvement late in his life, never fully involved in political life. Commentators have seen him as a forerunner of post-First World War democracy (he assisted in the preparation of the constitution of the Weimar Republic); others have seen his work as an anticipatory version of the Führer principle.[9] One thing is clear – he was a passionate German nationalist.

Turning now to the early work of Weber we can take note of the way in which problems were set which subsequently took him into diverse intellectual areas. From the outset Weber was preoccupied with capitalism and, in particular, with the nature of its development in Germany. His first important work was a study of landed estates in Prussia[10] and the incipient conflict between landowners and free labourers where these conflicts, in turn, generate problems of 'national policy'. The problem, as analysed by Weber, revolved around the changing economic and social character of the great Prussian landed estates. These changes involved, first, a steady flow of German workers from the agrarian, 'feudal', east towards the more advanced west. The shortfall in labour for the estates was met by the eastern Slavic nations, who provided a supply of cheap labour. The second aspect of these changes concerned the character of the labour force. There was a clear shift away from the bonded labour characteristic of medieval times towards the free day labourer characteristic of industrialism. The shift towards a commercial-type agriculture accentuated conflict between employer and employee. More generally, Weber took the view that the economic rationality of the Junker landowners – employing cheap imported labour – threatened the integrity of the German state. Weber's answer was simple, and, in terms of displaying the fundamental character of his approach to social theorizing, revealing. Weber argued that Germany's eastern frontier must be closed.

Here Weber is declaring, in opposition to economic deterministic social analyses, that invoking economic rationality was not sufficient to secure conclusions in social–political argument. (Indeed, invoking economic rationality was not explanatorily rich enough to cope with the observed behaviour of the labourers on the landed estates: the free labourers were often economically worse-off than the bonded labourers – motivations were not just narrowly economic.) Weber insists that the tendency to capitalistic relations, and patterns of life, was *not* an iron law of economics.

The solution proposed by Weber is political. Weber here reveals his intellectual background (with all its concern for human meanings and history) and declares his own ultimate value position (and here we see the acceptance of the 'irrational' in human life and history) which is the necessity of maintaining the integrity of the German nation state. If it is to survive, so far as Weber is concerned, it must act as a power state: this reflects Weber's view of political activity – the struggle for power, resolved by force.

This area of enquiry is developed further, and more systematically, in his inaugural lecture as professor (1895). In this lecture Weber advocates the centrality of the interests of the power state in German politics, and in this context identifies as crucial the question of the leadership of the state. Weber argues that the German state was constructed 'from the top', so to say, by Bismarck. The power of Bismarck was based on the power of Prussia and thus upon the power of the Junker landowners, the civil service bureaucracy and the officer corps. The problem now, thought Weber, was of transferring political power. The issue was whether or not the economically prosperous bourgeoisie could develop a political consciousness adequate to the task of leadership of the nation. Weber did not consider the claims of the proletariat (argued for by the marxist SPD) as he felt that their future lay within capitalism. On the other hand, the economically declining landowning class is dangerous if it retains the political power which should pass to the hitherto supine bourgeoisie.[11]

These early works centre Weber's attention upon the dynamic of capitalism, especially in Germany, and they reveal a complex set of commitments about political values, economics and social change, the nature of motivation, and the character and role of sociological analysis (objective characterization of means to (irrational) value-prescribed ends). The central problem for Weber now focuses upon the nature of the consciousness of the historically progressive bourgeoisie and the task of identifying for the German bourgeoisie its historical, leadership role. Now, clearly, these early concerns of Weber took him into preicsely those areas which preoccupied marxist writers. Weber's text *The Protestant Ethic and the Spirit of Capitalism* (1904–5) is his first general treatment of this complex of issues.

In *The Protestant Ethic* Weber discusses the role which certain religious doctrines played in facilitating the emergence of capitalistic social forms. Weber rejects the then current marxian view that Protestantism was simply the ideological consequence of earlier economic changes and instead advances the claim that ascetic Protestantism actually aided the emergence of capitalism.

The analysis begins with noting the apparent anomaly that

whereas it is usually said that those with a strong religious faith are comparatively indifferent, or hostile, to material advancement, it is also true that Protestants are disproportionately overrepresented in modern industrial enterprise. Weber then goes on to analyse, in an ideal-typical way, both the 'spirit' of modern capitalism and the particular belief system of Protestantism. Reduced to its bare bones Weber's argument points to an 'elective affinity' between the Protestant (in particular, Calvinist) notion of a 'calling' – which has been transposed from a monastic, reflective form into an outward, directed, active form – and the requirement of capitalistic material accumulation which requires, amongst other things, the habit of delayed gratification. As a historical phenomenon, then, the rise of capitalism can be seen to have been assisted by particular sets of religious ideas. The belief system of the Calvinists led them to act in such a way that they served as the catalyst for widespread changes in the economic character of society.

Weber seeks to demonstrate that the rationalization, characteristic of capitalism, is derived, in a sense, from irrational value commitments. Weber does this in order to 'create a space' within the historical process[12] for human willed action and to identify the role of ultimate value commitments. This is the way it serves as a 'reminder' for the German bourgeoisie. Weber also takes his work to refute decisively the naive mechanical schemes of historical materialism which were prevalent at that time. This is the basis of the claims, since made, that Weber refuted Marx. The point is that not only is this claim nonsense, but also it is a claim which Weber would not have made. Indeed, he was at some pains to disavow any intention of replacing a mechanistic marxian unicausal (economic) explanation – reducing social life to economics – with another unicausal explanation which reduced social life to the play of ideas.[13]

The Protestant Ethic combines and generalizes the conclusions that Weber had reached in studying the eastern German situation, and in his reflections on German politics. The disjunction between economics and politics made in 1892 remains: human willed action, political action, can decisively impact upon the massively complex and powerful 'logic' of history and economic events. That the German bourgeoisie can, and ought to, act to take over the direction of the German nation state from the faltering hands of the declining landowning aristocracy is the practical lesson, or message, of Weber's scholarship.[14] However, the exchanges between political concerns and scholarly concerns in the body of Weber's work are complex – he was not merely a 'sophisticated ideologue'. The exchanges between political and intellectual concerns are as complex in Weber as they were in Marx and, let us note, politics figure in Weber's life and work just as centrally as they do in Marx's. And here is a useful point at which to stop these present discussions; Gerth and Mills observe:

> In many ways, Max Weber's life and thought are expressions of political events and concerns. His political stands, which must be understood in terms of private contexts as well as public happenings, make up a theme inextricably interwoven with Weber the man and the intellectual. For he was a political man and a political intellectual . . . To judge politics and rhetoric in terms of consequences and to measure the motives of men in terms of the intended or unintended results of their actions remained a constant principle of his political thinking. In this fundamental sense, Weber the scholar always wrote from the point of view of the active politician.[15]

At this point, having reviewed Weber's early work and brought out the way in which scholarship and politics are inextricably intertwined, I want to move on to consider Weber's later works. It is in his book *Economy and Society* (1922) that we find a systematic exposition of sociological theory and, at the same time, discover the keys to Weber's analysis of modern capitalism. However, before I turn to that material I will offer a brief note on Weber's methodological writings.

Weber's methodological writings have been variously described. Some have claimed to see in his work anticipations of much of contemporary sociology's concerns,[16] some have seen his methodological work anticipating all the central concerns of twentieth-century philosophy.[17] Others have presented him as the arch-priest of 'value-free' sociology.[18] For Antoni[19] Weber is one stage in the *decline* of historicism into sociology; and, in this vein, both Giddens[20] and Hughes[21] focus their attention upon the complexity of the issues he addressed *and* the confusions of the period.

In respect of the general methodological commitments made by Weber I will pick out four elements. Thus, first Weber grants that social science is concerned with 'ideal phenomena' (meanings, intentions, etc.), but insists that objectivity and causal analysis must also be retained. Second, Weber further insists upon the absolute separation of matters of fact from matters of value. Scientific enquiry can identify means but it cannot provide the ends. Third, the human world for Weber is, in line with his ethical individualism, composed of persons. This is an anti-holistic, anti-organicist, voluntarist stance methodologically and it denies the possibility of a universal ethics: the social world comprises competing ideals. Fourth, these views inform his political theory:

politics can be oriented either to ultimate ends (and thus it is essentially religious) or to pragmatic calculation. Social science is of use to the latter scheme.

The particular mode of sociologizing associated with Weber is often called 'interpretive sociology' and the crucial procedural novelty is that of 'ideal-typical analysis'. The ideal-type[22] serves to resolve the dilemma for social scientific enquiry posed by Weber's disjunctions between fact and value/causes and meanings/practical means and ethical ends. Positive science cannot interpret the realm of human meaning for us and nor can it tell us what we ought to do. The social world is a complex of partial views, themselves embedded in a web of historical causes. The social world must be presented as a realm of meanings (interpreted) which are themselves subject to complex patterns of historical causation. Any social scientific enquiry involves choosing both a point of view and an area of enquiry: the tension between the factual description of a situation and its interpretive evaluation is resolved via the notion of an 'ideal-type'. The ideal-type is an intellectual construct – a model, so to say – which accentuates particular elements of the social world in the light of some value orientation. The ideal-type represents a reference-point in enquiry, so to speak, where the theorist presents some sort of fusion of empirical descriptive enquiry (the realm of causes) and interpretive evaluation (the realm of meanings) where this 'fusion' will be patterned by the theorist's own commitments as to values and useful explanations.

The text *Economy and Society*, which was published after Weber's death, was intended as the introductory volume to a collaborative series of texts on society. In this book Weber is concerned with elucidating concepts adequate to the analysis of society – that is, with presenting the key concepts of a systematic sociology. The method presented in *Economy and Society* is a reworking of the earlier material and is designated 'interpretive sociology'. Thus Weber speaks of explanations which are adequate at the level of meaning *and* causally adequate. One theme that lies at the back of these ideas is the distinction between sociological generalization and historical specificity – as before, Weber is trying to bridge the gap between idealism and positivism.

Step number one in analysis involves interpretive understanding; and this is the notion most readily associated with Weber in the light of the debate surrounding *The Protestant Ethic*. The key to plotting the patterns of meanings inhabited by social actors is via ideal-typical analysis. Weber, confronted by the bewildering fluidity of human meanings, found it convenient to use rational ideal-types in the first place – non-rational behaviour could then be treated as deviations from the rational. (Weber was actually impressed by the success of economics using a model, or ideal-type, of rational economic man.) The second step of Weber's method looks to causal adequacy of explanation and when we try to pin down this notion we find that Weber seems to be pointing to an explanation that invokes empirical generalization: that pattern of meaning x will (tend to) issue in behaviour pattern y.[23] In sum, we could say that Weber takes interpretive sociology to be concerned with elucidating the relatively stable patterns of meaning inhabited by given actors or groups: this elucidation both interprets and identifies antecedent social (or, more broadly, historical) causes (and possible future patterns).

We can now look at the substance of *Economy and Society* and take note, in particular, of the fundamental ideal-types of social action and Weber's discussions of legitimate authority: his political sociology. As Weber has insisted that sociological analysis must begin with persons, he is obliged to begin with generic patterns of social action. Four ideal-types of social action are presented. First, we have *purposive rational action* which is action based upon rational calculation designed to secure some desired end or goal. Second, we have *value rational action* which is behaviour oriented to some ultimate ideal – an ethical commitment, for example. Third, we have *affective action* which is action informed by emotional commitments. Fourth, we have *traditional action* which is action governed by custom or habit.

These ideal-types form the basis of Weber's enquiries: they are represented in his political sociology. Patterns of social relationships are seen by Weber to be stable to the extent that they are informed by beliefs that the social order structuring these relationships is a legitimate order. Weber identifies three ideal-types of legitimate order which can structure social relationships. That a social order is seen as legitimate entails that power relationships within the social complex in question are accepted: the power of the superiors in accepted by the subordinates as *legitimate authority*. The three types of legitimacy are:

(i) traditional authority, where patterns of social order are legitimated by custom;
(ii) legal authority, where patterns of social order are legitimated by rational bodies of rules;
(iii) charismatic authority, where patterns of social order are legitimated by the person of the ruler.

The notion of traditional authority has its principal application in examining pre-capitalist social formations. The notions of legal and charismatic authority are both crucial to the analysis of capitalism – and to Weber's political evaluation of Germany. Weber argues that modern capitalism is governed by legal–rational authority. The social institution which embodies such legal–rational authority is the modern bureaucracy. Contemporary capitalism, on Weber's view, could not function without bureaucratic organization. Weber also thinks bureaucratic authority tends to be conservative and expansionary: in the modern capitalist world ever greater areas of social life are subject to legal–rational rules. This is the key, so far as Weber is concerned, to understanding capitalism – the spread throughout social life of rationality. In political life he speaks of the 'iron cage of bureaucracy' and, more generally, of the 'disenchantment of the world'. As a historical process Weber viewed it with distaste: his own self-definitions seem to have involved, fairly importantly, notions of a cultured European individualism. And in very directly political terms he did not trust the German bureaucracy with its 'alliance' to the Prussian officer corps: he saw them as incompetent – blind to the needs of the German nation state.

At this point we can introduce Weber's notion of charismatic authority: legitimations of social order which flow from the person of the ruler, his or her special qualities. Weber's analysis of capitalism saw a process of bureaucratic rationalization periodically upset/revivified by the appearance of a charismatic political figure. Weber's individualism, with his disjunction between fact and value, presents itself – in the context of the politics of capitalism – in the view that contemporary legal–rational, bureaucratic capitalism requires periodic non-rational 'value-injections'. The modern capitalist state is typically a plebiscitary democracy: at periodic intervals the mass of the people elect a leader, who necessarily will have charismatic qualities (in order to, first, get elected and thereafter to lead). At this point we can see why Antoni[24] identifies in Weber the basis of the Führer principle. It is also fairly clear how this analysis was shaped by Weber's judgments in respect of the situation in Germany: from the ranks of the bourgeoisie there must spring a charismatic political figure capable of leading the nation state in the post-Bismarckian era.

Weber does not see any progressive trend in history – as did both Marx and Durkheim in their different ways. Weber centres his enquiries upon the nature of capitalism and he characterizes it in terms of the spread of rationality, which process he comes increasingly to regard as characterizing history itself. This is a tendency to which Weber acquiesces; he is not an optimist. Weber once remarked that the two most important figures in contemporary culture were Marx, with his elaborate social science; and Nietzsche, a somewhat mystical-inclined anticipator of existentialism: it is little wonder that Giddens speaks of Weber's analyses as a 'brittle synthesis'.[25]

At this point I will set aside the 'systematic sociology', with its important analyses of authority, and turn to Weber's work on world religions. I will link these discussions both with Weber's concerns to elucidate the nature of capitalism and to subsequent (mis)uses of Weberian ideas within development studies.

The matter of the exchange between religious doctrines and capitalist development which Weber had addressed in *The Protestant Ethic* were pursued in his extensive cultural analyses of the religions of ancient Israel, China and India. In these studies we find the histories of the peoples reviewed with a particular concern being the extent to which religious doctrines, with their impact upon social structure, tended to assist or inhibit the rise of capitalism.

Weber's preoccupation with capitalism and the effective 'role of ideas' in history is pursued in these studies. At the same time, more broadly still, the civilizations of the East and West come to be seen as fundamentally different: in the West, there has been demystification and the culturally pervasive extension of rationality; in the East, this demystification has not occurred.

The religion of China, revolving around Confucianism and linking to Taoist mysticism and ancestor worship, is diagnosed by Weber as essentially quietistic and myth-ridden. The pattern of religious ideals sits neatly with the society in which it was embedded. The vast empire of the Chinese emperors was ruled via a network of officials owing allegiance to the centre – which appointed them on the basis of examination – and drawing tax revenues from their spheres of authority. The aspirations of the educated, the literati, are to the ethical/aesthetic/social model of the Confucian gentleman: a figure in harmony with his environment – not challenging it as did Protestantism. This scheme was thoroughly conservative. Related to it is the myth-ridden 'mentality' of the peasantry with its additional handicaps of ancestor worship and thus geographical limitation to village. China had no equivalents of the medieval European towns, it never had Western ideas of private property, and it never did have a bourgeoisie.

A similar tale is told for India; of the development of the caste system and the ascendancy of the Brahmins – the equivalent of the literati – with a vested interest in the maintenance of their privilege. Acquiescence and magic again rule the culture; there is no shift towards that disenchantment which Weber diagnosed as the crucial element of Western culture. This element he traced to Judaism, the source of the rationality he saw in the West's culture.

However, the detail in these studies is beyond my scope, but we can take note of the way in which Weber's understanding of capitalism became subtly broadened – a manifestation of the *rationalization* of the world – such that later (mis)interpreters could see an evolutionary-type tendency against which the belief systems of 'traditional' societies could be characterized as *obstacles* (to development). At the same time there are signs of an uncertainty of focus in his work such that the complexity of historical causation, upon which he insisted, is elided in favour of an exclusive focus upon the contribution of religious ideas: in brief, *a* causal factor sometimes looks like *the* causal factor merely as a result of its being the one Weber concentrated on. Again, this allows the (mis)interpretation of Weber – as having proved the key role of ideas in history – to be deployed. Zeitlin sums up the drift of Weber's writing on the religions/cultures of China and India as follows:

> Ultimately . . . what he sees as really crucial is that despite the rational, scientific elements in the East, and the existence there of economic strata and forms seemingly conducive to the emergence of a modern rational economy, the East remained an enchanted garden. This meant that all aspects and institutions of Oriental civilization were permeated and even dominated by the magical mentality – which became a brake on economic developments in particular and on rationalization of the culture as a whole. On the other hand, Occidental civilization, already in its early stages of development, had undergone significant disenchantment . . . This disenchantment began with the scriptural Judaic prophets . . . and generated the process which has made Western civilization as a whole fundamentally different from that of the East.[26]

Turning now, finally, to the subsequent use of the work of Max Weber in contemporary development studies we find a familiar area of debate – again, the role of (religious) ideas in development.

The way in which Weberian ideas have typically been used in development studies work is discussed by R. I. Rhodes. Thus he notes: 'Two closely related approaches to development have emerged as a result of Weber's influence, the cultural and the psychological.'[27] In the first case, Rhodes points to the way in which theorists speak of 'traditional' patterns of thought and belief which severely inhibit the spread of economic rationality.[28] The characterization of Third World societies as 'traditional' is typical of modernization theory's approaches: Weber's work is drawn on to help characterize the cultural schemes of these 'traditional' societies. All the work on comparative culture and history from *The Protestant Ethic* onwards is drawn on so as to enable the refractory nature of non-Western cultures to the prerequisites of capitalism to be discussed. This misuse of Weber involves taking what he said was one element of the complex histories of these regions and making it a simple necessary condition of change. We saw with Alatas (above, p. 18) that Weber can be (mis)read in this way, in terms of the 'Weber thesis', but that to do so involves seriously misrepresenting the particular and historically specific characteristics of these societies.

In the second case, Rhodes has a series of specific targets: McClelland, Hagen and Lerner,[29] all of whom, in differing ways, attempt to characterize the psychology of the people in the underdeveloped countries *and* try to identify ways of encouraging those with the 'right' psychologies. This material is not now well regarded and the critique presented by Rhodes is very acute. Thus he observes:

> The weaknesses characteristic of the cultural and psychological approaches . . . are not empirical . . . One of the most serious problems is simply that of omission. When these findings are not placed in a proper historical context they lead to misleading conclusions.[30]

In particular the history of colonialism is simply omitted and along with it the historical record of the active suppression of local industries where they conflicted with the interests of the colonizers. These theorists thus: (i) vulgarize Weber, the 'Weber thesis'; (ii) proceed in a cultural/psychological reductionist fashion; (iii) neglect the actual histories, colonialism in particular.

Notwithstanding that these 'vulgar Weberian' approaches are not now well regarded, they are still proffered as explanations for lack of progress in the matter of development. In a recent work Brian May[31] argues that First World concern for the Third World is misconceived: development is a hopeless and unattainable goal. Prior to colonial contact 'Africans and Asians were almost totally gripped by superstition of unfathomable psychic depth';[32] and today development theorists 'are trying to push Third World countries towards economic and social goals, European in conception, that lie beyond impenetrable psycho-cultural barriers.'[33] May claims[34] that Weber identified this crucial difference in 'mentality'. May also writes from a position of (I think) sympathetic concern for the peoples of the Third World. In respect of Weber and the people of the Third World it is difficult not to think that with friends like this, one would not need enemies.

Part 3
Contemporary theories of development

Preamble

In the above chapters I presented a particular characterization of social science and, very briefly, reviewed the work of the 'founding fathers' in the light of the general characterization. The work of Marx, Durkheim and Weber I claimed was also of interest in that their thinking has been used in the construction of theories of development.

Thus I characterized social science as one way, amongst many, of making self-conscious sense of the social world. Within social science I identified two self-conceptions, and labelled them 'rationalist' and 'empiricist'. The former I claimed was broader in scope and interpretive in intent, whereas the latter tended to be narrowly technical and manipulative. Gellner was offered as an example of prospective, general, interpretive social theorizing.

The trio of Marx, Durkheim and Weber was considered in the light of the general claims: each theorist's work was presented as a circumstance-specific attempt to comprehend the dynamic of change that underlay emergent industrialism. Each theorist was shown to have recourse to a particular set of intellectual resources which were used in fashioning interpretative schemes ('theories'). The work of this trio has come down to the present day and is clearly visible in the theories of development which are the concern of Part 3.

Here I will consider the major approaches to theorizing development that have been adopted, under the headings of 'Bourgeois Liberal Theories' (Chapters 5–9) and 'Marxist Theories' (Chapters 10–13). I will then illustrate the application of orthodox and radical views to the situation of Southeast Asia. I will analyse the theories on offer in line with the claims I have made above: what we have on offer are two internally diverse and sharply divergent *interpretive schemes* and they have to be considered as such.

Through this period two principal theories have been presented: modernization theory and dependency theory.

Modernization theory was elaborated in the context of Cold War competition for allies in the Third World. Where the USSR offered 'socialism', the USA offered 'modernization'. Modernization theory is essentially evolutionist and involves the deployment of a series of dichotomous constructs (rural versus urban, agricultural versus industrial, communal versus associative, etc.) which purport to explain the fundamental dichotomy between 'traditional society' and 'modern society': modernization is the bridge across the gap. Theorists of modernization pursued a descriptive, general policy science. If the process of modernization could be characterized in such a fashion, then the process would admit of manipulative intervention: it could be engineered, *planned*. This approach reached its apogee in the late 1960s: in 1960 Walt Rostow published the manifesto of this line of thinking in his *The Stages of Economic Growth*. Thereafter, the theory fell rapidly into decline.

An important factor in the eclipse of modernization theory was the rise of dependency theory. Originating with the work of Prebisch the position became increasingly radicalized. Where Prebisch had pointed to the relatively disadvantaged location in the world economy occupied by the Third World economies, marxian-inspired writers such as A. G. Frank preferred to talk in terms of the socially, politically and economically deforming consequences of the subordinate incorporation of the peripheral economies within the world capitalist system. Frank has argued that the prerequisite of development (construed broadly) in the Third World is disengagement from the world capitalist system. However, as the 1970s wore on, revolutionary optimism rather went the same way as evolutionary confidence. Newly independent 'socialist' nations found themselves with a mass of problems, inherited from their ex-colonial masters (usually), which severely circumscribed their options. There was also much doubt as to intellectual coherence of the more radical and polemical versions of dependency.

The general lack of confidence within studies of development as to 'what to do next' has its counterparts within social science as a whole. The social scientific orthodoxy of the 1950s and 1960s, structural functionalism, is now in confusion and there are no signs of a replacement, or even agreement as to whether a replacement is necessary. This doubt within the social sciences, and development studies, has occasioned extensive rethinking of long-held assumptions – and these discussions are still in progress. However, for our present purposes these broader speculations can be safely set aside: what we have within development studies are two internally differentiated, competing approaches; and it is to these theories that I now turn.

Bourgeois liberal theories

I have followed Ankie Hoogvelt's[1] scheme of allocating theories of development into two very broad categories and I now want to consider the material of the orthodox category, what she calls 'bourgeois liberal theories'. I think it is well to bear in mind that these categories are designed to assist our enquiries, not direct them. Confronted with the output of government agencies, international agencies and academics over nearly forty years, some system of labelling is needed lest we become hopelessly lost.

Within the broad dualistic scheme presented by Hoogvelt I will offer a discussion of a series of 'schools'. Each school I will analyse in 'sociology of knowledge' fashion before reviewing the 'good points/bad points' of the finished 'theory'. Within the 'bourgeois liberal' category, my concern in this section, I will discuss five 'schools' – each a variation upon the basic orthodox theme. The five are: growth theory; modernization theory; neo-institutional social theory; international Keynesianism; and monetarism.

5 Growth theory

Growth theory is the earliest of the post-Second World War theories of development. Often this approach is relegated to the status of precursor to modernization theory, but it seems to me that there is both enough interesting material in growth theory and sufficient differences from modernization theory to warrant their separate treatment.[1]

I will begin with the broad history of the period and identify the backdrop to the pronouncements of the economic orthodoxy of the period. Then I will look at the fundamental structure of that interventionist scheme, treating the notions of growth, planning and aid. Finally, I turn to consider the earliest attempts to use the theory in the context of matters of Third World development.

We can identify four elements in this background to growth theory. These are:

(i) issues of economic theorizing and the rise of Keynesianism;
(ii) matters of the multiple conflicts of the 'Big Three';
(iii) the reconstruction of Western Europe and Marshall Aid;
(iv) the demands of 'nationalist developmentalism', the ideology of emergent new nations.

From discussions of the 'Keynesian revolution', as it has often been called, I will draw three points. First, the inter-war period sees the occasion of the Great Depression, an event which could not happen according to neo-classical economic doctrine. Second, there is the impact of the apparent contrast of the success of the USSR's planned economy; and, third, there is the radical overhaul of neo-classicism effected by Keynes. Kurihara, looking at the impact of history on Keynesian theory, remarks that two events were crucial: 'namely (a) the establishment of the first centrally planned economy in Russia, after World War I and (b) the Great Depression of the 1930s'.[2] Kurihara takes Keynes to have plotted a middle course through the alternatives of laissez-faire and authoritarian intervention. As regards the theses established by Keynes, three are identified flowing from the experience of depression and Bolshevism. They are: the notion of depression equilibrium; deficit finance and the idea of the multiplier; and the compatibility of full employment with liberty. In the 1930s the economic orthodoxy rested upon the work of the 'equilibrium theorists', men such as Jevons, Marshall, Walras and Pareto. Setting marxists and socialists to one side, amongst the criticisms voiced, Sraffa (in 1926) had argued, in effect, that the notion of 'perfect competition' was untenable as each firm not merely competes, but seeks to differentiate itself in the market. Ruling out 'perfect competition' denies the possibility of a general theory of equilibrium; it thus cuts at the heart of the project of the orthodox neo-classical theorists. Attempts at repair by Robinson ('imperfect competition') and Chamberlin ('monopolistic competition') in 1933 are deemed by the economic historian Napoleoni to have failed. The contribution of Keynes to this debate is introduced thus:

> Parallel with the revision of the theory of market forms another criticism was levelled at the theory of economic equilibrium. This criticism concerned the statement that a competitive economy, left to itself, will automatically achieve the full employment of resources in general and of the labour force in particular.[3]

Keynes shows that it is perfectly possible for economies to go into depression equilibrium, whereby factors of production were so used that optimum configurations were not achieved. The neo-classical scheme argued that this was impossible.

The question follows: what conditions, if any, will ensure full employment? The answers to this question provide for a new idea of the government's role in the economy. The laissez-faire scheme had been attacked on three points: (a) unemployment; (b) misuse of available resources; and (c) trend to monopoly. Policy proposals flow from this view: generally, if the level of total expenditure falls below that necessary to sustain full employment, then the shortfall is to be made up by government spending. This in turn rests on the two notions of the 'multiplier' and 'deficit financing'. Thus the role for a government is sharply altered in line with revision of the established conception of the market.

This counter-cyclical role with regard to unemployment does not necessarily alter any fundamentals in the system. Policy proposals which might flow from charges of misuse of resources or maldistribution of income would involve more radical change. So Keynes reassured doubters that full-employment policies did not entail significant diminution of ordinarily understood liberties.

What I want to take from all this is the observation that the work of Keynes grows out of two circumstances: first, the situation of protected monopoly capitalism working at greatly reduced capacity whilst simultaneously having massive unemployment, and the concurrent manifest theoretical absurdity of economic liberalism; second, the combined encouragement and awful warning of the apparently successful efforts at planning in the USSR. With Keynes, the economic orthodoxy was very sharply overhauled, resulting in a style of government regulation that was taken to have tamed the system's periodic crises.

Having looked at the roots of the Keynesian enterprise, I want now to go on to indicate the initial set of political factors which gave form to those subsequent efforts to make use of it in guiding policy with regard to 'development'. The crucial considerations here revolve around the determination of the USA to order the post-war world in a fashion acceptable to itself.

Of the war aims of the USA, Kolko argues that three issues dominated US thinking in the period 1943–5:

> First was the question of the left which is to say, the disintegration of the pre-war social systems and the growth of revolutionary movements and political upheaval everywhere in the world. Next was the problem of the Soviet Union, which at times appeared very much connected with the issue of the left. Finally there was the issue of Great Britain, invariably set in the context of the future of the world economy and its present and future relationship to the US.[4]

It is argued that the Americans, once they were in the war, quickly began to establish a series of economic war aims. This task is reported as falling to the Department of State under Cordell Hull, a disciple of Wilson's laissez-faire liberalism and a man marked, as was Keynes, by the experience of the depression. Yet Hull drew opposing conclusions: tariff blocks and controls were the road to economic ruin and war, and the solution was laissez-faire. Kolko wryly notes: 'The identification of the interests of the world and future peace with Hull's doctrines and American prosperity looked more and more like the classic pursuit of national self-interest in an ill-fitting wrapper of internationalist rhetoric.'[5]

There were two major elements in US thinking: finance and trade. The discussion of finance was initiated in 1942 with a British submission prepared by Keynes which envisaged the growth of world trade with an international fund to smooth over budget deficits and channel investment money into development projects. To this the USA replied with the White plan (Harry White was number two in the US treasury) and debate thereafter revolved around the control of these proposed institutions and the ground-rules of their operation. The debate continued right up until July 1944 and the Bretton Woods Conference. The deal that was eventually struck was much closer to the USA's view than that of the UK. It may be said that Bretton Woods established the US view of the post-war world economy – that is, one run by business on business principles. The Bretton Woods Conference led to the establishment of the International Monetary Fund (IMF) and the International Bank for Reconstruction and Development (IBRD, World Bank). A little later a body to regulate trading was proposed, the International Trade Organization (ITO), but this was not successful and eventually GATT (General Agreement on Tariffs and Trade) was established.[6]

The general way in which the USA was later to approach matters of development is also clear. Kolko argues that

> America's foreign policy at the end of World War II necessitated the ability and desire to employ loans, credits and investments everywhere to create a world economic order to its own desires.[7]

The interventionist aspect is clear: it is also clear that Streeten's[8] choice of Marshall Aid as one of the roots of what he calls 'development theory' is apposite. The European Recovery Plan (ERP, or 'Marshall Plan') evidently encapsulates a wealth of tensions and it is to the history of post-war Europe that I now wish to turn.

Streeten argues that it was the dramatic recovery of Europe's economy that lent credence to the notion that deliberate intervention in an economic system to raise its level of activity was possible. Postan also takes this view and argues that 'By far the most dramatic, as well as the most effective contribution to recovery was the announcement in the summer of 1947 . . . of the so-called "Marshall Plan." '[9]

The 'Marshall Plan' was American and, in the justification of ERP, crisis in Europe and fear of communism figure prominently. Thus Seymour Harris remarks that

> Self interest rather than charity inspired E. R. P. Frightened by the onward movement of communism, which feeds on distress, the American people rallied to the support of the Marshall Plan . . . Americans realized also that economic

recovery in Western Europe would rebound favourably on the American economy.[10]

In addition, Harris notes the pressure of particular US economic groups which had surpluses on their hands – for example, farmers. The mixture of both political and economic aspects is fairly obvious.

Politically, the major event of this period was the promulgation of the 'Truman Doctrine' in March 1947. The essence of the doctrine was that political change not agreed by the USA was to be arrested: 'Truman spoke for the bulk of American conservatives and allied himself with reaction around the globe.'[11] The Marshall Plan followed on from this stance, and in Western Europe the aid administration's powers were used, reports Fleming, 'to discourage social reform . . . the effect of our [American] economic intervention in Europe has been not only to oust communists from the governments but to put the socialists out or decrease their influence.'[12]

The second area indicated by Harris is the economic and, apart from the business of self-interest, what is novel is the view of government that is adopted. Zeylstra notes: 'For the first time the Truman Doctrine contained a concept of international aid based on the need to promote a suitable rate of growth in the receiving countries, a prototype thus of modern development aid.'[13] That growth could be described theoretically and actually promoted as a matter of policy were novelties. Zeylstra's words reveal both the essence of the orthodox notion that specific policy-guided interventions could be made to secure a targeted growth rate, *and*, in his ease with the terms, the fact that such ideas have become a part of the common coin of development theorizing.

To summarize: my remarks thus far indicate the general environment from which growth theory emerged. The possibilities opened up by the theoretical work of Keynes are squeezed between the twin pressures of popular demand for reform and the determination of the USA to hold the line against any radical change. Ordered reconstruction and development is now taken to be within the grasp of governments – but the ruling factor in any such efforts is the overwhelming economic and military power of the USA.

The shift from this point to treatments of the Third World is characterized usefully by Streeten,[14] who argues that discussion of 'development' had its origins in two general sets of thoughts: problems of resources and people are taken to be urgent in view of the population explosion and soluble in the light of the success of post-war European recovery; second, political change in the form of the rise of new nation states in the Third World[15] and the Cold War increases the concern of the West for the 'proper' development of these areas. The Marshall Plan is thus an appropriate symbol for the start of development studies. Now I will turn to the 'theory' that was presented: I begin with economic growth models as these schemes provided the general intellectual frame (and legitimating notions) for studies of development, growth theory proper.[16]

I want now to look at the basic logic of growth theory and my treatment rests on the claim that out of the *mélange* of theoretical possibility identified by Keynes, political and economic necessity as seen principally by the USA, examples provided by European recovery and with the further demand of 'nationalist developmentalism', the theorists distil an intellectually coherent and politically relevant scheme. They produce an ideology, a broad interpretive scheme, of *authoritative intervention*.

If we take this idea of 'authoritative intervention' and unpack it, we can offer a simple sketch of what the idea presupposes and entails. If we consider any particular occasion of an intervention, then it might be understood as a deliberate action whose objective is to bring about a particular change in some array and thereby achieve a preferred state of affairs. We seem to have three basic elements: the supposition that

(1) there is something to be acted upon, an object;
(2) that it will respond and do so in a predictable (anticipated) fashion;
(3) the idea that the intervention is accomplished by an actor in a precise manner according to a clear set of expectations (that is, authoritatively).

There are two related points we can make. First, that the story above requires that the actor confront (or constitute for his present purposes) an object – that is, there is implicit in the ordinary notion of intervention a subject–object dualism. An orthodox empiricist would see the 'real world' as a realm of potentially manipulable objects. Second, it is clear that for the intervention to be successful it must be a knowing intervention – that is, in the right place at the right time and of the right kind. Thus authoritative intervention demands a descriptive, general theory. What is needed is natural-science-type knowledge: authoritative and manipulative. This is what Brian Fay calls a 'policy science': it designates the assumed product of mainstream social science such that in response to the question 'why have a social science?' the answer is given: 'it will enable men to control their social environment.'[17] Authoritative intervention requires a legitimating intellectual core; thereafter, it needs organizing and implementing.

With development growth theory, intervention is legitimated by being based upon economic discussions of growth. These in turn centre upon extensions made to the work of Keynes. Kurihara notes that Roy Harrod (with Domar later) 'established growth economics as a going concern on the foundations of Keynes's saving investment theory'.[18] Kurihara summarizes the reworkings of Keynes involved:

> If Keynes effected the transition from micro-analysis (with emphasis on profit maximization for the firm *à la* Marshallian price theory) to macro-analysis (with emphasis on employment maximization for the whole economy *à la* General Theory), then Harrod can be credited with effecting the post-Keynesian transition from short run macro-statics to long run macro-dynamics. Harrod emphasized the long run importance of the growth-promoting, capacity-increasing aspect of saving, whereas Keynes had concentrated on the employment-impeding, demand-decreasing aspect of saving; Harrod also emphasized investment both as a cause and as an effect of capacity expansion, whereas Keynes has treated investment mainly as a source of effective demand.[19]

The influence of the Harrod–Domar model, as it is called in the literature, has been extensive. Brookfield notes that it was this theory that 'underlay the growth policies actually put into effect'.[20] This economically technical material is difficult for the non-economist but I will, none the less, pick out the bare bones of Harrod's arguments.

Harrod's work is in the style of Keynes as regards terminology, assumptions and techniques. His famous essay[21] focuses on 'the necessary conditions for equilibrium between aggregate saving and investment in a dynamic economy'.[22] The basic proposition is that Ga=s/v where 'Ga' is the actual rate of growth of national income, 's' is the marginal propensity to save and 'v' is the marginal capital–output ratio. This 'fundamental relation' can define a growth path if it is linked to a statement of the entrepreneur's estimations. The notion of 'warranted growth' (Gw) is introduced to fulfil the Keynesian role of the entrepreneur: the entrepreneur invests and his investment today depends upon his estimation of tomorrow's possibilities. If he is to be reassured that his reading of the economy is correct, then Ga will have to be equal to Gw. In addition to Ga and Gw, Harrod has 'Gn' which is the 'natural' rate of growth flowing from given rises in population – more people, more production.

If all these are put together we have the first major conclusion to issue from his work. Thus, 'If, by coincidence, the actual rate of growth equalled the warranted rate, which itself equalled the rate of growth of the labour force, then steady growth at full employment would occur.'[23] The second conclusion he makes is that such a happy state of affairs is unlikely to come about and, even if it did, would be unstable. Harrod's work *does* identify a long-term stable growth path, but suggests that it would be difficult to find and difficult to keep to.[24] This view, in an economic theory underpinning an approach to development predicated upon the notion of authoritative intervention, came to be seen as awkward and then, in modernization theory, intolerable. However, Harrod's work was widely used and elaborated and, in any case, remained serviceable in its legitimating role. Growth theory – as a 'school' within development studies – was elaborated from the 1940s to the mid-1950s when it was absorbed into modernization theory.

Having looked at the legitimation of intervention, I now turn to its organization – that is, to ideas of planning. The conceptual relation is, in outline, straightforward. Thus, given that we know what we want to do to the system, how do we set about the task? How do we organize, initiate, monitor and control our intervention? How do we plan? Indeed, can we?

The debate about economic (and social) planning begins, it may be argued, not with Marx and Engels (who advocated but did not treat the notion of a 'planned economy') but with an Austrian economist, Von Mises, who, reacting against 'socialism' and the example of the USSR, argued in the 1920s that a planned economy could not work rationally. The gist of his argument is that, separating the economy from its institutional frame, it is the job of the economic system to allocate scarce resources between competing ends. This requires *indices of scarcity* and these have to be established by allowing market determination of prices. An economy with no free market cannot provide any index of scarcity and so cannot rationally allocate scarce resources.

Unfortunately for Von Mises, it was possible to answer his argument by manipulating the formal machineries of neo-classical economics so as to abolish the need for a market to determine indices of scarcity. Throughout the 1920s and 1930s, debate centred on whether – and if so, how – the theoretical possibility of planning could actually be translated into practice. We need not pursue this:[25] for our purposes it is enough to note that when, in the post-Second World War period, a demand arose for a planning system, the notion was already well known.

It was 'real world' changes, so to say, that called planning machines into being. Brookfield notes that a contributory factor in the rise of the preoccupation with growth was the reconstruction of capitalism that was evident in the 1920s and 1930s. Specifically, monopoly forms of enterprises and a recasting of the relationship of state and industry. Brookfield remarks that 'there is nothing new about the partnership between capital and state';[26] what is novel is its *respectability* and *organization*. The changes were evident in the 1930s but it was Keynes who made them acceptable and, thereafter, the war that ushered them in fully. When it came to dismantling war economies, the legislative, institutional and 'psychological' requirements of a Keynesian-managed economy were in place. In sum: in matters of respectability and organization, the work of Keynes legitimated and permitted a reworking of the relationship of state and industry, and a reworking of public altitudes thereto. Keynesianism, it could be said, was the particular intellectual/ideological form in which a prior economic–political need to 'intervene' manifested itself.[27]

Now I turn to the implementation of intervention – that is, to aid. Aid we can understand generically to be specific, piecemeal interventions in the system, having the aim of contriving a preferred state of affairs. Aid can take the form of single projects, sets of related projects, programmes, emergency 'one-off' jobs, etc.[28] What I want to do here is look at questions of the origins of aid-giving: intellectual and 'real world'.

The intellectual source of the idea of aid can be identified clearly: it is a simple corollary of economic growth models and is a logical consequence of the structure of (authoritative interventionist) growth theories. The concern of theorists, at the time of the promulgation of growth theories, was *technical*. Thus Mikesell writes that

> aid theories provide an analytic framework for determining the amount of the aid and the policies which must be followed by the recipient country for achieving a given target rate of growth which can be sustained without further external assistance.[29]

Such technical aid theories are categorized by White[30] as being either political transaction theories (how does the exchange work and who gets what at what cost?) or economic transfer theories (how much and with what impact?). White notes that the most familiar type is economic *supplemental*: and this, in the light of my above arguments, is precisely what we would expect.

The 'real world' counterpart, the demand, can be sketched by referring to the work of Zeylstra. Two sources of interest in aid-giving are identified. Zeylstra's first source is aid to allies, exemplified by the ERP. Subsequently, as political need dictated, aid was given to other allies – particularly in Asia. With the shift of aid to the Asian sphere its perceived task is broadened and the notion of development comes to the fore: there are a variety of reasons for this, chief amongst them being the changed nature of the recipients (economies and societies unlike those of Europe) and aid-donor competition, with the USSR amongst the newly emerged 'non-aligned group'.

The second source of interest in aid-giving flows from the process of withdrawal from empire. In the case of Asia, withdrawal was understood as marking the end of any 'responsibilities' the ex-colonial power had for its ex-colony. In the case of withdrawal from Africa, there was an assumption of continuing assistance – of aid. What we can note, by way of an interim conclusion in respect of this tangled historical tale, is that aid-giving is increasingly understood in *non*-context-specific terms: the idea that the 'rich' have a responsibility to aid the 'poor' comes to be taken for granted. Specific exchanges come to be understood within a generalized perspective: it might be said that this is a hindrance – both to clear thinking and effective action.

I have now dealt with the historical and intellectual milieu within which growth theory was constructed. I have also offered an explanation of its basic logic in terms of the trio: legitimation, organization and implementation. Now I want to turn to the actual use of this theory and I will look at two influential texts: the 1951 UN report and Arthur Lewis's 1955 book, *The Theory of Economic Growth*.

The United Nations report, *Measures for the Economic Development of Underdeveloped Countries* (1951), was written by a group of 'experts' who were invited to prepare 'a report on unemployment and underemployment . . . [in underdeveloped countries], and the national and international measures required to reduce such unemployment and underemployment'.[31] The experts begin by redefining their task as concerned with 'economic development rather than . . . unemployment'.[32] Their treatment involves the following elements.

(1) They consider the preconditions of progress; thus they see as a necessary condition the establishment of 'proper cultural orientations'. This rather reveals the economic orthodoxy of the experts: that which distinguishes underdeveloped countries (UDCs) from developed countries (DCs) is labelled/dismissed as 'prerequisites'.

(2) They go on to take note of the role of the government; whilst the Keynesianism is here blurred, the central role of the state is acknowledged. The argument rests upon the analogy of

underdeveloped countries' governments facing development and developed countries' governments facing depression.

(3) They also treat technical matters. Domestic saving is discussed and a tacit definition of their assumed goal is offered. In DCs they observe a 10 per cent of national income rate of capital formation, whereas in the UDCs this rate is only 5 per cent. A key problem is thus how to raise the rate of capital formation. Several techniques are discussed and what is most interesting is how matters of politics and economics are casually jumbled together. Thus they remark that 'people of middle and higher incomes in many UDSs are well known for their tendency to conspicuous consumption and there is no doubt that a fall in their consumption would be in the public interest.'[33] The authors neither pretend to be neutral social scientists nor do they come out and explicitly argue a case – as my scheme of social theorizing, introduced in Part 1, enjoins. Rather, they take the role of 'experts' and offer an argued case against a backdrop of unexamined, unacknowledged assumptions.

(4) The role of the expert is crucial in respect of the fourth element, where they treat planning. They offer an anodyne definition and then consider neo-classical economics: adequate, they say, at the micro level when precise data are available, but inadequate at the macro (structural) level when precise data are not readily available. The experts suggest that it is not possible to offer any general rules governing economic (again, the narrow focus) planning: 'those who are responsible must soak themselves in the facts of each particular case and must then use their best judgement as to what will be the most desirable directions of movement.'[34] This is one of the most breathtakingly optimistic sections of this report: the world of orthodox laissez-faire is left far behind. Indeed, the experts call for nothing less than *carte blanche* for the economic planner!

(5) The experts then turn to look at terms of trade. On this they affirm a loose internationalism that is in accord with the style expected of a UN study and, more relevantly, it fits in with the views of the USA on the proper development of post-war trade. They affirm that international trade is important and are confident that the DCs can sort out problems: fluctuations in trade cycle, protectionism, decline in terms of trade, etc.

(6) Finally, they tackle the matter of external sources of capital. Here we see two points of interest. First, they answer the question of the extent to which capital is needed from abroad by seeking to indicate a quantity. This, they grant, is difficult – so why do they do it? I would suggest that it is in line with the orthodox desire for precision; and the immediate thought must be that they

are arguing in the light of the experience of Marshall Aid, where large sums were shifted about. This impression is reinforced (and this is the second point) when, discussing the government's role as provider of infrastructure, they say: 'we do not suggest that aid should be given unconditionally . . . This would not be wise. Each grant should be linked to a specific function, and there should be international verification that the funds are used only for the purposes for which they have been granted.'[35] Thus aid is targeted and monitored according to 'wise' prescriptions. This is what we would expect to find: it is the practical expression of a 'policy science', and indeed it is how the Marshall Plan worked at first.

Arthur Lewis worked on the 1951 UN report. It was one of the earliest attempts to make sense of the matter of Third World development. I want to pursue, a little further, this business of the 'export of Keynes' by considering Lewis's text *The Theory of Economic Growth* (1955), which offers a more 'theoretical' statement of those views which were oriented to practical expression in the UN 1951 report: Lewis's text is a formal treatise.

Lewis declares in the book's preface that he is not presenting original ideas, but offering a framework for studying economic development. The level of enquiry is general. Lewis identifies three 'proximate' causes with which we can grasp matters of growth and development. These are: first, the 'effort to economize', which notion Lewis uses to characterize the DCs: included within it, or, as illustrations of it, we find listed: experimentation, risk taking, mobility and specialization. We can take it as fairly straightforwardly descriptive of his world. Its liability to criticisms developed with the notions of oversimplification, aggregation and value-insensitivity is evident. The second proximate cause which Lewis cites is the increase of knowledge and its application. This, I think, can be taken as a simple corollary of the first point: thus Gellner remarks that 'science is the mode of cognition of industrial society.'[36] Finally, we are reminded that growth depends upon increasing the amount of capital: a fairly obvious reflection of economic ideas.

From these three elements Lewis sketches a procedure of unpacking; thus he shifts closer to 'history', to the 'real world', by asking why do these proximate causes operate in some societies more strongly than in others? This is a search for consistency: non-economic factors must be consistent with the demands of economic logic. Just what does an environment conducive to growth look like? These questions are then reformulated to focus on the evolutionary aspects: how do 'environments' change, becoming more or less conducive to economic growth? This is the area of historical and social scientific research: and in his concern for 'non-economic' factors he anticipates directly the interests of modernization theory.

I have now discussed the historical milieu of growth theory, its logic of explanation, and looked at two influential early 'applications' of the position. By way of a summary, I would offer the following three comments. First, it is clear that these theorists were sensitive to the difficulties of shifting established intellectual tools to the Third World and they appreciated the complexity of the issues themselves. Given the demand that they produce something by way of a 'theory of development', their procedure was what we would expect. They began with the intellectual tools at their disposal and fashioned a plausible scheme around the notions of authoritative intervention and the economics of Keynesian growth theories. Second, we can note that their work subsequently fell out of fashion: tackling development was not like tackling unemployment, the basic metaphor was false, and the range of reworked analytic tools, consequently, unhelpful. Paul Streeten[37] remarks that they *miscast* their starting-point and confused complex problems of social, political and economic change with the range of technically detailed aspects of managing sophisticated economies. Their work did, however, prepare the ground for modernization theory: I would hesitate before dismissing their work in its entirety. This is because, thirdly, their work saw the initial presentation of a whole series of ideas that have, subsequently, become the common coin of studies of development: intervention; growth; the role of the expert; aid; and planning. These ideas run through the whole of orthodox, 'bourgeois liberal', thinking.

6 Modernization theory

Modernization theory is the label applied to an extensive body of work which was very influential in the late 1950s and early 1960s. The field of development studies is, like social science more generally, riven by a multitude of debates: modernization theory, though now not well regarded, was, for a brief period an almost unchallenged orthodoxy.

I will review the background to the emergence of modernization theory and then go on to consider its logic of enquiry. Having reviewed the criticisms that undermined the theory, I will add a short note on the work of W. W. Rostow.

The background to the construction of modernization theory can be said to have three elements: (1) bipolarity; (2) containment; and (3) aid-donor competition.

The post-Second World War period sees the decline of European power and the rise to pre-eminence of the USA and USSR. Raymond Aron in his study[1] of the US in the post-war period attempts, amongst other things, to explain the nature of the US's diplomacy. Here he suggests that after the end of the Second World War the nature of the 'interstate system', as he terms it, changed. What had been a European-style negotiation between states – a sort of diplomatic free market, its theory flowing from Machiavelli – becomes a bipolar situation where two 'great powers' confront, and accommodate to, each other's interests. So in this period the style of US 'interstate' activity is, with regard to its allies, that of generalship; and with regard to the USSR, one of accommodation. Bipolarity represents for Aron a change in diplomatic style, or perception of role, and Cold War hysteria is to be understood as a mask – worn by the actors for the benefit, largely, of their respective populations: in reality, bipolarity involves accommodation.

One seeming implication of Aron's 'realist' history is the reduction of the Cold War to the status of a grandiose 'PR job' designed to placate the US public. It is easy to find evidence that supports such a view: Caute,[2] in his history of the Cold War, indicates that its inception and development owed not a little to matters of party politics *inside* the USA. However, to deny – explicitly or implicitly – the Cold War a broader relevance seems misleading. Kolko[3] details the economic interests of the USA during the war and argues that the USA prepared for its global role. If this is true, then the Cold War was more than 'PR' for a change of diplomatic style: it was an integral element of a clearly articulated resistance to the left in general and the USSR in particular. However, for our purposes it is enough to note the division of Europe, and the developed First and Second World, into two camps. Also we can note that the Third World thereafter became an arena within which both sides manoeuvred for advantage.

Turning to the notion of containment we can consider a second element in the background to modernization theory. The idea was promulgated by President Truman and expressed the resolution of the USA to halt what it saw as the spread of communism. US concern was initially focused upon Europe in the wake of wartime upheaval, both the occupation of Eastern Europe by the USSR and the activities of the left in Western Europe. Subsequently, attention is extended to the Third World.

The domestic political background to the inauguration of 'containment' in the announcement of the Truman Doctrine is described by Caute. It is noted that when President Truman assumed power 'federal and state statute books were already bristling with anti-communist legislation. All that was required, and conspicuously lacking under F. D. Roosevelt, was the will to enforce it.'[4] This political will came to be provided in the period immediately following the end of the war when Truman (a Democrat) came under increasing pressure from the right and gave ground to it. Caute argues that Truman's response was coloured by considerations of short-term electoral advantage: he tried to steal a vote-catching strategy from the Republicans. By 1947 red-baiting, as an integral element of the US political scene, was well under way.

In the period of the 1950s when the first work that was to issue in modernization theory was undertaken, the model of the modern was not merely the image of the USA writ large, but an image suffused with the demands of the 'patriotic imperative'.[5] It was widely supposed that it was the business of the USA to reconstruct the world in its own image. The ideological position typical of

American thinking equated: (a) the interests of the USA; (b) functioning liberal market economies; (c) resistance to communism; and (d) the future prosperity of the world. This doctrinal package was labelled the 'Free World'. The mere existence of the USSR was a challenge and it seemed, within the logic of this ideology, that peace and stability required that the USA adopt the role of protector of the Free World. It was Truman's March 1947 address to Congress that officially launched the doctrine of 'containment': what the US government was attempting to do was to proscribe any change (political/economic/social) not agreed by it.

Element number three of the background to modernization involves 'aid-donor competition'. In respect of the history of aid-giving, White[6] distinguishes between two broad phases: thus, at first, aid was *internally oriented* and concerned with reconstructing Western Europe. This is the period of the construction of growth theory. In phase two the attention of (First World) theorists was *outwardly oriented* and concerned with development in the Third World. This is the period during which modernization theory was constructed. White identifies the Bandung Conference as marking this shift: there is also the entry on to the aid-giving scene of the USSR.

Until 1953 the USSR can be taken to have regarded the world as split into hostile camps and hence any suggestion of non-alignment was viewed with disfavour. With Stalin's death there was a relaxation in that stance which coincided with a 'thaw' in the Cold War. The first sign of this new line was the pledge by the USSR of 1 million dollars to a UN aid programme. This shift was further reinforced when the Bandung Conference of 1955 asserted the notions of 'non-alignment' and anti-colonialism. In 1956 Khrushchev announced that the USSR was now willing to offer UDCs development aid. This offer saw practical expression in that in the wake of the USA's withdrawal of financial support for Nasser's Aswan High Dam, the USSR stepped in.

As a consequence of these events there opened up, with regard to aid-giving, an area of competition. This competitive aid-giving took the form of offers of, on the one hand, 'socialism' and, on the other, membership of the 'Free World.' With the USA the latter scheme was presented within the ambit of development studies as 'modernization theory'. So where above we looked at the crystallization of Keynesian-derived growth theory, here we look at the construction of modernization theory. From the above three elements of background it is easy to see how modernization theory was crucially shaped by the demands of doctrines of containment.

Turning now to the construction of modernization theory we see that the intellectual resources available to the theorists comprised two major areas. First, there was the work of the economists who confront the problems attendant upon the scale and complexity of the macro-economics of growth. Second, we have the work of the sociologists, historians, psychologists, and so on: the social sciences more broadly. I will review the work of the economists very briefly and take note of their continuing optimism and internal disputes. I will pay much more attention to the work of the broader group of social scientists who produce the body of work recognizable as modernization theory.

Jones[7] remarks that the history of growth economics can be characterized as a sustained attempt to weaken the unpalatable implications of Harrod's work. This debate around Harrod and the possibilities of growth can also be seen as one element of a wider debate around the implications of the work of Keynes for economics in general. Two tendencies can be identified. First, the 'new Cambridge school', which seems to have taken Keynes to have reinvented political economy, understood as a style of social theory. Second, the continued neo-classical line, promoted by scholars at Cambridge, Massachusetts, which takes Keynes to be assimilable to the neo-classical line where economics is taken to be a matter of the construction of formal economic–analytic calculi.

I will not pursue this wider debate, save to note that the hesitant rediscovery of political economy made by the 'new Cambridge school' is echoed and elaborated by later theorists of development whilst the work of Keynes is, simultaneously, so to say, absorbed into a revivified neo-classical orthodoxy. Recent years have, indeed, seen the *anti*-Keynesian ideas of economic monetarism attain a measure of fashionable acceptance.

In the more restricted area of growth economics I will again eschew any treatment of detail. Brookfield remarks that 'growth theory quickly became highly elaborated and often esoteric: contact with the real world was not often established.'[8] It will not help this study to attempt to pursue the economists through their labyrinth.

I will offer a tentative summary of all these discussions by making two points. The first relates to the basic economic growth model itself. Harrod's work was rather pessimistic in character: in 1956 Solow[9] presents a revised model of economic growth in which the uncomfortable elements of Harrod's work are simply struck out. Economic growth is made virtually freely available, in theory, to those who would have it. No longer is the growth path difficult to find and hard to keep to; on the contrary, it is easy to find and thereafter self-sustaining. Clearly, in terms of aid-donor competition, this is a much more attractive view. My second point is this: Mikesell, looking at the history of growth modelling identifies a twofold pattern of revision. Initially taken as presenting an oversimplified model of the growth process, they have 'become more complex by the introduction of larger numbers of economic and non-economic factors and have borrowed heavily from theories dealing with the processes of social and institutional change.'[10] Thus models have become more complex and less narrowly economic. The distinction between economic growth theories and theories of social change grows increasingly blurred. And at this point we can turn to the theories of social change – to modernization theory.

Theories of social change constitute the second area of substantive interest that carries over from the earlier discussions of growth theory. In that context these matters were touched upon as 'non-economic aspects' of a process seen as essentially economic. Here we trace the emancipation of the broad range of the social sciences from their status as 'under-labourers' to economics.

With regard to the origins of modernization theory, Tipps notes that 'the idea of modernization is primarily an American idea, developed by American social scientists in the period after the Second World War and reaching the height of its popularity in the middle years of the 1960s.'[11] He goes on to note that 'Two features of this period stand out: a widespread attitude of complacency toward American society and the world.'[12] This complacency has its counterpart in social theory: a mixture of structural functionalism, social psychology and empirical survey analysis was deployed in order to elucidate the nature of *industrial* society. It was claimed, reports Hawthorn, that all societies were 'converging towards a common destination dictated by the technical and organizational imperatives of advanced industrialization'.[13] The fate of the Third World was one of disintegration and reformation in line with this trend. Hawthorn reads all this in the light of US intellectual traditions of social thought and current preoccupations. He notes: 'in such a way contemporary history was assimilated to the foreshortened historical understanding in American social thought so that the diverse peculiarities of other societies and the worrying features of America itself could always be explained away.'[14]

Thus far I have presented modernization theory as being an American ideology. But what of its character and typical pattern of argument? I will now turn to the 'logic' of modernization theory and will consider, first, A. D. Smith's treatment which (i) usefully links modernization theory to neo-evolutionist ideas of change; and (ii) offers a categorization (one of many) of modernization theories. I will then go on to look at some lines of criticism which are suggested by Brookfield.

A. D. Smith[15] argues that the revival of interest in evolutionary analyses of change owed much to the response of functionalist theorists to their critics in the late 1950s and early 1960s. Smith also argues that neo-evolutionism came to underpin theories of modernization.

The early critics of functionalism accused the approach of being static, blind to social conflict and biased towards political conservatism: in sum, that it could not handle social change. The functionalists responded by attempting to build a functionalist theory of change: Smith calls this the 'expansionist' response and he offers a series of reasons as to why this response, and not 'consolidation', was chosen. These include: trouble within the USA itself so that functionalism had to cope with conflict or lose all credibility; competition with the USSR for friends in the Third World; intellectual developments – sophisticated statistical and modelling techniques; a tendency within functionalism itself to become ever more general; and, finally, an ideological need to rebut charges of bias *and* affirm the model of the USA. Smith comments: 'Neo-evolutionism . . . is the form taken by functionalism in its attempt to meet the charge that it cannot cope with social change.'[16]

The basic logic of neo-evolutionism involves three notions: *differentiation; reintegration*; and *adaptation*. The first of these can be traced back to Durkheim and his notion of the division of labour with its increasing complexity and specialization in modern industrial society. The neo-evolutionists greatly expand the scope of Durkheim's idea: where the original focus was on occupational specialization, the new notion looks to *structural* differentiation and identifies it as 'both motor and central trend of all historical development'.[17] The idea is taken to have *general* applicability: to political entities like nation states, to economies, to institutions, to patterns of culture. The idea of differentiation, Smith also notes, entails an immanent notion of change – change arises 'from within'.[18] The second notion is called forth by the first: thus if structural differentiation continued unchecked, so to say, then society would tend to disintegration. Hence the notion of reintegration: this 'becomes a second major postulate of neo-evolutionism. Tendencies to disintegration are inevitably counteracted by reintegratory mechanisms, which re-equilibrate a disturbed system.'[19] These mechanisms are chiefly 'ideologies and organizations like the state'.[20] Once again, we have an echo of Durkheim and, once again, Durkheim's specific analysis is generalized. Finally, we come to the idea of adaptation which gives these patterned changes a direction: adaptation is both cause and consequence of differentiation/reintegration. Systems adapt to their environment and systems become more adapted through structural differentiation. Once again, an organic metaphor is being used (in a thoroughly confusing way, it has to be said) and, once again, Darwinian evolutionary theory is being drawn upon.

This 'logic' underlies modernization theory: theorists of modernization looked to see *how* UDCs were changing to *become like* DCs.[21] Smith offers three models – three sorts of modernization theory.

Model number one can be called *social maturation*. Thus modernization involves a shift from traditional societies, which have characteristic patterns of ideas/culture, to modern societies, which have their own typical patterns of belief and culture. Traditional society is seen as hidebound and static, whereas modern society is energetic and innovative. The shift from one to the other is a means to a higher adaptive level: and change is essentially, or crucially, a matter of changed patterns of ideas/culture. Smith remarks that what we 'are watching here [is] the application of Parsons's pattern variables and a diluted notion of Weberian rationalization to contemporary change.'[22] This model is criticized for confusing classification with the explanation of change (from one classification to the other): notions of 'maturation' are not good enough to cover this flaw.[23]

Model number two is called *differentiation–integration*. This approach relates changes in external circumstances to internal adjustments within society. Thus the rise of the capitalist industrial societies transmits a series of impulses which the recipient society simply has to adapt to. However, there is a gap between the initial impetus to change (to differentiate) and subsequent completed and successful adjustment (reintegration). The presently developing countries, the UDCs, fall into this gap. This explains (a) their problems; and (b) what must be done. Smith suggests that this approach to modernization can be traced back to Herbert Spencer and Durkheim: and this modern variant is criticized for its remarkable vagueness.[24]

Model number three is called *generating and absorbing change* and here models one and two are run together. Thus it is argued that all societies change and that the question therefore is: how do they generate change and absorb its impacts? The present UDCs are experiencing multiple structural change as they experience differentiation and reintegration. Smith cites an American theorist called Eisenstadt, and rightly notes that he is rather more sophisticated than the run-of-the-mill modernizer. None the less, this approach in the end does no better than the two noted above:

the problem is not merely in the handling of detailed material it is, more fatally, in the logic of the approach itself. I will pursue this matter a little further with Brookfield.

Brookfield begins his treatment of modernization theory by taking note of the general matter of strategies of explanation. Thus he says he is writing 'about dichotomies in the theory of development'.[25] The whole episode of modernization is taken as characterized by its adherence to *dichotomous characterization* of the issue of development. Brookfield argues that having conceptualized the whole business in terms of the dichotomy traditional/modern theorists of this school then proceed to attempt to elucidate matters by deploying a further set of dichotomous constructs – rural/urban; religious/secular; literate/pre-literate; modern sector/traditional sector, etc.

The argument strategy of modernization theory has been well summarized by S. P. Huntington. He begins by taking note that the terms 'traditional' and 'modern' are merely 'the latest manifestation of a Great Dichotomy between more primitive and more advanced societies which has been a common feature of Western social thought for the past one hundred years.'[26] Thus we can note, as do both Brookfield and Huntington: Maine's status/contract; Durkheim's mechanical/organic; Tönnies's Gemeinschaft/Gesellschaft; or Weber's traditional/rational. The strategy of argument can now be indicated: 'The bridge across the Great Dichotomy between modern and traditional societies is the Grand Process of Modernization.'[27]

It is with the work of Parsons that we find the basis of contemporary attempts to flesh out the modern. Parsons advanced a series of five 'pattern variables'[28] whereby human action could be characterized. The theorists of modernization rework these variables so that they become a way of characterizing social systems. In the case of the 'pattern variables' the set of characteristics is explicitly linked, but in the literature of modernization other, more descriptive, characterizations are added. The result, of course, is the familiar division between the dynamic modern world and the moribund traditional world. It seems clear that what we have in these 'modernization' schemes is an attempt to construct a descriptive general policy science which characterizes the process and goal of 'modernization' and identifies specific points of intervention.

Modernization theory has been extensively criticized. We can begin with the attacks that have been made on the two central notions used: 'traditional' and 'modern'. Both have been criticized as highly dubious descriptions: the modern world is thus only restrictedly universalistic – society is fissured by class, ethnic and religious affiliations. The extent of achievement-orientation may also be questioned: the attitude of the middle-class careerist is not that of either the landed aristocrat or the working-class labourer. When we turn to the model of the traditional, we find that the criticisms have been sharper: the image of 'traditional society' contains in addition to the above-indicated type of imprecision an ethnocentric bias.[29] If it is now retorted that these are 'ideal-typical' characterizations (and thus inevitably problematic in concrete application), then we can say: (i) that as heuristic devices they are low grade, because of their imprecision; and (ii) that their manner of construction, and internal relationship, are less than satisfactory.

The first objection of this second, theoretical, type is to the way in which the category 'traditional' is simply defined negatively in relation to 'modern'. The procedure of the modernization theorists has been this: first define modern and then non-modern is what is left over. The category, or ideal-type, 'traditional' is a *residual* category. Residual categories are beset with problems. If we begin by taking note that the modernization theorists aspire to produce a policy science – which understands knowledge of the social as being the same as knowledge of the natural – then it is clear that the fundamental concepts they use must (on their own arguments) stand in some clear relationship to the 'facts': to the concept's 'empirical referents'. We can agree that the category 'modern', even if the characterizations produced are faulty, does at least stand in some sort of clear and direct relationship to the material circumstances it would grasp: and even, to go one step further, if we note that abstracting and generalizing are faulty procedures,[30] we can none the less grant that with the 'modern' the procedure is at least minimally plausible. This is not so with 'tradition'. This concept is not made by abstraction and generalization, but by detailing the way in which non-modern societies fail to measure up to the model of the modern: 'traditional' is thus a residual category and, as Huntington notes, 'Dichotomies which combine "positive" concepts and residual ones . . . are highly dangerous analytically. In point of fact, they are not properly dichotomies at all.'[31] It is from this fundamental incoherence that the (intellectual) problems of modernization flow: they are trying to use *half a dichotomy*! It is little wonder that their characterizations of 'traditional' were attacked as vague, unconvincing and ethnocentrically biased.

If we move on to the issue of bias we can see that it is inherent in the use of residual categories. I will offer an illustration of this from the sociology of deviance and then return to our concern with development.

I want to argue with a dichotomous typification which affirms one category and then identifies the other as a concatenation of non-prime category elements, is immediately biased. Consider the idea, taken from studies of deviancy, of the 'non-medical use of drugs'. This term was introduced into discourse for the stated purpose of allowing cool-headed discussion of social, or recreational, drug use. It is taken to be a movement forward from simple condemnation. But we can ask: just when, and by whom, was the *medical* use established as the prime category against which other uses might be classified? Clearly, when the dichotomy 'medical/non-medical' is written in full, then the implicit criticism of any drug use that is other than prime case – that is, which is not legitimated by an authoritative medical practitioner for approved use – is revealed. The expression 'non-medical' purports to be non-judgmental, but clearly it is not. Outright condemnation can be replied to. But if condemnation is disguised, or is implicit in the formulation of the problem, then it is harder to discuss. I hope the point of all this is clear: the notion of 'modern' operates in modernization theory in the same way. The 'modern' is taken as the *self-evidently given*, and the non-modern constitutes just so many deviations from it.

With modernization theory this bias works in several quite interesting ways. I will note one: the abolition of the history of Third World nations. Thus A. G. Frank[32] notes, of Rostow's 'stage theory', that the scheme supposes a primitive starting-point from which the presently developed are taken to have emerged. Frank thinks this reasoning is flawed: 'This entire approach to economic development and cultural change attributes a history to the developed countries but denies all history to the under-developed ones.'[33] The presently 'rich' have the history of their emergence whilst the 'poor' have yet to move, so to say, and consequently have no history. Now clearly this is ludicrous, but what is happening is that classifying the Third World as comprising 'traditional societies' neatly begs the issues in respect of their character: Frank then argues that far from the Third World nations having no history, it is precisely the history they do have that explains their present circumstances. And their history involves, crucially, the episode of colonialism and the manner of their insertion into the expanding world economy of First World capitalism. The modernization approach is condemned as theoretically incapable of treating what, on any plausible account, would be part of the common sense of enquiry. The formulation 'traditional/modern' is thus skewed, or biased, in that it rules out consideration of the part played by the 'rich' in creating the present circumstances of the 'poor'.

There is one final point which we can note in respect of dichotomies, and this was mentioned in respect of Smith's model number one, above: I call it the problem of 'collapsing arguments' and I take this line of criticism from Huntington. In his 1976 paper, Huntington remarks that the characterizations of 'modern' and 'traditional' are unsatisfactory, but in comparison with the idea of 'modernization' they are lucid and clear: he adds, 'Inevitably . . . the dual character of the concepts undermined the conceptual dichotomy.'[34] The problem is that all societies display 'traditional' and 'modern' characteristics. This is not a problem if all the theorist wants to do is collect static comparisons. If, however, you want to analyse pattern of change within specific societies, then you have to start talking about 'intermediate societies': intermediate between 'traditional' and 'modern'. Huntington remarks that this makes problems for modernization theory (which rests, *inter alia*, on the distinction between 'traditional and modern') because 'the addition of a transitional category tended to exclude the traditional and modern stages from the historical process.'[35] The two notions, 'traditional' and 'modern', come to represent, it is suggested, the start and end of history: 'But if all real societies are transitional societies a theory is needed which will explain the forms and processes of change at work in transitional societies. This is just what the dichotomic theory failed to provide.'[36] So we are back where we started! It seems to me that this is a crucial attack: the fundamental argument strategy of modernization theory, the elucidation of change across a general dichotomy by means of the presentation of a series of particular dichotomies, fails when the scheme is brought to bear on the 'real world'. The scheme is unable to grasp change and can only offer static comparisons in abstract and ahistorical terms. This is not just empirical inadequacy; it is, rather, a fundamental conceptual incapacity.

I want to conclude this discussion of modernization by looking at the work of W. W. Rostow, who produced the single most (in)famous book on development in the post-Second World War period. It is with Rostow's *The Stages of Economic Growth* (1960) that we can examine the apogee of modernization theory. I will begin with a straightforward exposition of (a) the stages, and (b) the mechanism which Rostow claims underlies the stages.

Rostow identifies five stages of economic growth and then observes: 'They constitute, in the end, both a theory about economic growth and a more general, if still highly partial, theory about modern history as a whole.'[37] To this he adds that 'the dynamic theory of production . . . is their bone structure.'[38] The stages and mechanism combined thus address the issues tackled by Marx: hence the book's subtitle – *A Non-Communist Manifesto* – and Rostow's claim to have replaced Marx.

The stages comprise the following:

(1) *Traditional Society*: which is characterized as having low technological/economic power-based, pre-Newtonian science. Traditional society is agricultural, clan-based, and the 'mentality' is fatalistic.
(2) *Pre-conditions for Take-off*: this is exemplified by Western Europe in the late seventeenth and early eighteenth centuries. Medieval society disintegrates, modern science grows, trade develops. Traditional societies are 'dislodged' by incursions of external powers – in seventeenth-century Europe 'reactive nationalism' was generated by Spanish/Dutch/English wars.
(3) *Take-off*: now economic growth becomes normal as the last blockages are overcome. Investment rises from 5 to 10 per cent of national income and growth is inegalitarian – a particular group has to seize the opportunities provided by their resources.
(4) *Drive to Maturity*: there is now a long period of progress with 10–20 per cent of national income invested. Industries forge ahead, mature, level off. New ones arrive on the scene. There is a period of social, institutional fine adjustment such that eventually a mature economy/society is established which rests on the absorption of home-generated new technologies.
(5) *High Mass Consumption*: leading sectors shift to consumer durables and services, welfare provisions are made.

Rostow links this stage theory to a mechanism – which he has to, of course, otherwise all he's produced is an arbitrary periodicization of history. Thus he speaks of a 'dynamic theory of production' and notes that his stages 'are not merely descriptive . . . They have an analytic bone-structure, rooted in a dynamic theory of production.'[39] Rostow's dynamic theory of production is a derivation, it seems, from Keynesian work: thus he looks at savings, investment and sectoral performance and postulates, for an economy, a set of optimum paths of sectoral development. History will, of course, see divergences from this optimum path but, essentially, development is 'the effort of societies to approximate to the optimum sector paths'.[40] In terms of a mechanism, what we have (in addition to the above-noted element of 'reactive nationalism') is a mixture of growth economics, after the style of Harrod, and sectoral analysis, after the style of the economist Colin Clark.[41]

What was the response to Rostow's text? Amongst laymen it was well received – a matter I will return to below – whilst amongst specialists it was badly received.

Higgins[42] argues that Rostow's work adds nothing to knowledge; and he offers a series of criticisms:

(i) To stage theories in general: they are vague and internally logically indeterminate (i.e. it's never clear just what is being claimed about history and its stages and their sequences).

(ii) To Rostow's stage theory in particular: the stages ought to be distinct, relations between stages clearly specifiable, and the scope of the claims being made ought also to be clear and in all particulars Rostow's effort fails.

(iii) To Rostow's facts: he is not reliable.

We might care to note that Higgins is, if anything, 'on Rostow's side'; so too is Hagen,[43] who similarly argues that Rostow's work does not advance knowledge of matters of modernization. Baran and Hobsbawm are not 'on Rostow's side' (both are marxists) and having dismissed Rostow's stage theory much as the orthodox critics did, remark that the closest the author actually comes to offering a mechanism of growth (as distinct from banal redescription) comprises 'little more than verbiage . . . based on . . . coffee-house sociology and political speculation'.[44] Baran and Hobsbawm suggest that Rostow's work is (so) defective precisely because of the book's subtitle – *A Non-Communist Manifesto*. Rostow takes himself to have replaced Marx – which claim Baran and Hobsbawm then demolish. Not a difficult task, it must be said.

So why was Rostow's book so very influential? A sketch of an answer to this question of popularity – amongst laymen – can be presented in terms of 'ideological fitness'. So we ask: how does Rostow's *mélange* of proffered explanations sit with the political needs of those embroiled in matters of development? We can identify two broad areas: the timing and origin of his message, on the one hand, and, on the other, the optimistic generality of its content.

Rostow's 'stages' analysis is the pre-eminent theory of modernization in the early 1960s. The work was first presented in a 1956 essay[45] and represented in its now familiar form in 1960. Thus its initial publication coincides with the shift from US exclusivity in aid-giving to competition (as noted above) and the subsequent search for an elaborated theory of modernization. In the 1960 publication the policy-scientific core of the scheme plus its anti-communist theme fit Rostow neatly into the 'New Frontier'.[46] It is here that we find the highest expression of the notions of 'interventionism'. Rostow was a part of this establishment.

The counterpart is the message's acceptability. In the 1960s a confluence of factors had effectively shifted international discussion of aid and development on to a very general level. Debate came to focus on the 'rules of the game'; and questions about what aid was actually for, how it was supposed to work, and what existing conceptions supposed and entailed, all dropped away. In their place there was a presumption of 'self-evidence'. Here the descriptive, unreflective generality of the Rostovian scheme was, it can be suggested, wholly appropriate. It can also be suggested that the scheme had 'detailed stylistic' advantages: thus 'take-off' was scheduled to take twenty years – a period that was, for any policy-maker, both short enough to be conceivable and long enough not to be oppressive. Rostow's theory also offered quantitative criteria. Brookfield summarizes the scheme's persuasiveness as follows:

> It seemed to give every country an equal chance; it 'explained' the advantage of the developed countries; it offered a clear path to progress – without spelling this out in detail; it identified the requirements for advance with the virtues of the West; it suggested comfortingly that the communist countries were in fact following Western recipes, with a difference; it debunked the historical theories of Marx.[47]

7 Dissenting economics: neo-institutionalism

The orthodox tradition within development theory is an internally diverse one and the more narrowly economic traditions that it draws upon are themselves diverse. In considering the work of mainstream economists it is possible to identify a position which dissents from the central idea of the regulative discipline of the marketplace. In place of this idea the proponents of 'dissenting economics' substitute a scheme of rational and reasonable control of the market via mechanisms of planning and regulation.

In the wake of the 'marginalist revolution' of the 1870s, we find a steady stream of these dissenters: they include Veblen, Galbraith and Myrdal. Common to all these various schemes of dissenting economics is the stress upon economics as social economics. Economic analyses are routinely and self-consciously couched in terms which acknowledge that economies are simultaneously social systems and have their own distinct socio-cultural patterns and histories. Elsewhere,[1] I have called this a 'sociologized economics'; here, I want to consider the work of one variant of this approach, neo-institutionalism, via the work of the noted development theorist and planner Gunnar Myrdal.

The school I have labelled neo-institutionalism can be taken, despite its internal diversity, to represent a coherent and distinct position within the orthodox line of development theorizing. These theorists – with the figure of Myrdal made central – tended to the view that development studies was a novel and distinct social science. This is not a view I would share, but these theorists' self-understanding gave their writings a theoretical self-consciousness and part of this self-consciousness involved a denial of the simple transferability of social scientific concepts that had been produced in the First World to the circumstances of the Third World. Thus we can see that Dudley Seers, in a celebrated article[2] published in 1963, argues that the concepts of orthodox economics are not applicable to the economies of the Third World. (And this point, by extension, is true of all social scientific notions.) Attention must be paid, he argues, to the institutional and social contexts of the economies in question and to their position in the world economy. This emphasis on 'situating' analysis is taken up by Paul Streeten.[3] Streeten is, to my mind, the most theoretically subtle member of this group and, additionally, he can usefully be taken as Myrdal's exegetist. It is Myrdal who is the pre-eminent figure of the neo-institutionalists.

The particular occasion for the work of the neo-institutionalists is to be found in the late 1950s and early 1960s as the European colonial powers withdraw from Africa south of the Sahara: 'black' Africa, in other words. I take neo-institutionalism to be an interventionist scheme, but in this case the political and socio-cultural contexts (both for 'intervenors' and their new nation 'clients') of calls for intervention have changed. The neo-institutionalists are not immediately concerned with confronting a supposedly expansionist communism, as was the case with modernization theory. Nor are they attempting to interpret a rather general commitment to development, as was the case with growth theory. What they are concerned with is the project of *reworking long-established colonial relationships* such that over a period of time a replacement ruling elite, which would affirm ideas of nationalist developmentalism, could be safely installed. This project of 'reworking' is thus understood as involving: (a) First World 'experts' deploying a *reflexive* social science; (b) indigenous replacement rulers; (c) continuing 'aid' from the departing colonial power; (d) a long period during which the exchanges between the various actors will be for mutually agreed goals – that is, co-operative. It is with these general thoughts in mind that I label neo-institutionalism – the approach that comes out of these peculiar circumstances – an ideology, in my sense, of co-operative (revised authoritative) interventionism.

The resources invoked by the neo-institutionalists include: the actual experience of the colonial episode; a history of close relationships between social scientists and governments which generally has had a 'liberal reformist' character; and a distinct European tradition of social thought which we can, for our purposes, trace back to Thorstein Veblen and which is concerned with controlling the free market.

The resources available to the neo-institutionalists from the colonial episode were of great significance. This is clear if we compare the idea of intervention as it appears in US modernization work with how it appears in neo-institutionalism. The European colonial powers had long years of experience with their colonial territories, and even if such knowledge was partial, it was none the less available. The USA never had an equivalent stock of knowledge. When the demand came to theorize 'development', the neo-institutionalists could draw on the body of knowledge and local contacts established over the years (merely by being there) and within this body of knowledge there was the idea of 'stewardship' because, however grudgingly, it has been acknowledged that the ethical end of colonialism was the abolition of the system. Stewardship is a richer idea (and presents a subtler view of the relationships of First Worlders and Third Worlders) than that of containment, which was the notion central to modernization theory. To put the matter very simply it can be said that neo-institutionalism evolves out of an ongoing European colonial situation, whereas modernization is cobbled together in the USA in response to a developing competitive situation.

To this element of the lessons available within the experience of the colonial situation we can add our second element: again, it points up differences in the European and American situations. Hawthorn[4] argues that 'national' sociologies can be identified, and characterized, and that the peculiar characters of such 'national sociologies' owe much to the relationship of the community of social scientists to the state. Hawthorn's comparative history is a complex tale but from it we can draw one, rather general, point. In Europe there has been a tendency for social theory and political practice to be distinctly liberal reformist in character. In contrast, in the case of the USA, such liberal reformism has not been the general rule. This general intellectual/social milieu provides neo-institutionalism with its characteristic political ethic: these theorists' work centres upon the ideal of rule by men of enlightened goodwill.

Turning now to the intellectual resources available to the theorists of neo-institutionalism, we find a particular variant of the tradition of 'dissenting economics' which goes back to the turn of the century and, in particular, to the work of Thorstein Veblen. Institutional economics are associated with Veblen, who was a stern critic of the unregulated market, and centre upon the matter of government control of business. In the 1930s in the USA, neo-institutionalism was, to simplify, the intellectual counterpart to President Roosevelt's 'New Deal' – a programme of government public works designed to ameliorate the effects of the Great Depression. Myrdal's precise relationship with the neo-institutionalists is a matter of some debate; however, the label neo-institutionalist does capture the spirit and character of his work:

he makes the planner central and advances the idea of 'world welfarism'.

Myrdal's writings are very extensive and often rather repetitive: Brookfield calls him a 'generalist'.[5] I will offer a brief sketch of what I take to be the core of the Myrdalian position. I can begin by noting that Myrdal's work involved a strong reaction against neo-classical equilibrium theory and in its place offered a new 'sociologized economics' which had as its central dynamic the idea of 'circular cumulative causation'. The social and economic system is no longer seen, contra the orthodox economists, as a self-regulating system; instead, Myrdal argues that once a direction of change is set then the social system adjusts to reinforce that direction of change. In addition to this revision, Myrdal also includes *people*, whom he treats naturalistically so that they become causal agents of change. What we have, I think, is an idea of social inertia. However, this 'dynamic' is fitted into a vague evolutionist framework such that the present result of the process of cumulative causation is the modern welfare state. The next logical step is 'world welfarism'.

With regard to the Third World, Myrdal applies his notion of circular cumulative causation both to the Third World position *vis à vis* the world economy and to its internal social and institutional structures. His conclusions are notoriously pessimistic. The Third World nations are, he suggests, locked into a debilitating position in the world economy and are internally crippled by outmoded social forms. The remedy is to use national planning to shift individual economies into an upward dynamic – 'what in fact we all mean by development is the movement upward of the whole social system.'[6] It is with the notion of planning that we meet the clue to understanding Myrdal's work: he is writing the ideology of the First World planner in its most 'obvious' form. The state planning agencies are the vehicle for contriving an upward dynamic: Myrdal observes:

> what a state needs, and what politics is about, is precisely a macro-plan for inducing changes, simultaneously, in a great number of conditions, not only in the economic, and doing it in a way so as to co-ordinate all these changes in order to reach a maximum development effect of efforts and sacrifices. This may, in popular terms, be a definition of what we should mean by planning.[7]

I remarked above that Myrdal was the figure made central to this school: and his approach to development has been reflected in a diverse group of 'liberal reformists', all of whom attempt to use a sceptical and 'reflexive' approach to the construction of *realistic*[8] models upon which piecemeal planning can be based. I want now to pick out three issues which flow from the approach adopted by the neo-institutionalists.

The first is the matter of the use made of the resources of social science. The neo-institutionalists' scheme is, as I have noted, typically piecemeal, sceptical and empiricist. It pursues realism in modelling as means to order planned social change and the key idea in respect of the construction of such models is that a concept has an ecology, so to say. That is, concepts are seen as working only in particular circumstances. So, for example, Seers[9] looks at the familiar economist's term 'unemployment' and points out that far from this notion being an abstract, generally applicable notion, as the orthodox economists would be obliged to claim, it is only usable in a particular context. When the economist uses the term, he *thereby supposes* all the social and institutional arrangements of mature capitalist society. The corollary is clear: in the case of any Third World economy a detailed knowledge of the society is a prerequisite of concept-formation. Further than this, not only does social scientific 'data' enable the neo-institutionalist's epistemology of concept-formation to function, it also provides the general conceptual framework for analysing social systems.

The second point in respect of the neo-institutionalists' argument strategy concerns their attempts to resolve the 'problem of values' in social science. Myrdal's solution involves, in addition to a reflexive (or self-critical) effort to extirpate bias, invoking the notion of 'crisis politics'. This argument (if that is what it is) involves the key claim that in periods of 'crisis' (political, social and economic) value issues are rendered 'obvious' and therefore unproblematical. In periods of crisis, it is claimed, it becomes generally obvious what ought to be done. Development, for the neo-institutionalists, is one such 'obvious crisis'; and, as I will point out a little later on, there is a distinct element of appeals to crisis-engendered obviousness in talk of 'basic needs'. As a solution to the problem of values in social science it is, of course, a non-solution.

Finally, I wish to discuss the neo-institutionalists' scheme of agency: the mechanisms which will actually effect the social changes they deem necessary. This, in other terms, introduces the question of the neo-institutionalists' conception of the relationship of theory and practice. Myrdal argues their typical position. The state (planning) machine run by reasonable men will order and implement programmes of social change. What Myrdal does is reduce politics to planning. It seems to me that this scheme is absurd and I think Myrdal recognizes this, for, having taken note that the typical Third World state cannot (for reasons of inefficiency, corruption, lack of skills, etc.) fulfil the role allocated to it by the Myrdalian scheme, he goes on to introduce the idea of the 'soft state'. The character of the 'soft state' explains why his scheme is not yet ready to go.

In the end it seems to me that the neo-institutional approach is the most plausible of the post-Second World War orthodox theories of development. The general procedural dictum of neo-institutionalism is the pursuit of problem-specific formulations and not general theories. Its analytical machineries are subtle, in contrast to those of growth and modernization theory, and the claim to the 'obviousness' of their reformist stance may well, as we shall see below, be taken as a part of the 'common sense' of development studies. However, whilst the work of the neo-institutionalists is valuable and instructive, it is none the less flawed, for reasons noted above. It remains a policy-scientific and interventionist scheme, for all that it is a subtle version.[10]

8 After modernization

Thus far I have dealt with the way in which the 'bourgeois liberal' line of development studies was assembled into a, momentarily unchallenged, orthodoxy in the guise of modernization theory. What I have done is reviewed the process of the construction of an ideology. I now turn to the business of the decline and disintegration of that position: this is an intrinsically more awkward task and here I will rely upon the exposition offered by Hoogvelt.[1]

Hoogvelt's treatment of what she calls 'new directions' in orthodox thinking revolves around the substitution of the idea of global interdependence for recapitualation (where the Third World has to 'catch up' with the First World) and the programme (the policy expressions of these ideas) of international Keynesianism for modernization. I will break up my treatment into three parts: (i) overview; (ii) NIEO (New International Economic Order); (iii) basic needs.

Hoogvelt identifies a series of circumstances which together conspired to redirect the attention of orthodox development theorists, and which, in particular, undermined their (remarkable) optimism. Thus she takes note that the post-Second World War economic 'boom' faltered through the late 1960s and then, in the early 1970s, came to a halt. Subsequently, the world economy has moved into a depression situation. A second factor is the impact of the 1973 oil price rises instituted by OPEC (the Organization of Petroleum Exporting Countries) which she reads as contributing to inflation and thus depression, and as an act of political defiance which rather challenged the 'recapitulation' idea at back of modernization theory. Third, there is a shift in the international terms of trade in favour of the First World: thus the situation of the Third World deteriorated. Again, the optimism of modernization theory looked inappropriate. A fourth point relates to the arrival on the intellectual/political scene of a new series of concerns: overpopulation and (new) food crises; arms production – both its total sum and the extent of Third World spending on imports of sophisticated weaponry; there were also fears for ecological problems – resource depletion, pollution.

Running alongside these particular reasons was the fact of the presentation of a counter-view to modernization theory: dependency. The dependency view originated (as we will see later) in Latin America and, in its watered-down versions, has been used by international agencies, like the UN and the World Bank. Dependency theory contains, as one central element, the idea of a 'world system' and this was picked up by First World orthodox theorists. The upshot is, as noted, that 'recapitulation' gives way to 'global interdependence'.

The circumstances of Third World countries are now not to be discussed in terms of how they can modernize, and thereby 'catch up', but in terms of their role within the world system. This role has to be characterized so as to display the responsibilities of the powerful: in an interdependent world system the onus for achieving growth or development no longer rests exclusively with individual nation states. Their possibilities for the future are highly circumscribed by the world contexts within which they operate. The rich are now implicated in the business of development – at least in principle.

Hoogvelt then turns to the 'kaleidoscopic diversity'[2] of those theorists who have tried to peer into the future. She calls their work 'World Futures Theories'[3] and offers an interesting note on their methods. What we find is the production of models, the extrapolation of trends, the simulation of alternatives: generally, the production of scenarios. Hoogvelt points out (a) that this rests, as did modernization, on systems theory, and (b) that it is interventionist and, crucially, attempts to reduce the intervenor to extra-systemic cause. This is, of course, impossible and so is usually disguised as appeals to 'the reasonable men acting for mankind'.

The members of what Hoogvelt dubs the 'first generation' include people like Herman Kahn, Walt Rostow and the various 'eco-doomsday' theorists of the Club of Rome reports.[4] I shall ignore these people as they are peripheral to the main trend of development thinking. (This is one problem of tracing decline – large fragments break off and pursuing them is interesting, but also dispersive of our attention.)

The 'second generation' Hoogvelt calls the international Keynesians. The rationale for this label is clear: where Keynes urged national governments to stimulate demand within their economies during times of depression so as to preserve the system, the international Keynesian line urges the necessity of international agreement on a new international economic order lest the Third World nations collapse into a miserable poverty and, in so doing, damage the economies of the First World. In order to bring the diversity of material under control, I will distinguish two areas of concern for international Keynesianism: first, the business of the 'rules of the game' which I shall discuss in the context of the NIEO programme; and, second, the business of reforms in aid and resource transfer and its utilization – which can be tackled under the heading 'basic needs'. The first-noted area looks to the business of stimulating economic growth in the Third World (and thereby providing markets for First World exports), whilst the second-noted area looks at 'welfare' – resource transfer and use.

The presentation of the NIEO, in the United Nations, is (as might be expected) a complex little story in itself; Hoogvelt compresses the tale thus: 'the *Declaration on the Establishment of a New International Economic Order*[3] . . . and the accompanying *Program of Action*, were adopted without a vote at the Sixth Special Session of the UN General Assembly in May 1974, and were confirmed in November 1974 in the *Charter of Economic Rights and Duties of States*.'[5] These texts contain declarations of principles, programmes of development of the principles and, on Hoogvelt's account, all have been further elaborated in a series of subsequent and related conferences. I will set aside all this instutitional detail and speak simply of the NIEO and its concern to adjust the 'rules of the game' in favour of the Third World nations. The NIEO can be taken to have had five principal areas of concern. First, international trade reforms: concern here, on the part of the drafters of the NIEO, focuses upon the declining value of primary products – the major source of earnings for Third World nations. Proposals include the establishment of 'buffer stocks' to smooth out price fluctuations, the establishment of targets for a shift in balance of global industry and liberalized trade preferences for Third World economies. Second, international monetary reform: as the Bretton Woods arrangement falters the Third World nations have sought to have *their* interests acknowledged in the processes of reformulation. Third, debt relief: the burden upon the budgets of some Third World nations of debt-servicing is now severe and the NIEO was concerned to seek alleviation. (Since 1974, of course, the debt problem has begun to assume crisis proportions.) Fourth, technology transfer: here attention is focused upon maximizing the benefit to host nations of multinationals and minimizing the costs of bought-in technology. Fifth, there is concern to foster interregional co-operation.[6]

After the presentation of the NIEO programme the First and Third World manoeuvred for position, the First World endeavouring to block change. In this goal it not only seems to have succeeded but, with the ideas of 'basic needs', it actually seems to have turned the tables on the Third World nations. Where the pursuit of development was taken to be a matter of increasing the autonomy of peripheral economies now – on the 'basic needs' view – it (development) now requires submission to greater levels of external direction.

The idea of basic needs originated with a group of Latin American theorists[7] and, reports Hoogvelt, 'was officially launched at the ILO [International Labour Organization] World Employment Conference in 1976'.[8] The Barlioche model was constructed so as to deny the pessimistic position of the first Club of Rome report: they argued that in a radically changed world economic system *all people* could have an acceptable standard of life. Rather more specifically, they argued that with a little more egalitarianism, national and international, basic needs could be achieved with much lower growth rates than are needed in the present inegalitarian world system.

The idea of basic needs was immediately picked up by theorists in the orthodox tradition, and by international institutions – the World Bank, in particular – and used to justify a reworked interventionist stance. The autonomy which the Third World nations had been pursuing in the NIEO debate was subtly undermined: aid and development project work had to be targeted at the poorest and success monitored. Recipient governments were required to acquiesce in their own downgrading, so to say. The Third World nations quickly came to view the 'basic needs' approach as thoroughly ambiguous!

The 'basic needs' approach, to simplify matters, involves the following elements: (i) it calls attention to the needs of the poorest of the poor, those whom Hoogvelt calls the inhabitants of the Fourth World; (ii) the attempt to define basic needs in operational terms – food, water, health and thereafter education, work and political participation; (iii) the establishment of targets for countries and the specification of criteria of performance; (iv) the acknowledgment of the necessity for structural – *internal* – transformations in the economic and socio-political patterns of societies.[9]

The 'basic needs' approach, thus summarized, has, in the light of what I have been arguing in respect of the character of Hoogvelt's 'bourgeois liberal orthodoxy', three rather obvious characteristics. These are, first, an appeal (covert) to obviousness. The distress of the poorest of the poor is such as to constitute a presently extant crisis. What must (ought) to be done is not, in general, in doubt: this crisis must be confronted in terms of immediate attempts to alleviate this distress. The second point which is immediately striking is that the scheme is interventionist: we have not left the realm of targets/aid flows/projects/performance criteria/monitoring etc. Thus far, then, the 'basic needs' approach is not new. There is a superficial novelty in the third characteristic: the business of urging the necessity of internal social, economic and political reform. It is here, with internal reform, that we come across the reasons why Third World nations have viewed the approach as ambiguous. More interestingly, we now confront the blindness of the theorists of basic needs to: (a) the role of the international system in creating the problems (of corruption, inefficiency, wastefulness, etc.) of which they are complaining; and (b) the impossibility of reducing the political realities of the present world system to a size that can be managed by a planner's ideology.

The politics of the real world (patterns of power and economic advantage) are presented as a problem for the planners. The recalcitrant world, on this view, must pull itself together so that the planners can get on with their jobs! However, it seems clear that matters of internal social, political and economic change cannot be treated thus. The substantive realities of Third World societies cannot be thus elided: making social reforms the precondition of effective planning begs the question of *how* such changes might be brought about. The problem for the basic needers is, in my view, that development cannot be reduced to a problem amenable to solution by recipe knowledge.

Paul Streeten,[10] an eloquent proponent of a 'basic needs' approach, manages to illustrate my contentions whilst simultaneously scoring a spectacular 'own goal' (it might even be a self-refuting 'own goal'!). Basic needs, says Streeten, are concrete goals, they are obvious, they are specific. Streeten goes on to say that the 'basic needs' approach:

(1) reminds us what development studies is all about – making better lives for people;
(2) spells out in detail the *human* requirements – food, water, health, housing, etc;
(3) reminds us that economic and social models are abstract and that theorists should be specific;
(4) appeals to the international community – the idea is clear;

(5) has great intellectual organizing power, all other development problems fall into place around it.

He then adds:

> In one sense, this is a home-coming. For when we embarked on development 30 years ago, it was surely the needs of the poor of the world that we had in mind. In the process we got sidetracked, but we also discovered many important things about development . . . We are now back where we started in the 1950s . . . But we are back with a deeper understanding . . . [and] with a clearer vision of the path.[11]

The work of thirty years has, so Streeten thinks, been very useful in learning what development studies is all about! It is true that there is something in this claim[12] – though it would be more remarkable if *no* learning had taken place – but it is not clear to me that Streeten has learned very much: basic needs are crisis-engendered obvious goals for technical expert intervention in a context of world community approval!

To summarize this review of the decline of the orthodoxy we must note that the relationship of NIEO and 'basic needs' is complex. The relationship of both to the interventionist ethic of the orthodoxy in development studies is also complex. The key idea to have come to the fore in this general line – Hoogvelt's 'bourgeois liberal' – is that of global interdependence. The present world system, it is suggested, can be 'saved' only if this is acknowledged. The First World has acted cautiously and defensively in the area of the overall setting of the rules of the game (NIEO). Its constituent countries have acted more aggressively with respect to 'basic needs' analyses which focus attention upon the recipients' uses of resource transfers. Interventionism – both in rule-setting and resource-using – continues to be the core of this orthodox position. However, in recent years another view has become fashionable. This analysis of the present world economic situation begins from the diagnosis of far too much intervention: a return to the joys of the 'free market' is urged. These people are known as 'monetarists' and it is to their ideology that I now turn.

9 Monetarism

Monetarism does *not* represent another school within development studies: however, there have been 'monetarist experiments' (most notoriously in Chile) and we can also identify a few details of the doctrine's general impact on Third World nations. I will offer a few notes on these matters a little later. Generally, however, this discussion of monetarism is little more than a footnote to the various characterizations of the 'bourgeois liberal orthodoxy' presented above. My own interest in monetarism is twofold: it represents, arguably, the 'residual common sense'[1] of orthodox economics; and it also offers a (rather vulgar) social and political ideology whilst simultaneously claiming the status of 'positive scientific' economics.

A simple technical characterization

The ideas which are embraced by monetarists can be traced back to the equilibrium theorists of the late nineteenth and early twentieth centuries, in general, and an American economist named Irving Fisher, in particular. Equilibrium theory is central to twentieth-century economics and may be characterized, in brief, as the theory of laissez-faire capitalism: the free market, left to its own self-regulating devices, will ensure a maximum of individual utilities and their equitable distribution. Irving Fisher was one of the major contributors to the elaboration of equilibrium theory and paid particular attention to the market which determined rates of interest. It was, on Fisher's view, the rate of interest that was the key mechanism for ensuring system equilibrium. If the system's 'activity level' (my term – not, I think, any economist's) were to fall, then interest rates would fall, making it cheaper to borrow money, and thus encourage spending which in turn would lift the economy's 'activity level'. On the other hand, if the system's 'activity level' is rising too fast (above, presumably, a 'natural' level given by, for example, population increase and technological innovation), then higher interest rates will slow things down and re-establish equilibrium.

Fisher also argued that the economic system needed an appropriate amount of money in it so as to finance (facilitate) all the multiplicity of exchanges (of goods and services) taking place within it. There was a distinction drawn between the 'real economy' and the 'monetary economy'. Moreover, the prices of goods were determined, relatively, by the equilibrium system, and they were determined absolutely by the quantity of money available; it was governments that literally *made* money. This is the point that present-day monetarists have seized upon: it was 'rediscovered' by Milton Friedman, a vehement free marketeer and anti-Keynesian, in a context of problems of inflation in First World economies, and he argued that inflation was solely a monetary phenomenon. Inflation was created by governments operating their economies with too large a quantity of money in them.

But before we pursue these arguments, let us ask what happened to equilibrium theory? What happened was the Great Depression – idle plant, idle workers, idle money: a set of circumstances which, according to the equilibrium theory was not possible. Clearly, the situation was something of an embarrassment to the theory and, indeed, it was replaced by Keynes.

The economy, argued Keynes, *could* settle into low-level equilibrium and, moreover, it *could* be shifted from it although not by relying upon manipulating the interest rate. Instead, governments had to use fiscal policy (as opposed to monetary policy): government spending and taxation. In the post-Second World War period, as the economic 'boom' continued, monetary policy was forgotten and government planners spoke of fiscal policy and of 'fine tuning the economy'. Keynes's work was radical not only for the reasons noted here and above (with growth theory), but also – as I will bring out below – for the *revised conception of economics* itself that he advanced: his work was that of a liberal reformist.

Keynes's work was received less than wholeheartedly in the USA and the 'reformism' quickly fell away. Slowly, Keynesianism became a depression-relevant special case of the neo-classical equilibrium orthodoxy. Milton Friedman's work, seen in this context, is not so novel.

Throughout the 1970s a new 'problem' came to dominate economic thinking – inflation. And it was within this particular setting that Friedman's work attained its fashionable, almost 'conservative guru', status. Friedman argued that inflation was a phenomenon generated in the monetary economy (as opposed to the real economy) and that it was caused by government 'overspending': putting too large a quantity of money into the system. The remedy was simple: governments should stop their oversupply of money. It also involved reinstituting the laissez-faire market. This too was a good thing, argued Friedman, because competitive capitalism was the necessary condition of human freedom. Once again, we meet a version of the ideology of the 'Free World'!

The debate between Keyenesians and monetarists has been fierce. I will venture into this area with the intention of indicating how the contending parties regard the issue of inflation and, more broadly, how they regard the nature of economics: the work of Celso Furtado will usefully link up these two matters in the context of a discussion of how to theorize inflation in Third World economies.

The debate with Keynes

Narrow: how to tackle inflation

This debate, which is complicated in its detail, may be seen to turn on the matter of the cause of inflation. Keynesians (who do not distinguish 'real' from 'money' economies) have spoken of two varieties of inflationary pressure: cost–push inflation, so called because costs push up prices, and here wage costs have been of particular concern; and demand–pull inflation, which occurs when many consumers compete for scarce goods. The Keynesian concern with inflation, secondary, of course, to maintaining high levels of employment, centres upon curbing rises in prices and incomes: thus there have been, typically, statutory controls on price increases made by firms and conversely attempts to hold down wage costs by curbing wage increases. The right mix of policies has been a matter of debate and, indeed, until the slump of recent years the US and the UK (to offer two examples) managed for a few years, in the 1970s, to combine very low growth with inflation – 'stagflation'![2] As a political/social/economic phenomenon, inflation (like any other circumstance) is hugely complex.

The monetarists, in contrast, offered a 'simple cure': the cause of inflation was too great a quantity of money in the economy. Distinguishing 'real' and 'money' economies, Friedman could boldly announce that 'inflation is always and everywhere a monetary phenomenon'[3] which is caused by governments taking the easy way out of problems by 'printing money'. The solution is equally clear – curb government spending and thereby reduce the quantity of money in the system.[4] This message has the great merit of simplicity: analogies can be drawn between profligate householders who spend all they have, and responsible householders who budget carefully and live within their means. Profligacy in government is the problem – so say the monetarists. To this central stand are conjoined several other laissez-faire notions. Thus the monetarists do not believe – unlike the Keynesians – that governments have much influence on rates of economic growth or rates of unemployment. The monetarists do think that governments have a powerful impact on the rate of inflation.

As the government cuts its spending – reduces welfare budgets, usually – so will the inflation rate drop and the self-regulating system attain its equilibrium position; thereafter, it will function smoothly.[5] In the short term there will be a few rather unpleasant 'side-effects' – a dramatic fall in the output of the economy and an equally dramatic rise in the rate of unemployment. All this, say the Keynesians, is little more than a recipe for a slump and there are no reasons to suppose that the slump will be self-removing.

This debate continues and I cannot follow the economists: what I can do at this point is take note that in the UK (where the government has been explicitly monetarist) the economy has, on the face of it, deteriorated steadily over the years of Conservative power. Again, in the USA, another monetarist government has presided over cutbacks in welfare, a huge expansion in arms spending,[6] a rising government deficit (*sic*), and now seems to have a growing economy on its hands! In Chile, *the* Third World 'experiment', there has been what is widely seen as an economic disaster.

I will now turn to the debate between monetarists and Keynesians about the *nature* of economic science: but before I do that the issues at stake can be illustrated by the critique of orthodox discussions of inflation in Latin America offered by Celso Furtado.

Furtado: a structuralist analysis of inflation

In his *Economic Development of Latin America*[7] Furtado presents a structuralist analysis of inflation. Structuralist economics begins with a denial of the relevance of orthodox economics (Keynesian and neo-classical) to the circumstances of Latin America. The economies of Latin America must be modelled directly and not with reference to *a priori* schemes imported from the First World.

The 'typical' Latin American economy is seen as split into a very loosely related set of quasi-autonomous 'sectors' each of which represents either a residue of the historical process of the expansion of European capitalism or a present requirement of the newly dominant capitalist centre of the USA. The distinctively 'autonomous national economy' of orthodox economics simply does not exist: there is, rather, a concatenation of 'residues', 'enclaves', and various 'parasitic forms'. As O'Brien puts it: 'An underdeveloped country is underdeveloped precisely because it consists of different structures each with a specific type of behaviour.'[8]

The structuralist analysis of inflation – as propounded by Furtado – begins by noting the inflation-proneness of traditional primary-product-exporting economies and then goes on to note that 'Industrialization based on import substitution started a new inflationary cycle'[9] Weaknesses in the 'capacity to import' were met by generating local credits (printing money, a monetarist would say!) and this 'sparked off a number of structural tensions which were translated into an inflationary process.'[10]

The debate around the matter of inflation lets Furtado counterpose a structuralist approach, to those orthodox discussions (and Furtado does not separate out very clearly Keynesian and monetarist approaches) which regard inflation as a matter of the poor functioning of money flows. Thus Furtado insists that even if familiar patterns of inflation did occur,[11] then they were, more often than not, the outcome of 'more complex processes, whose main ingredients were structural inflexibility and the determination to press ahead with a development policy.'[12] This argument is unpacked in terms of the various responses contrived by the different sectors of the economy in endeavouring to avoid the burden of financing (through increased taxes or reduced subsidies, etc.) the government's deficit. Thus Furtado deploys notions such as: 'basic inflationary pressures', 'circumstantial pressures', 'propagation mechanisms' and, crucially, 'decision centres'. The last-mentioned involves the financial authorities of the state. It is here, of course, that monetarist arguments get started. In sum, Furtado attempts to provide an analysis of inflation that acknowledges the particular circumstances of Latin American economies in contrast to the analyses presented by the orthodox which rest – more or less sophisticatedly – upon ideas of integrated (maybe), self-regulating equilibrium systems.[13]

Broad: what is economics?

Furtado's view of economics requires that it be adequate to specific situations: he 'writes in' sociology and history. The orthodox tend not to – and the monetarists deliberately write them out. This issue of the scope of economics is one I will now, briefly, pursue.

Friedman's conception of the status of economics is, in terms of my distinction between 'empiricists' and 'rationalists' presented in Part 1, firmly empiricist. Economics is a narrowly technical discipline dealing not with 'values', but with 'how things in fact are'. In a noted essay, 'The Methodology of Positive Economics',[14] Friedman claims that:

> Positive economics is in principle independent of any particular ethical position . . . Its task is to provide a system of generalizations that can be used to make correct predictions about the consequences of any change in circumstances. Its performance is to be judged by the precision, scope, and conformity with experience of the predictions it yields. In short, positive economics is, or can be, an 'objective' science, in precisely the same sense as any of the physical sciences.[15]

A little later we are told that the role of *theory* is twofold: systematization and abstraction of essentials. Theory, in other words, is a complex summary description. Prediction is difficult and testing awkward, but not insuperably difficult – the absence of laboratory experiment can be accommodated. Assumptions in economics are, Friedman argues, relatively unimportant: accurate predictions are the key. In sum: 'Economics as a positive science is a body of tentatively accepted generalizations about economic phenomena that can be used to predict the consequences of changes in circumstances.'[16]

As I made clear in Part 1, I personally am not persuaded of the correctness of this view: indeed, I do not think a 'positive' social science is possible. Furthermore, it seems to me that its pursuit distracts attention from the task of discovering just what social science can and cannot do.[17] However, matters improve when we turn to monetarism's target.

Keynesianism in its original form was an economics and politics of social reform. Joan Robinson offers a series of points on this matter. She contrasts Keynesian economics with the neo-classical orthodoxy which it had (she thought) replaced. Keynes, Robinson argues, brought back into economics the 'hard-headedness of the Classics'[18] – i.e. he speaks directly of capitalism. Keynes reintroduces history (no more non-specific enquiry), morals (no more easy value-freedom: economists must necessarily make and defend choices), time (no more timeless perfect equilibrium worlds). Robinson summarizes the impact of the work of Keynes by saying that these revisions made

> it impossible to believe any longer in an automatic reconciliation of conflicting interests into a harmonious whole, [Keynes] brought out into the open the problem of choice and judgement that the neo-classicals had managed to smother. The ideology to end ideologies broke down. Economics once more became Political Economy . . . The Keynesian revolution has destroyed the old soporific doctrines . . . We are left in the uncomfortable situation of having to think for ourselves.[19]

The ideology of monetarism

Monetarism is the ideology of social conservatism: this is made perfectly clear by Friedman when he argues that laissez-faire capitalism is a necessary condition of political freedom.[20] In a competitive capitalist society individuals freely enter into exchanges – in the marketplace and in society. The role of the state is minimal: economic power is dispersed in a competitive capitalist economy and political power, too, must be dispersed. The separation of economic from political power lets the former act as a check on the concentration tendencies in the latter: the proper role of the latter, the state, is in setting the rules of the social game (so as to outlaw coercion) and arbitrating on disputes. Friedman takes this ideology to rule out not only (his version of) socialism, but also the welfare-state-type of societies of the post-Second World War First World.

If Friedman's work on methods is unpersuasive, his efforts in the realm of political thought are rather depressingly stupid: C. B. Macpherson[21] offers a sharp critique of the ideology underlying monetarism and here I will rehearse a couple of Macpherson's points.

It is Friedman's contention that competitive capitalism entails no coercion – people freely choose how to earn their money and how to spend it. This proposition is established in two steps. We begin by considering the situation in a 'simple traditional society', where production is for subsistence and any surplus is exchanged if the participants so wish: if they do not want to enter the market, then they do not have to. Co-operation is freely entered into. This is the simple market model. Step number two in the argument shifts us to a consideration of modern society. This is the 'actual complex market model'. Co-operation is free if (a) productive enterprises are privately owned, and (b) if individuals can choose not to enter any particular exchange. The complex model repeats the essence of the simple model and hence we can see, Friedman argues, that competitive capitalism entails no coercion. The logical slide is this: in the simple market model actors were free not to enter *any* exchange, whereas in the complex market model they are free not to enter *any particular* exchange – they now cannot refrain from entering exchange at all. Macpherson comments that Friedman has shifted from

> the simple economy of exchange between independent producers, to the capitalist economy, without mentioning the most important thing that distinguishes them . . . [namely] the separation of labour and capital, that is, the existence of a labour force without its own sufficient capital and therefore without a choice as to whether to put its labour in the market or not.[22]

This is enough to undermine Friedmanite 'liberalism': but we can pick up one more of Macpherson's points.

Friedman's ideology is anti-socialist and anti-welfare state. On Friedman's view, capitalism is a condition of political freedom and socialism is therefore incompatible with political freedom. Friedman offers a historical argument: thus capitalism is historically associated with political freedom. This, remarks Macpherson, is true so far as it goes, but what is the causal relationship? On Macpherson's view, political freedoms had to be won in order to get capitalism going: here we could cite the English, French and American revolutions (the first and last in the forms of civil war). Friedman, however, also offers a logical argument: the economic dispersal of power restricts the tendency of political power concentration. Macpherson comments that the market may *enable* the offsetting of political power, but the market does not necessarily *lead to* such offsetting. Indeed, the probability runs the other way: if the state is weak, then economic power is enhanced and as capitalist society is unfree (labour/capital) this enhances unfreedom – coercion. It is only welfare or socialist systems that have reduced such capitalist market coercion.[23]

The impact on the Third World: the Chilean experiment

The view of economic systems propounded by monetarists rests upon, as we have seen, the idea of equilibrium. Economies, if left to their own devices – that is, with no state intervention – will tend to settle into an equilibrium position that is 'optimal' (that is, roughly, most generally efficient) for the economy. Whilst ideas of equilibrium and optimal configurations can be developed in several ways – in particular, as I have noted in discussing Keynes earlier, to assist economic planning schemes – the monetarists have sought to reduce planning intervention by the state.

There has been one notable experiment with, or test of, monetarist theory in the Third World – Chile. The history of the Chilean experiment has been simply reviewed by Hurtado[24] and here I will present the gist of her discussion. Thus we can note that prior to the monetarist experiment, the Chilean economic strategy was, like others in the region, concerned with industralizing behind tariff barriers. In this process the state played a major role. The Allende government added to this programme extensive redistribution policies and the role of the state increased – as did inflation, which reached a remarkable 600 per cent. Through the early 1970s the USA organized a 'destabilization' programme which bore fruit in the 1973 coup of Pinochet. Hurtado comments:

> General Augusto Pinochet's 1973 military coup buried the old Chile. Fired by the Milton Friedman doctrine, Chile's new economic team [known as the 'Chicago Boys' began to engineer an economic counter revolution to end inflation and stimulate production and exports by opening up to international competition and freeing the domestic market.[25]

Seven policy initiatives are noted:

(i) sharp reductions in import tariff barriers;
(ii) removal of controls on the private financial sector;
(iii) tight restrictions imposed on government spending (money supply);
(iv) government spending levels cut sharply;
(v) removal of subsidies;
(vi) privatization;
(vii) liberal rules for foreign investment.

After a steep recession in 1975 the approach seemed to be working: by 1979 inflation had fallen dramatically and exports were growing. However, in the conditions of world recession of the 1980s the Chilean economy quickly sank into debt, unemployment, bankruptcies, and so on. There has also been a political price to be paid for the 'experiment' and its failure. Richard Gott recalls that Pinochet came to power with 'the initial support and encouragement of Chile's comparatively large middle class'.[26] Their enthusiasm, reports Gott, drained away as Pinochet established a dictatorial regime that was unpleasant even by Latin American standards. With the collapse of the exposed economy the issue now, so far as Gott sees it, is: how will Pinochet be removed? So much for the Chilean monetarist experiment.[27]

Marxist theories

In Chapters 10–13 I will review the major elements of the 'marxian' approach to matters of development.[1] In earlier chapters I have looked at the several varieties of orthodox, 'bourgeois', approaches and indicated how they grew out of rather different circumstances and presented theories with differing characterizations of development and the way in which it could be secured. Roughly speaking, the various shifts in emphasis could be expressed as a process of broadening (social scientifically and ethico-politically) of approach around an essentially similar common approach that is authoritative and interventionist.

When we turn to look at marxian approaches there are – in addition to analogous internal complexities and confusions of discussion – a number of 'strategic' points to be made so that enquiry can proceed in a rational fashion. Thus most generally it has to be acknowledged at the outset that what we confront in the work of the marxian tradition is a completely different strategy of making sense. The intellectual traditions invoked are different from those of the orthodox. In respect of conception (that is, ideas about *how* social theoretic enquiry should proceed), the marxian line is, to put the matter simply, rationalistic. Social theorizing is essentially a matter of argument and not, contra the orthodox, description. In respect of intention (that is, ideas held about the *purpose* of social theoretic enquiry), the marxian line is practical – in the sense of attempting to uncover the dynamic of the social world so as to be able to act politically in it – rather than, as with the orthodox, technical – where theorizing is done on behalf of the authoritative interventionist planners.[2] Terrel Carver sums up the idea of scientific enquiry that Marx had in the following way: 'The searching process for Marx was essentially active, investigative, critical and practical; a scientific presentation, in his view, seems to have been one which solved conceptual mysteries and presented the human world accurately, intelligibly and politically.'[3] In sum, we must first adequately characterize before we go on to criticize (or complement) the approach.[4] It is pointless to condemn the work – as is often done – on the grounds that it fails to improve on orthodox material when judged by orthodox standards!

In addition to this 'strategic' point, there are two other notes to be made. First, debate within the marxian line has been routinely concerned (albeit with differing stresses) with uncovering the fundamental characteristics of the approach. The marxian line has only reappeared on the general intellectual scene in the last twenty years. Marxists have thus had to decide just what marxian analysis entailed at the same time as they addressed specific issues – and my present concern is with their treatments of 'development'. The orthodox, in contrast, have not had this sort of problem as their work was essentially concerned with refashioning established intellectual tools for novel uses (even if the extent of refashioning was, occasionally, very extensive as it was with, say, Seers or Streeten). Second, debate within the marxian line has been 'severally located' – that is, geographically, politically and intellectually (different 'readings' of Marx). Often within reviews of the marxian approach vital distinctions between the various elements are neglected: splendid confusion is generated!

Both these points are captured in Figure 1, which I have prepared after the work of Palma.[5] This diagrammatic summary of marxian debate presents us with three distinct areas/stances and one contemporary summary concern. The three areas are: dependency theory; neo-marxism; and the work of A. G. Frank (around whom several debates turn). The summary issue – what is to count as a properly marxian analysis? – is the point at which the issues noted above as latent within the approach are now explicitly addressed.

To a significant extent – as will become clear in the following chapters – the whole marxian line treating development has been shaped by the Latin American theorists of dependency. These theorists – with Celso Furtado as the particular figure whom I will consider – have, in the post-war period, effected a thoroughgoing revision of long-established patterns of Latin American social theorizing and political notions. Accident and design are conjoined in the presentation of the early structuralist approach: a scheme designed to make sense of changes set in train by the impact of the depression and the war years. A notion of disintegrated, multisectored economics was advanced and a broadly social scientific approach was favoured. Disappointment with

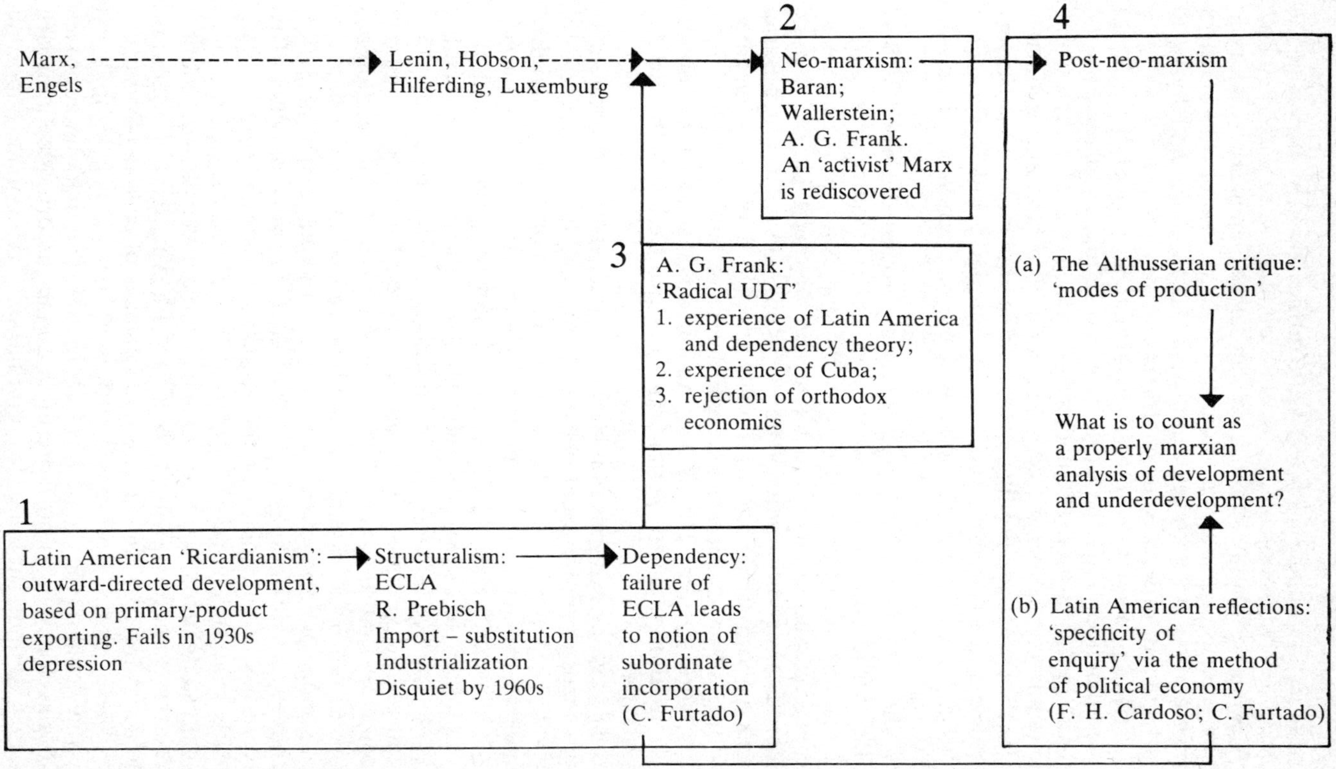

Figure 1 The relationship of the various elements of the 'marxist theories'

structuralist policies coupled with further thought issued in the dependency position. Third World economies were to be seen now as being peripheral, subordinate capitalist. Dependency theory in this guise is, arguably, a 'radical orthodoxy' rather than outright marxian, as it continues populist and nationalist and looks to government-ordered reform strategies.

The dependency work of Latin American scholars was one of the influences upon the work of A. G. Frank. Frank is a pivotal figure in this history: detailed attention to historical data, a strong commitment to socialist activism, and a trenchant and distinctive (English-language) writing style, combined to make his work very widely read and discussed. I will consider Frank's work both directly and as a part of the approach now often labelled as 'neo-marxian'.

The neo-marxian approach revolves around the work of Paul Baran who published a seminal text on development and under-development in the late 1950s. Baran makes use of the notion of economic surplus to characterize the internal logic of what he identifies as a monopoly-capitalist system – a system which Baran sees as both stable and irrational. The Third World is relegated to a position of subordinate and deformed incorporation within the world system. This is a condition which is likely to endure, thinks Baran, unless peripheral areas are 'rescued' by socialist revolution.

The neo-marxist position has come under strong criticism – and this leads us into present debate on marxian analysis *per se* – for what, to simplify, has been seen as its moralizing generality. Indeed, it has been suggested by more than a few (largely academic critics) that neo-marxism is not really marxian at all! I will take note of two particular lines of criticism, which together I label 'post-neo-marxism', and which have it in common that they address the summary issue of the nature of a properly marxian analysis of development. The notion of modes of production has been used in an attempt to combine sensitivity to the detail of particular patterns of life with a rigorously elaborated analytical framework which links up to the 'scientific' work of Marx. This work has been inspired by the French marxist philosopher Louis Althusser. In contrast, the second line of criticism of the neo-marxists which I want to consider invokes the idea of political economic enquiry. This material is Latin American in origin and looks to the identification of the dynamics of class conflicts.

These various positions and present debates will be followed up in detail in the chapters which follow. The marxian approach to 'development' is no more unified than the orthodox approach and it is important to be clear on this point. It is equally important to remember the 'strategic' differences between orthodox and marxian approaches.

10 Latin American dependency theory

I will discuss dependency theory in the following way: first, a brief note on Latin America's experience of the inter-war depression; second, a note on the work of Raul Prebisch; and, third, a discussion of Celso Furtado's dependency theory.

Up until the depression of the 1930s Latin American nations had pursued policies of primary-product exporting – an outward-oriented development. This approach was the result of the political victories of the European-oriented elites in the nineteenth century. (A. G. Frank[1] identifies two factions: the 'Europeans', who were advocates of free trade and thus a continuing role as primary-product exporters; and the 'Americans', who were nationalistic and advocates of industrialization behind protective tariff barriers.) Alongside this outward-orientation there was the 'available theory' of Ricardianism which served to explain and legitimate the status quo. David Ricardo was a nineteenth-century English political economist who – rather pardoxically, given the use made of his work in Latin America – was *the* theorist of the rising industrial bourgeoisie in England. The particular element of Ricardo's work which was invoked was the idea of international specialization. Each area of the world produces just that for which local circumstances best fit it and thereafter there is extensive exchange between areas, with the result of maximum general benefit.

This view of the benefits of international specialization was essentially an ideological (in the familiar sense also) justification of the UK's position in the world economy during most of the nineteenth century, when the industrial world economy was more or less equivalent to the UK economy. The theory guaranteed the industrial pre-eminence of the UK and relegated the rest of the world to the status of raw material suppliers and consumers of finished products.[2]

In the depression years the economies of Latin America were very badly hit as demand for their products fell, in line with falls in production within the industrialized economies of the First World. The automatic defensive reaction of Latin American governments, seeking to adapt to these adverse circumstances, had the effect of initiating a programme of import-substituting industrialization. As exports of primary products fell, so too did the income Latin America derived from them. Goods which had been bought abroad were now produced locally.

The work of the influential development theorist Raul Prebisch grows out of the experience of the Latin American economies after the crisis of the depression when their traditional patterns of economic activity – primary-product exporting – were severely disrupted by the contraction in world trade. The measures initiated by Latin American governments at this time in an attempt to reduce the disruptions to their economies had the effect of initiating a process of import-substituting industrialization. After the end of the war there was a revival in world trade and the process of industrializing was now in need of a general explanatory theory. Prebisch and a team of economists on the staff of ECLA (Economic Commission for Latin America) provided this theory.

The principal position against which Prebisch[3] developed his views was the claim of traditional Ricardian theories to the effect that international specialization conferred benefits upon all those involved. Against it, Prebisch uses a version of the centre/periphery idea. This idea was available not only in marxism, but also in indigenous Latin American anti-imperialist and anti-marxian writings. Prebisch argues that within the orthodox theory, and pre-depression status quo, Latin American economies were condemned to a secondary and relatively declining position. The solution was to pursue industrialization behind protective barriers: precisely the pattern which had grown up in the wake of the depression crisis. In addition to this reworking of the conception of the position of Latin American economies within the world economy, there is a concurrent reworking of the explanations of the nature of peripheral economies. The equilibrium model of neo-classicism is rejected in favour of an empiricist-style, pragmatic and problem-oriented approach known as *structuralism*.

The structuralist approach starts with the attempt realistically to model the local situation. The putative single national economy is seen as split into a very loosely integrated set of quasi-autonomous 'sectors'. Each sector represents either a residue of the historical process of the expansion of Western European capitalism or a present requirement of contemporary capitalism – where, of course, it is the USA that is predominant. The distinctively 'national economy' does not exist –instead, there is a collection of 'residues' and 'enclaves' and various 'parasitic forms'. As O'Brien puts it: 'An underdeveloped country is underdeveloped precisely because it consists of different structures each with a specific type of behaviour.[4]

The reformist structuralism of ECLA belongs to the first of what the noted dependency theorist Celso Furtado has called 'three easily identifiable periods'[5] in the economic history of post-war Latin America. The first is characterized as one of rapid growth based upon favourable terms of trade, accumulated reserves from the war years, and currencies strong enough to be able to withstand gradual devaluation in the face of already active inflationary pressures. By the mid-1960s the position was changed and the strategy of import-substituting industrialization was apparently failing: in this second period there was a sharp deterioration in the terms of trade and a slackening of the rate of growth.[6] On top of this the Cuban revolution provoked widespread questioning of the nature of Latin America's recent development history.

The deteriorating situation was interpreted by ECLA in terms of problems with small local markets (and associated difficulties of securing overseas markets) and disadvantageous international exchanges. Girvan reports that 'ECLA thus pursued a two pronged strategy of presssure and persuasion in the 1960s: the first, on Latin American governments in favour of regional integration; the second, on governments of the developed countries for more liberal trade and financial policies.'[7]

However, by the late 1960s O'Brien argues that 'this model was in crisis.'[8] A variety of problems are noted: the continuation of economic dependency despite import substitution; income inequality was becoming worse; large sections of the population were marginalized; the role of foreign capital was increasingly in evidence; and the military were in power in many places. O'Brien remarks that 'The theory of dependence emerged as an attempt to explain this failure.'[9]

It is out of this complex pattern of debate, which revolved around the exchange of metropolitan centres and Latin American economies, that the notion of dependency crystallizes. Familiar structuralist themes are firmly lodged within an explanatory frame which locates crucial elements of local problems beyond the local state's control: the familiar themes of external dependency and internal fixity of social and economic structures and presented.

I will consider dependency theory as it is presented by Celso Furtado[10] whose work usefully covers a number of issues.

Furtado's early study *Development and Underdevelopment* (1961) begins with a chapter called 'The Theory of Development in Economic Science', which treats the issue methodologically and in terms of the history of ideas in economics. Thus Furtado observes that:

> The theory of development endeavours to explain, from a macroeconomic point of view, the causes and mechanisms of the persistent growth in productivity of the labour factor and the repercussions of this growth on the organization of production and on the distribution and utilization of the social product.[11]

This is how Furtado understands the work of the classical school of economics and from this point he goes on to identify two further and related areas, or styles, of enquiry. Of the first, 'in which abstract formulations prevail',[12] Furtado argues that it 'comprises analysis of the actual mechanisms of the process of growth'[13] and the strategy of enquiry involves 'building models or simplified schemes of existing economic systems'.[14]

What we have here is an acknowledgment of the view of the classical theorists in respect of the fundamental nature of economic 'laws', transposed into the post-war, neo-classical-informed language of the precise identification of mechanisms via model-building.

Furtado continues by introducing his second, related, style of enquiry. It is the 'historical plane, [and] comprises critical study in the light of a given reality and on the basis of the categories defined by the abstract analysis.'[15]

This establishes Furtado's 'early general method': what he is going to try to do is to construct a set of models of Latin American economies which will reveal how they have changed through time and how they are presently constituted. What is most intriguing in this early work – itself a collection of essays written through the 1950s – is the way Furtado mixes together attention to historical detail with deference to orthodox ideas of scientific generality of formulation. This early work is both: (a) theoretically unstable – Furtado vacillates between the pursuit of relevance and the presentation of results of enquiry in a scientifically general form (later he will abandon this explanatory inhibition); and (b) narrowly policy scientific, notwithstanding his historical sensitivity (later he will abandon this inhibition about praxis).[16]

The substance of the analyses he presents at this time already contains, in outline, the dependency position. The approach is historical and attempts to characterize the various economic types produced during the expansion of what Furtado calls industrial capitalism.

Thus he observes: 'The advent of an industrial nucleus in eighteenth-century Europe disrupted the world economy of the time and eventually conditioned later economic development in almost every region in the world.'[7] This nucleus expanded in three directions: internally, in Europe itself; into the 'empty lands' of North America and Australasia; and, third, into already inhabited lands. It is the matter of the types of economies and societies produced – especially in the last-noted case – that is of interest to Furtado. Thus he argues: 'The effect of the impact of capitalist expansion on the archaic structures varied from region to region; the result, however, was almost always to create hybrid structures.'[18] Thus we have a first statement of the core of the dependency – and marxian generally – analysis: underdevelopment is not an 'original condition', but a historically generated one.

The impact of the expansion of industrial capitalism upon the various colonized territories has the effect of producing economies comprised of distinct *sectors*. Furtado identifies three typical sectors: 'one was the "remnant" economy with a predominance of subsistence activities and a minor money flow; the second comprised activities directly connected with foreign trade; the third consisted of activities directly connected with the domestic market.'[19] Using this scheme, Furtado goes on to look at the situation of the Brazilian economy – and he concludes his remarks by noting, 'Again we see that underdevelopment, specific phenomenon that it is, calls for an effort of autonomous theorizing.'[20]

These matters of Furtado's ideas of an appropriate theory are pursued in the text *Diagnosis of the Brazilian Crisis*, first published in 1964. Thus far we have met the ideas of sectors and structures. The importance of historical analysis has also been stressed. Furtado has, most importantly stressed that enquiry into the circumstances of underdevelopment in Latin America (his particular area of concern) must focus upon the actual local situation: hence his calls for 'autonomous theorizing'.

In the 1964 text, which was written at a time of political crisis in Brazil, we find, arguably, three crucial revisions to the analysis thus far made. Furtado, first, invokes the Hegelian and marxian idea of dialectical change. This, argues, Furtado, is the best available general orientating frame for enquiry – however, Furtado immediately goes on to say that at a 'practical' level it is not much use and other modelling exercises are needed. The second revision made involves acknowledging the idea of class and class struggle. Furtado has discovered the diversity of political class interests in

Brazil – however, again, he quickly softens his arguments by treating 'class' in the style of orthodox sociology. Indeed, he seems to want class analysis without political commitment. Finally, the third revision entails speaking of institutional flexibility, and here Furtado extends his argument into the 'political' realm. The Brazilian economy/society lacks a ruling class committed to industrialization and the emergence of such a group will depend upon the flexibility of present institutional arrangements. Unfortunately for Furtado's analysis, and Brazil, the actual result of the crisis was a military coup.

In the text *Economic Development in Latin America*, first published in 1969, the dependency line is now fully presented. In this text it is a central commitment that the economic and social structures of present-day Latin American countries are a result of the manner of that continent's incorporation into, and present role within, the world capitalist economy.

Norman Girvan characterizes the production of the dependency position over the period we have noted as follows:

> the developments in thought, generally, took the forms of (i) adding a historical perspective and analysis to the structural and institutional method, (ii) giving the historical/structural/institutional method the kind of theoretical and empirical content needed to construct a general theory of dependence and underdevelopment.[21]

The nature of this 'historical/structural/institutional' method is exemplified in the analyses presented. Thus, given circumstances which admit of a description (or disaggregated modelling informed by generally true economic propositions) in terms of economic structure also admit of a complementary description in terms of a functionally necessary institutional framework. Historical analysis provides data for examples and the construction of a sequence of models; and, further, borrowing from classical economics and marxian traditions, an overarching frame which firmly locates the Latin American economies in the dependent peripheral area of the world capitalist economy. Problems of 'development' are then treated in terms of the lack of fit between, on the one hand, the possibilities for development provided by technological levels and, on the other, the restrictions and possibilities attendant upon given structural/ institutional circumstances.

In his 1969 text Furtado presents a detailed analysis in line with this procedure and treats the historical genesis of the contemporary situation. The work ends with a chapter summarizing his argument and identifying the necessary conditions of any future advance. He observes that

> There can be no doubt that development based on exports of raw materials and import substitution industrialization has reached the limits of its possibilities . . . Similarly the institutional framework inherited from the colonial period . . . seems to have exhausted its possibilities of adaptation to development needs.[22]

And he adds that discussion has increasingly turned – not surprisingly – to the business of structural/institutional reform. When we look at the two broad areas of specific policy proposals he then makes, what is abundantly clear is that the dependency approach is both politically explosive in its implications and that the tasks it identifies are daunting ones. The key dilemma for the theorist is neatly captured by Philip Ehrensaft, who sums up the lessons of dependency analysis by saying that subordinate peripheral capitalism 'is associated with the rise of powerful indigenous groups which benefit from the distortion and skewing of resources; they control capital formation and state power . . . the linkage of their interests to a political economy based upon "outward growth" remains fundamental.'[23] Furtado confronts this dilemma with a reform package. Externally, there are three problems:

(1) re-entry of regional economies into the expanding mainstream;
(2) reshaping economic relations with the USA;
(3) reshaping economic relations with the multinational corporations.[24]

And, internally, five problems are noted:

(1) reconstruction of economic structures to permit the use of modern technology;
(2) avoidance of social marginalization of large sections of the population;
(3) reorganization of the state sector (so as to enable the state to assume its proper role as the agent of development);
(4) the pursuit of 'technological autonomy';
(5) the establishment of regional co-operation.[25]

It is clear that these represent an essentially political programme cast in terms of policy proposals: here I have followed Furtado in noting the broad 'headings', but it is clear that they admit of detailed elaboration. However, for my purposes what is interesting is the political reform strategy they embody. Furtado's dilemma is that of reform-minded theorists generally: his own work disposes him to reliance upon reason and persuasion, but his circumstances are not obviously conducive to the efficacy of reasoned debate. Furtado's 'solution' revolves around the key role of the state – but the present state represents, crucially, the interests of specific groups whose interests are *not* general. The vehicle of the solution to the problem of development is actually a part of the problem. Furtado offers a reformist politics and I will pursue this complex issue of the relationship of theory and practice (a long-established issue for marxists!) with later theorists – A. G. Frank in particular. For the moment, however, we can note that in Furtado's later work the dependency approach emerges with all its subtlety and intellectual power.[26]

11 Neo-marxism and Paul Baran

Contemporary marxian enquiry into the issue of development has been heavily influenced by the particular context of the social scientific rediscovery of Marx in the late 1960s.[1] This was a period of political and social conflict in the First World and, consequently, it was an activist Marx who was represented. This activist movement, when it came to theorize development/underdevelopment made reference to the work of Paul Baran and thence to the intellectual tradition of marxism. Neo-marxism can be counted as the third major attempt within the marxian line to theorize development.[2] First, there was the work of Marx and Engels, who saw capitalism as destructive of non-capitalist social forms and, thereafter, as progressive. Second, there was the work of the classic theorists of imperialism, who initially expected capitalism to act progressively once the colonial system had been dismantled but who later became more pessimistic. Third, and most recent, we have the material presented here under the general heading of 'Marxist Theories' and, included within that, neo-marxism.

The neo-marxian line revolves around the work of Baran, who speaks of monopoly capitalism which he analyses in terms of the idea of economic surplus. Monopoly capitalism, argues Baran, cannot realize the full potential of modern economies and, moreover, is irrational and wasteful. Baran analyses the situation of the Third World in terms of how local economic surplus is realized and used: like dependency theorists, he diagnoses subordinate and deforming incorporation within a world capitalist economy. The key to development is via socialist revolution and disengagement from the world capitalist economy. Baran's work has been subject to much criticism, as has the neo-marxian position: however, he is a significant and influential figure. In this treatment of neo-marxism I will focus upon Paul Baran and proceed in the following way: first, a discussion of the rediscovery of Marx; second, a discussion of Baran's work and of some of the principal criticisms made of it.

Prior to the late 1960s, social scientists generally and students of development in particular did not pay very much attention to the marxian tradition of social theorizing. Marx and marxism were condemned to the status of intellectual and historical curiosities at best, and, at worst, were seen as the ideological prop of a malign regime and its unsavoury representatives (the various national Communist Parties). The intellectual and political 'rediscovery' of Marx in the late 1960s was an abrupt and 'heady' experience for those concerned, it was also an experience with very definite social roots (or changes in the 'real world'). Although there would be disagreement amongst commentators about the precise social occasions of this rediscovery of Marx and about the weight to be allocated to various factors, there would, I think, be a measure of agreement on the broad reasons. I will approach these reasons using a distinction between: (i) internal and immediate reasons; and (ii) external and adoptive reasons.

Kay has observed that the rediscovery of Marx was brought about by 'the collapse of consensus politics, the decomposition of the affluent society and the failure of the Americans to win a decisive victory in Vietnam . . . [and] academic social science [having] stood still.'[3] The 'new politics' rapidly acquired the label New Left: a broad progressive movement.

The dissolution of social and political (and, shortly thereafter, social scientific) consensus was abrupt and surprising. Birnbaum, writing in 1969, observed that 'It was only yesterday that we were assured that our western societies were immune to severe disruptions.'[4] The image of security varied. Liberals saw a securely established pluralism, socialists a solidly engineered consent, and conservatives a vulgar consumerism. In the USA the collapse of consensus and the gradual awakening of critical scholarship from the quietude of the Eisenhower years was bound up with three major issues: civil rights, university reform and the episode of the war in Vietnam. These last two factors are central to the experience of Europe.

The civil rights movement, in the USA, has, arguably, two major early events to mark its rise. The first was the Supreme Court decision of 1954 which desegregated the public school system and the second was the Greensboro demonstrations of 1960. The latter began with a group of black youths demanding food at a segregated Woolworth's departmental store lunch-counter. They were refused food and promptly staged a 'sit-in' which quickly gained support. Many students, at this time, came to the south of the USA in order to aid the civil rights movement. One commentator reports that a body called 'the Student Non-Violent Coordinating Committee . . . represented the earliest actual appearance of the New Left,'[5] and the SNCC was established to assist civil rights workers.

A second element in this dissolution of consensus was the 1960s movement for reform of the universities: here, as Birnbaum notes, the New Left became to a significant extent transformed 'into a youth movement'.[6] At this point we can also include the European experience. Thus Statera[7] argues that for European students the prototype was Germany: in particular he cites the students of the Free University of Berlin. This institution was set up, largely as a propaganda exercise aimed at the University of East Berlin, with a very liberal organizational form. Through the 1940s and 1950s, these liberties were gradually curtailed and, eventually, in 1959 the students protested.

From this point, reports Statera, the scope of protest was ever-widening. 'Vietnam was the crucial issue; but from the attack on American imperialism protest extended to the repressive nature of capitalism, to authoritarianism, to the "manipulation of consciousness".'[8] The universities quickly came to be seen as exemplifying, in microcosm, the character of the society of which they were a part. The universities, like the society, were paternalistic, authoritarian, hierarchical and, in a broad ethical sense, non-democratic.

Much of the ideology of the New Left came to revolve around notions of technical–rational knowledge and its increasingly central role in society. Just as society was experiencing (it was claimed) a substitution of technical for practical discourse, so the universities were experiencing a substitution of technical expertise for scholarship. This diagnosis entailed a critical praxis. Thus Statera reports that:

> Authoritarianism and repression were regarded as dominant themes in the social, political and cultural life of industrial societies whose aim is to establish an immutable order both internally and internationally. The extra-parliamentary opposition, and the students above all, could therefore become the counterpart, on the internal political level, of the Vietcong.[9]

This introduces the third reason for the dissolution of consensus: the experience of the Vietnam war. Birnbaum remarks that the Vietnam war offered an unparalleled opportunity for self-discovery for American society: 'mobilization for the war in Vietnam has exposed for all the world to see . . . the brutal visage of our ambiguous society: a monstrous technological apparatus tended by moral dwarfs.'[10] Again, as in the two cases noted above, students came to play a major role. In Europe there were extensive demonstrations against the war, and in the USA this was also the case – indeed, for US students the problem was a pressing one as they were liable for drafting into the armed forces.

Turning now to the external and adoptive reasons for the renewal of interest in Marx, I will indicate those events in the Third World which allowed First World thinkers to 'co-opt' the experiences of the Third World.

In the works of many students of Third World affairs there is a sense of disappointment, of promise unfulfilled. In the 1950s, during the time of extensive decolonization, there was a widespread spirit of optimism. This optimism was misplaced. Far from it being the case that new nationalist elites were inevitably innovative, they were, if anything, the reverse (and circumstances often conspired to reinforce any such tendencies).

Basil Davidson is one commentator who has analysed the circumstances of decolonization with reference to the particular expectations of the foremost groups. It is Africa he has principally in mind, but his comments will serve more generally. Davidson distinguishes between the 'few' and the 'many'. The former are the (often) Western-educated elite who (simplifying Davidson's history considerably) see 'the world of the European nation state as the manifest destiny of the colonial state . . . decolonization, when it came, was bound and fettered within the terms of this nationalism.'[11] As for the latter group, the 'many', Davidson reports that they were detached from the nationalists and made a variety of accommodating responses to colonial rule. However, during the 1930s depression and subsequent war years the 'many' saw their old patterns of life very severely undermined. The two groups came together, briefly, in the post-war period: 'The new parties moblized the clamour in the streets. They became movements of mass support or mass acclaim. They did not become movements of mass participation. The distinction is important.'[12] The interests of the nationalist elite in political power and the interests of the masses in social reforms came together, in the period of decolonization, 'as a mutual opportunism'.[13] It is precisely this gap that Davidson sees opening up later so that the new ruling elite quickly comes to stand in the same relationship to the masses as did the colonial authority.[14] The imported political model collapses. The spectacle of corrupted elite groups and successions of military coups led to the recognition that any affirmation of the notion of democracy would entail a sharp revision in political theory and practice.[15] This new politics slowly began to emerge: it proposed ditching elite-ordered capitalist nation-building in favour of an identification by leaders with the problems of the masses. 'This new politics . . . became known as the politics of liberation. Its development after 1966 occurred in many forms.'[16] The examples of the independent states of Tanzania and Somalia are cited; and the efforts of the then non-independent are noted. Thus Cabral and PAIGC (the African Party for the Independence of Guinea and Cape Verde), Mondlane and FRELIMO (Front for the Liberation Mozambique), and the MPLA (Popular Movement for the Liberation of Angola) are listed. Of them, Davidson observes that they 'may be said to have been the first in Africa to have fully indigenized a marxist analysis . . . But what their evolution really displayed was an African politics of mass participation in a mature phase.'[17]

The struggle against a repressive and often brutal and unjustifiable colonial authority; the creative revision of democratic/socialist/marxist theorems; the identification with the masses, with the corollary of the affirmation of the centrality of social reform – all these, it would seem, are the bases whereby activity within the Third World might be embraced by radicals in the developed nations. Davidson focuses his attention on sub-Saharan Africa, but the claim may be extended to the Third World in general. Thus Chaliand[18] follows Davidson in making Cabral and PAIGC genuinely revolutionary; he also adds China, Korea, Vietnam and Cuba as places where political and social revolution has occurred.

The experiences of Vietnam, Algeria and Cuba are central to the manner of co-option by the New Left of the experience of groups in the Third World. Chaliand treats it as myth-making; he observes:

> A sort of Third-World euphoria began to be felt at the close of the 1950s, during the Algerian war, and it was soon given a boost by the radical turn of events in the Cuban revolution in 1960–61 . . . the Algerian revolution, geographically so close to Europe, came to symbolize the anticolonialist struggle.[19]

In the case of Vietnam: 'The war in Vietnam embodies the very model of the Third World myth: a war of the people victoriously resisting the most powerful imperialism.'[20] In sum, it would seem to be the case that the pervasive activism of the New Left, when confronted with genuinely relevant events in the lurid light of the circumstance of brutal warfare, issued in an anguished, and inevitably overemphatic, co-option of the proffered lessons: hence Chaliand's 'myth'. Of the myth, Chaliand notes:

> Third Worldism saw the revolutionary potential of the Third World as deriving from two main factors: on the one hand, the grinding, humiliating poverty of the masses, and the contradictions that produced it, and on the other hand, the crisis that could not fail to erupt in industrial countries, once revolutionary regimes put a stop to their pillage of Third World materials.[21]

He adds that

> Third Worldism was a phenomenon born of the crisis of Stalinism and fed by a policy of peaceful coexistence. It prospered in the 1960s because of the new hopes in the spread of socialist revolution in and by the Third World. But it has turned out to be a myth.[22]

Myth it may have been, and Chaliand's argument is persuasive. Yet this is not to say that the original impulse to embrace these novel contributions to theorizing/reforming mature capitalism were wrongheaded. They were not, as we see below.

We have, then, two sets of reasons for the rediscovery of Marx: how plausible were the links between the two – were they, as Chaliand suggests, wholly unfounded?

I think that we can quite plausibly identify three broad areas of similarity in the experiences of the New Left, on the one hand, and, on the other, the Third World proponents of what Davidson calls a 'new politics'.

The first area is the struggle against a repressive or unjustifiable authority. That the struggle of the peoples of the Third World (both old and new politics) was against just such regimes must, now, not be in doubt. The history of the exchange of rich and poor nations has (in general) been one of the unprincipled exploitation of the latter by the former. But to what extent can it be argued that the mass of the people in the First World stand in an equivalent relationship to their rulers? This is the basis of the claimed analogy. The gist of the New Left's answer is to grant that the level of living of First World masses is indeed far higher than that of the masses in the Third World. But they add that it is also true that First Worlders do inhabit inegalitarian, unequal, class societies. The resemblance, evidently, is more one of form than substance. But, in terms of the ideological (formal) justifiability of authority in metropolitan and colonial areas, there is much more to the analogy than first meets the eye.

The second area of similarity is in the centrality of the task of social reform. I have noted Davidson's view that the paying of genuine attention to the social reform problems of 'the many' is the key to what he calls the new 'politics of liberation'[23] and it is certainly true that the New Left adopted a similarly broad notion of democracy. The New Left called for, to simplify, participatory democracy and this entailed, amongst other things, paying routine attention to the problems of those who were 'marginalized' – either as 'consumers' or 'disadvantaged'.

The third area of similarity is the creative revision of democratic/socialist/marxian ideas. Here, on an 'idealist' level, I think the claimed resemblances are very clear. There are even direct linkages in the cases of Regis Debray (who interpreted the Cuban revolution to European marxists) and Franz Fanon (the spokesman of the Algerian revolution), both of whom contributed not only to Third World liberation politics but also the ideas of the New Left.

Let me now summarize this chapter. The rediscovery of Marx and the marxian tradition took place in the period of the disintegration of the post-Second World War mood of consensus within the First World. The experience of the civil rights movement, the reform of the universities and the awful lessons of the Vietnam war all contributed to a revival of radical thought. To these 'internal' reasons we can conjoin the 'external' reason of the (more or less plausible) example of the new politics of liberation in the Third World. The upshot of these events was that, once again, social theorists paid serious attention to Marx. When the radicals of this period, in the First World, turned their thoughts to a general theory of development and underdevelopment there was an available explanation in the form of the work of Paul Baran. It is to his work that I now turn.

Paul Baran was one of a very small number of marxists based in the West who kept the intellectual tradition of marxism alive at a time when, as I noted above, the line had almost effectively died out in the form of its enshrinement within official Marxism – Leninism, the official ideology of the USSR.

Baran actually presented a quite novel marxian analysis of the post-Second World War condition of capitalism. This characterization is the stepping-off point for his analysis of the Third World presented in the text *The Political Economy of Growth*, first published in 1957. Baran (with his co-worker P. Sweezy) advances the idea of monopoly capitalism. The capitalist system, according to this characterization, can no longer be regarded as having a competitive market and nor can it be regarded as a progressive social form. In a monopoly-capitalist situation, argues Baran, the economy is dominated by a handful of giant firms and they operate – in a variety of ways – so as to control competition. They use their monopoly power so as to defend the status quo in which they, as giant corporations, have a crucial interest and dominant position. In general, they become 'historically conservative': it is a moribund capitalism Baran sees. It is also a wasteful and immoral one, as we shall see when we consider the idea of surplus.

The crucial idea of *The Political Economy of Growth* is that of surplus; thus Baran remarks: 'I consider [economic surplus] to be the key to the understanding of the general working principles of capitalism.'[24] The idea of surplus used by Baran is not that of Marx (a point I will come to below); it is, rather, an essentially orthodox idea of economic surplus: the total material output of an economy. What Baran is going to do is to argue that monopoly capitalism: (i) fails to realize the economic surplus that could be generated with presently available factors of production; and (ii) diverts much of the economic surplus that it does realize into wasteful and immoral consumption. Baran identifies three related notions of surplus. Thus he speaks of actual surplus, potential surplus and planned surplus: it is the relationships of these three terms that lets Baran make his analysis of monopoly capitalism and, by extension, the Third World. Thus the idea of actual surplus is just that which an economy produces. The idea of potential surplus is that which the economy could produce, given the available factors of production. The idea of planned surplus is what could be produced by a rational and humane (socialist) society.

In a monopoly-capitalist economy there is, so far as Baran is concerned, an inbuilt tendency towards stagnation[25] and this is due to there being insufficient consumer demand within the economy. This idea of 'underconsumption' is a matter of interest for economists, but I do not wish to review these debates here: suffice it to say that the monopoly-capitalist system actually faces, continually, the problem of avoiding a slump. The remedy identified by Baran – and Keynes, albeit with a rather different evaluation of the resulting state of affairs – was the role of the state as consumer. State spending underpins the monopoly-capitalist system. In particular he cites military spending, as this is the one kind of spending that does not obviously raise general questions about social arrangements in society.[26] Baran's view of monopoly capitalism was thus that it was irrational and wasteful.

In the case of the Third World, Baran again uses the trio of notions of surplus to analyse and prescribe. The world capitalist economy is, so far as Baran is concerned, divided into two groups: what the dependency line and Frank call 'centres and peripheries'. Baran, like these theorists, sees the division of the world into two (the Second World of state socialism is set to one side) historically generated sectors. In Baran's argument, which explains this division is to be found in the mercantile capitalist appropriation of surplus from (what are now) the peripheries in the fifteenth, sixteenth and seventeenth centuries. This view is subsequently used by A. G. Frank.

As regards the present-day circumstances of the Third World, again the idea of surplus is used. Two issues emerge: how is the economic surplus realized and, crucially, how is it then used? Baran's answer to this double question entails the identification of a series of sectors within the Third World economy. Thus we have: first, the agricultural sector of either peasant farming or commercial plantation. Neither part of this sector is progressive: surplus is realized and either consumed immediately or removed, as profits, immediately. Second, there is the merchant sector – the money lenders, traders, middlemen, and so on. This essentially parasitic grouping is not progressive either: Baran sees a tendency for the roles of middlemen (etc.) to be shared out. There is no likelihood of concentration (and thus, presumably, potential progressivity) and surplus is merely diverted into the consumption of the middlemen (etc.). Third, there is the local industrial group. Because its members face daunting problems of internal handicaps and external competition, their contribution to total economic surplus is depressed and they too are not progressive. The fourth sector, or grouping, identified by Baran is the state. The state absorbs, thinks Baran, a large measure of the available economic surplus: if there is to be 'development', then the state must use this surplus to foster it. However, this does not happen. The state, even if uncorrupted, has the unenviable task of trying to balance the conflicting demands of internal agricultural (plantation or commercial, in particular), mercantile (middlemen, etc.), and industrial capital. Additionally, the state employees come to have a powerful interest. Externally, there is the power of overseas capital (multinationals, International Monetary Fund, metropolitan firms, etc.). Baran thinks that the state is either probably incapable or already corrupted and thus available economic surplus is either (a) drained away to the metropolitan centres, or (b) misused in the peripheral states. The economic surplus that the Third World economy does produce is not effectively utilized and nor, within the context of the world capitalist system, can it be. The solution to which Baran points is that of withdrawal from the world capitalist system and the state-socialist pursuit of development.

I want now to consider some of the criticisms to which this influential analysis has been subjected. I will consider these criticisms under three headings: (i) objections to the notion of surplus;

(ii) objections to the characterization of capitalism; and (iii) objections to the ethics affirmed.

The notion of 'surplus', in its three guises, is the key to Baran's analysis of underdevelopment. There have been two main lines of criticism of the notion of 'economic surplus'. The orthodox have lodged charges of ambiguity and difficulty of measurement – these attacks I will not pursue as they are (to oversimplify) rather beside the point: what we have in Baran's work, recalling the introductory remarks on pp. 121–5, is a different way of making sense from that used by the orthodox. From the marxist camp, too, there have been, sometimes fierce, criticisms; it is these attacks that I will take note of here. These criticisms have been energetically presented by, in particular, those working within an Althusserian-inspired framework (all of which objections we will encounter in the final part of this chapter).

Picking up this last-noted line of criticism we can note that it has been argued that Baran's notion of surplus – and therefore the idea used by all the 'neo-marxist' thinkers – is not marxian. Indeed, it has been suggested that Baran's 'surplus' owes more to the aggregative reformist economics of Keynes than it does to Marx. Sutcliffe reports that

> The conceptual difference is that Marx's 'surplus value' is defined in relation to the ownership of property while Baran's 'surplus' is defined more in relation to consumption needs. It is therefore to Baran something which exists in all societies.[27]

What we have here is a fairly complex distinction: what is most obviously relevant in the present context is that, on the one hand, we have (with Marx) an essentially economic notion defined with reference to the historically specific circumstances of capitalism, whereas, on the other hand, we have an abstract and idealist notion.

I can elucidate this distinction by citing the work of Lorraine Culley, who, arguing from an Althusserian position, says: 'In *Capital* the concepts of necessary and surplus labour are strictly economic concepts and are not derived from any extra-economic concept of human needs.'[28] She then goes on to discuss the ideas of surplus labour and surplus value, indicating that surplus, understood thus, is specific to capitalist social relations. In contrast to this, Baran's idea of 'economic surplus' relates to the excess of production over consumption: it is, as Brewer puts it, a pre-marxian notion which understands surplus as a material quantity of goods produced.[29] Baran introduces an idea of 'human need' so as to characterize different production schedules (wasteful or rational). Culley is arguing that Baran's notion of surplus is not strictly economic, as was, she thinks, that of Marx, and it is distinctly idealistic – a point I'll pursue in a little while, when I look at objections to 'ethics'. For the moment, though, we can note that it is true that Baran's notion of economic surplus differs from that of Marx, but we can also ask whether this is really all that interesting a point. The real question must be not whether Baran alters elements of Marx, but whether or not the resultant theory makes good or bad sense – clearly, a rather more awkward issue.[30]

The characterization of capitalism within Baran's work, and the closely related issue of class analysis, have been extensively debated. These criticisms attach to the entire 'neo-marxian' position.

At this point, I will make reference to the essay by Robert Brenner,[31] in which he develops a powerful criticism of the 'neo-marxist' stance on the character of capitalism. I will focus on two points.

First, Brenner says that neo-marxist theorists argue in a circular fashion: they assume the existence of capitalistic social relations in their attempts to explain the rise of capitalism. Brenner analyses Sweezy's work[32] (*The Transition from Feudalism to Capitalism* (1976)) by unpacking the model offered and asking after the plausibility of its assumptions about the behaviour of the historical actors mentioned. The conclusion presented is that: 'the entire account of the transition from feudalism to capitalism is based on the implicit assumption that capitalism already exists.'[33] Sweezy's work is taken to reduce to the view that the transition from feudalism to capitalism is a matter of the appropriate adjustment in society to the demands of the market. But the relationship of economics to society is not one of simple determination of social relations by economic forces and nor can capitalism be defined just by the existence of a market. Brenner is suggesting that Sweezy and the rest offer an economistic reading of Marx (and, here, the shift from feudalism to capitalism) which contains, amongst its assumptions, precisely those individualistic assumptions (pursuit of individual satisfactions in the market) that underlie orthodox economics.

The second point I want to take from Brenner is the claim that the entire 'neo-marxian' line in this area of debate reduces to a polemical inversion of Adam Smith. Most broadly: where Smith argued that the 'free market' would maximize progress, the neo-marxists argue that it actually has generated a moribund monopoly. In more detail: Brenner argues that the neo-marxists follow Smith in equating capitalism with a trade-based division of labour where innovation (and thus, in the end, progress) is determined by market pressure. Class relations are taken to adjust thereafter. This is characterized by Brenner as 'historical functionalism' and 'economic determinism': it is also wrong. Instead, he wants to reduce economics to social (and thus class) relations. This links up, as did Marx, economic and social analysis. The core of the matter is the particular set of class circumstances that trigger and sustain the innovative dynamic of capitalism.

The neo-marxists, by seeing capitalism in these economistic terms, displace the system's dynamic element from the social relations of production into the business of market exchanges in pursuit of profit. Development and underdevelopment are seen as aspects of this same world market. One theorist, Wallerstein, 'straightforwardly defines capitalism as a trade based division of labour, and it is here that he locates the dynamic of capitalist . . . development.'[34] To this Brenner counterposes his own view which he presents via detailed historical discussion of the shift from feudalism to capitalism in Europe. The core of his claims is the rejection of capitalism as primarily an exchange relationship in the market: it is rather a specific social form which, uniquely, requires that productive forces (science and technology) be continuously upgraded. Thus, he says,

> In short the uniquely successful development of capitalism in Western Europe was determined by a class system, a property system, a system of surplus extraction, in which the methods the extractors were obliged to use to increase their surplus corresponded to an unprecedented, though imperfect, degree to the needs of development of the productive forces.[35]

It is in this conjunction that the search for an explanation of the genesis of capitalism is to be conducted, not in any behaviour of an abstractly regarded world market.

A. G. Frank, whom we will meet in the next chapter, repeats this neo-marxian line. Development and underdevelopment are explained by reference to international trade-based extraction of surplus, and not the particular conjunctions of class circumstances and technological possibility. Brenner argues that 'the *method* of an entire line of writers in the [neo-]Marxist tradition has led them to displace class relations from the centre of their analyses of economic development and underdevelopment.[36] And the upshot of these errors is, it is suggested, a wholly implausible analysis of the present circumstances of the underdeveloped: an analysis which is both economistic and heavily skewed to the single issue of the deleterious effects of external dependency. These erroneous analyses generate unhelpful political/policy proposals.

So, picking up the issue raised at the end of the first objection – do the neo-marxists make good or bad sense – can we now say anything more? Evidently there are good reasons for doubting that Baran *et al.* had their historical and economic–social enquiries rigorously worked out. Both Baran and his early co-worker Sweezy were writing in a period of Keynesian reformism, and they were more or less isolated, so it would be easy for them to go astray (scholarship is communal). And Brenner writes with the benefit of 'hindsight', so to say. At the time Baran and Sweezy produced their material it was novel and, we can now see, anticipated many subsequent areas of debate – this is surely evidence of the value of their work. Wallerstein and A. G. Frank, as general theorists, have, perhaps, less to be said in their favour. But Frank, in any case, is best regarded as a political pamphleteer 'sensitizing' people to problematical issues: his 'contribution' is easily secured on those grounds.

There have been a variety of objections to the ethics embodied in the work of the neo-marxists, and I will tackle these in three parts: the ethic, the idea of development and the politics. All are closely related and, indeed, are closely bound up with the ideas of economic surplus and capitalism noted above.

It has been argued that Baran's (and hence the others') analysis is, fundamentally, a moral critique that is not marxian and not helpful. This line of criticism again focuses on the idea of 'economic surplus'. Culley reports that the idea of potential surplus is significant: 'It is primarily by an analysis of their potentialities that types of society . . . are assessed.'[37] The potential surplus represents some sort of a theoretical maximum of production in an economy and planned surplus that which could/would be produced in a socialist (rational and humane) society. Culley argues that 'The Utopian nature of this conception is quite clear. It allows Baran and his followers to launch an attack upon capitalism as an irrational phenomenon with respect to his own ethical position.'[38] Culley takes Baran's effort to be 'humanistic', 'idealistic', 'relativistic' and 'teleological' – all damning criticisms so far as Althusserians are concerned. The whole of the work undertaken by Baran and his followers is reduced to the status of an elaborate and disguised expression of disapproval.

Now, as I have (repeatedly) said that I take social theorizing to be concerned with making politically and ethically relevant sense of society, I am obliged to pursue this matter. First, we must note that – on the view of theorizing presented in Part 1 – what is at issue is not whether or not Baran's work is 'tainted' by ethical valuation, for all social theorizing necessarily rests upon, or generates, value positions. With the work of Baran it is certainly the case that we have what looks like an 'idealist' argument. The notion of 'economic surplus' is, it must be granted, not obviously marxian. Further, the notion of 'economic surplus' is distinctly redolent of Keynesian aggregative macro-economic analysis, and of the liberal reformist ethic affirmed in Keynes's work. One also thinks, at this point, of Galbraith or Myrdal. It seems to me that Baran's notion of 'economic surplus' does have a built-in value position and, more importantly *prima facie*, that this ethic is actually borrowed from the stance he is attacking!

But, again, that Baran's work is politically (and thus ethically) engaged, or committed, is not in doubt. Nor is it in doubt that the notion of 'economic surplus' will serve as a core element of a political economic analysis. What is at issue, and here Culley's position is rejected, is the *precise nature of the moral core* of Baran's analysis (because we can rationally discuss ethics) and the *manner of its insertion into analysis*.

In the case of Marx the moral core of his work – a 'philosophical anthropology', which issued in the notion of alienated labour – was central to his substantive, political, analyses. If we compare Baran's evaluative stance – the ideas and the way they are used – then there is some cause for concern. Baran's evaluative stance, which condemns the system's present irrationality of use of economic surplus and points to a rationally ordered future, is pitched at such a general level as to tend to be indistinguishable from any other 'liberal' critique. Related to this is the manner of 'insertion' – how the ethic is used. It is suggested by Culley that Baran's economics are not linked to his ethics and, indeed, the economics are merely a vehicle for the application of otherwise established moral views. It seems to me that there is something to be said for both these points – but we can, for the time being, rewrite these criticisms thus: Baran offers a simple political–economic analysis affirming an easily recognizable ethic. Let us now look at the idea of development present in his, and the neo-marxists', work.

The idea of development is, as I argued in Part 1, best seen as an ethico-political term which has to be 'cashed' in specific circumstances. What then of the 'cashing' (if such it is) made by Baran? Two points occur: first, that Baran is talking in rather general terms – that is, he is not saying this will count as development in that country or region; he is, rather, discussing the plight of the Third World in general. In addition to this, we can see that his ethic is relatively unconsidered: his stance does, as critics complain, look distinctly reformist liberal. Thus far Baran stands condemned (if that's not too harsh) of being rather general – and, again, we can read this in terms of the situation–boundedness of his theorizing: as Brewer[39] remarks, this work was novel – that is, exploratory – and maybe we shouldn't expect too much. But there is a further criticism that has more force: it has been suggested[40] that the idea of development affirmed by Baran is both pessimistically static and, in marxian terms, incoherent. Baran, with his idea of monopoly capitalism as historically moribund – that is, non-progressive – is offering a view that in marxian terms is arguably incoherent. Marx always regarded capitalism as historically progressive. Related to this is the suggestion that Baran has made the system distinctly static: what progress there is likely to be he has displaced from the metropolitan capitalist core and lodged in the periphery; and, additionally, he sees little chance for change even there. Again, there is force in this charge and I will return to it after noting the third line of criticism of the ethics embodied in neo-marxism.

The politics proposed by the neo-marxian line is criticized as naive: Third Worldist. Wrong conceptions of capitalism, of the development of underdevelopment and of the chances for change in the metropolitan centres, coupled with an enthusiasm for activism that was a compound of guilt and overexcitement during the 1960s, on the part of the theorists, have issued in an apocalyptic politics of disengagement in the peripheries, the location that is also seen as the 'next step' in world history given that the First World proletariat has been 'bought off' by consumerism. The critics suggest – again, with good reason – that this simply is not plausible.

Let us now review these 'objections to ethics': the blanket objection to 'valuation' made by Culley is, I think, absurd. All social theorizing is suffused with valuation. It is true that the political–economic analysis offered by Baran (with Sweezy) is, when analysed, fairly simple – but there is an easy reply here: their work was 'path-breaking' and, in contrast to other available approaches (predominantly modernization theory), it was distinctly sophisticated. The more specific criticisms are harder to deflect: the idea that capitalism is now moribund – in terms of being historically progressive – is, whilst distinctly plausible, a major departure from Marx and one with very pessimistic implications. Likewise, the politics are overly simple.

If we add these remarks on the 'objections to ethics' to those made at the end of the earlier objections, what can we say in summary? The sense that Baran makes is, on balance, good sense. The neo-marxian line, of which he was the 'founding father', has opened up a host of novel questions and, it is fair to say, thrown much light upon the historical dynamic of capitalist exchanges with peripheral areas. It is as well to recall, even after having granted that marxists might wish today to make extensive revisions to theses of the development of underdevelopment – in the light of debate occasioned by these very formulations – the remark of Colin Leys: the neo-marxists may have got much of the story wrong, but they did rescue enquiry into matters of development from the veritable 'intellectual deserts'[41] of modernization theory. This was no mean achievement.

12 A. G. Frank

A. G. Frank is probably the best-known theorist working within the general marxian line, and his writings have been influential. His work has also been extensively and heavily criticized: much of this criticism has come from the 'left'. I will review the work of A. G. Frank under four headings: first, the background to his work; second, the main arguments advanced; third, the principal criticisms offered of his work; and, finally, the recent 'reworking' of his stance.

I remarked at the outset of this examination of marxian material, that we now confronted a radically different way of making sense (of development) from that adopted by orthodox theorists. This is nowhere more obvious than in the case of A. G. Frank. Frank's background is that of an economist turned political activist.[1] The decisive events in Frank's career centre upon his experience of Latin America in the early 1960s. David Booth remarks that a 'brief spell of teaching and research in Latin America . . . sufficed to convey to Frank the largely fictional character of what he had been taught.'[2] Frank's response was to fashion an entirely new position – a remarkably bold move if one recalls Galbraith's remarks about the difficulty of acquisition of knowledge in the realm of the social.[3] Brookfield speaks of Frank's 'most rapid conversion to radical ideologies'.[4]

Out of a general milieu of long-term foreign (and, in particular, US) dominance of the area and the experience of the Cuban revolution,[5] and within the context of a rejection of orthodox approaches, Frank conceives the task of contributing to a revolutionary critique of orthodox theorizing and expectations. The available resources are threefold. First, the orthodox economics of the neo-classical, economics-informed theories of 'modernization' provide an object against which the new departure may be defined. Second, the analytical machineries are largely provided by the structuralist line associated with ECLA. These constitute, it has been argued,[6] the principal intellectual resource used by Frank, whilst the political reformism associated with ECLA provides another negative defining element of Frank's stance. Third, a simple strategic metaphor (which involves a crucial analytical notion of surplus) is borrowed from the marxism of Baran – that is, the notion of the debilitating metropolitan extraction of economic surplus from the peripheral areas (which are understood to have been integrated into the world capitalist system for centuries, and their national bourgeoisies 'bought off').

The product of Frank's critique has been variously labelled: in so far as his work can be separated from the 'neo-marxian' stance associated with Baran, Frank and Wallerstein, it is probably easiest to designate him a 'radical underdevelopment theorist'.[7] In a text written in 1975, Frank presents his intellectual/political 'manifesto' in these terms:

> All serious study of the problems of development of underdeveloped areas and all serious intent to formulate policy for the elimination of underdevelopment and for the promotion of development must take into account, nay must begin with, this fundamental historical and structural cause of underdevelopment in capitalism. Indeed, all serious study of development must take into account the fundamental relation the development of development has had, and continues to have, with the development of underdevelopment. All serious study of capitalism, of its manifestations in the development of the metropole and of that in the underdevelopment of the periphery, and especially the study of the contemporary single world capitalist system and its development in the past and future, must begin with capitalism's unity and its fundamental internal contradiction, which has always and everywhere expressed itself in diffusion and exploitation, development and underdevelopment.[8]

The fundamental contradictions of capitalism alluded to in the quotation above is, I presume, the private appropriation of social wealth: in any case, the idea of appropriation figures importantly in Frank's theoretical writings.

This fundamental contradiction is further elucidated in a 1967 text, *Capitalism and Underdevelopment in Latin America*, where Frank identifies three contradictions: these characterize capitalist development and the development of underdevelopment. The contradictions are:

> the expropriation of economic surplus from the many and its appropriation by the few, the polarization of the capitalist system into metropolitan center and peripheral satellites, and the continuity of the fundamental structure of the capitalist system throughout the history of its expansion and transformation, due to the persistence or re-creation of these contradictions everywhere and at all times.[9]

The first-noted contradiction (expropriation/appropriation) deals with the way in which the economic surplus generated within an economy is removed from the hands of those who actually produce it. Frank argues that this results in the poor functioning of the economy and the division of society into 'haves' and 'have nots'. The image he uses is of a chainlike expropriation/appropriation of economic surplus. This chain stretches from the poorest landless labourer (whom the orthodox would regard as a 'traditional' figure outside the ambit of the modern world), up through landlords, regional elite groups, national elites, and finally joins the metropolitan capitalist centres. An economic model is conjoined (apparently without noticing – a point for which A. G. Frank was criticized) with a geographical pattern: surplus shifts up the chain and moves from peripheries to centres.

This is pursued in the second contradiction (polarization), where Frank argues that the immanent tendency towards centralization within capitalism has manifested itself on a world scale in the form of a split between metropolitan centres and peripheral satellites. Thus, he argues: 'Economic development and underdevelopment are the opposite faces of the same coin.'[10]

The third contradiction (continuity in change) allows A. G. Frank to urge that capitalism does not and has not changed its character. The view of ECLA, with their structuralist analysis, is opposed here: to understand the circumstances of Latin America one has to think in terms of *capitalist* underdevelopment. All other economic/social phenomena revolve around this basic point. Latin America, argues Frank, has been capitalist ever since the Conquistadors arrived.

With this basic position sketched, Frank then goes on to review the history of Chilean incorporation. A series of phases are identified, beginning in the sixteenth century and culminating in the twentieth-century situation which is characterized in terms of the incapacity of national bourgeois groups to fulfil their classical historical role[11] of securing development; only socialist revolution can now advance matters. At this point we can take note that we now have two of the characteristic elements of the Frankian mode of analysis: the analytical framework – a mixture of Latin American social science run together, in a distinctly 'activist' fashion, with the marxism of Baran; and the detailed attention to history. This historical material I have not reproduced, but the extensive role of historical research/illustration in Frank's work is something I will make clear below. The next issue I wish to consider is A. G. Frank's style of argument: this matter can be usefully introduced by looking at his 1969 text, *Latin America: Underdevelopment or Revolution*.

Frank begins thus: 'These essays were written to contribute to the Revolution in Latin America and the world.'[12] The central argument is this:

> Underdevelopment in Latin America (and elsewhere) developed as the result of the colonial structure of world capitalist development. This structure has penetrated all of Latin America, thereby forming and transforming the colonial and class structure of underdevelopment throughout the continent on the national and local levels. As a result, the development of underdevelopment will continue in Latin America until its people free themselves from this structure the only way possible, by violent revolutionary victory over their own bourgeoisie and over imperialism.[13]

The first essay of the collection, entitled 'The Development of Underdevelopment', offers a review of this general theme. I will not, however, rehearse the argument: what I will do is use this particular essay to analyse, in a preliminary fashion, the characteristic Frankian style of argument. The aspects of his 'style' that I wish to call attention to are: his repeated appeal to history; his use of institutional and structural ideas; and his attempt to persuade.

Frank begins the essay by advocating an approach to theorizing that is sensitive to history: that grants that societies, and theories, change through time. He argues that an 'adequate development theory and policy . . . [requires] first learning how . . . past economic and social history gave rise to . . . present underdevelopment.'[14] This injunction is used to consider orthodox material: there has been a gross neglect, argues Frank, of the episode of colonial empire. He says: 'for this reason most of our theoretical categories and guides to development policy have been distilled exclusively from the historical experience of the European and North American advanced capitalist nations.'[15] Undoubtedly this is true; but it is interesting, in relation to this charge against orthodoxy, to note how redolent it is of the critiques made by Seers, Streeten, Myrdal, and so on. A lack of knowledge of history, argues Frank, results in an inadequate theory: one which neither 'fits the facts' nor displays the options for the future;

instead, we have theorems of recapitulation. The Third World will travel the same set of stages as the First World did.

Frank thinks this last claim, generated by an ignorance of history, is ridiculous. The conclusion he draws is this: 'consequently, most of our theory fails to explain the structure and development of the capitalist system as a whole and to account for its simultaneous generation of underdevelopment in some of its parts and of economic development in others.'[16] Now, what is clear here is that this sentence *presents* his counter-theory *vis à vis* the orthodox. That is, Frank does not offer a formal argument and his final stance does not flow logically from his observations on the role of historical aspects in theorizing. A. G. Frank thus *introduces* his point of view in a distinctly misleading fashion. Having got this far, Frank goes on to present a series of fuller statements of his view in a question-and-answer fashion.

First, Frank remarks that 'It is generally held that economic development occurs in a succession of capitalist stages,'[17] where the presently developed are the model and all other countries are, being underdeveloped, fated to repeat this sequence. Frank observes: 'Yet even a modest acquaintance with history shows that underdevelopment is not original or traditional . . . The now developed countries were never underdeveloped though they may have been undeveloped.[18]

Second, Frank notes the widespread view, amongst orthodox theorists, that 'contemporary underdevelopment of a country can be understood as the product . . . of its own economic, political, social and cultural characteristics.[19] Once again, A. G. Frank invokes history: 'historical research demonstrates'[20] that underdevelopment is generated by the world capitalist system.

In reply to this strategy of invoking history, it must be said that 'history' *per se* cannot tell us anything. History does not provide its own interpretation – the historian has to do that. A. G. Frank's appeal is not to some given body of data; it is to a *reading* of history. As I remarked above, Frank introduces his material in what I think is a misleading fashion.

Third, Frank continues by noting the orthodox thesis of the diffusion of growth impulses via contact with the developed nations, and he denies it. A 'historical perspective . . . suggests that on the contrary, economic development in the underdeveloped countries can now occur only independently of these relations of diffusion.'[21]

Fourth, Frank considers and rejects the 'dual society' thesis. This leads to, fifth, a general declaration of his position: 'A mounting body of evidence suggests, and I am confident that future historical research will confirm . . . [the idea of the development of underdevelopment].[22]

Having presented his counter-view, and further elucidated it in a question-and-answer fashion, Frank goes on to consider the case of Brazil. I will not pursue him into the realm of historical reportage. What is relevant for my present purposes is the demonstration of the way Frank claims to draw his theory from the historical data: this is not the way theorizing works and it is not (even) the way Frank works. None the less, this methodologically orthodox syntax is retained by A. G. Frank throughout his work and it causes confusion.[23]

All the foregoing material is taken by Frank, if I have understood him, to relate to the history of the world economy. He then goes on to say: 'The same historical and structural approach can also lead to a better development theory and policy by generating a series of hypotheses about development and underdevelopment such as those I am testing in my current research.'[24] There are three points that can be made in respect of this quotation. First, we can recall Girvan's 'historical/structural/institutional' method (discussed on pp. 131–2) and ask whether or not Frank's work is at base any different from that of Furtado's? The second point relates to the idea of a 'better development theory and policy': on the orthodox view a better theory will be the more factually accurate one and it seems, here, as if Frank might be making such an appeal. Third, we have (again) Frank presenting his work as, in some sense, historical and empiricist. I do not think he is running an empirical research project, but I do think he is revising and elaborating an ideological position. The repeated appeal to history is, it seems to me, an attempt to *persuade*.

Frank concludes his essay in the following way: 'All of these hypotheses and studies suggest that the global extension and unity of the capitalist system . . . deserve much more attention . . . than they have hitherto received'.[25] Again, it seems to me that Frank's syntax is unhelpful in that the core of the 'research project' he sketches is precisely the core of the ideological stance that has informed his work. All this should be *declared*, and then he could get his epistemology and methodology straightened out. This would enable him to avoid sentences of the following sort: 'Though science and truth know no national boundaries, it is probably new generations of scientists from the underdeveloped countries themselves who most need to, and best can, devote the necessary attention to these problems and clarify the process of underdevelopment and development.[26] This strikes me as a descent into nonsense. In the above essay he has criticized the orthodox and presented an outline of his stance in *orthodox terms*.

Arguably, this is reasonable in terms of an introductory (persuasive) effort in that, again arguably, it makes the work accessible. But to conclude with a series of claims to 'scientific status' is absurd: it deflects attention away from the real problems of locating the theorist (in the society of which he speaks) and considering how to evaluate ideological schemes.

The final note offered by Frank is again revealing. The citizens of the Third World have a job to do and must fashion their own intellectual tools:

> To change their reality they must understand it. For this reason, I hope that better confirmation of these hypotheses and further pursuit of the proposed *historical, holistic, and structural approach* may help the peoples of the underdeveloped countries to understand the causes and eliminate the reality of their development of underdevelopment.[27]

Again, one wonders *what method* is being used by Frank. In 1972 Frank published a short book with the engaging title *Lumpenbourgeoisie–Lumpendevelopment*. This text represents a first reply to his critics and the first reconsidered presentation of his thesis in respect of the historical development of underdevelopment. For my purposes there are two major points of interest: first, his idea of revision; and second, the overt politics.

The text begins with a preface entitled 'Mea Culpa' (a declaration of 'guilty as charged') in which he lists a series of criticisms made of his earlier work. He notes that he has been accused of being: overly schematic; historically shallow; neglectful of class; and overly emphatic in respect of external aspects of dependency. Frank denies these lapses and offers the present text as a clarification of his position. He declares that he will defend three claims. First: 'the conquest placed all of Latin America in a position of subjection and colonial and neo-colonial economic dependence in relation to the single world system of expanding commercial capitalism.[28] Second: 'this colonial or neo-colonial relationship to the capitalist metropolis formed and transformed the economic and class structure, as well as the culture of Latin American society, with the transformations in national structure occurring as a consequence of changes in the forms of colonial dependence.[29] Third: 'this colonial and class structure established the very direct interests of the dominant sector of the bourgeoisie. Using governmental cabinets and instruments of the state, this sector spawns policies of economic, social, cultural and political under-development for the "nation" and for the people of Latin America.'[30]

The dominant class of Latin America with its self-interested alliance with the centre, Frank dubs the 'Lumpenbourgeoisie' and the politico-economic consequence of their rule 'Lumpendevelopment'. And in respect of the criticisms of his earlier works Frank notes that 'instead of discarding the methodology or rejecting the thesis, I should attempt to strengthen the methodology and clarify the dialectical relationship between the actors and their changing setting.'[31] This is the task of the 1972 text. What is clear, it seems to me, is that little has changed in terms of either Frank's thesis or his style of argument: his idea of revision seems to involve working harder at the old task,[32] although we can grant that his *language* is rather more marxian in flavour (the notions of class, etc.).

Frank follows up these discussions/declarations and produces a political pamphlet, of no little elegance and power, which interprets the historical experience of Latin America in line with his central notion of the development of underdevelopment. Along the way, two points stand out. The first is the corollary of a critique of dependency – a notion of autonomy. In respect of economic surplus appropriated and misused, Frank notes that it could have been employed in the 'promotion [of] self-sustained economic development'.[33] We are told little of where this image comes from or what is involved: critics will subsequently argue that A. G. Frank and the neo-marxists generally have in fact little idea of their alternative to dependent capitalism. The second point – and the second major point of interest I noted above – is that Frank declares himself and his work politically. Thus 'Lumpendevelopment' and its problems are amenable to just one solution: 'the only true development strategy: armed revolution and the construction of socialism',[34] and he concludes by quoting from a speech he made in Havana in 1968 to the effect that the immediate enemy are the national bourgeoisies of Latin America, as they are the local representatives of imperialism. It is at this point, I think, that Frank is revealed as a political pamphleteer and political activist. This is, evidently, a quite distinctive way of making sense of the social world – and it certainly has little obvious connection with the orthodox-type invocations of natural science that Frank himself, with his appeals to history, was looking to in the earlier essays discussed above.

I want now to consider some of the criticisms that have been made of the work of Frank: I will take note of criticisms made by Laclau, Brenner, Leys and Bernstein.

Ernesto Laclau argues that the notion of capitalism that Frank uses is not, however interesting it and its author's general schemes may be, the same as the notion used by Marx. Frank's arguments are *not* marxian – and they *are* confused. Laclau begins by characterizing, in a reasonable enough way, Frank's thesis of the development of underdevelopment. He then comments that

> It can be seen that Frank's theoretical schema involves three types of assertion: 1. Latin America has had a market economy from the beginning; 2. Latin America has been capitalist from the beginning; 3. the dependent nature of its insertion into the capitalist world market is the cause of its underdevelopment. The three assertions claim to refer to a single process identical in its essential aspects from the 16th to the 20th century.[35]

These three are considered in turn. Thus the criticism of dualism (the first point) is granted, but from the fact that Latin American economies have been market economies it does not follow that they were *capitalist* economies. Laclau then considers what Frank understands by capitalism and concludes that it is a system of production for the market in pursuit of profit. Laclau objects to this: capitalism is a particular *social* form. Laclau introduces the idea, taken from Marx, of a mode of production: a complex of economic, social and cultural relationships. The upshot of this critique is that – focusing now on the third point – Frank's thesis is *overgeneral*. The idea of capitalism used is so all-encompassing that the derived idea of dependence becomes similarly general. All these failings Laclau traces back to Frank's 'wrong' definition of capitalism.

These matters are pursued by Robert Brenner in his 1977 paper.[36] Brenner begins his paper – as we saw in the discussion of neo-marxism above – with a question about, to simplify, the dynamic of capitalism: how did this mode of production start and how has it expanded subsequently? Brenner argues that Frank's answers to these matters are quite clear. Frank, says Brenner,

> was unambiguous in locating the dynamic of capitalist expansion in the rise of a world commercial network, while specifying the roots of both growth and backwardness in the 'surplus appropriation chain' which emerged in the expansionary process: surplus appropriation by the core from the periphery and the organisation of the satellite's internal mode of production to serve the needs of the metropolis.[37]

This is Brenner's summary of Frank's position and the crucial objection to this position is that capitalism is redefined as essentially an exchange relationship and, relatedly, the dynamism of the capitalist system is removed from innovation in the core-to-surplus creation in the periphery. Brenner comments:

> In this way, Frank sets the stage for ceasing to locate the dynamic of capitalist development in a self-expanding process of capital accumulation by way of innovation in the core itself. Thus for Frank, the accumulation of capital in the core depends, on the one hand, upon a process of original surplus creation in the periphery and surplus transfer to the core and, on the other hand, upon the imposition of a raw material-producing, export-dependent economy upon the periphery.[38]

The upshot of these errors, so far as Brenner is concerned, is that Frank collapses into a Third Worldist ideology: a view of the present world system that sees the only chance for progressive change arising within the peripheral areas. Brenner cannot accept this view: Frank is wrong to rule out change in the core (by displacing the system's dynamic) and, in any case, Frankian disengagement looks like autarchy rather than socialism.

Turning now to Leys and Bernstein, we confront two critics whose papers are rather more 'academic' in tone. Colin Leys, in a 1977 paper,[39] addresses the character of 'radical underdevelopment theory' in general. Leys's criticisms are quite severe, but they are suffused with an appropriate regard for the contribution made by 'radical UDT (underdevelopment theory)'. The difficulties Leys has in mind with the theory are listed: the meaning of development is unclear; the term 'exploitation' is much in evidence, but its meaning is left vague; the theory uses 'primitive concepts' – it is very general; the theory is economistic and mechanical; it ignores the notion of imperialism; its units of analysis are unclear; and, oddly enough, it offers no answer to the causes of underdevelopment. Leys labels the approach a 'marxified structuralism': it is, he says, the ideology of the guilty progressive intellectuals.

All of which may indeed be true: Leys, however, constructs his criticisms from a position of adherence to Althusserian canons of explanatory propriety. It is not easy, consequently, to separate out sensible criticisms from foolish (if presently understated) calls for a 'rigorous marxian science of development/underdevelopment'. Leys's critique does display its sensitivity when he notes: one, that 'radical UDT' had the positive benefit that it 'stimulated the empirical study of institutional and structural mechanisms of underdevelopment;[40] and two, that 'in the context of the early 1960s, when UDT emerged as a militant critique of the ruling ideas of developmentalism, its thrust was unquestionably a progressive one.[41] Leys is right in both these particulars.

Turning now to the work of Bernstein, we find a similarly Althusserian-inspired critique of Frankian material. Bernstein considers both modernization theory and UDT to be unsatisfactory. Affirming a distinction between science and ideology, both are condemned as ideological and UDT is finally damned for its 'mystifying use of a marxist terminology'[42] and 'the use of a moralistic and idealistic critique of capitalism based on philosophical humanism'.[43] I will not pursue Bernstein's critique: elements of it have been treated in the context of looking at Baran and its Althussarian-inspired elements will be looked below (pp. 163–7).

In the final part of this discussion of A. G. Frank I want to look briefly at his subsequent reply to his critics and then offer a final summary note. In a recent work, *Dependent Accumulation and Underdevelopment* (1978), Frank recalls that he has contributed to the formation of the 'dependency' school, and that his early efforts have been heavily criticized for tending to the economistic and lacking any genuinely dialectical analysis. Of the 1978 work, Frank says that it represents 'an attempt to transcend the "dependence" approach, but without yet abandoning it or the focus on underdevelopment, and to proceed on towards the integration of dependence and underdevelopment within the world process of accumulation.'[44] The book tackles a set of particular questions of analysis: issues occasioned by the criticisms of the earlier work, though not flowing directly from them. The criticisms are treated in an introductory chapter that indicates Frank's line of research interest. Thus he declares: 'This book and these introductory questions to it are an attempt to break out of the vicious circle of development theory.'[45] The hoped-for replacement is characterized in three ways. The first is by reference to method:

> To free ourselves from the irrelevance of narrowly limited neo-classical theory . . . we may take the global historical vision of Adam Smith and the dialectical analysis of Karl Marx as points of departure in an attempt to advance toward a whole world encompassing holistic, real world historical, socially structural (and therefore in fact theoretically dialectical) theory of development and underdevelopment.[46]

Second, as regards procedure, he says: 'This will require the scientific examination of the historical evidence and record of capitalist development and the better reading (in the sense of Althusser) of Smith and Marx in the light of this evidence.'[47] Third, Frank indicates the expected manner of emergence of the product:

> With this purpose and in this spirit we review the participation of Asia, Africa and Latin America in this world wide

> historical process; and we emphasize the subordinate dependence of these areas within the process of world capitalist development as the cause of their development of underdevelopment.[48]

It seems to me that this does not represent the rethinking of his position that his critics had looked for. The resolutions noted above reveal that there is no general reconstruction being undertaken. Rather, Frank continues to use the syntax of the natural sciences: thus he seeks to revise his theories with a closer, more detailed reading of history in the light of concepts that are already established in his work, yet are liable, it seems, to relocation within a subtler frame derived from Smith and Marx.

In this 1978 text what we see is, I think, an intellectual/political relocation. That which was characteristically Frankian is not so much lost as partly submerged. In the attempt to accommodate to (largely academic) criticism, Frank's work shifts from that of the political pamphleteer towards that of the academic, scholarly commentator and simultaneously adopts a more general academic frame of reference (more thinkers are embraced). I do not find it persuasive, and in his most recent work the 'old' A. G. Frank has returned.[49]

How then might we sum up A. G. Frank? In conception (notions of *how* to explain) it seems clear that Frank's work is a curious mixture of Latin American social science, Baran-style marxism, and historical exegesis: the whole considered in – it has to be said – a methodologically awkward (indeed, even orthodox) fashion. All these points I have discussed above. It is with the business of Frank's intentions (notions of *why* the explanations are worth making) that, particularly within the general context of my ideas about social theorizing (recall Part 1), we find the clue to appreciating his work.

Thus Ehrensaft labels Frank's effort 'satellization', and remarks that 'the satellization approach deals with the same phenomena as does the structuralist. The difference consists largely in the interpretation given to these phenomena.'[50] There is certainly a large element of truth in this (even if Ehrensaft doesn't appreciate the force of his own observation): Ehrensaft goes on to quote Frank (from the essay 'The Development of Underdevelopment') to the effect that where he, Frank, differs from some other structuralists is that he is *not* ideologically blinkered. Here, I think, is the crucial novelty of A. G. Frank's work: it resides in his overt political (and activist) commitment. Not only is this political engagement obvious, but it is made central to the whole effort. Thus he has said of his earlier-noted work: 'These essays were written to contribute to the Revolution in Latin America and the world';[51] and, again, he argues that problems of underdevelopment can be resolved 'with the only true development strategy: armed revolution and the construction of socialism.'[52] It is for these reasons that I prefer to think of A. G. Frank as a political pamphleteer – it is a quite distinctive mode of social theorizing[53] – even though he makes use of (and contributes to) the work of sociologists, economists, historians, political scientists, and so on.

13 Post-neo-marxism

I use this label 'post-neo-marxism' to designate a fairly broad area of concern within contemporary marxian discourse. At the present time an issue that was, it seems to me, latent within the broad marxian tradition, which I've reviewed in this Part 3, has come to be explicitly discussed. This issue is the nature of a properly marxian analysis of development and underdevelopment. That this question should come to exercise marxian theorists is not all that surprising: marxism, both generally and in respect of treatments of development, has only returned to intellectual respectability over the last fifteen or so years. As this process of rediscovery progressed, attention was directed not only to substantive issues or problems but also, reflexively, to the very intellectual machineries being used. There is, of course, a simple contrast to be drawn here between orthodox and marxist theorists: the orthodox theorists had by the post-war period an agreed approach – a consensus: – the major problems of social science and methods appropriate to it were, they thought, known. Theorizing development simply entailed the application of known intellectual tools to novel situations. For the marxists – emerging from the deserts of 'Marxism–Leninism' – there was no such confidence: the marxist revival was self-conscious from the outset. Amusingly, the consensus of the orthodox has now disintegrated[1] and they face analogous problems to those working in the marxist tradition.

The discussion of what is to count as a properly marxian analysis of development and underdevelopment has been extensive and I will pick out two broad tendencies. The first is a rather deterministic and distinctly scientistic approach; the second is more voluntaristic and concerned with politics. These two tendencies can be associated with the ideas of *modes of production* and *specificity of enquiry*, respectively. What both these two approaches, or areas of concern, are trying to achieve is a method of analysing under-development (in particular) in a way that is both clearly linked to the intellectual machineries of Marx and which is also sensitive to the detail of the various 'forms of life' of the Third World.

The idea of mode of production, evidently marxist, has been represented in Louis Althusser's[2] reading of Marx: it is used to designate a particular sort of social production. The concept permits, its adherents claim, the pursuit of enquiry which is faithful to Marx, sensitive to detail (as noted) and scientifically rigorous. All this is taken to be in marked contrast to the over-generality of A. G. Frank and the neo-marxists. Thus the Third World is taken to comprise many modes of production: these can coexist with each other for long periods of time and the business of the transition from one pre-capitalist mode of production to the capitalist mode proper is typically a long-drawn-out and thoroughly complex business. The idea of a sequence of modes of production, which can be discerned in the work of Marx, is thus revised and the crucial question – given an interest in development – becomes the way in which different modes of production interact, either facilitating or retarding the emergence of capitalism. This is referred to as the *articulation* of modes of production. The most important articulation is that between capitalism and various precapitalist modes of production.

The value of this approach is much debated. The rather scientistic notion of marxism affirmed, plus the influence of Althusser as a *philosopher*, issues in a tendency to produce elaborate, rather general and formal schemes. None the less, the insistence upon paying attention in a detailed/rigorous way to the differences, and differing patterns of change, between modes of production within the Third World is a useful corrective to the, arguably, overschematic style of A. G. Frank.

A similar insistence upon attention to detail and patterns of change is found in the differently premissed and oriented work of F. Cardoso and E. Faletto.[3] What they take from Marx – although not quite directly – is the idea of political economy. The two theorists characterize political economy as a total approach to analysing society: they contrast it with orthodox social science with its many disciplinary sub-divisions. Political economy is thoroughly practical and political in character: it was the premier mode of social analysis in the nineteenth century, and Cardoso and Faletto take Marx to be the leading exponent of this style of enquiry.

Cardoso and Faletto analyse the present situation of Latin American societies using this approach. They consider the particular balances of class forces in various countries as they have successively presented themselves in history. The contemporary conjunction of classes is analysed and it is upon such analyses that political alternatives to dependent development are identified.

As with the 'mode of production' approach, Cardoso and Faletto seek to go beyond the analytical schemes of the neo-marxists. I will review the main points of these two patterns of concern with properly marxian analysis. However, it should be noted that these are very much 'live issues' and what I have to say here is, therefore, tentative.

A. G. Frank (and the neo-marxists more generally) has been heavily criticized, as we saw in the preceding chapter, for oversimplifying the issues of development and underdevelopment by taking capitalism as essentially an exchange relationship. That is, for equating the existence of the individual pursuit of profit within a market with capitalism. His critics pointed out that Marx had understood capitalism as a particular sort of social production. Marx, most famously in the 'Preface' of 1859,[4] deployed the notions of 'forces of production' plus 'relations of production' and summarized their complex patterns of interaction under the heading of 'mode of production'. A 'capitalist mode of production' is characterized as involving, centrally, the private control of social production: the system was characterized as historically dynamic and inherently unstable.

Marx also identified other modes of production: primitive communism, ancient slave-based production, feudalism, capitalism, socialism, and the Asiatic mode of production. The list varies somewhat[5] and there is a large amount of then contemporary ethnographic material discussed – but, except for some work published by Engels, little of this material was ever set out in an ordered form. However, we need not pursue this: the point for us to note is that Marx (and Engels) did indeed use the notion of 'mode of production'. We can now look at how it has been used in recent studies of development.

The idea was reintroduced by French writers: Althusser I have already mentioned. The gist of the approach is as follows. The Third World is no longer seen as being an 'underdeveloped' social form – as A. G. Frank would characterize it – but as comprising very many 'modes of production'. Each of these modes of production represents a particular, historically generated, pattern of life – an arrangement of social relations around a particular sort of production. These modes of production have their own internal dynamics: *any* mode of production must be able to reproduce itself. Further, it is pointed out that these modes of production interact in specific and complex fashions: pre-capitalist modes with each other, and all these with capitalism. So, to analyse any particular part of the world, we have: first, to specify the character of the local modes of production, indicating how they reproduce themselves and how they accommodatively interact with one another; then, second, to detail the way in which these local modes of production interact with the capitalist mode of production. This complex set of circumstances will have its own dynamic and this will condition the chances of development.

P. P. Rey[6] makes use of the notion of modes of production, in the fashion indicated above. The way in which the term was used by Marx and Engels was, as indicated, largely unformalized. Subsequent orthodox marxists presented the idea of modes of production as a set of stages, or a sequence punctuated with periods of transformation where one mode of production turned into the next. Rey reworks this image so that transition is seen as typical: the two modes of production (or, in principle, more than two) will coexist and the process of replacement is slow. Rey calls this the *articulation* of modes of production.

The expanding mode of production is capitalism, and Rey here returns to the old marxian idea of capitalism as progressive (in contrast to the scheme of the neo-marxists). Why, then, have some areas advanced and others not? Rey's answer is, predictably, that it depends upon the other mode of production with which capitalism is interacting – or is articulated. In the heartlands of capitalism, in Europe, the historical articulation of the feudal mode of production with the nascent capitalist mode issued in the (relatively straightforward) succession of the latter. Elsewhere in the world, pre-capitalist modes of production did not generate their own internal progressive dynamic and have subsequently been drawn into the general world system via exchange with the established, and external, capitalist mode of production.

Rey analyses in detail the case of the Congo in West Africa. First, he identifies the local mode of production which he calls a 'lineage mode'. This lineage mode is analysed as comprising two classes: chiefs (or elders) and dependants (or juniors). Allocation of tasks is by kinship relations and the whole is a subsistence-type production. A crucial aspect of this lineage mode is the exchange of slaves between related groups. Slavery within the lineage mode was not slavery as we would now understand it; it was, rather, a small-scale circulation of population and not the 'chattel slavery' of plantations in the New World.

The lineage mode interacted with the capitalist mode via the slave trade. The slave trade was supportable for the lineage mode for a long time: slaves were drawn from the interior and shipped out by coastal lineage modes and European goods moved inwards from coastal trading stations. Thus were the two 'modes' articulated.

As the slave trade declined, European traders looked for other goods (ivory, rubber, etc.): the typical products of the subsistence pattern of the area. The colonial power (having taken formal responsibility) attempted to rationalize production by allocating areas to trading companies. However, this did not succeed – and Rey points to this as evidence that purely economic exchanges could not effect any radical change in the lineage mode: when the chiefs had enough prestige (European) goods, they simply stopped supplying the ivory, etc. At this point we have the imposition of colonial authority and the creation of what Rey calls the 'colonial mode of production'. The imposition of the colonial mode involves the forced destruction of the lineage mode simultaneously with the implantation of modern production forms. Subsistence farming is replaced and the key is the setting-up of a money economy. In this period we have the usual range of colonial developments – railways, ports, plantations, mines, towns – *plus* all the social changes that go alongside these obvious changes. The upshot is that the traditional lineage mode is effectively destroyed. A final shift, for this area, was from the colonial mode to the 'neo-colonial mode' of production: patterns of economic and political dependence on the metropolis assume their present and familiar form and within the peripheral territory we find the familiar disintegrated sectoral pattern. Rey argues that development within the peripheral territory is held up by the alliance of the 'neo-colonial mode' with the 'capitalist mode' and the majority of the people continue in their (now degenerate) lineage mode. Politically (and here Rey's analysis comes to resemble Frank's), a socialist revolution is a prerequisite of change. The present alliance of peripheral and metropolitan capitalism will only advance development for the mass of the people at a very slow pace.

Thus does Rey offer his version of an analysis of the Third World that is sensitive to the detail of actual Third World societies and rigorously marxian. To offer a criticism of Rey's work would entail a simultaneous criticism of Althusserian material: this I do not want to tackle in this text. There are two points which I would make: first, the insistence upon conceptual rigour and sensitivity to 'empirical' detail are unobjectionable (although whether it is fair for the proponents of this approach to contrast their work with that of the neo-marxists is much less clear); second, the Althusserian syntax of scientificity is, for my own part, unpersuasive. Further than this I do not want to go, as the debate gets very tangled.[7] What I will do instead is offer a contrasting attempt to conceive a properly marxian analysis of development and underdevelopment: that presented by, in particular, F. H. Cardoso.

The work of Cardoso (with his early co-worker, E. Faletto) eschews the deterministic style of the Althusserians: the work is geared to elucidating the nature of class dynamics with an eye to political action. Cardoso and Faletto have their own procedure of reworking Marx and, as it happens, I think that their reading of Marx is preferable to that discussed above. This reworking involves a central appeal to the method of political economic enquiry. Here I will look, first, at the idea of political economy and, second, at the use made by Cardoso and Faletto of that style of analysis in the context of Latin America.

Political economy as a general style is touched upon by Carver. He notes that 'much of the effort of the political economists went into what appears today to be a very general enquiry, with statements and defences of their views on definitional questions, and some of the moral and political issues entailed.'[8] In addition to this catholicity of intellectual interest involved in the construction of their effort,[9] we must also note their thoroughgoing practical intent. Carver offers a summation which will stand as general. Noting that Marx's critique is subtle and allusive and consequently none too easy to follow, he remarks: 'Also, he does not limit himself to criticism, but investigates the questions which interest him, and then develops his own point of view – a characteristic Marxian procedure.'[10]

This characteristic breadth of scope is picked up by those who would affirm the propriety of this mode of enquiry. The explicit contrast is often drawn with the restricted, partial, institutionalized discourses of the various orthodox sciences of the social. This rejection of compartmentalism is the most general starting-point for Cardoso and Faletto, who, in recording in most general terms their intellectual history, take note of the impact of US academic social science and detail their response to it. They state: 'We attempt to re-establish the intellectual tradition based on a comprehensive social science. We seek a global and dynamic understanding of social structures.'[11] Beyond this they lodge themselves specifically within a tradition; hence, 'we stress the socio-political nature of the economic relations of production, thus following the nineteenth century tradition of treating economy as political economy . . . which found its highest expression in Marx.'[12]

Political economy not only differs from orthodox social science in the case of the catholicity of its intellectual interest and practicality of intent, but it also differs in the overall 'shape' of its method. According to Carver, Marx draws a distinction between logical analysis 'in which something complex is resolved or broken up into simple elements',[13] on the one hand, and, on the other, logical synthesis which 'proceeds in the opposite direction in order to reproduce the concrete in a conception'.[14] It is the second procedure that is taken by Marx to represent the proper direction of enquiry for political economy.

The effort is one of the intellectual 'reconstruction of the real'. Thus it is noted that

> Marx develops the view that this concrete result, achieved by a process of synthesis, is also the 'actual starting point', the starting point which actually exists; in other words to perform the synthesis properly he must, at the beginning, presuppose actuality in order to arrive at the summarized conceptualized concrete.[15]

As a scheme of enquiry/explanation, political economy is clearly sharply distinct from the orthodoxy. Enquiry does not proceed by abstraction from the given, generalization and model-building; nor is explanation linked with, or made in some fashion analogous to, causal predictiveness. Instead, enquiry proceeds by the technically explicit, categorial 'reconstruction of the real'. To explain is to make sense. Of Marx's notion of 'science', Carver notes: 'The searching process for Marx was essentially active, investigative, critical and practical; a scientific presentation, in his view, seems to have been one which solved conceptual mysteries and presented the human world accurately, intelligibly and politically.'[16]

The differences just noted have been represented in recent critical-theory-inspired work[17] in the guise of a distinction between validation and authentication. Cardoso and Faletto seemingly anticipate this distinction when they treat the issue of 'measurement'. They reject the model of social scientific explanation presented in orthodox US work, and assert that 'The accuracy of a historical–structural interpretation has to be checked by confronting its delineation of structural conditions and trends of change with actual socio-political processes.'[18] They speak of two elements, 'construction of interpretation and . . . its practical validation',[19] and note that 'the demonstration of an interpretation follows real historical process very closely and depends to some extent on its own ability to show socio-political actors the precise solution to contradictory situations.'[20]

So much for the style of enquiry of political economy. I now want to turn to the work of Cardoso and Faletto and, in particular, their noted 1967 text, *Dependency and Development in Latin America*.[21] Rather than continue with general exegesis, I will offer an example (taken virtually at random) from this text by way of illustration of the claims made above.

In the new (1976) preface to their book, the authors remark that

> If the analytical effort succeeds, general platitudes and reaffirmations about the role of capitalist modes of production can turn into a lively knowledge of real processes . . . It is necessary to elaborate concepts and explanations able to show how general trends of capitalist expansion turn into concrete relations among men, classes and states in the periphery . . . This is the methodological movement constituting what is called the passage from an 'abstract' style of analysis into a 'concrete' form of historical knowledge.[22]

An example might be this. Discussing the post-Second World War adjustments in societies to shifts in pre-war class alliances occasioned by changes in relations with the world economy, Cardoso and Faletto make the following report:

> In Argentina, where the agro-export sector continued to be economically important, industrialization, although accompanied by substantial redistribution, was not significant, especially in the basic industries. The new situation of the world market presented the alternatives most dramatically: to hold down wages and public expenditures at the expense of the working-popular classes; or to re-organise and raise the productivity of the agro-expert economy in order to use it to continue long term financing of the modern industrial sector. After the fall of Peron in 1955, the anti-populist opposition chose the latter policy. Nevertheless, the export sector could not by itself impose this objective on the rest of the country, nor could it counteract the pressure of the masses through an alliance with the politically weak industrial sectors, as was attempted by the Frondizi government (1958–62). Military intervention became frequent both as a form of arbitration and as an open reaction against a return to populism. This course of economic development was vigorously blocked by broad sectors of wage earners. It could not be imposed as a policy that, if not legitimate, was at least efficient. Therefore, there was neither development nor political stability.[23]

It is in this fashion that Cardoso and Faletto trace the patterns of class relationships over time: it is the key to their approach. Latin American economies are presented in terms of a shifting scene of competing, co-operating, cohabiting, and mutually unconnected groups. The whole is subject to the impact of the world capitalist economy and that is beyond any one group's control. In his recent work Cardoso has gone on to look at the spontaneous organizations produced amongst the masses of the people: he is interested in their chances of effecting change and in the role of the intellectuals in relation to them. This is the reason why, following Palma,[24] this line of analysis of the Third World revolves around the idea of specificity of enquiry.

So much, then, for the two main areas of enquiry into the issue of the nature of a properly marxian analysis of development and underdevelopment. It must be kept firmly in mind that this is very much 'work in progress' and not only are the debates noted here still being pursued, but there are also other discussions, which I have not treated, and which also claim the label 'marxist'. I find it difficult to imagine that this debate will subside to any appreciable extent in the near future – as I see matters, there are signs of a return to the 'classic tradition' of social theorizing; but, equally, there is a diversity of interests in matters social. These are issues I will pursue in the Part 4.

Orthodox and radical views of Southeast Asia

In the preceding chapters I have presented the idea that social theorizing is, generically speaking, concerned with making sense. The work of the 'founding fathers' was reviewed as a series of examples of prospective and general social theorizing – or, using the word in my sense, ideology-making. I have argued that thc post-war career of development studies can be interpreted as having seen the presentation of a series of 'ideologies'. Following Ankie Hoogvelt, I used a general twofold scheme and spoke of, first, bourgeois liberal theories and then, second, marxist theories. The work of these internally diverse theoretical schools has been presented and reviewed. The question that now faces us is: how might we make sense of the circumstances of Southeast Asia? To offer any sort of a 'definitive' answer to this question would require another volume of essays: I am not going even to attempt that task! What I will do here is to review the work of a series of scholars and attempt to illustrate how the two approaches to development work in the context of Southeast Asia.

14 Analysing Southeast Asia

This chapter is offering an essay in 'comparing and contrasting' orthodox and radical approaches to development in Southeast Asia. I am not directly interested in the substance of these analyses; rather, I am interested in the formal patterns of argument and how they follow established traditions. Above, I spoke of a multiplicity of approaches subsumed under two headings – modernization and marxism. Here, I will speak of three broad headings by sub-dividing the orthodox tradition: there are straightforwardly modernization-theory approaches and there are revised schemes which I will label 'dissenting economics' lines of argument. Put simply, these approaches fall between the main two.[1] I will begin by reviewing these three approaches so that we can be reminded of their typical argument strategies.

Any social theory can be analysed in terms of its conception of how enquiry should proceed and its intention in respect of the use to which enquiry is directed. I shall look at modernization theory in this way and then add a list of its typical arguments and concerns.

In conception, modernization theory is, with some variations,[2] empiricist: social theorizing is understood as the value-neutral modelling of how things are in fact. To this conception is joined the intention of providing authoritative and manipulative knowledge of the dynamics of social systems. The theorists understand themselves to be the equivalents in the realm of the social to the natural scientists in their realm. They are experts pursuing the task of providing reliable technical knowledge. However, in my view, their mode of engagement is not as they understand it – that is, detached, scientific, expert – but is, rather, via the provision of crucial elements (general/legitimating, and particular/manipulative) of a prevalent technocratic political ideology. Politics is reduced to planning and this is to be ordered by the experts.

Substantively, modernization theory is offering an elaborated authoritative interventionist ideology of development, where the idea of development affirmed rests upon a concern for economic growth. The theorists of modernization, after an initial growth-theory-based pessimism, offer a thoroughly optimistic scheme. Economic growth, they argue, is fairly readily available to any government that is prepared to make the initial effort to get growth moving. Added to this optimistic economic model of growth is a broad social scientific view of the shift from pre-modern to modern societies, and this has given the whole theory its name – modernization.

Modernization theory, accepting the optimistic economics, rests upon a definite theory of social change. It makes use of neo-evolutionist models of stable, ordered change. A dichotomy is presented between 'traditional' and 'modern', and this gap – the crossing of which constitutes modernization – is explored by reference to a further set of dichotomous comparisons. Typical argument elements would include the following: (a) a neo-evolutionary theory of change, borrowed from Durkheim's notion of the division of labour, which presents change as cumulative, endogenous and progressive; (b) an ethnocentric stance which affirms the model of the West – its ethics (often in a crude materialistic guise), its science (understood as an empiricist style which entails that social science is also generally applicable), and its history and present social form (the model of the modern fuses with that of the West); (c) a conservative politics which focuses upon the problem of order; (d) a dichotomous analytic procedure centred upon the prime dichotomy of traditional/modern; (e) an acceptance as 'given' of the optimistic orthodox economics of growth; and (f) a focus on the elites as the primary agents of change.

Turning now to the 'dissenting economists', we can begin by noting that it could be argued that the key story of the post-war career of development studies has been the sustained attempt made by a series of dissenters to constitute development theory as an autonomous social scientific discipline separate from other social sciences and encompassing their lessons. The dissenting economists have in particular insisted upon their separateness from orthodox neo-classical economics, and some of them have even gone so far as to claim to have replaced orthodox economics in studies of both First and Third Worlds. I do not think that any of these claims was ever finally secured, but much of what they had to say was of value. I will consider the distinction between orthodox and dissenting economics below.

In conception their work is piecemeal, sceptical and pragmatic: their central concern is the pursuit of realistic models of problem situations and this necessitates extensive familiarity with the social–cultural circumstances. Their approach is thus a version of empiricism which is typified by its reflexivity – concepts are automatically checked against sociological data. This links up to their intentions. These theorists are, *par excellence*, the theorists of planning. They aspire to the possession of technical manipulative knowledge. As with advocates of the orthodoxy above, I think these dissenters are aiming to provide policy-scientific knowledge – but their mode of engagement is differently understood, even if in practice it is pretty much the same. The dissenting economists do not pretend to be neutral experts; instead, they take themselves to be ethically and scientifically engaged. They argue on behalf of the reasonable men in control of the state – the planner technocrats – who are in pursuit of development understood as broad, ordered social reform.

The typical argument elements used by these social economists will include the following: (a) a variation on neo-evolutionary ideas of change; (b) a mitigated ethnocentrism where the model of the West is not simply taken for granted; (c) a reformist politics which stresses planning; and (d) a modified, reflexive empiricism focused upon realistic modelling of problem situations.

In the First World, marxian social theory has recently been revived as an intellectually reputable, and indeed politically plausible, line of enquiry, following its many years under the shadow of both the official doctrine of Marxism–Leninism and the image of Stalin. The marxism of Western European theorists has returned to the work of Marx and Engels directly and, in particular, to the work of the 'early Marx' and his analysis of alienation. Today, theorists speak of the 'humanist marxian tradition'. It is this version I will characterize here.

In conception, marxism adopts a historical materialist approach with the intention of displaying the possibilities for the future lodged in the present, so as to inspire and inform effective political action. The approach thus differs sharply from both the above with their 'policy science'.

As Marx has been 'rediscovered' only recently, there exists an extensive literature attempting to recover his 'real meaning'. Generally, however, we can see marxism as concerned with the class dynamics of capitalism and the possibilities for development understood as movement towards radical democracy.

The typical elements of a marxian analysis of the Third World would include the following: (a) change is to a very significant extent exogenous as the world capitalist system expands and impacts upon non-capitalist social forms; (b) the position taken is non-ethnocentric on the grounds of its thoroughgoing reflexivity;[3] (c) the analysis affirms a radical democratic politics; (d) it uses a historical materialist approach centred upon political economic analyses and the matter of surplus; (e) it rejects liberal market economics and speaks of capitalism; and (f) it looks at class dynamics as the key to change within societies and at relations of dependence between 'centres' and 'peripheries'.

In sum, we can identify three approaches to the business of development: orthodox economics and dissenting economics – both of which fall under my general label of 'modernization' – and marxist approaches. Each has its own ideas about procedures and goals, and each offers a different development strategy.

I now turn to the main business of this chapter – the provision of illustrations of how development theorists draw upon the above-noted approaches when they endeavour to make sense of Southeast Asia. My discussions here, it must be stressed, are illustrative only: I am not offering any substantive argument about Southeast Asian development. I will begin with the orthodox theorists, Hoogvelt's 'bourgeois liberals';[4] within this discussion I will treat the social economists, the dissenters. Then I will go on to look at the marxists.

The orthodox liberal modernization theorists' view

The material dealt with here is organized around the typical modernization theory division of intellectual responsibilities. Thus Evers notes of a collection of essays edited by him that it is 'loosely grouped into four parts, each focusing on a major area in which "modernization" is said to take place: in the political, economic, social and religious spheres.'[5] I will therefore look, in turn, at political modernization, economic modernization, social modernization and, finally, religious modernization.

Political modernization

S. P. Huntington, a noted orthodox theorist, remarks, in a 1971 paper, that political theorists came to the business of 'modernization' rather slowly. He cites four reasons for this: the habit of focusing upon the stable (*sic*) societies of the First World; the aspiration to the status of scientists and the consequent eschewal of history; the strategy of explaining politics as derived from more basic features of social life which they tended to focus upon, thus reducing politics to formal political processes and events; and, finally, they ignored comparative politics. Huntington notes:

> Not until the mid-1950s did a renaissance in the study of comparative politics get underway. The renaissance began with a concern with modernization and the comparison of modern and traditional political systems. It evolved in the early 1960s into a preoccupation with the concept of political development . . . In the late 1960s the focus on political development in turn yielded to broader efforts to generate more general theories of political change.[6]

Discussion of political modernization thus went through a 'career', just like modernization theory generally, and this movement involves a progressive broadening and revision of the basic traditional/modern dichotomy. As we shall see in a little while, orthodox theorists of politics still use these dichotomies.

In the 1950s when political scientists turned to look at politics in the Third World they used the material that lay ready to hand – ideas of structure, function, evolution, and so on – as did other social scientists who were also looking for the first time at the Third World.[7] They spoke of traditional and modern societies and conceived the process of modernization. Huntington quotes Ward and Rustow as offering the neatest example of the modernization theorists' characterization of a 'modern polity' – in contrast to a 'traditional' one. Here is the basis of talk about political modernization, this is the goal towards which the nations of the Third World must strive:

> 1. A highly differentiated and functionally specific system of government organization; 2. a high degree of integration within this governmental structure; 3. the prevalence of rational and secular procedures for the making of political decisions; 4. the large volume, wide range, and high efficacy of its political and administrative decisions; 5. a widespread and effective sense of popular identification with the history, territory, and national identity of the state; 6. widespread popular interest and involvement in the political system, though not necessarily in the decision-making aspects thereof; 7. the allocation of political roles by achievement rather than ascription; and 8. judicial and regulatory techniques based upon a predominantly secular and impersonal system of law.[8]

Huntington reports that it can be said that, generally, the modern is distinguished from the traditional by having '– rationalized authority, differentiated structure, mass participation and a consequent capability to accomplish a broad range of goals'.[9]

This first phase of theorizing political development took 'modernization' for granted, but it quickly became clear that the modernization approach was far too simple. A period of revision set in. Political scientists likewise revised their theorems: away from the traditional/modern dichotomies towards a 'more dynamic and developmentally oriented set of concerns'.[10] In the end (even) Huntington thinks that it did not get them very far, and he proposes abandoning the notion of political development (or modernization) in favour of speaking of political change. Huntington sums up his feelings on 'political development' by remarking that the concept's key role was to legitimate the ideals of the political scientists: that is, the term was disguised ideology (in the usual pejorative sense).[11]

The key ideas of 'political modernization' are these. First, that the process of political modernization entails movement towards the model of a 'modern polity'; that the goal is a stable political system like that of the First World, where power is diffused to a greater or lesser extent through society – that is, the system is a pluralist democracy. Second, that in the presently developing world this movement towards a pluralistic modern polity can be 'uneven' – that is, the basic evolutionary process can suffer 'break-downs' and authoritarian, totalitarian and bureaucratic politics can emerge. Third, the process of political modernization can be analysed as a species of technical social science and knowledge useful to policy-makers generated – that is, political modernization theory is elite-oriented in the sense that the theorists argue on behalf of the elite and organize their enquiries around the supposed needs of the elite.

Recalling my characterization of modernization theory as an ideology of elaborated authoritative intervention, it is rather easy to grasp the broad outlines of the work of political modernization theorists, and the rest is just detail and illustration which may or may not be interesting.

Huntington cites Eisenstadt as a 'revisionist modernization theorist'. I want now to turn to the work of this theorist as he will let me link the business of political modernization with analyses of Southeast Asia. In the text edited by Evers, *Modernization in Southeast Asia* (1973), an essay by Eisenstadt forms the point of departure for the collection as a whole. This essay is entitled 'The Influence of Traditional and Colonial Political Systems on the Development of Post-traditional Social and Political Orders'; from this title we can see that it is in line with Huntington's suggestion that studies of political modernization were moving into the main areas of modernization theory by looking at change generally. It is also clear that Eisenstadt's work is similar to Darling's in approach.

Eisenstadt begins by offering as the major premiss of his argument the observation that

> while we witness today throughout the world a breakdown of traditional socio-political orders, this does not necessarily mean that the development system or order will be patterned according to the initial modern model that developed in Europe, that, in fact, there may arise a great variety of post-traditional orders, and that such types are developing now in Southeast Asia.[12]

The approach he takes to analysing these issues is via 'a reconsideration of some of the assumptions which have guided the initial studies of modernization.'[13] He goes on to speak of an interest in stable change as central to modern sociology (and it was, as we have seen, central to structural functionalist sociology in the 1950s and 1960s). Eisenstadt, speaking simply of traditional and modern reports that early, sharply dualistic formulations, have given way to 'a growing interest in the *conditions of emergence* of modern societies . . . asking about the *pre-conditions* of . . . successful "take-off" into maturity'.[14] Eisenstadt characterizes the early modernization theorists as optimistic constructors of indices of modernity, who took the process for granted. But in the early 1960s doubt crept in as 'take-off' turned, in not a few cases, into 'breakdown'. The idea of 'traditional' received, in consequence, very much more attention: it was seen to be, roughly speaking, much more resilient, complex and viable than the simple optimists of modernization had first thought.

The modernization approach, having come to be seen as implausible in the light of 'real world' events, is to be revised. One might ask, to what extent is this an *ad hoc* revision? – as it was, say, with Myrdal's idea of the 'soft state' or Durkheim's idea of the anomic division of labour. One might also note that it was initially the model of the traditional that was to be reconsidered, rather than both models and their putative relationship. Thus Eisenstadt observes that the story of the 'breakthrough into modernity' is now seen to be much more complicated than first thought: so he revises, in a mechanical fashion, the assumed process.[15] None the less, there are still 'basics' – and here the original duo of traditional/modern are reaffirmed as 'cultural premisses'.

Eisenstadt adds that a key cultural premiss is the split between 'centre' and 'periphery'. The 'centres' maintain the general stock of a society's 'cultural premisses', and so it is at the 'centres' that the breakthrough to modernity has to occur. Put simply, it is the political elite that have to make the move and replace the static polity of traditional society with the dynamism of the modern. Eisenstadt speaks of 'breakthroughs to mass consensual post-traditional societies'. The new polity has to be able to deal with continual change or, 'in other words, the problem of sustained development'.[16]

Eisenstadt then turns to look at nation states, the model of politico-cultural 'centres'. The rise of nation states in the eighteenth and nineteenth centuries in Europe is noted, as are their typical characteristics. Modernization theory, remarks Eisenstadt, has assumed that the 'breakthrough to modernity' will repeat the First World experience but this, he insists, is not inevitable. The nature of present new nations, their position in this movement towards maturity, now depends upon traditional patterns of political life and the nature of decolonization. Their pasts shape their presents. Eisenstadt, as he takes notice of a historical approach, correctly notes that in the case of the First World the forms of nation states were 'historically generated'. In the case of the Third World,

> In most general terms it can be said that the centres that tended to crystallize in these societies were characterized by what may be called 'modern patrimonialism', that is, the establishment or continuation of new political and administrative central frameworks which have a tendency to maintain the external contents of traditional or of modern symbols without simultaneously maintaining any strong commitments to them. Such centres display almost exclusive concern for the preservation of the existing weak frameworks of power, thus giving rise to a continuous succession of weak centres.[17]

Eisenstadt's label of 'modern patrimonialism' is one variant of a focus upon tradition and bureaucracy. Thus Darling[18] offers us 'bureaucratic polities' amongst a series of other 'breakdowns of modernization'. Girling,[19] too, speaks of 'bureaucratic polities' in Southeast Asia. Both these theorists are following the lead of the noted modernization theorist Fred Rigg.[20] The common characteristic of these analyses, as in the case of Eisenstadt, is that the basic modernization-theory commitment to the model of the West/USA is left in place and other polities are ordered and ranked around this model.

In sum, Eisenstadt replaces the simple linear recapitulation model of early modernization theory, where the Third World followed the First World directly, with a complex historical borrowing/sedimentation model, according to which the Third World follows the First World in a shambling, uneven sort of a way. The counter-tradition, the marxists with their historicist approach, would dismiss this whole enterprise. Instead, they would speak of peripheral incorporation into the world capitalist system and the end of colonialism seeing the installation of neo-colonial regimes.[21] These are arguments we will come to. For the moment I will simply note that Eisenstadt's analysis is criticized by his co-essayists: (1) for the notion of 'breakdown', which is untenably Westerncentric and rules out other patterns of development – for example, that of the People's Republic of China; (2) for the stress Eisenstadt puts on cultural symbols and breakthroughs to modernity at the centre, which both emphasizes 'symbols' too much and, relatedly, gives notice of Eisenstadt's neglect of economics; and (3) and for the focus on the centre/elite, which is seen to be just plain wrong and the success of the rural-based Vietnamese nationalists is cited. Eisenstadt's co-essayists all attempt to 'go beyond' modernization theory, but I cannot see that they actually get very far.[22]

Modernization theorists are often insistent upon the 'scientific status' of their work. Often there is a tension between 'scientificness' and informativeness. I will illustrate this with the following four theorists and then, taking the example of Singapore, look at the key modernization-theory issue of elites.

Nawawi,[23] in his essay 'Tradition, Mobilization and Development in Indonesia', urges that 'To be highly objective, the concept of political development must deal firmly with the extent of authority or the degree of government itself.'[24] This seems to be a variation on the concern for stable order that is so central to political modernization thinkers – as is the assumption that it is governments that create order. This concern is unpacked in an empiricist fashion: 'One way of directly evaluating the capacity of the political system is to measure the quantity of its products and services . . . Assuming that these political goods can be satisfactorily measured and aggregated, their extent or amount can give a valuable index to the performance of the government.'[25] The author then goes on to consider road provision, health and educational provision, judicial services and, most important, tax takes. These he considers and compares across regions in Indonesia and, having noted the minimal political modernization seemingly achieved, concludes that: '*The essence of political development is the upward spiralling process of increasing political wealth and intensifying mobilization of the required resources.*'[26] To the extent that this conclusion is intelligible, it seems to be both tautological – development requires development – and derivative in its borrowing from economics syntax. More interesting is Nawawi's explanation of the lack of political modernization. His explanation is couched, as we might expect, in terms of 'tradition', and he speaks of parochialism, personalism and unsystematic resource mobilization and use. Thus, as he begins to speak directly about the situation, he becomes both more interesting and more plausible. However, his work is couched in terms of a very restricting theoretical perspective which postulates a shift from traditional to modern: thus he remarks, 'From this perspective, the real complaint against the Dutch is not that they came and subjugated but that they were not dominant enough.'[27] The view that the Dutch routinely destroyed opposition, economically exploited the area and only belatedly introduced a limited reform programme – the 'ethical policy' – is not treated by Nawawi. Colonialism, dependency and neo-colonialism do not fit into his theoretical perspective and thus when he does speak of the colonial power it is in this thoroughly peculiar fashion.

Agpalo,[28] in an essay entitled 'Political Modernization in the Philippines', begins in the same way. He declares in an empiricist orthodox style how he will deploy certain concepts and he refers to: political elite, ruling power elite and counter-elite. The descent from this formal 'theoretical' level to history is considerably more abrupt than in Nawawi's essay and thus Agpalo's work is more interesting: fairly routinely analysed historical material is presented and the detail need not concern us.

In contrast, Ahmad's[29] analysis of the Malaysian political structure is a markedly less self-consciously political–scientific piece of analysis. Here, matters of style of enquiry are not permitted to override matters of substance. Thus Ahmad both adopts a political modernization framework and focuses directly on the concrete issue of race: he speaks of the 'racial paradigm'.[30] It is around this substantive issue that he discusses, in the style of a historical review, the business of modernizing the political structures of Malaysia – clearly seeing it as a task characterizable in terms of: (1) a likely lengthy duration; (2) a political, not technical, process; and (3) continuing communalist tension. The understated 'scientificness' enhances the essay.

An interestingly unselfconscious use of the idea of political modernization is provided by the historian Pandy[31] who, reviewing the post-Second World War histories of South and Southeast Asian nations, discusses their present political systems in terms of the idea of 'falling away'. The model Pandy affirms, with utter unselfconsciousness, is that of liberal parliamentary democracy and when he searches amongst his stock of nation states he cannot, to his evident dismay, find any good examples of functioning liberal democratic systems and, instead, he can find a large number of non-liberal democratic forms which he interprets as failures: these political systems have 'fallen away' from commitment to the true model. He reviews the period's political history by noting, first, that: 'Never during the colonial period did the Asian nationalists ever question the suitability of a democratic system';[32] and after the Second World War, 'Democracy was in fashion.'[33] Subsequently, however, 'the liberal face of Southern Asia began to change'[34] and Pandy chronicles the sequence of what the theorists cited at the outset of this discussion would designate as 'breakdowns of political modernization'. The upshot being that, generally, political systems of liberal democracy had gone. In seeking to answer the question 'why these democracies collapsed in South and South-East Asia',[35] Pandy remarks, interestingly, that the system was called on to do jobs never demanded of it in the West. Here, the genuine issue of 'transferability' of simple models is raised, but not, unfortunately, pursued. Instead, the metaphor of 'falling away' (mine, not Pandy's) is in evidence and he identifies the culprits for us: 'They are mainly three: the undemocratic competition for power and the lack of national consensus among the political elites; the political role of the military; the communist challenge and American intervention.'[36] Pandy's analysis of South and Southeast Asia seems to me to be a pleasingly direct piece of work: like Ahmad, he brings the substance of his enquiries to the forefront and leaves the laborious machineries of 'scientific' political modernization in the background – though clearly he is drawing upon them.

Turning now to the issue of elites, we find an area of major preoccupation for theorists of political modernization as it is the elites who are the agents to whom the modernization theorists look to translate their theories into practice. It is the elites for whom the modernization theorists argue. And on this matter of elites, we can look at a series of essays collected by Chen and Evers:[37] Evers on the role of the professionals; Chen on the power elite; and, finally, Chan and Evers on nation-building. All the essays focus on Singapore and all cover similar ground.

Evers is concerned with the changing role of professionals in 'new nations' and especially Singapore. He begins with the claim-*cum*-observation that it is professionals who come closest to modernization theorists' ideals of a modern person – as opposed to a 'traditional person'. Evers argues that professionals are disposed to affirm liberal democratic systems because in them they can deploy their skills of argument, reason and persuasion. Evers claims that professionals played crucial roles in the bourgeois revolutions in Europe and he also notes that professionals have been active in decolonization movements because they had the time, legitimacy and interest. However, there was a decisive change 'during the 1960s. In most countries the political role of the professionals declined; parliamentary democracies broke down and were replaced by military dictatorships or authoritarian one party systems.'[38] In answering the question – why this decline? – Evers makes two points: first, that military or one-party rule does not need liberal democracy (which, he has claimed, is the 'natural political environment' of professional people); and, second, the professionals become absorbed both occupationally (with jobs in the bureaucracies) and ideologically (which is to say that they become caught up in positivistic notions of policy science). Habermas, a noted German social theorist who has treated these issues, is cited and Evers reports:

> The impact of this ideology on the Third World was substantial. The question of 'development' was, in the thinking of academics and developers, removed from the realm of politics and became a matter of 'technical rationality'. Development strategies were not to be determined by politicians but by professionals in the guise of 'experts'. Professionals were thus turned into politically castrated technocrats.[39]

The point Evers is making here is that the professionals contributed to the demise of the systems of liberal democracy by arguing for the ideology of technical rationality. Ironically, they also lost their independence by being absorbed into the authoritarian political systems they had unwillingly helped to create.

Evers is not a narrowly orthodox figure – indeed, he is drawing on the work of Habermas[40] – but he is followed by a distinctly more orthodox figure, Chen, who picks up the same point – technocratic rule – and discusses it with reference to the ideas of power elite, functional elite and counter-elite. Chen also speaks, rather confusingly, of a political/bureaucratic elite which he seems to take to be the central part of the power elite. Setting this problem aside, we find that his analysis traces the shift from a 'loosely structured, laissez faire society to a planned, development oriented state. In the process of these changes elites, especially the political elite have played a significant role.'[41] The upshot is that members of the political elite have become undisputed masters. Chen, it would seem, neither approves nor disapproves of this situation and he rests content with a non-committal report. This is, of itself, interesting: Chen adopts the 'role of the expert', commenting in a technical rather than ethically engaged manner.

More broadly, theorists of modernization have displayed a tendency to downgrade liberal democracy (the model of political modernization, according to them) and rest content with authoritarian systems if they seemed to deliver the economic goods. Critics of modernization theory have spoken of the 'erosion of the democratic ideal'.[42]

A critical note is sounded in the essay of Chan and Evers entitled 'National Identity and Nation Building in Singapore'.[43] They observe that nationstatehood, the predominant mode of political organization at the present time, requires national identity – an idea of nation. Constructing such an identity has, typically, involved either: (a) the regressive invocation of a proud cultural tradition; or (b) the progressive invocation of a radical programme for the future.[44] In the case of Singapore, neither of these options was open to the new rulers: the regressive strategy would have created a 'Third China' in the midst of a predominantly Malay region which might have exacerbated communalist tensions,[45] whilst a progressive strategy would have looked communist in a geopolitical sphere that was within the non-communist, indeed Western capitalist, sphere. The solution was the pursuit of a 'non-ideological' identity – a celebration of pragmatism. The result of this was that, within Singapore, 'Discussion of basic questions of political philosophy and ideology, even political discussion in general was severely curbed until it flowed at a low ebb out of public purview.'[46] This 'depoliticized society', as Chan elsewhere calls it,[47] affirms, officially, an ideology of multiracialism, multiculturalism, and so on. Malay- and Chinese-educated have been pushed to one side and a curious English-language-using culture is emerging. Chan and Evers think that the system is inherently unstable: the PAP (People's Action Party) has forged a national identity with 'development and economic success as the symbols of identification',[48] thus creating the risk of an obvious problem of legitimation if ever economic growth falters. They conclude with a most interesting statement:

> Our discussion of nation building has concentrated primarily on Singapore because we see this to be a new type of political system that is still gaining shape. It also moves to be the first to implement many of the features that social scientists have espoused as crucial steps in the process of nation building. Our case study shows clearly what an authoritarian model in pursuit of nationbuilding in fact implies.[49]

Put simply, Chan and Evers think Singapore is a good example of modernization theory 'put into practice': an intriguing idea and evidently the authors are unsure about how to judge the results.

Later, we will look at other judgments which draw on material outside the orthodox frame within which Chan and Evers remain.

Now, to conclude this discussion of political modernization, I will turn to a recently published survey of Southeast Asian polities. The survey, prepared by Darling,[50] will give us a brief summary of the sorts of judgments that political modernization theorists actually make about this region. This summary thus indicates how the typical argument strategies of political modernization noted above are put to use and, in Darling's case, we are spared any subtlety of argument. The author speaks of present political systems being the result of a mix of traditional, Western and 'fusional' inputs. Six types of political system have been produced:

> These types are the quasi-democracies (India, Pakistan, Ceylon, Burma, Malaya, the Philippines), the bureaucratic polities (Nationalist China, Japan, Thailand), the truncated totalitarian polities (Communist China, North Korea, North Vietnam), the truncated authoritarian polities (South Korea, South Vietnam), the hybrid polity (Indonesia), the dynastic polities (Cambodia, Laos) [*sic*].[51]

Given that this book was published as recently as 1979, some of Darling's listing is bizarre: in addition to using several incorrect names, one of the countries mentioned ceased to exist long before 1979, royalty was swept out of the two dynastic polities before 1979, and Singapore has evidently escaped his notice altogether!

I will not pursue the detail of Darling's analyses; instead, I will simply note his characterizations.

(1) The quasi-democracies: here, the notion we met with in Eisenstadt of breakdowns in modernization via 'reversions to traditional type' is invoked. Traditional authoritarian rule reasserts itself and the masses acquiesce because: 'In most cases the struggle for independence had touched only a small number of indigenous political activists, and a vast majority of the local populace was completely untouched by the gradual transfer of political power from Western to indigenous control.'[52]

(2) The bureaucratic polities: originally modelled on Thailand, the notion entails a 'ruling elite composed of career government officials (civilian and military), while "extrabureaucratic" elements such as political parties, interest groups, public opinion etc. exert a minor role.'[53]

(3) The truncated totalitarian polities: Darling's analysis here is little more than orthodox conservative description. We have small bands of Marxist–Leninist revolutionaries seizing the chance offered by the confusions attendant upon world war. Darling acknowledges the military skill of leaders but 'Also, the acqui-

sition of power . . . was enhanced by . . . much sheer "good luck".'[54]

(4) The truncated authoritarian polities: here, Darling uses the distinction between authoritarian and totalitarian: the latter are communist (and cannot ever modernize), whilst the former, although hardly pluralist democrats, may advance in time. More specifically: 'Authoritarianism in South Korea and South Vietnam was also bolstered by memories of grandeur from former empires . . . a factor which acquired special importance in these new societies devoid of an elaborate revolutionary ideology . . . prevailing nationalism sought only the end of foreign colonial rule . . . it wanted no further major changes . . . the United States became the prime source of external support for the preservation of these two non-communist societies.'[55]

(5) The hybrid polity: with Indonesia in mind – often routinely cited as a thoroughly complex nation state in geography, peoples and history – Darling offers this characterization of a hybrid polity: 'It is a composite polity blending or seeking to blend significantly dissimilar cultures and behaviour.'[56]

(6) The dynastic polities: both Darling's instances are no longer in existence but he notes the minimal change in Cambodia and Laos under the French. At that time a small privileged elite sought to hold its authority: 'The dynastic quality came from the pursuit of dominant political and administrative power by the royal family and leading members of the aristocracy.'[57]

In these summaries Darling is drawing upon the stock of ideas available under the heading of political modernization. Change is analysed in a mechanical fashion where 'factors' impel societies this way or that: analysis centres on the model of the West, so the characterizations of Asian nations are thus generally a detailing of failure, or breakdowns and reversions to pre-colonial, non-democratic forms. The whole is presented in the syntax of 'science' – systematicness is stressed and many summary comparative tables are presented, some of which we will meet below. I do not think that it would be unfair to comment that if one wanted to understand what was really going on in Asia and wanted an orthodox analysis, then Pandy would be a much better read.

Economic modernization

Discourse on economic modernization is centred upon liberal market economics. However, 'orthodox' economics are not a monolithically fixed set of notions, but are – as might be expected of any area of social science (and as I briefly noted above) – internally diverse. When I looked at growth theory and modernization theory above I began to sketch, implicitly, two sub-areas of the orthodoxy and noted that one area was distinctly more challenging to established patterns of economic thinking, and political and social arrangements, than the other. Thus growth theory was thoroughly Keynesian in approach and challenged many of the cherished notions of the neo-classical orthodox. Joan Robinson remarks that Keynesianism left economists (and those whose own work rests upon the efforts of the specialists) 'in the uncomfortable situation of having to think for ourselves'.[58]

However, the orthodoxy reasserted itself and the radicalism of Keynes was fairly quickly stifled and thereafter the approach was either marginalized[59] or assimilated into a revamped neo-classicism.[60] The post-Second World War orthodoxy in the First World has been, therefore, neo-classicism. But there have been voices of dissent and they include those Keynesians who have taken Keynes to have represented political economy and have pursued this broader style of enquiry.[61] Recently – to add a final element of confusion! – the neo-classical line has found a vigorous, non-apologetic, and indeed atavistic, proponent in Milton Friedman. I will try to avoid these confusing debates within economics and will simplify the story by identifying two rather different versions of the economic orthodoxy: first, an unmodified (or atavistic) neo-classicism; and second, a modified (or superseded) neo-classicism.[62]

A final point can be made in respect of the attitude of various practitioners to the economics they are using. The first-mentioned – the type-one orthodox – tend to accept orthodox economics as basically correct because the whole is a positive science and knowledge will accumulate over time; whereas the second-mentioned – the type-two orthodox – adopt a very much more sceptical stance towards the products of their own efforts.[63]

In this discussion of economic modernization the variety of economics that I have in mind is, in the first place, the type-one orthodoxy: I will sketch its main tenets and then go on to look at its use in Southeast Asia.

Clements[64] characterizes this type-one orthodoxy in terms of two main principles. The first of these is economic rationality and the second is consumer sovereignty.

(1) Neo-classicism is based on ideas of human economic economic rationality and this is taken to entail the strategy of securing a maximum return for a minimum input – 'efficiency'. The notion of economic rationality serves to establish a relationship between human intention and action and thus to render human behaviour amenable to 'scientific study'. The realm of human meanings is acknowledged, but only in terms of a model of rational economic

activity. The idea of 'economically rational behaviour' allows economic life to be analysed in terms of formal modes and in a detached fashion. Orthodox economic models are the economist's analogue of orthodox sociology's models of social systems. The human world is made an object of study: an empiricist approach.

However, there are various objections to be made to this procedure of analysing the social world via the principle of economic rationality. It has been argued that, as a model of human behaviour, this is an impoverished piece of philosophical anthropology – little more than a crude abstraction from liberal market capitalist society. Arguments which move from the specific to the general are unreliable in form and, in this case, the upshot is the affirmation of a model of human beings that was never very plausible and is now no longer relevant to the present.[65] It is also said that constructing this model of rational economic behaviour will not serve to establish a 'scientific' study of society, as its adherents claim, as the principle is so obviously value-based. Finally, it has been objected that the goal of a 'scientific economics' – or social science – is unattainable. The reasons for this we discussed in Part 1. So, for these three broad reasons, neo-classicism has come to be regarded by its critics as ideological in a pejorative sense.

(2) Related to the above are the notions of consumers and 'consumer sovereignty'. Neo-classicism affirms a notion of human beings as rationally calculating in pursuit of consumption. Clements reports that the consumer is a key figure in neo-classical schemes:

> Consumption . . . is the starting point for neo-classical theory at micro, macro and international levels. The consumer is sovereign and will determine . . . what is or is not produced and in what quantities. Producers compete with one another to satisfy consumer demand in the most profitable way. Prices, therefore, both at national and international level, are determined by forces of supply and demand. It follows that the market will guarantee that factors of production (land, labour and capital) respond to changes in prices and wages in the most efficient/profitable way possible.[66]

And, Clements continues:

> The key principles of the neo-classical view of development are, therefore, profit maximization for individual consumers and producers, the mutual benefits to be gained from national and international trade and the achievements of economic and social progress by the pursuit of enlightened self-interest.[67]

Clements then takes this basic twofold model – economically rational consumers operating in a free market to maximum mutual benefit – and picks out the main general lines of policy advice. I will paraphrase his main points. (a) Regulation of the market is to be avoided, save for crises and the removal of malfunctions or inhibitions to full functioning. (b) Thus intervention to remove causes of price distortions is correct, so subsidies should be abolished, tax rates adjusted to 'encourage enterprise', tariff barriers removed along with other disguised restrictions, and so on. (c) The government's role in the economy should be minimized because private enterprise can usually do the job better, and when government does become involved the rule should be the pursuit of profit and not the provision of subsidies to weak industries. (d) Labour unions should be curbed so as to keep the cost of labour low. (e) International trade should be 'free trade', and, argue the neo-classicists, the more trade the better: 'They therefore argue heavily in favour of "export led growth" as a major policy for LDCs (less developed countries).'[68]

Clements remarks that this broad set of policy proposals has been advocated with renewed enthusiasm in recent years as the West has struggled to deal with a long and severe post-1973 depression. Clements offers a plausible set of reasons for the general popularity of the neo-classical approach, namely that its core assumptions

> leave the world economic system intact . . . do not demand any radical restructuring of domestic economies . . . can be accommodated to by most conservative political philosophies . . . seem to have 'worked' in the so-called 'Boom economies of South Korea, Brazil and Taiwan, to name just three countries which have had high growth rates in recent years; and . . . Keynesianism has failed to solve the current depression with the result that most Western economies now suffer from 'Slumpflation'.[69]

To the list of economies that have, over recent years, 'worked' is usually added the name of Singapore. The noted local scholar Peter Chen has argued, as we will see below, that Singapore is indeed a model for rapid growth that others can invoke to illuminate their own circumstances. So as an illustration of a type-one-informed analysis, I will look at the discussion of Singapore's track record offered by Lim.[70]

Lim begins by presenting the familiar type of raw economic data in respect of Singapore. Thus he begins: 'If one studies the figures of average annual growth of real GNP per capita between 1960 and 1977 . . . one finds that Singapore had the second highest growth rate among Third World countries.'[71] He gives the relevant data and then adds: 'surpassed interestingly enough only by Iran'.[72] An intriguing remark indeed! Lim continues by noting that Singapore's growth rate has enabled the country to 'close the gap between the rich industrial nations and herself'.[73] External trade balances have been – thanks to 'invisible trade' – good, and the currency stable or appreciating. Statistical tables are presented with all the appropriate data for these various elements.[74]

Structural changes are then discussed. The rise of the manufacturing sector is noted: '11.9 percent of GDP in 1960, this enlarged steadily to 26.1 per cent of GDP in 1978.'[75] The trade sector experienced a relative decline 'from 35.9 percent of GDP in 1960 to 27.9 percent of GDP in 1978, although in terms of value-added in current prices the trade sector expanded from $712.5 million in 1960 to $4541.1 million by 1978.'[76] The growth of the tourist industry is noted and then it is further noted that '–another remarkable area of growth is the emergence of Singapore as a financial centre.'[77] More statistical data are presented. We can note: (a) the familiar style of Lim's quantification and its apparently automatic equation of economic growth with political–social success; and (b) that the general analysis is in terms first of economics and then social impacts.[78]

In respect of this 'social impact', Lim remarks that 'The rapid increase in GDP . . . has its impact . . . This can be seen particularly conspicuously in public housing, in increases in contributions to the Central Provident Fund (CPF) and in the infrastructural facilities developed.'[79] Again, data are presented and the general social scene reviewed – all very briefly. One peculiar example of an economist's analysis of matters social is found in the observation that 'To the extent that man-hours lost [in strikes] is a reflection of an aspect in the quality of life, Singapore has improved quite impressively.'[80] Others, as we will see, would talk of an authoritarian politics.[81]

Lim then goes on to discuss the causes of growth and attempts to 'seek out the fundamental factors'.[82] He identifies: political continuity; political stability; the relentless pursuit of development; and meritocracy.

Political continuity is interpreted by Lim to mean the continuation in power not just of the PAP, but of Lee Kuan Yew and his 'inner circle'. Proceeding to political stability, Lim observes: 'fortunately political continuity has also been accompanied by political stability.'[83] Others, whom we will meet, have spoken of 'depoliticization' and looking at Lim's next set of figures one can gather a hint as to why this should be so. Thus he adds: 'Indeed the ruling PAP has been so successful that for three general elections (1968, 1972, and 1976), the various opposition parties have failed to secure a single seat in Parliament. Taking the country as a whole, however, 13.3 percent of the electors voted against the PAP in the General Election of 1968, 29.6 percent in 1972 and 25.9 percent in 1976'[84] – and won no seats! And in the 1984 election 38 per cent of the vote won only two seats.[85]

Turning to areas closer to the narrowly economic, Lim speaks of a 'relentless policy of pursuing economic development [which] took top priority'.[86] Investment was encouraged wherever it came from: diversity was pursued, competition encouraged and wages regulated. All of which, it is fairly obvious, reads the situation of Singapore in orthodox terms whilst hinting at the official ideology of the state – which includes, *inter alia*, ideas of survival and, the last factor cited by Lim, meritocracy.

Lim continues: 'If two factors are to be singled out as fundamental . . . I would put them as political stability and correct economic policy.'[87] Only as an afterthought, it seems, does Lim cite geographical location, culture, historically established trading links – surely the sensible starting-points. He concludes by adding in the factors of racial harmony and a 'symbiotic' relationship between unions and government. But these are all seen as 'raw materials', they have to be blended – again, we return to modernization theory's focus upon a technical manipulative elite.

Lim's essay is a good example of reading political, economic and social history through the eyes of a type-one theorist. Also sketched out for us are major elements of the official ideology of Singapore. Lim would follow Chen in offering Singapore as a model to be emulated.

I now turn to the work of another Singaporean, John Wong, who both offers a useful survey of ASEAN (Association of South East Asian Nations) and presents us with an example of a type-two economist. I will pick up this second aspect first, and offer a brief note on the idea of 'dissenting economics'.

Within economics there is a long and distinguished tradition of dissenting economics. Theorists who have dissented from the neoclassical orthodoxies have done so in a variety of social and political circumstances. They have also offered a variety of intellectual schemes as replacements. Within the narrow area of concern for development we can find theorists dissenting from then prevalent ideas of 'free trade' as long ago as the eighteenth century. Thus Alexander Hamilton, an adviser to the very earliest governments of the USA, urged the course of independent industrialization rather than continuing with the policy of perpetuating an agricultural economy which looked to Europe. In the nineteenth century the German economist F. List[88] urged the course of industrialization behind tariff barriers. These thinkers were, I suppose we must say, 'pre-neo-classical'.

Yet with the rise of neo-classicism after the 1870s 'marginalist revolution', we find a steady stream of dissenters: Thorstein Veblen in the USA; Werner Sombart and Schumpeter in Germany; Cassels in Sweden; Kalecki in Poland; Boeke in Holland; and Keynes in the UK. Recently, we could add the distinguished names of J. K. Galbraith, Joan Robinson and Gunnar Myrdal. The list is casually presented and a full discussion lies beyond my competence: however, what can be said is that all these theorists have it in common that they see economics as social economics. That is, their economic analyses are routinely and self-consciously couched in terms which acknowledge that economies are simultaneously social systems and, moreover, have their own distinct socio-cultural patterns and histories.

Social economics, as a composite of various material presented in this 'dissenting' tradition, can be characterized in terms of conception and intent as follows. Thus, first, in respect of these economists' conception of how enquiry should proceed they typically: (1) acknowledge that concept-formation is context-dependent; (2) adopt a sceptical and reflexive stance in respect of enquiry; and (3) centre their enquiry, in its formal aspect, upon the pursuit of realistic models of the sets of 'real world' circumstances that they confront. And second, in respect of their intention, the commitments they make in respect of the intended practical use of their theorizing, typically we find: (1) a strong disposition to argue on behalf of the 'planners'; (2) a commitment to reformist-style politics.

I want now to turn to an example of this general style of analysis by way of an exposition of John Wong's treatment of ASEAN.[89] This text offers two lessons: first, an example of the sorts of revisions to orthodox economics that are made when theorists shift towards social economics; and second, it illustrates how type-two economic theorizing can, and often does, stay close to the basic economic claims of type one. Thus in Wong's case it is quite clear that he is displaying in his analysis a range of concerns of a social economic nature: income distribution; government legitimacy; neglect of rural areas, and so on. Simultaneously, he stays close to the orthodox type one by accepting the familiar injunctions to export orientation.

It is this retention of type-one elements that is perhaps a clue to the differences between those whose dissent gets them as far as social economics and those who move to adopt a marxian frame which reduces economics wholly to social life.

Wong begins, appropriately enough, by reviewing in a concise way the 'track record' of the ASEAN region. It is noted that all the ASEAN countries are 'middle income' (according to the usual measures of Gross National Product, and so on) and that they have all recorded high annual growth rates over recent years. Wong adds, first, that it is 'not just the rate of economic growth but also the nature of growth that will emerge as the dominant issue in the future';[90] and second, he takes note that the ASEAN governments have identified closely with economic success – 'With the . . . move towards more rigid, centralized patterns of control, further economic success will be needed to enhance the legitimacy . . . of present political leadership, or just to maintain the political and social status quo without revolutionary upheaval.'[91] A record of economic success has been established, thinks Wong, but this success is both fragile and, more awkwardly, the sole or key claim to legitimacy for these governments. In the future, thinks Wong, not only will this economic prosperity have to be maintained, but there will also have to be a broadening of the idea of progress affirmed by governments. At the outset, then, matters of economics are taken to be linked to matters of society and politics.

From this point, three matters are discussed: first, the record of dependent industrialization in ASEAN; second, the problems of the vital but neglected rural sector; and third, the crucial problems that will have to be tackled in the not-too-distant future – and these are political, social and economic.

The key to grasping the recent history of the ASEAN nations is trade which is 'both an engine for growth and a mechanism for dependency'.[92] It is trade which slots the ASEAN economies into the dynamic world economy: however, trade is also an ambiguous phenomenon. Wong is, at this point, clearly aware of the Latin American dependency analysis, but what he does is: (a) to narrow the idea down to focus on economic trade relationships (thus striking out the political, social, and cultural analytic heart of the Latin American dependency approach); and (b) to treat the term as a non-political one. Thereafter, analysis of 'track records' proceeds in terms of how successful the ASEAN economies have been in diversifying – that is, reducing the economic vulnerability of the ASEAN economies to outside forces. Diversification took the form initially of import-substituting industrialization.

Import substitution as a strategy involves protecting home-based manufacturing (with tariffs, quotas, and the like) and making at home that which was previously imported. Typically, the strategy is 'low-tech' and the sorts of industrial imports that are substituted are food processing, and simple consumer durables. This economic activity can be reworked so as to attract the MNC (multi-national companies): local assembly for either local consumption or re-export. It is the business of shifting from local 'low-tech' substitution to a 'higher-tech' manufacturing and exporting economy (that is, to a different and more materially rewarding role in the world economy) that has preoccupied government economic planners. The strategy of import-substituting industrialization has, we might say, a fairly low ceiling to it – and once that ceiling is reached, other strategies are needed. Wong summarizes the general position thus:

> Import substitution industries are usually set up to produce simple low priced consumer goods using imported machinery and often using cheap labour . . . the problems . . . are well known . . . industries set up behind protective tariffs tend to be small, inefficient and inward looking . . . rarely look beyond their national boundaries for the competitive foreign markets.[93]

The crucial test of economic development is, thinks Wong, whether or not the shift from import substitution to 'export substitution'[94] can be made. Wong then reviews the industrialization experience of the ASEAN countries: I will not reproduce here the detail but I will summarize the main points.

First, Indonesia: in the pre-1965 coup period economic development was inhibited by constant political, social and administrative problems. In the post-coup period Wong thinks the 'New Order' of Suharto has produced coherent plans, but the old problems remain. Later, we will meet the idea of a 'bureaucratic polity', a socio–economic–political system with its own logic; a logic which takes it outside the ambit of Wong's economics.[95]

Second, Malaysia: the economic history of Malaysia involves, crucially, a social and political aspect. The country's total population is primarily made up of two large groups: Chinese and Malay. This division of population into two main ethnic groups is repeated in geography (the west is Chinese and the east is Malay), mode of life (the west is industrial and urban whilst the east is rural), and economic level (thus the Chinese have dominated the economy's 'modern' sector). After the 1969 riots the government introduced the New Economic Policy (NEP). Designed to eradicate poverty and restructure the economy, this was supposed to remove, in time, the dichotomies associated with ethnicity. Wong comments:

> As a result of intervention from the government, the industrialization process in Malaysia has borne two distinct hallmarks . . . First . . . the central development strategy in Malaysia must be a rare example of one promoting

> industrialization and retaining a strong rural bias at the same time. Second . . . the development patterns have had a distinct trade-off tilted toward distributional objectives albeit structured along a specific racial line.[96]

Third, the Philippines: of all the ASEAN countries the Philippines have been pursuing industrialization the longest – and with restricted success. Wong notes: 'In fact the many problems experienced . . . can be used as examples . . . to highlight the shortcomings of the import substitution industrialization strategy.'[97] The economy of the Philippines has run through the easy stage of substitution, but has subsequently failed to upgrade its role in the world economy. Wong speaks of 'typical failure examples'[98] – inward-looking industries, dependence on foreign inputs, overreliance upon a few primary products, regional imbalances, inequality. The present crisis in the Philippines would seem to be the latest manifestation of a chronic condition.

Fourth, Singapore: often hailed as a model for others of successful industrialization – a point Wong immediately denies: the circumstances of Singapore have been very particular. Wong notes:

> For a 'typical' underdeveloped economy, like those in the other four agrarian ASEAN countries, industrialization basically involves the transfer of resources from the primary sector to industrial development in the urban sector, which has proved to be infinitely more difficult than in the case of a city state like Singapore or Hong Kong where industrialization simply involves the transformation of the entrepôt trade sector.[99]

In short, Singapore had a head-start on its ASEAN neighbours.

From this point, Wong goes on to review the problems/prospects of the region in general: these revolve around the fragility of industrial development and their external dependency. The role of the MNCs is of increasing concern. The character of Wong's treatment of the industrial sector is largely descriptive; when it is prescriptive, he writes on behalf of the planners. This indeed is the most 'orthodox' part of the book (it is also the major part of it!). Matters become more interesting, from our point of view, in the next two parts.

Turning to his second area of concern, the rural sector, Wong begins with an arresting statistic: 'Roughly 65% of the total economically active population of ASEAN are in agriculture.'[100] It is the crucial sector and Wong characterizes it with reference to the idea of dualism. The agricultural sector is 'backward . . . and remains stagnant'.[101] The agricultural sector can be divided into a subsistence and plantation element; in neither case have they 'measured up'[102] to their task. In food production ASEAN can barely feed its growing population! In the rest of his discussion it is the rural sector in general that Wong speaks of – the sub-sector of plantations is not picked out. Wong reviews attempts made by ASEAN countries to tackle the problems of their rural sectors: the 'high-tech' solutions of the 'Green Revolution' days are now seen to have been misconceived. Rural development is a complex socio-economic (and politically sensitive) issue which does not admit of authoritatively constructed and imposed solutions. Calling in the experts is not good enough. Rural reform will have to involve: (1) land reform coupled with mass participation; (2) the expunging of the bias against the rural sector which is evident in orthodox theorizing and planning; (3) the establishment of an integrated rural development approach. It is at this point that Wong's enlightened orthodoxy meets the real world head-on, for to make these changes would involve enormous shifts in the balance of political forces in Southeast Asia. The only country cited by Wong as having tackled these problems with any success is the People's Republic of China!

The third area of concern is the socio-economic framework of development. In the future, the population of ASEAN will grow sharply and Wong observes that this necessitates a vigorous response in the shape of enhanced agricultural, industrial and export performance. Securing this enhanced performance will require that attention be paid to a range of economic and social issues. Wong notes:

> It has been stressed at the beginning that conventional development strategies are not likely to measure up to the new purposes of future development, and they will probably create as many problems as they may have solved. Foremost among these problems are the twin issues of poverty and income inequality, which were often dismissed in the past under the orthodox neo-classical paradigm as inevitable short term 'externalities' in the development process.[103]

The major problem now is that of meeting basic needs: poverty and inequality are now crucial issues.

In ASEAN, reports Wong, there is no very bad absolute poverty as in, say, parts of India or Africa, but there is still extensive relative poverty.

> To this matter of poverty must be linked the issue of the pattern of income distribution. In ASEAN it is skewed with

> the upper 20% of families taking as much as 50% of the total income whilst the lowest 20% receive only 5% of the total . . . In short, the extent of income inequality with the associated problem of poverty is clearly uncomfortably high for the region as a whole.[104]

The elimination of such gross differentials ought, thinks Wong, to be a major policy goal. Reviewing the efforts made in the region, he notes that only Malaysia has addressed the issue. Moving farther south, he adds: 'Obsessed with the problem of survival on account of the lack of natural resources, Singapore has continued to stress the policy of "grow now and redistribute later".'[105] As for the other ASEAN countries, they are still at the stage of 'paying lip service to the issue'.[106] Wong summarizes the complex of problems thus: 'Distribution of income is closely related to the distribution of wealth, and ultimately of political power . . . it would be exceedingly difficult to suggest a fast and effective solution of the poverty problem without overhauling or adjusting the existing social and political system.'[107] His proposals are, as we might expect from a reform-minded, type-two orthodox theorist, modest. An 'integrated' and 'multidimensional' policy approach is needed. This approach will have to look at broader social objectives. Planning will continue to be vital, but there must be participation. All this, it is said, represents an evolutionary approach to 'drawing the poor into the development process'.[108]

So much for Wong's intriguing analysis – the likelihood of its being successful (or even implemented) can be considered later, when neo-marxian approaches are presented. In sum, we can recall that Wong's material offers us, in addition to the useful little survey of ASEAN, the example of a shift away from simple type-one analysis. The approach is revised and a different sort of attention is paid to matters social, cultural and political. Rather than seeing these phenomena as aspects of a process basically economic (which is what Lim, discussed above, did), they come to be seen as integral parts of a general process centred upon economics.

Social modernization

Turning now to the business of social modernization, I will offer a fairly brief note as the areas of concern are reasonably familiar and are routinely pursued in a policy-scientific fashion. Rather more interesting, and in respect of Southeast Asia, relevant, is the business of rural life, both plantation and subsistence farming.[109]

Following my earlier typification of modernization, the business of social modernization must present itself as entailing evolutionary change, dualistically analysed, from traditional to modern societies where the latter is the model of the West. So where economic modernization, as analysed by orthodox economics, is a matter of systemic changes, the notion of social modernization takes note that the elements of the system are persons. The typical areas of concern are thus patterns of social change attendant upon economic growth. Four areas of changes can be readily identified: the sphere of work, the family, community and social mores.

Patterns of working change as new technologies are introduced. At the most general level modernization theory sees a shift from very low-tech rural life to urban industrial life. This pattern can be revised to treat changes in work relationships attendant upon technological and political changes. Thus in, say, Singapore, the social modernization of the workplace would entail both changes in the technological component (from, say, *entrepôt*, service and informal sector types to manufacturing, banking and high-tech types), and in the personnel component (from a division of labour reserving middle and senior ranks for colonials to one based on local people). In the workplace, in new nations, there is thus usually a double pattern of change.

Patterns of family life also undergo change in the broad shift from traditional to modern societies. Orthodox modernization theory sees a shift from extended families to nuclear families. This shift involves a complex alteration of roles within the family, and an equally complex reworking of the particular family's linkages with its surrounding social environment.

Flowing from elements one and two is the third element: the inevitable reworking of community life. Orthodox modernization theorists have, like other social scientists in this period of the 1950s and 1960s, rather tended to think in terms of a 'loss'. A contrast is made, or taken for granted, between the static, relaxed, personal style of rural life and the dynamic, pressured, anonymous qualities of urban life. The drift to the towns, coupled with new work patterns and family patterns, leads to, or goes along with, changes in community life. In the First World this is a well-worn sociological theme and it is all expressed as the twin theses of the decline of community and the rise of mass society.

Finally (element four), patterns of social mores change as communal ethics give way to individualistic ethics. In Southeast Asia, with its complex mixture of ethnic, religious and economic modes, the nature of the changes in patterns of social mores attendant upon the shift to the modern type of society will be thoroughly complex.

All these issues are familiar in orthodox sociology and social planning, and I do not want to pursue them.[110] However, I will add one note, which flows from the modernization theorists' concerns and is of particular relevance in Southeast Asia. Thus within the modernization frame there are generated the related notions of, first, adjustment problems (or even breakdowns) in the shift to modernity, and, second, obstacles to change. As regards the matter of obstacles, it is often the peasantry who are cited. As Wong[111] calculates that 65 per cent of the population of ASEAN are peasant farmers, this is an issue that can usefully be pursued.

Wertheim[112] begins by taking note that much of modernization theory's work on the peasantry recalls the colonial episode in that both have spoken of the 'backwardness' of the rural peoples: unadventurous, irrational, incompetent. In the literature of modernization, as Wertheim points out, all this has been understood as resistance to change. But this, argues Wertheim, is a wrong view. The reason for the wariness of peasant farmers in respect of the efforts of rural development planners lies in the marginal relevance to them of such programmes. John Wong details the way in which the authoritative and high-tech approaches of the 'Green Revolution' generally failed; and where they did not, it was the richer peasants who benefited.[113] Wong calls for a broad approach to rural development – an 'integrated approach' modelled on the example of the PRC, the only real Asian success story in rural development. For Southeast Asia, Wong remains pessimistic. Wertheim makes the same point – against the orthodox modernizers – 'Gradually we may realize where the true obstacles to change are to be found. It is those who benefit from existing inequality and from the distress among the broad masses who, usually with some support from the authorities, oppose any attempt on the part of the underdogs to effectuate some basic change in their lot.'[114] Wertheim, in a thoroughly polemical piece, ends by speaking of 'neo-colonialism' in current approaches to rural development. The occasion of this critique is clear when he observes: 'And on the rare occasions that the poor peasants in a certain country effectuate fundamental change, the Western "resistance" to change assumes a more extreme form: that of napalm, fragmentation bombs and herbicides used against people who are impertinent enough to pursue real change.'[115] The Vietnam episode led to many otherwise orthodox figures revising their views: both Wong and Wertheim stress, against straightforward modernization approaches, the political (internal and external) dimensions of attempts to secure change. When I look at the 'radicals', I will pursue this issue.[116]

To round off this brief commentary on social modernization it can be noted that just as the focus on policy-scientific planning is typical, so too is the talk about problems of adjustment/obstacles/breakdowns. This strategy of analysing resistance to change is one of prejudging: any rationally based legitimate, defensible objections to change engendered at the elite/expert level are ruled out from the outset. Thus, most notoriously, Walt Rostow speaks of communism not as a political position which has some rational occasion in unsatisfactory economic and social relations and as therefore worth debating with, but, instead, as a 'disease of the transition'. This strategy of dismissing problems and issues by a trick of definition just will not do. There are many instances where 'obstacles' to development had perfectly good reasons for objecting.

Religious modernization

The sphere of religious modernization is the final sphere identified by Evers in the introduction to his 1973 collection. It has to be said that I find the phrase 'religious modernization' thoroughly curious. Within the ambit of modernization approaches the business of patterns of religious ideas has usually entered theorizing in terms of their being potential inhibitors of development. Often, too, there is an echo of a vulgar Weberian argument about the importance of Protestantism for development and the problems occasioned (apparently) by its absence from whatever set of circumstances is under review.[117] An alternative way of looking at the role of religion in development is to look at specific cases. Here, the abstract schematism of modernization theory drops away and more straightforward social scientific and historical analyses are presented. These are much more interesting but, arguably, not really modernization approaches.[118]

Here, I will do two things: with the help of Darling I will present a typical (indeed, caricature) example of modernization work on religion and then go on to look, in detail, at an essay by Alatas which – somewhat confusedly – does advocate an approach which centres on specifics.

Darling begins his analysis by discussing the traditional patterns of religion–culture–society: six are identified in Southeast Asia: Hindu, Therevada Buddhist, Islamic, Atomized Animist, Confucian, Japanized Confucian. Each of these is then characterized in a threefold fashion: element one, the cultural system, deals with the traditional belief patterns; element two, class structure, examines patterns of authority associated with cultural system; and element three, societal structure, deals with social organization-

cum-focus of life, and the range in scale of polity with empire at the top and village at the bottom.

Having offered this characterization of the various 'traditional societies' found in Southeast Asia, Darling then goes on to look at the impact of colonialism. The nature of the various colonial regimes is noted and the response of the colonized polities is analysed in terms of urbanism, nationalism, secularization and population growth.

The shape of the new independent nations is a matter of three elements on Darling's analysis: first, traditional inputs; second, Western inputs; and third, 'fusional' inputs, where this is a mix of elements one and two. The upshot of all this is the list of present-day polities that we met earlier when we looked at political modernization.

What is notable about Darling's treatment is its simple 'traditional/modern' dichotomous form and, in respect of religion, the way the various Asian religious schemes are treated in terms of their fit or lack of fit with the demands of modernization. There is little concern evidenced in Darling's analysis with what has actually been the relationship of religion to processes of change in history in the region. We are offered a systematic survey which is of very limited use.[119]

Now I turn to consider in detail an analysis of the relationship of religion and modernization in Southeast Asia prepared by Alatas.[120] Alatas's treatment is revealing for several reasons. Thus he illustrates the claims I have made earlier, and repeatedly, for the importance of looking at the work of the 'founding fathers'. Alatas's analysis also reveals the importance, as the 'rationalist' tradition of conceiving social science would insist, of the starting-points of analyses: he does so by getting roughly the 'right answer', but by accomplishing this via a thoroughly odd route. One last preliminary: Alatas's starting-point, an unhelpful one, reveals one crucial problem which the modernization frame both generates and cannot solve – that of distinguishing modernization from Westernization.

Alatas begins with a remark that links up to the 'orthodox' position in two ways: substantively (focus on modernization) and formally (an empiricist syntax). Thus he observes: 'The relation between religion and modernization in Southeast Asia is . . . complex . . . [and requires] preliminary methodological and conceptual clarification.'[121] This task of clarification is then pursued as the study of the process of modernization has not been helped by the confused terminology employed. Alatas distinguishes five related notions which have to be carefully separated from each other. First, the identification of modernization with social change has to be avoided and essential/consequent changes specified. We have to be able to say what is crucial in any pattern of change. Second, the equation of modernization with Westernization has to be avoided.[122] Third, the equation of modernization with the establishment of liberal democratic systems is to be avoided (and Alatas cites Eisenstadt as making precisely this error).[123] Fourth, the focus on particular aspects of Western experience, such as industrial and capitalist elements, is to be avoided. Fifth, the business of modernization (process) is not to be confused with modernity, by which Alatas seems to mean Western 'style'.

Alatas then offers a definition of what he understands to be modernization:

> the process by which modern scientific knowledge covering all aspects of human life is introduced at varying degrees, first in the Western civilization, and later diffused to the non-Western world, by different methods and groups with the ultimate purpose of achieving a better and more satisfactory life in the broadest sense of the term, as accepted by the society concerned.[124]

Alatas then characterizes science (referring to a couple of US modernization theorists) in a simple, common-sensical fashion. Around this core commitment to modernization as the spread of science are then arranged a series of 'consequences'. Thus we can go on to look at the cultural circumstances of the adoption and use of science; we can now easily distinguish Westernization and industrialization; we can see that modernization can be of particular cultural forms – for example, magic – and not just 'societies'. Alatas's strategy here is to pursue the essence of modernization and, like Wilbur Moore, whom we briefly came across above, and many others, he ends up by finding 'rationalization' – or the spread of science. On my reading of modernization as an ideological position, Alatas's strategy fails even to address the problem. (Later we shall see how those working within the marxist tradition handle all this with their idea of the 'spread of world capitalism'.)

Alatas then declares that his paper will focus on 'the relationship between religion and modernization in Southeast Asia'.[125] Asking whether religion hinders, helps or is neutral, Alatas reports that 'data derived from the South-East Asian setting . . . point to the fact that it is impossible to sustain any generalization after concretely analysing cases.'[126] He immediately adds, 'nowhere do they hinder modernization and economic development.'[127] Alatas goes on to argue that claims to hindrance are erroneous and usually based on unfamiliarity with either the religion or the region, or both.

Alatas notes that Islam has been presented as inhibiting growth in Malaysia and argues that this is an indefensible claim. It is true, he grants, that the Malays do not 'perform' as well as the Chinese, but this cannot be put down to Islam, and four arguments are advanced: (a) 'The teachings of Islam encourage diligence, frugality, discipline, a rational approach';[128] (b) South Indians in Malaysia are Muslim and successful; (c) other local Muslims are active economically; and (d) contrariwise, many Southeast Asian non-Muslims also live like the Malays.

Alatas then identifies a pattern of thinking which he claims is both widespread in Southeast Asia and a leftover from the past. This pattern of thinking has five traits. First, it regards a government job as better than entrepreneurship. Second, it views work instrumentally. Third, non-agricultural manual labour is seen as degrading. Fourth, it favours consumption rather than saving. And finally, fifth, it values wealth in land. Alatas also comments: 'It is this value system, a hangover from the feudal past and consolidated by colonial influence, that forms the greatest obstacle to modernization in contemporary South-East Asia.'[129]

The author then calls, correctly I think, for specific enquiry. He cites Weber on 'Chinese magical animism' – a non-rational religion whose devotees have, none the less, been successful. Contrast this with the Malays who, although professing a rational religion, have not been successful. The clues to unravelling this situation are 'to be sought in the historical and sociological backgrounds of the two communities'.[130] Alatas points to the immigrant status of the Chinese; of the Malays, he reports that there were four main reasons for their lack of development, 'the most significant of which was the despotic nature of Malay rule, the other three being the small size of the country and population, the geographical barriers, and the social values.'[131] Malay society was stagnant, invoking Islam is not necessary: 'Considering the factors which had been cited to explain the stagnation of Malay society prior to the expansion of British rule, it is apparent that Islam had not been the cause of that stagnation even if we take the interpretation of Islam current in those periods.'[132]

Thus does Alatas approach an answer to his initial question: the relationship between religion and modernization in Southeast Asia is not one that can be discussed in simple cause-and-effect terms – as Darling, with his schematic history, tried to do. Rather, it is perfectly clear that 'the historical, cultural, sociological and political factors had been much more decisive in their influence on modernization and modern economic activity among both the

Chinese and Malay communities than their religious backgrounds.'[133]

It is at this point that Alatas's essay coincides most closely with a coherent answer to the issue of the relationship of religion and the shift to the modern world: from this point on we slip into repetition and falling away – thus he returns to talk about doctrine and world, rather than what the various communities of believers actually did. Answering the question about religion's relation to the business of modernization requires specific, and not general, analyses.[134]

Summary

I have followed Evers's list and looked at political, economic, social and religious modernization in turn and have reviewed with illustrative intent a selection of uses of the approach to analyses of Southeast Asia. The basic theme of modernization theory is the model of the West. It is, in my terms, an ideological position – an exercise in 'making sense'. By way of a concluding note, we can ask after the overall sense the theorists of modernization would make of Southeast Asia. This will generate a very short comparative review which I will compare later with the equivalent set of marxist-inspired judgments. I will focus on political and economic characterizations and set the other two aside as too remote from the core of the theory of modernization.

In respect of political modernization the matter is judged according to the model of liberal parliamentary regimes. And whilst the modernization theorists never either (a) question the plausibility of that model in general, or (b) record that the West's liberal democratic systems are the result of past, and present, socio-political struggle, they none the less use this model to judge new nation states, both ethically (though this would be denied) and in terms of their political 'maturity'. The essential question asked is: how closely do new nation states resemble the West?

With economic matters, modernization is based on neo-classical economics, the economics of liberal market systems. And although the economics of the orthodoxy comes in two varieties, as I have noted, both schemes coincide, in contradistinction to the neo-marxists in their commitment to development within the world capitalist system. The differences between the two economics can be profound but, simplifying greatly, orthodox theory has looked at economic modernization in terms of two phases: (1) import-substituting industrialization, followed by (2) export-oriented industrialization. In sum, and including religious and social modernization, what we have is the story of the shift from 'traditional' to 'modern' societies. I shall finish with the comparative survey of Southeast Asian nations.[135]

Independence without decolonization[136]

The Philippines were colonized by the Spanish in the sixteenth century. When the colonizers arrived they found, reports McCoy, an archipelago which boasted dozens of 'micro-states'. The colonial regime of the Spanish is characterized by McCoy as economically comparatively benign: the economy was left to its own devices and not drained. A local elite began to grow, and so, at the same time, did a dispossessed peasantry. It seems that the Spanish had a preoccupation with disseminating Catholicism rather than plunder.

The notion of a Filipino identity – that is, an emergent nationalism – took shape through the nineteenth century and a rebellion was launched in the late years of that era. However, on the point of success it was, in turn, overwhelmed by the USA. The colonial regime of the USA had a very distinct style in that, having acquired this territory in pursuit of the status of a great power, the Americans promptly declared their intention to establish democracy and free the islands! In the inter-war years the Philippines pursued a bizarre policy of 'bi-nationalism' such that the inhabitants of the archipelago were both American and Filipino. In the event, a very close relationship was established between the USA and the Philippines: a relationship that tied the economy of the Philippines to that of the USA.

Decolonization, having been interrupted by the Japanese occupation (when the elite collaborated and the peasantry provided the resistance), was made awkward by the existence of a powerful group called the Huks whose radicalism endeared them to neither the local elite nor to the US. After a brief guerilla war the Huks[137] were, temporarily, disposed of and the familiar Philippines polity established.[138]

Most commentators seem to be agreed upon three things: (1) that the Philippines have been economically absorbed into the US sphere and that this was deliberate US policy from the start; (2) that the Filipino elite has been 'bought off' by its economic linkages to the US and is now sharply separated from the Filipino masses; and finally (3) that the contemporary Philippines political scene is degenerate – a dictatorship.

In sum, the Philippines have ever been operating at a low level of political modernization and, presently, a new low has been reached in the 'conjugal dictatorship' of Marcos. Economically, there is little to report which will give cause for optimism: the Philippines are locked into a long-established, import-substitution, phase-one situation. The economy has come to a 'ceiling' behind its long-established tariff walls and, indeed, is a 'classic example' of the ills attendant upon the import-substituting industrialization strategy. The restoration of democracy, in some form, plus a meaningful drive for industrial development are prerequisites of change in the Philippines.

Revolution without socialism[139]

The Dutch began trading in what is now Indonesia back in the sixteenth century. And the Dutch were, when they came to establish a formal colonial authority, preoccupied with profit: they ran Indonesia as one vast agricultural holding. The impact of the regime, both economically and socially, is usually regarded as having been very damaging.

The movement towards Indonesian independence is of interest for several reasons. It is here that we find the first example of a colonial nationalist movement with a mass base. Over the period 1912–26 Serekat Islam recruited large numbers of followers: 'At its height . . . Serekat Islam had become the voice of national awakening.'[140] The Serekat Islam grouping was 'open' in character, and anyone who wanted to join could. A few Indonesian communists did so, but broke away in 1923 to form the Indonesian Communist Party (PKI). A further element in the rise of Indonesian nationalist sentiment in this pre-Second World War period was the exposure of small numbers of Indonesians to European political thinking – other than marxism – whilst studying at Dutch universities.

The Dutch, in the inter-war period, responded to the upsurge in nationalist sentiment with repression. Reid notes:

> Nevertheless, the national ideal continued to develop rapidly . . . Taking from Marxism the opposition to capitalism, from Serekat Islam the solidarity of 'us' against 'them', and from European scholarship the name of Indonesia and the rediscovery of a glorious pre-European past, secular nationalism became the dominant political force after 1926.[141]

And, Reid adds, 'alienation from the colonial regime was universal by 1942, and the Japanese were welcomed as liberators.[142]

As the Japanese collapsed, the nationalists – who had been encouraged by the Japanese, with Sukarno and Hatta at the helm – declared a republic on 17 August 1945 and then moved, in a hesitant and patchy way, to secure their control over Indonesia. The British assisted the return of the Dutch and a confused period of manoeuvring followed: eventually, after two 'small wars' the

Dutch withdrew and the Indonesian republic was formed in 1949.[143]

The Indonesian army was thus, from the outset, shaped by the experience of anti-colonial warfare: this had a reinforcing tendency for Indonesian nationalism, and helped shape the subsequent pattern of development in the country. Reid notes: 'The result was neither socialism nor capitalism but a system in which the state dominated the formation of capital and the crucial relationships with foreign enterprise . . . the revolutionary experience had weakened or broken most of the political, administrative and economic institutions of pre-war Indonesia.'[144] The new pattern of economics/politics/society has been characterized as a 'bureaucratic polity'. The army is to a large extent coterminus with the state. Such political life as there is revolves around the development programmes and economic activity of the army, with its intimate linkages to the bureaucracy and the business world: public politics centres on the official ideology of 'pancasila' and the Islamic church is the only potential source of opposition, the rest (especially the PKI) having been swept away. In terms of notions of political modernization, Indonesia is not a success story. And the same is true of the economic sphere. Indonesia is still locked into phase one of the recommended programme – import substitution. This is facilitated by the vast size of the internal market, and the shift to phase two, export-oriented industry, is hindered by corruption and the MNCs' engagement in the economy. For the future, Indonesia needs an extensive political reform and the coming to power of a regime committed to development because, as things stand, Indonesia has reached a ceiling in its progress to the modern world.

New state, old elites[145]

The manner of incorporation of what is now Malaysia into the British colonial empire has two major points of presently relevant note. First, the local rulers – the sultanate – were co-opted and the Malays effectively marginalized. And, second, the British encouraged the inflow of immigrants (Chinese and Indian). Bedlington sums up the tangled story thus: 'British policies . . . were designed to mollify and in part co-opt the ruling class, while keeping the Malay peasantry physically and psychologically down on the farm.'[146] He goes on: '[the sultanate joined] the British Imperial club, with all its pomp and splendor . . . [As for the rest] the Malay peasantry did not enjoy any substantial socio-economic progress, but remained immured in a separate and unequal, if tranquil, social system.'[147] This general state of affairs persisted largely unchanged (and unchallenged) until 1942. The colonial regime thus pursued the exploitation of the territory in a fashion that minimized the disruption to established patterns of life (of the Malays), whilst simultaneously (by encouraging immigration) storing up very complex problems for the future.

It is in the inter-war period that we can identify the first stirrings of nationalist sentiment. The Malays began to show signs of reaction to the influx of immigrants, whilst the immigrant groups themselves looked to their respective mother countries. They were all, therefore, 'communalist' in character.

The Japanese invasion had, as elsewhere, a devastating impact: the British were swept away and the three communities were left to adjust as best they might. The contribution of the Japanese episode to the formation of nationalist sentiment is complex: Bedlington tersely summarizes the exchanges by saying that the races were forced apart.[148] The Chinese resisted the Japanese, who treated them with particular harshness (they were simultaneously fighting in China) and the Malayan Communist Party (MCP), which was predominantly Chinese, fought back. The Malays rather tended to acquiesce and there was, it seems, an element of collaboration in pursuit of nationalist goals. The same applied with the Indians.

As the British returned to take over from the Japanese there was interethnic fighting,[149] and the subsequent history of Malaysia has been to a very significant extent shaped by this communal split: Chinese/Malay, in particular. The British eventually left Malaya, after defeating the MCP revolt, and handed over power to an alliance of the three ethnic groups: such attempts as have been made to establish non-communal parties have not been successful.

An early arrangement between the elements of the ruling group – political power to the Malays and economic power to the Chinese – broke down in 1969 with race riots in the wake of an election. A new arrangement was insisted upon by the Malays and the New Economic Policy (NEP) was promulgated. The plan has the objective of alleviating poverty and effecting a shift of economic power by quickly advancing the interests of the Malays. The system has many areas of tension built into it – but the Malaysian economic and political system had, paradoxically, a familiar look to it for Westerners: it has been said that Malaysia has 'democracy by default', as no one group is strong enough to assume complete authority. And apart from this ethnic bifurcation, the Malay elite – in the view of some commentators – might well have moved towards a 'bureaucratic polity'.

The present political situation is thus complex, consisting now of latent communalism, restrictions on freedom of speech, active opposition parties, an active sultanate, and a politically and socially contentious 'positive discrimination' programme. Malaysia epitomizes a politically ambiguous modernization. Likewise with economic modernization: present circumstance is in the midst of a switch from phase one to phase two. Generally, the economic sphere could be described as a success story, but there are problems: (1) the size of the economy is not large enough for modern efficient firms and consequently, whilst export orientation is necessary, the switch is difficult; (2) the manufacturing sector is dominated by foreign firms; and (3) industrial development is regionally concentrated and, notwithstanding efforts to alleviate this (as part of the Bumiputera Programme), it remains a problem – as does the lack of linkages generated by recent projects. None the less, Malaysian development has been, in the main, a story of success over the post-war period.

The city state[150]

Singapore was not incorporated into the colonial orbit in the sense in which we can speak of the above three nation states (as now are) being incorporated. Singapore was, in contrast, constructed from a small part of the 'traditionally held' sphere of the local sultanate. A sultan of Singapore was installed to legitimize the British control of the island, but the sultanate was discarded by the British once their hold was secure.[151] Bedlington remarks: 'modern Singapore is an artificial creation born out of imperial economic expansion, and down to the present economic affairs dominate political realities.'[152] Singapore was designed to be, and to an extent still is, the 'middleman' of Southeast Asia.

In regard to the rest of Southeast Asia, it was, as we have seen, the experience of the Japanese occupation that, in diverse ways, both destroyed the old order and fostered the new. The situation in Singapore was somewhat different. The territory had, even in 1945, a fairly high proportion of migrants: they serviced the manpower needs of a great trading port. The step from trading port to independent nation state was not an obvious one. Such pre-war nationalist sentiment as there was would seem to have been either externally focused (India or China) or couched in terms of membership of the surrounding Malay world. In the post-war period, both the eventually dominant PAP and the leftist populists looked, in different ways, to some sort of linkage with the wider Malay world. An independent nation state of Singapore does not seem to have been in anyone's mind during the decolonization period – the late 1950s and early 1960s.

During this period the British, who had held on to Singapore for military and 'geostrategic' reasons, looked around for a group to whom internal self-rule could be devolved: initially, the Marshall government and, in 1959, the PAP – both of whom had looked for a scheduling of independence. The politics of the period are labyrinthine in their complexity: in 1961 the idea of a Malaysian Federation was floated, and it attracted hostility from radicals in the two countries (or three, if we include the northern states of the island of Borneo), and hostility from Indonesia and the Philippines. None the less, the federation was formed in 1963. It disintegrated in 1965 and the PAP adopted, perforce, a 'go it alone' strategy.

The subsequent character of Singapore has been shaped by the relentless drive for economic security as a base for political security within a (potentially) hostile Malay world. The upshot has been the creation of, arguably, a unique city state.[153] The result has attracted a variety of labels. Politically, a modernization view would be of an authoritatively led democracy (albeit somewhat restricted). Economically, it has been a remarkable success story: the economy has successfully shifted from import substitution to export-oriented growth – the region's only Newly Industrializing Country (NIC). Problems for the future revolve around the authoritarian aspects of the political system and the relatively heavily MNC-dependent nature of present economic growth.

A bureaucratic policy[154]

In Thailand politics now takes place within the state apparatus, as individual factions manoeuvre for position. An important part of the process is the army – as in the case of Indonesia. The situation in Thailand is made more awkward, from the point of view of political modernization, by the fragile nature of the state's hold on power in many of the rural areas. This situation has obtained for so long that movement towards a modern polity is difficult to envision, even if it is necessary to economic well-being. On the economic front, Thailand is still in phase one of industrialization. The Thai economy is still predominantly a rural agriculture economy, despite some bursts of growth. It is an untidy pattern and there is no really coherent strategy for growth. For the future, both democratization and the establishment of coherent development plans are necessary.

So much for my 'modernization' summaries. They are not to be taken too seriously, but neither are they wholly unreasonable or unhelpful. They do give us a rough idea of the way in which modernization theorists make sense of Southeast Asia and, when we have gone on to look at the efforts of the marxists, we will be able to compare these summaries with those produced by marxian analysis.

The view from the marxist perspective

In looking at marxist work we confront a wholly different school of thought: one which draws fairly directly upon Marx's work and which operates within the rationalist tradition of social theory. In conception, the marxist line draws on the notion of historical materialism and, in intention, aims to display the possibilities for the future lodged in the present. Its typical argument style is thus a broad, investigative, critical, and politically engaged political economy. All this requires that we must first understand the marxian project in its own terms. It is simply no use dismissing marxism because it is not very good policy science (as the more foolish orthodox tend to) because it does not try to be. What it does try to provide is a prospective, politically effective analysis of historically located sets of economic, social and political circumstances, where the key to understanding is the notion of the world system as a capitalist system.

Marxists are concerned with analysing the totality of social, economic and political circumstances expressed by any national state and doing so in a historical fashion. Thus there is considerable concern for the following issues.

First, in location within the world economic system:

(a) How is this position to be characterized?
(b) How was this position historically generated?
(c) How does this historical record shape the present?

Second, the nature of the exchange between peripheries and centres:

(a) What are the links and who are the agents?
(b) How do these linkages impact upon local circumstances?

Third, the internal dynamics of nation states:

(a) What are the internal patterns of class relations?
(b) What can be said about the overall pattern of life?

Fourth and finally, possibilities for the future:

(a) What are the likely sources of change?
(b) What are the likely directions of change?

In this illustrative review of Marxian analyses of Southeast Asia, I will begin with discussions of the world context and look at the various characterizations of the circumstances of the Third World that have been offered. From this point, I will turn to substantive discussions and look at illustrative material in respect of the economic base of Southeast Asian societies, and their social and cultural superstructures. And, in a final section, I will offer a country-by-country summary of how marxists see the present situation of Southeast Asia.

The world context variously characterized

The earliest self-consciously marxian work to be produced in the post-war period centres on the writings of Paul Baran. This particular effort at marxian political economic analysis was given an influential – and quite idiosyncratic – presentation in the work of A. G. Frank, who speaks of an active process of the development of underdevelopment. The general stance adopted we can call neo-marxism.

Bob Catley, looking at Southeast Asia, and following Baran and Frank, argues that: 'what is now in evidence throughout the poor capitalist countries is a system of economic and social relations which have been established to ensure that economic surplus is extractd from the "satellite economies" for use in the "metropoles".'[155] Catley presents a historical periodization of the phases of this relationship of surplus appropriation: 'Mercantilism I, II, and III'. But he begins – as his theoretical position invites – with pre-contact days.

The familiar and static notion of the 'Asiatic mode of production' is reworked and evidence is discerned to support the theory-derived expectation of pre-contact economic and social dynamism: the germ of a movement that might have generated a 'route to the modern world' in these Southeast Asian areas, but which was snuffed out by the arrival of the European colonial powers. The theory requires that this be so, and Catley presents some empirical evidence to support the view.

From this point on, Catley reviews the history of European capitalist penetration into the region and attempts to show how Southeast Asian colonial penetration has altered in character over the period but has never really altered in its basic economic intentions.

The first phase of European involvement Catley calls 'Mercantilism I', and he dates it (with remarkable precision!) as 1511–1870. In this period, the colonial powers make their initial inroads. The goods they sought were those of the traditional economies and societies of the area. The earliest colonial contacts were thus those of traders – and little damage was done to established patterns of life (save for the 'theoretical snuffing out' which was noted above). Catley notes:

> During this period, with due allowance for varying intensity of penetration – more so in the Philippines and later Java, less so in Indo-China – the effect of imperial penetration on the social structure of South East Asia was limited. For that mode of production produced already the goods required and the great trading monopolies of the era were able to extract them by exchange and where necessary with the compliance of a local ruling class.[156]

'Mercantile I' provided, argues Catley, a vast flow of capital into the metropoles and it was this period of mercantile capitalism which paved the way for the industrial capitalism of the nineteenth century. With the rise of industrial capitalism in the metropoles the requirements which the metropoles had of the peripheral areas changed. It was no longer simply traditional trade goods, but was, instead, the raw-material demands of industrial economies – rubber, tin, oil, coffee, tea and sugar. Catley argues that: 'The immediate result was the age of colonialism and, like the rest of Asia and Africa, Southeast Asia was carved up into colonial states as the metropolitan governments assumed responsibility for overseeing their exploitation.'[157] This Catley labels 'Mercantilism II' (1870–1945). The general social, economic and cultural impact was extensive. Pre-contact patterns of life were extensively changed and, as Catley notes, 'resistance was widespread and frequent.'[158] This general pattern of resistance eventually attained what was to become its potent form with the early twentieth-century rise of nationalism.

'Mercantilism III' (1945–70) is the system generated by the circumstance of war, nationalism and continued surplus extraction by the capitalist world system. 'Mercantilism III' represents a reworking rather than an abolition of the familiar idea of colonial exploitation. Herbert Feith, as we will see, uses the notion of 'neo-colonialism'. The upshot of this 'reworking' is summarized by Catley as follows: 'The major consequence was the preservation in modified form of the colonial economic and social structure: the production of raw materials, free trade with the metropoles and the preservation of the prerogatives of foreign capital.'[159]

As we saw earlier, the theoretical position adopted by Baran and Frank entails the view that a prerequisite of development (as opposed to the continued development of underdevelopment entailed by integration in the world capitalist economy) is disengagement. Catley cites Vietnam as a country which has, after its long war, disengaged from the world capitalist economy. The possibility of development is thus present – and Catley looks for, and finds, supporting empirical evidence. That Catley should look to Vietnam is not surprising, given the theoretical machinery he is using. We can, however, add two points in respect of his choice. First, that Vietnam in the early 1970s was a *cause célèbre* for First World radicals,[160] and second, that to the present day that country continues embroiled in war and it might not therefore be thought an easy historical example to interpret.

'Mercantilism IV' (1970 to date) is the tag that Catley uses to characterize recent changes. The integration of peripheral areas continues largely as before, with the significant novelty of the incorporation of some peripheral areas as overseas bases for transnational companies. The success of Southeast Asian countries depends on the extent to which their ruling groups have 'made themselves useful' to the international economic system.

Catley offers a very broad sketch of a neo-marxian analysis. It is only a sketch and its weaknesses are those of such exploratory enquiries. However, we can see quite clearly how the marxian analysis adds in those elements typically neglected by the orthodox. Historical and international contexts of change are looked at, as are patterns of internal (and external) political alliances.

Looking at the Indonesian example, we can cite the text of Arief and Sasono[161] as a further, more detailed, but still fairly direct neo-marxian analysis. Arief and Sasono offer a slightly different style of theorizing: where Catley offers a preliminary illustrative argument of a key neo-marxian concept, the two present theorists simply take available theory and try to apply it to their own circumstances. Their text falls into two sections: a discussion of theory and an investigation of the Indonesian experience in the light of the theory.

There are a number of interesting points we can note in respect of their treatment of theory. They begin by looking at Baran and their discussion is absolutely straightforward: they seem concerned to spell out the key ideas so as to be able to apply them directly. Their interest is quite different from Catley's. Having introduced Baran, they go on to review, in the same fashion, Frank, Wallerstein and Samir Amin. Also mentioned are Cardoso and Faletto. We may note that others have been at pains to separate out these various strands.[162] Again, direct usefulness seems to be Arief's and Sasono's concern. And the work has, to simplify, an empiricist tone. The various criticisms of the various positions reviewed are absorbed in a similar way. Rather oddly, it seems, they combine the above 'political economic' material with a narrower economic focus: we see this when they turn to the second part of their treatment.

In this substantive section they begin by considering the impact of the Dutch and, in particular, they note the pattern of class alliances formed at that time. In the post-independence period a similar set of class arrangements has persisted. The independence period is discussed under the headings: growth process, employment, industrialization, financing of development, and food production. The story, to anticipate later material, is one of neo-colonialism. Their application of the notions of underdevelopment drawn from the Baran line of marxist approaches issues in recommendations that are noticeably not spelt out: they affirm, like Furtado above, a nationalist–populist stance.

The early explorations of the neo-marxian position centring on Baran, whom we considered above, have, subsequently been much criticized and much revised. I want now to look at work which operates under the notion of dependency, and which plays down the marxian elements of this broad area of approach. (In my final preliminary, when we look at the use of the notion of the Asiatic mode of production, we will find an approach which stresses the marxian roots of the material.) An interesting revision of the Latin American dependency approach, looking in this case at Southeast Asia (at least in part), is offered by Bienefeld,[163] who argues that the success of the NICs over recent years is evidence that dependency theory – appropriately purged of radical politics – is correct.[164]

Bienefeld begins by offering an argument to the effect that early dependency theorists (and he often seems to mean A. G. Frank and, at other times, Furtado) were wrong to talk about both disengagement and socialism in their analyses of the position of peripheral economies within the world economic system. Beinefeld argues instead for specific enquiry organized thus: '[we] should ask the question whether or not a greater degree of social control can be imposed on the development process through the mechanism of the state, and whether this control can be (or is being) exercised in the interests (short or long term) of the great majority of the members of that society.'[165] Then the position of the NICs is reviewed and they are diagnosed as the somewhat fortunate benefactors of competition between capital in the First World. The NICs are taken to confirm the dependency theorists' stress on the nationalist state: the NICs owe their success not simply to the passive receipt of world market forces, but to state-ordered responses to opportunities in the international situation. Bienefeld adds that the inegalitarian, non-democratic forms of the NIC societies reinforces the requirement for a more humane model of development as the peripheral capitalism on offer in the NICs remains liable to the ethical criticisms lodged against peripheral capitalism by the dependency theorists. Both these general points are good, but the tone of Bienefeld's analysis seems to hint strongly at a commitment to 'better policy science'. This point I will pursue below. For the moment, though, I will take note of a thoroughly ambiguous follow-up to Bienefeld offered by Lamb.[166]

Lamb seems to grant, like Bienefeld, that world political economic circumstances have ushered in the NICs. Then Lamb goes on to berate both dependency and marxist theorists (unspecified) for not tackling the politics of dependent accumulation. This is most peculiar. His remarks on the politics of the 'fast track' developing nations mention: (a) the role of the overseas links – MNCs, IMF, development planners, etc.; (b) breaking the power of organized labour; and (c) established authoritarian states with the local bourgeoisie well and truly 'bought off'. But, can one not suggest, all this has been said – often? And by, amongst others, A. G. Frank?

At this point one can make a general interjection: the thrust of the revisions to dependency being proposed are such as to focus not on disengagement plus socialism, but, instead, upon a more effective linking to the world economy. And the question must be raised as to whether or not it is legitimate to posit this apparent substitution of a policy-scientific orientation (dependency as external constraint requiring effective state action) for the broader politico-social analysis of the dependency theorists. Any position can only absorb so much revision before it ceases to be that position and becomes another stance altogether. One can recall both Wong and Lim Chong Yah[167] who, talking about Singapore, reduce the whole approach to a matter of trading relationships. We can pursue this matter in a further text.

Bienefeld and Godfrey's text[168] is avowedly theoretically eclectic and they focus on the contexts for Third World policy planners: how action is constrained. This is, it seems to me, arguably a type-two orthodox economics approach. However, by way of a partial defence it could be suggested that Bienefeld is picking up from Cardoso – whom he cites favourably – the notions of specificity of enquiry via political economic analysis. Yet Bienefeld's eclecticism, avoidance of politics and celebration of the role of the state does seem to take him far from Cardoso's project. The idea of dependency, originally looking at the Third World within the world capitalist system, is now, it seems, an 'abstract principle' around which Bienefeld looks, in a political economic fashion, at choices facing actors (states) in the world system. It might be thought that this material is a regression to work in the style of earlier 'dissenting economics'.

A third way of characterizing the world context within which any particular economy and society would be operating entails using Marx's notion of the 'mode of production'.[169] This we considered above, and here I will add one further note on the Asiatic mode of production: this is one of the ways in which Marx looked beyond European capitalism.

On Melotti's[170] account there are three key elements to the Asiatic mode of production (AMP). There is no private ownership of land; the society is village-based; and there is a despotic central authority. What we have, then, is an image of an essentially rural society, owning land in common and subject to the depredations (taxes, tithes, etc.) of a remote overlord. The moribund nature of the whole system resides in the absence of private property rights in land. The notion of private property is absolutely central to Marx's analysis of capitalism: the accumulation of capital is possible only when there are extensive rights to private property. Without private property the capitalist system is unimaginable; thus the AMP was fatally handicapped, in terms of its internal historical dynamic, by the absence of private property in land – the means of production in a rural society. As it had no internal dynamic, it was moribund. Marx went on to argue that the great service performed by the colonial powers had been to introduce the idea of private property and thus to breathe life into these moribund forms. It is easy to see why Marx has embarrassed some of his followers!

Malcolm Caldwell observes that the 'awkward appendage to the corpus of marxism – the Asiatic Mode of Production (AMP) – has been laid to rest with even greater frequency than the general body of which it forms an apparently rather casual member.'[171] One might ask: why did Marx write about the AMP? And if we look at Marx's work overall what is immediately apparent is that his central concern was with the dynamics of change in the capitalist system of Western Europe. Economies, societies and cultures he characterized as 'modes of production' and he concerned himself with the dynamics of the capitalist mode, and, secondarily, those of the feudal mode from which capitalism had sprung. These are his overriding concerns and all else is peripheral. It is true that there is a large mass of such 'peripheral' material: Marx was extremely widely read; he engaged in an extensive correspondence with other social theorists in Europe and America; he also wrote pamphlets, journalism and substantial drafts of his major works. It is within this peripheral material that we find discussions of the AMP.

Marx's consuming passion for social research gives us half an answer to the question of why he produced the notion of the AMP. His studies made it clear to him that there was a world outside Europe, and so he drew it into his schemes. The other half of an answer involves the notion of historical materialism: this strategy of analysis was extremely powerful and we can speculate that Marx found it interesting to try out. This use of the method served to sketch out a context within which discussion of feudalism and capitalism could rest, but again, this context was a peripheral concern – one remote from Marx's major preoccupations. Worsley remarks that 'Marx became more tentative and exploratory the further back he went from capitalism and the further away from Europe.'[172]

When we turn to the sources which Marx drew upon to characterize the AMP we can see how present-day marxists could feel embarrassed at the efforts of the tradition's founder. Melotti devotes a chapter to Marx's sources and identifies three. The first is the work of the thinkers of the Enlightenment who, in characterizing types of polities (so as to argue for democracy), spoke of 'oriental despotism'. Their sociology, as Gellner noted above, was not too good, but the idea became part of the stock which subsequent theorists used. The second source for Marx is the first, but as reworked by Hegel: now the Asian pattern of life – static – became one moment in the realization of 'World Spirit'. The third source was contemporary work: 'the parliamentary records and reports of British officials, from the original writings of European travellers or references to them by other authors, and lastly from historical, geographical and ethnographical works on the Middle and Far East'.[173] All this material was prepared by people within the mental set generated by colonialism: the distinction between civilized Europeans and barbarian non-Europeans was burnt deep into the European mind and it must, to an extent, have shaped this work of Marx – one of the sources he drew on was a certain Thomas Stamford Raffles![174]

The notion of the AMP relates to pre-capitalist social and economic forms of life and to pursue the matter further – by offering examples – would take us into the realm of marxian historiography, and this would take us too far away from our present concerns. So we can turn to an essay which uses the idea of modes of production to look at Indonesia. Crucial to this essay is the idea that the pre-colonial mode of production (AMP) could not itself generate the shift to a capitalist mode and that the violence of the colonial mode of production is of primary importance. Thus discussion of the colonial mode centres on the implantation of a form of economy and society which the pre-colonial mode could not generate and which itself rested upon the extensive use of violence.

Gordon[175] begins by noting that discussion of capitalism in Asia has been (setting the orthodoxy aside) either in Frankian dependency terms or cast in terms of modes of production. The author declares that he will pursue the second line and argue that

> The specific form modern colonial domination took in the process of underdeveloping Indonesia – the plantation system – could not survive the Dutch loss of direct control of the state. The overwhelming presence of the plantation system – and its most important and unique form, the Java sugar system – dragged down the rest of the socio-economic structure with it when it collapsed following change in state power on the achievement of Independence. No new dominant mode of production emerged in the period 1942–1965. So although chronologically 'post colonial' there was no post-colonial mode of production. Instead an indeterminate form of socio-economic formation was dominated by no specific mode of production. A post colonial formation did not appear until after the military coup of 1965–66.[176]

Gordon then goes on to run through his argument in detail. The idea of mode of production which he uses follows the general position we met above with Rey: to the idea that violence was necessary to implant the system is added the idea that violence was necessary to sustain it. Thus when the Dutch were expelled, the whole system simply collapsed.

Gordon discusses in detail what he calls the colonial mode of production, from 1870 to 1942. The earlier date marks the shift from the 'culture system' to plantation agriculture, primarily sugar and rubber. These plantations were Dutch- and English-owned; local capital was confined to 'petty manufacturing', except for a few bigger Chinese enterprises. There was no national bourgeoisie.

Of the plantation system Gordon notes that it required cheap labour and cheap land – both were provided by the state: the system rested on crude exploitation and force. In Java the sugar industry had a very particular structure: smallholders were contracted to supply cane to mills. These were effectively forced contracts and demanded up to 50 per cent of the best land. Rubber was grown in a more familiar plantation way. Gordon concludes: 'I maintain simply that the plantation system (and hence the colonial economy) could operate only with the permanent backing and participation of the colonial state.'[177]

The period from 1942 to 1965 Gordon labels an 'Indeterminate Socio-economic Formation'.[178] With the defeat of the Dutch, the sugar system collapsed – and along with it the rest of the economy. Thus a Dutch neo-colonialism was impossible. Any social revolutionary change was halted by 1948 as Sukarno consolidated power, and thereafter Guided Democracy acted only to delay the rise of the military–bureaucratic polity of Suharto. This, argues Gordon, is a neo-colonial regime, and thus the post-1965 period sees a coherent post-colonial mode of production established.

To summarize: in this short section I have made reference to three ways in which those in the marxist tradition have tried to grasp the overall situation of the Third World in general, and, as illustrated here, Southeast Asia. The positions adopted vary somewhat and, indeed, have been the subject of sometimes heated debate. I am neither going to join nor try to resolve these debates: given my earlier remarks on the recentness of the 'rediscovery' of Marx, the fact that there are these debates is wholly unsurprising. The particular trio cited here – neo-marxism, dependency and modes of production – call attention to the way in which internal economic and class relationships were, and are, shaped by particular linkages to the world capitalist economy. I will use this general synthetic, and very simple, formulation as the point around which subsequent illustrative material can be presented: I will call attention to the disputes between strands of the marxian argument only when it seems helpful to do so.

The local economic base

Southeast Asia has lately been a source of much interesting debate within the marxian line. This is because of its apparently successful recent capitalist industrialization and discussions of the Asian NICs; Singapore figures under both headings. The post-independence success of these various countries has been presented as a vindication of orthodox economic analyses. And these success stories have also been presented as clearly establishing that neo-marxist and dependency analyses are wrong. Bill Warren[179] has argued this general case forcefully. Thus we have disputes between orthodox and marxists, and within the marxian tradition. I will now turn to look at two essays which focus on ASEAN and the NICs.

Limqueco, arguing against Baran and Frank, begins by declaring that he will look at 'the current process of capitalist industrialization [in ASEAN] from the perspective that the development of productive forces and class struggle are the prime movers of society.'[180] ASEAN is seen to have played 'host to a great flood of Japanese and American capital'[181] with consequent implications for economic growth and democracy. Economic data for ASEAN show remarkable results, but these aggregated data hide structural problems. First, there is the problem of labour absorption as the agricultural workforce has shrunk. Many workers have been absorbed into the 'informal sectors', services and bureaucracies. The author notes: 'The generation of an unemployed and under-developed workforce is a key structural contradiction, which leads to severe social problems.'[182] However, Limqueco is not too clear on how severe these problems are; neither is it too clear how the author is using the word 'contradictions'. A second area of 'hidden' problems attaches to the drive to export manufactures. Running these industries involves many necessary imports. The author notes, correctly, that ASEAN's contribution is cheap labour. The export of manufactures also involves, argues Limqueco, a drift into indebtedness. A third area of concern is that of wages/prices. Limqueco diagnoses sharply inegalitarian systems with the mass of the people receiving stagnant, or even declining, real wages. The author comments: 'The consequences in human suffering as a result of the deterioration in income are politically and socially explosive.'[183] From this point, the author takes a short step and notes that all ASEAN governments are repressive – some more than others.

The author then concludes by insisting – implausibly, I think – that the data he has presented (all World Bank, IMF, ESCAP – Economic and Social Commission for Asia and the Pacific) establish the irrelevance of dependency and neo-marxian analyses to 'East Asia'. ASEAN's industrialization – an 'early phase'[184] – rests on cheap labour and this is the clue to analysis. If we read this as an injunction to specificity – and this is a charitable position – then we can agree. Otherwise, Limqueco's rather crude effort only serves to introduce a few elements of agency data. Comparing Limqueco's work with Gordon's (above) or Hamilton's (below) neatly establishes, *contra* Warren and his followers, that there is much more to marxian political economic analysis of a given situation than merely reinterpreting the standard data and invoking Marx on the expansionism of capitalism.

Hamilton[185] offers a discussion of the Asian NICs which is of more help than Limqueco's work. Thus he begins by noting that the NICs have been esteemed by the orthodox as vindicating their optimism and have posed an awkward question to dependency theory. The orthodox position is set aside by Hamilton, who remarks that the orthodox insistence on focusing on economic indicators and ignoring the social realities of inequality and the political realities of repression is unsatisfactory. He goes on to look at discussions within the marxian camp. At the outset, he notes that 'The broad consensus of radical economic analysis was that capital in the imperialist centres was alone capable of self-expansion and that any sporadic industrial growth in the periphery occurred solely at the behest of transnational corporations.'[186] Hamilton cites Warren as attacking this view and rehearses his argument that 'the imperialist powers favoured Third World industrialization, that in any case their ability to restrict the latter had been and is being markedly eroded, and that imperialism will disappear.[187] This is referred to, by Hamilton, as the 'impossibilist–inevitabilist problematic'[188] and he declares that he wishes to escape its confines. The strategy he adopts, to anticipate what follows, is to deploy what seems to me to be an economic metaphor whereby the NICs are taken to have been 'annexing space in the world economy . . . at the expense of other capitals . . . [whereas others] have industrialized largely on the basis of new spaces.'[189] This metaphor is then pursued in terms of linkages to the world economy and internal relationships of class, and his general view of the Asian NICs is that their industrialization was fortuitous, has exhausted its potential (it cannot annexe any more space), and is unstable due to the mix of rising expectations and political repression – where the former is a result of success and the latter a condition of continuation.

The analysis begins with a discussion of the world context of the NICs which, it is reported, have managed to 'occupy a larger and more diversified space in the world economy by specializing in the production and export of light consumer goods'.[190] The multinationals have played a role but, with the exception of Singapore, local capital has been responsible and this is 'essential to the argument'.[191] Local capital has opened up an economic space which rests on goods having no very great capital or technological input and whose manufacturing can utilize cheap labour: light consumer goods. Hamilton then considers the sets of class circumstances that fostered, and now sustain, this particular role.

The appropriate starting-point is the colonial period. Korea was occupied by Japan and played the role of agricultural supplier: patterns of agricultural life were much disturbed by the colonial power.

> The traditional Korean landed aristocracy was seriously weakened by colonial occupation and annexation of land, but it was not destroyed. It continued to exist effectively in alliance with the colonizers and was to suffer the opprobrium of this collaboration in the future. The twin exactions of pre-

> colonial feudalism and Japanese colonialism caused widespread agricultural pauperization.[192]

In Taiwan a similar agricultural role was pursued, albeit with less reworking of patterns of life. In neither territory was there any appreciable industrialization: 'During the period of intense colonial rule there was no potential, indigenous leadership stratum to speak of, except perhaps for scattered cabals of intimidated nationalists. No strong merchant class could develop, nor was indigenous industry allowed to flower.'[193]

In Hong Kong and Singapore there is a different story: both were founded as trading ports and both European and Chinese capital serviced the trading role.

From this context the shape of the post-war political, social and economic situation emerged. The time of the formation of new nation states in Asia, as elsewhere, was a period of confusion. American concern for resisting communism was of importance. In Korea the obvious nationalists were also largely communist: with the defeat of Japan, a series of local political initiatives were taken – factories seized from the colonialists, local government organizations formed (although here Hamilton gives very little detail). The Americans arrived a couple of months later 'and there began the process of crushing all popular political activity.'[194] Syngman Rhee became the US stooge. Again, Hamilton – remarkably – fails to tell us just how the split between North and South Korea came about, and fails even to mention 1945 as the date of the division! However, he then – rightly – goes on to characterize Rhee's subsequent rule, to 1960, as that of a US puppet whose power was rested on a police force and bureaucracy both tainted by collaboration. South Korea, like Taiwan, received massive military and economic aid from the Americans. Hamilton comments:

> In both countries, aid constituted the largest proportions of national budgets for several years . . . foreign direct investment was extremely low in both countries until the late 1960s. The effect of the US intervention was not only to sustain conservative, anti-communist regimes but also to foster the development of nascent bourgeoisies whose members profited from close ties with the US.[195]

Politically, in Taiwan the Koumintang (KMT) came to power with the aid of the USA which, as above, backed with aid the party's fight against communism. Hamilton makes it clear that the KMT were no puppets, but adds that the US had massive influence via aid for reconstruction and development.

Of Hong Kong and Singapore Hamilton has little to say: local nationalism never appeared in Hong Kong and Lee's regime was wholly acceptable to international capital.

The business of industrialization is then considered. It is noted that 'the role of indigenous capital accumulation varied from relative insignificance in Singapore to the main bearer in Hong Kong, Taiwan and Korea.'[196] Close study reveals, claims Hamilton, that 'the primitive accumulation of capital is as much a political process as an economic one.'[197] The role of the state is examined, and for each of the four it is found to be extensive – especially in enforcing a shift from merchant to industrial capitalism via land reforms, urbanization–industrialization programmes and the use of US aid to build appropriate infrastructure. This drive to industrialize coincided with the post-war economic boom: thus all four were able to carve out new 'economic spaces' for themselves.

The nature of the local capital formed and the industries developed are discussed in some detail by Hamilton. Summarizing his points, we have the claim that local industrial capital was: (1) firmly backed by local states themselves firmly lodged within, linked to, metropolitan capital – especially US; (2) 'inexperienced' and therefore cautious, thus making use of relatively 'low-tech' developments having a high labour input; (3) larger-scale, and 'high-tech', enterprises required more extensive link-ups with overseas capital.

Recent changes in the world economy have, argues Hamilton, posed problems for these four economies. Both the circumstances and nature of their success were very particular. This appraisal forms the basis of Hamilton's view that their path of capitalist industrialization has, at the present, come to a halt. Hamilton notes that their 'entry into the international division of labour has been largely on terms laid down by the dominant capitalist powers, and in consequence the four have been left with economies which are heavily biased towards a few consumer goods industries, except in Singapore where foreign capital has been responsible for a broader, but no more independent, industrial base.'[198] Recent attempts to diversify have not broken the mould whereby Asian capital links to world capital via the use of cheap labour. Hamilton judges this – as I noted above – a limited 'economic space' and a vulnerable one.

By way of comment upon Hamilton's essay we can make the following points. First, that the use of the metaphor of 'annexing economic space' is both pleasing in that it lets us grasp the totality of the various nation states' recent histories, and, arguably, misleading. Evidently, it is a spatial metaphor and this has two effects: (a) success is understood as more/less space; and (b) the whole matter is curiously static, thus the ideal implied is of an autonomous space rather than a particular set of relationships, internal and external, which would let the economy/society be seen in terms of process – as responding to and/or initiating movements which implied political and ethical goals on the part of the societies. Second, we could note that the 'initial conditions' of colonialism are not properly handled: Singapore and Hong Kong really are very different from South Korea and Taiwan in terms of their positions within the world economy. Neither began its 'annexing of space' from a situation of, so to say, having none at all. Both territories have always been integral parts of the world capitalist economy. I wonder if there is not an oversimplification at this point of Hamilton's analysis: thus Hong Kong and Singapore do not simply contribute cheap labour to the world system, they also contribute as mercantile centres. The third point to be made about Hamilton's work is that, although he clearly demonstrates that there has been significant capitalist industrialization, he understates the cost – notwithstanding his acknowledgement that three, certainly, of the four are authoritarian states. Related to this apparent neglect is an absence of any real discussion of internal political processes: a 'depoliticization' effected by repression seems to be granted with a few 'tensions' acknowledged, but this, surely, won't do. Fourth, Hamilton's treatment of external linkages seems very schematic. The early role of the US is noted in detail, but the subsequent rise of the Japanese is mentioned only in passing. And the historically imminent retrieval of Hong Kong by the People's Republic of China does not seem to merit inclusion at all – and it is surely impossible not to expect major changes in Hong Kong's economy and society as 1997 draws closer.

However, setting these criticisms aside, what Hamilton does offer is an overview of capitalist industrialization that is thoroughly plausible. And he also, correctly, calls attention to the role of the state in these matters: this will be considered below.[199]

In respect of the 'impossibilist–inevitabilist' debate Lim,[200] discussing the experience of the Philippines and its implication for the position taken by Warren *et al.*, considers in turn: the nature of Philippine industrialization; the elite; and the role of the state. Lim's discussion of Philippine industrialization notes improvements in Gross National Product figures – he is seemingly more impressed than Wong – mentions the Export Processing Zone in Bataan, and finally doubts that much can be said for Warren's thesis or the industrialization achieved by the Marcos regime. On industrialization, Lim is unsatisfactory. As regards the role of the elite, he is clearer: 'The elite of the New Society consists basically of the extended families of Ferdinand and Imelda Marcos.'[201] It is a corrupt elite and Lim comments that Warren's discussions of nationalism and its role in fostering development are, in the case of the Philippines, useless. Moving on lastly to the role of the state, Lim picks up Warren's point that nationalism in the Third World is articulated in state action. In the case of the Philippines, the corruption of Marcos's 'conjugal dictatorship' renders debate unhelpful. However, it might be said that Warren's pointing to the enhanced role of the state establishes very little that is new. One of the key ideas of recent marxist work has been precisely the way in which the local state could act to articulate the interests of the capitalist world system. And the case of the NICs is atypical and not an occasion for making broad generalizations.

So for all Lim's reluctance to dismiss Warren's thesis that, it seems to me, is what should be done. However, setting that particular debate aside and returning to the arguments followed with Hamilton, I will continue this discussion of the marxist view of the 'local economic base' by considering an argument that does look at the Japanese role and which also takes note of Asia as an arena of conflict between 'socialism' and 'capitalism'.

Halliday begins his discussion of the pivotal role of Japan by observing that 'Since 1945 East Asia has been the centre of the world struggle between capitalism and socialism . . . East Asia has also witnessed some of post-war capitalism's most impressive achievements.'[202] Halliday will analyse the present situation, focusing upon the role of Japan which he sees as absolutely crucial. Taking note[203] of the way Asia came to assume its present form – sharply divided between capitalist and socialist countries – the author observes that

> Behind these barriers a remarkable capitalist transformation has occurred, creating a series of new social, political and economic structures . . . The Taiwan and South Korean regimes achieved what the anti-communist governments in Indochina found impossible: they established a real social base through land reform, industrialization, greatly increased export earnings, and correspondingly more efficient systems of political repression.[204]

Halliday speaks of an 'inner arc' – Taiwan, South Korea, Hong Kong, Macau and Singapore (as it resembles Hong Kong) – and an 'outer arc' – ASEAN – all oriented towards Japan. The countries of the inner arc are seen to have broad resemblances: repression of their populations and militarization. In this latter case, Taiwan and South Korea are heavy military spenders, so for its size is Singapore.[205] Of the former pair Halliday notes: 'The political apparatuses, economies, and cultures of both states have been profoundly influenced by their role as forward bases of American imperialism in Asia.'[206] This he discusses under the heading of the 'Politics of Ultra-dependency',[207] seeing both as dependent on MNC links. Of Hong Kong and Singapore the author notes their regional and world importance financially[208] – but says no more![209]

Halliday then considers Japan and this inner arc: 'Just as Japan's restoration and reinsertion into the world economy were precipitated by the fight against socialism, so South Korea and Taiwan were reshaped not only to "contain" the Korean and Chinese revolutions, but also Japan's periphery.'[210] Halliday talks of Japan benefiting from the 'hyper-militarization'[211] of this periphery by being relieved of defence-speaking burdens and, economically, through favourable trade balances. The structural relationship of Japanese capital to the inner arc is also tackled and where Hamilton stressed that capital in Hong Kong, Taiwan and South Korea was indigenous, Halliday presents a different view. Whilst direct Japanese investment has been low, there has been very extensive credit involvement – all in all, thinks Halliday,

> its capitalist periphery has been of inestimable importance to post war Japan, not only because of the size of the markets involved, but also because of the structural integration with the metropolis, the long term trade imbalance, and the dependence of many smaller Japanese firms (aggregated through the shosha) upon the periphery for maintaining profit margins.[212]

Halliday continues: 'In some respects it is fair to consider Taiwan and South Korea as extensions of the Japanese domestic market.'[213] The Japanese economy is now equal in Gross National Product to that of the USSR and has *per capita* GNP roughly equal to the USA. Growth over the last decade has bettered OECD (the Organization for Economic Cooperation and Development) averages easily, and industrial restructuring has been achieved more smoothly than in other industrialized economies. The Japanese also have large current account surpluses. Halliday notes: 'Japan is, in general terms, well positioned to take advantage of the next phase of economic development in East Asia.'[214]

Of the future, Halliday notes the re-entry into the world market of the People's Republic of China and, to an extent, North Korea, the former especially offering opportunities for Japan. But, insists Halliday, Japan 'needs and depends on some Taiwans and South Koreas. Japanese capitalism would be sorely challenged by the prospect of other East Asian states pursuing the economic road of the DPRK – Democratic People's Republic of Korea – or

Vietnam.'[215] The real threats to the present Pacific rim status quo, centring on Japan, lie, thinks Halliday, in the fundamental instability of the 'whole East Asian pattern of capital accumulation through mass repression and super-exploitation'.[216]

So much for Halliday: by way of a comment I will add two notes. First, Halliday restores the historical context to Hamilton's narrowly economic reading. The major role of the Japanese is identified – they are *the* Asian capitalist power and their influence is extensive. Hamilton's stress on the indigenous capital nature of South Korean and Taiwanese industrialization is undermined – Halliday moves us away from Warren and back towards Frank, the vehicle being his indication of Japanese power. Hamilton's argument is also undermined in that, where he discusses the four NICs and the world economy in general, Halliday speaks clearly of the world economy's 'regional representative', Japan. Again, it seems to undermine Hamilton's suggestion of a measure of autonomy for the NICs. Hamilton is also contradicted for the future: these capitalist industrializers may not have reached a ceiling because they are, to a significant extent, locked into the Japanese 'space' in the world economy and that, evidently, has not reached a ceiling.

Second, both Hamilton and Halliday do agree on two things. First, that the repressive, exploitation systems of the four NICs are fragile – and whilst I think these authors may be right, I would also see them as wildly oversimplifying: thus they focus on instability in South Korea in recent years; some instability in Taiwan just after the war; the relative stability of Hong Kong is set aside; and, finally, the wholly passive Singaporean population is not considered at all. Instability for the future may well not revolve around a repression/liberalization axis, but rather centre on events disturbing the status quo – for example, Hong Kong's reversion to the People's Republic of China, or US military withdrawal from South Korea, or Lee Kuan Yew's demise, and so on. I think in looking at these Asian NICs the fact that they are Asian might be as important as Western perceptions of repression. The other point on which Hamilton and Halliday agree is that these four NICs constitute a homogeneous entity. However, they seem to me, looking at the arguments advanced, to be 2 + 2 (Taiwan, South Korea; Hong Kong, Singapore) or, more plausibly, given Hong Kong's uncertain future, 2 + 1 + 1 (Taiwan, South Korea; Hong Kong; Singapore). Given that both authors above treat them as a group, I think my reservations are appropriate. Thus both authors advance a general case and evidence is adduced from any one of the four as appropriate; that any one piece of evidence is found in only one of the four is not noticed. If we suggest that the four are really 2 + 1 + 1, then the general argument is shown to be invalid because it switches from specific to specific in an entirely *ad hoc* fashion.

However, clearly Halliday's article is a useful corrective to Hamilton: we are reminded of the world historical scale of the changes under consideration, the importance of the Japanese presence and the possibly extensive changes in the future as the People's Republic of China attempts to 'modernize'.

Thus far in this section, we have looked at examples of marxian analysis which have focused upon the local economic base and, more generally, the way in which local modes of production are lodged within the world capitalist system. As these discussions proceeded, references were made to rural peasant classes within Southeast Asia. Hitherto, however, the examples presented reveal marxian analysis to be centred on matters of industrial life. There is, consequently, a correction to be made to these illustrative discussions. As was noted with John Wong[217] above, the rural sector in Southeast Asia comprises approximately 70 per cent of the population: we need to know what marxists have had to say about this large grouping. Worsley,[218] a marxist and an anthropologist, has recently presented an interesting general review of these matters and I will begin with his material and then go on to look at some more specific discussions before turning, finally, to the work of Scott and the notion of 'the moral economy of the peasantry'.

Worsley begins his discussion of the peasantry by recalling that for 95 per cent of our history human society has been of the hunter-gatherer variety. Industry is thus wholly novel and agriculture is not that much older – a few thousand years only. Two kinds of agricultural production are identified: (a) small-scale peasant, and (b) plantation.

Worsley characterizes type (a) as a form of production which is household-based and lodged within a complex web of social dependencies and obligations (to family and village). This household is a centre of production and consumption, both focused upon land:

> The unit of production in peasant society is . . . the household, a multiplex entity whose collective productive activities, however vital, are only a part of its wider social activities. If the household is the core unit of production, it is also the core unit of consumption. Crops are grown primarily to satisfy the wants of the household's members . . . The same people are both the producers and the consumers of the product . . . [and] the household . . . is the crucial unit for all social

> purposes, economic and non-economic: a unit of residence, of marriage, and of kinship relationships; a unit for the purpose of worshipping . . . And it is always located within wider structures of corporate kinship . . . The crucial resource . . . is the land.[219]

Small-scale peasant farming is to be regarded as a coherent cultural form and not as some sort of essentially degraded pre-modern form of life. This is the starting-point for Worsley.

From this point Worsley goes on to review the shift of the peasantry to the modern world: to capitalist agriculture and to the collective farm. In both instances, the process of the effective abolition of the peasantry is reviewed: a long-drawn-out business in which Worsley is at pains to show the peasantry as an active (if increasingly superseded) force and not, as is usual, passive. An exception to this general story of removal is, so far as Worsley is concerned, Mao's China. Here, the peasantry were sustained as an equal attention was paid to rural life and urban industry.

The overwhelming trend identified by Worsley is towards the elimination of the peasantry. He notes a handful of initiatives which have tried to assist the peasants – 'community development', co-operatives, land reform[220] – but all these have failed. Overall, Worsley's report on the 'decline of the peasantry' is regretful: the trend seems to be inevitable. Peasants have generated rebellion and other forms of resistance, but rarely have they accomplished effective revolutionary change in their circumstances. I will discuss the nature of peasant patterns of thought when I come to consider Scott; for the moment, it is to the second typical mode of agricultural production – the plantation – that I wish to turn.

Looking at the plantation sector, we find that it was the expansion of this form of agricultural production in the nineteenth century, as metropolitan capital shifted from mercantile to industrial modes of accumulation with a consequent new schedule of resource demands, that ushered in the period of maximally penetrative and disruptive colonialism. Above, we looked briefly at Gordon on Indonesia; a recent text by de Silva[221] discusses plantations both generally and in the Sri Lankan context.

Picking up de Silva's general remarks, we find a treatment of plantations which centres upon what the author terms their 'metropolitan orientation'.[222] Others have looked at the plantation as a straightforward economic phenomenon or, drawing on social psychology, as a 'closed institution': de Silva, working within the marxian tradition, looks to uncover both external linkages to the world capitalist system and the consequent internal patterns of life as they have been fashioned, and sustained, through time.

The character of plantations has been shaped, on de Silva's account, since the seventeenth century. In the West Indies, there was initially settler plantation agriculture and these 'personal' enterprises tended to absorb the available labour, leaving the larger managed estates short of workers. The response of the plantation owners was to bring in slaves: this both provided labour and led to the settler plantations disappearing as the white settlers withdrew. The upshot was the familiar plantation pattern: 'The use of unfree labour, of one form or another, with a highly authoritarian structure of labour relations, as an answer to this problem was the mainspring of the plantation system.'[223] The owners were now absentee mercantile capitalists represented on the plantations by managers who oversaw large slave workforces.

De Silva argues that plantation crops were essentially simple and that they could be grown by local peasants quite effectively. There is thus no particular market advantage to plantations as such, and the author comments: 'The large size of the plantations is the result of the historical and institutional circumstances in which the plantation system developed, with high overhead costs due to absentee ownership and the use of immigrant labour.'[224] Evidently, this is not an argument that would impress an orthodox economist, but we might note that there is more than an echo here of Worsley's unease at the displacement of peasant agriculture by 'agribusiness': analyses centred on 'economic efficiency' and the holistic approach of marxists do produce very different interpretations.

The size of the holdings increased, reports de Silva, as corporate owners took over. Working at a low technological level with cheap land and cheap – often forced – labour, the plantations were dominated by 'merchant capital'.[225] Thus they exist to produce an exploitable – that is, tradable resource – and little local processing is done. The plantations grow the material and ship it out. This, thinks de Silva, is underdevelopment *par excellence*. Via the big agency houses, merchant capital controls the local economy – which is thus integrally linked to the capitalist economy of the First World. The point here is that this system is not just a matter of exporting agricultural products; rather, the whole social, economic and political nature of the plantation country is shaped around the demands of this form of agriculture.

De Silva distinguishes between settler and non-settler colonies: 'It was in the non-settler colonies that the plantation system developed as a form of agriculture distinguished by its organization and technology and by its role in the world economy.'[226]

This entailed a narrow dependency and it shaped the dependent economy and society: industrialization was discouraged, peasant production of some crops was discouraged, and monopolies for colonial powers were maintained against other First World competitors. Overall, we find that wages had to be kept low as the system was labour-intensive. Land had to be available cheaply – and, indeed, colonial authorities did make land available by various statutory means. Governments provided extensive support in the way of credits, agricultural extension services, and so on. They also buttressed the system – with its key requirements of cheap land and labour – with violence. Gordon (above) made the same point when discussing Indonesia. Plantation economies could be sustained only by extra-economic coercion. And the present-day legacy of this historical experience is characterized by de Silva as a narrow economic dependency and a distorted economy: recently, he notes, substitutes have been developed for some plantation crops, which further weakens these already underdeveloped countries.

Turning to a substantive discussion of the nature of colonial plantation agriculture, we can look at the work of Gordon – whom we met briefly above – on Indonesia. The plantation system of the Dutch, in their vast colonial territory of the East Indies, is often regarded as one of the more brutal and damaging modes of surplus extraction pursued in the later (post-slavery) colonial period. Indeed, Gordon reports that in the later nineteenth century: 'The United States Congress even passed a law to ban the importation of goods from Sumatra on the grounds that they were produced by slave labour.'[227]

In an earlier essay, Gordon[228] characterizes a thousand years of Indonesian history – rather like Catley – in order to focus on specific modes of surplus production and appropriation. In the earlier periods, Dutch mercantile capital comes to displace politically the power of the Javanese aristocracy. But it is not until the imposition of the 'cultivation system' (1830–70) that the general socio-economic pattern in Java begins to change. Gordon offers a summary characterization:

> The form of exploitation was the compulsory allocation of one-fifth of village land cultivated by forced labour for the growing of export crops, mainly sugar, for the government. A monopoly of foreign trade in these crops was held by government institutions.[229]

This marked the beginning of the destruction of village self-sufficiency. The process is continued in the period 1870–1900 which saw, first, the abolition of the culture system and then the shift to nominally free labour and a plantation system. There is a rise of commodity circulation, landlessness and market relations. These changes sent 'free' recruits into the rubber and sugar plantations, whilst further reducing the self-sufficiency of the village. However, most crucially, the plantation system of the Dutch required the extra-economic force of the state, with its law and monopolies of legitimate violence, to support it with cheap labour, cheap land and monopoly control of the product. Gordon comments: 'Whether analysed in terms of a combination of modes of production or as within a colonial mode of production, the indigenous, non-capitalist "sector" had been totally changed.'[230] And this plantation system continued in the period 1900–41 until, in the wake of the Japanese interregnum, the Dutch were ejected; when the extra-economic prop was removed, the system collapsed.

An economy similarly dominated by plantations was Malaya: Baharrudin speaks of the 'underdevelopment of the Malaysian peasantry'[231] having taken place alongside the capitalist development of the nineteenth and twentieth centuries. What is crucial is the division into sectors – plantation and subsistence/cash crop. Commenting on the effects of colonial agricultural policy, Baharrudin notes that the 'consequence of this external-oriented agricultural policy, coupled with a total disregard of the needs of the internal market, was that on the eve of her independence Malaya was importing about 50% of her rice requirements.'[232] Further, as the plantations were largely worked by immigrants and the peasant sector by Malays, 'there was an ethnic identification in terms of area and economic function.'[233]

Looking at the subsistence/cash crop sector, Baharuddin notes that the sector is predominantly Malay and that 'Malay peasant settlements can be divided into three types: (i) the fishing villages; (ii) padi settlements; (iii) settlements in cash-cropping and mixed cultivation areas.'[234] A purely subsistence economy does not now exist, and even the most remote areas have been drawn into the capitalist system. This has had the familiar consequences of 'social differentiation and polarization':[235] along with private property in land and cash cropping, came landlords, money lenders, debts and class differentiation.

Baharuddin concludes, first, that Malaysia is locked into a hierarchical surplus expropriation/appropriation chain – a scheme redolent of A. G. Frank – and, second, that government planners have failed to see this and thus government's efforts have been misplaced. At which point one might be inclined to note the linking of what many have called a poor theory to an arguably naive politics which would seem to rely upon the planners solving what must, on Baharuddin's scheme, be seen as complex problems of neo-colonial political and economic dependence. Matters of political action reappear in my last example.

So, finally, I want to look at the work of Scott,[236] whose analysis argues for regarding the peasantry as an active historical force rather than, as is usual, seeing them as the victims of history as capitalism expands and shatters/absorbs their form of life. This unusual revision is reminiscent of Worsley in some respects: thus both invoke the idea of 'culture' and insist that the coherence of the culture of the peasantry be acknowledged. However, where Worsley sees the peasantry being overwhelmed in the ongoing shift to the 'modern world', Scott sees a spontaneous hope for politically radical change.

Scott argues against the familiar marxian position which would tend to dismiss the peasantry as a superstitious, conservative and socially non-progressive class, destined to be swept away by the rise of capitalist industrialization. Instead, it is argued that close attention should be paid both to the nature of peasant life and to the character of peasant rebellion. Scott argues, plausibly, that peasants are detached from the dominant industrial hegemony of state machines and have therefore a nascent class consciousness: an idea of themselves as a distinct group within society, a group possessed of a different set of ideas and interests from those views, prevalent in society, which reflect the interests of the elite. In contrast, suggests Scott, the industrial proletariat is closely bound to the status quo and thus has neither this ready experience of separateness nor an alternative moral tradition to draw upon when fashioning interpretations of the world.

Now, clearly, there is something in this approach. Scott has rightly drawn attention to the 'cultural/anthropological equality', so to say, of the peasantry with other, familiar, groups in the modern world. Peasant culture is to be acknowledged. Thus far, we have advanced to the point of Worsley's basic argument. Beyond this, however, matters become more difficult because Scott wants to argue – and does – from this cultural/anthropological equality to a superior revolutionary potential. This, I think, is a shift from sense to romanticism. It involves a sensible, if not particular well-expressed, understanding of social change as often engendered 'accidentally', rather than 'engineered' in the self-conscious pursuit of a specified goal. On the other hand, Scott's approach evinces a failure to distinguish rebellion from revolution.

There are five steps to Scott's argument. The author begins, as I have noted, both by recording that marxists have tended to dismiss the peasantry and insisting that their experiential distance from the dominant hegemony confers revolutionary strength. From this point, he moves to discuss the Gramscian[237] notion of 'hegemony' the set of controlling and pervasive ideas, formal and, crucially, common-sensical, within society which reflect and sustain the interests of the ruling group. Then, in step three, Scott notes that this hegemony has to be institutionally articulated – via schools, government offices and officials, police, media, and so on (all this in addition to basic economic linkages which will carry their own sets of ideas); and that in the rural areas these institutional vehicles are often weak. In other words, the government's 'routine presence' is weaker than it is in the urban areas. And this 'experiential distance' from the hegemonic centre allows the peasantry to formulate and express, in a variety of ways, a counter-position. Now, step four, the peasantry has established patterns of life to draw upon – its own 'moral economy', the base for an articulated counter-position. This moral economy involves commitment to the local community and it is precisely these commitments that are threatened by the arrival of states and capitalist economic relations: this is the fundamental occasion for resistance. And from this point, Scott moves on to the manner of resisting. Vanguardism is set aside as liable either to co-option or timidity. Instead, spontaneity and voluntarism are affirmed. Thus may peasant rebellions be formed and expressed.

It is fairly easy to grant that Scott is reasonable when he asks that we pay attention to the culture of the peasantry, and it is also easy to acknowledge the claims of 'distance' between peasant and elite/urban–industrial peoples – but I think the political message is easy to dismiss. It seems to me, as noted above, that Scott's romanticism involves a fatal confusion between rebellion and revolution. However, to pick up my early point about change, I think Scott is right to remind us that change can be initiated in various ways. Far too often the orthodox marxists celebrate political organization, just as the liberal democrats look to planning to the exclusion of everything else. Scott leaves room for chance – and he is surely right. However, looking at the history of the twentieth century one might wish to choose world wars rather than peasants as the prime agents in the matter of social change.[238]

In summary, we can see that the local 'economic base' of Southeast Asia is to be read, within the marxian framework, as peripheral-dependent capitalism. This is as one would expect. The interesting questions in respect of the economic base centre upon the ways in which it was established through the colonial period and its present economic, class and political character. The general position of the writers noted above is this: first, that there has been some recent capitalist industrialization in Southeast (and East) Asia, but of a restricted and limited kind and secured at rather a high cost to the inhabitants of these regions; and second, that the peasantry of Southeast Asia is in long-term decline – although here there would be considerable debate as to the extent of the colonial system's effective present impact and the pace of future change.

On the question of the extensive role of the various state machines Bienefeld (pp.216–17), and those analysts of capitalist industrialization whom we have just considered, made some interesting points. These are worth pursuing. It would seem that the role of the state has been centrally important in securing the successful capitalist industrialization of the last thirty years or so. The nature of the state is a matter that has exercised marxist thinkers in recent years and it is an issue that shifts us neatly to the business of the 'superstructure'.[239]

The local superstructure

It is not usual in marxian analyses of the 'superstructure' to begin by talking about the state, but in the case of peripheral capitalism it is increasingly taken to be wholly appropriate as the role of the state is paramount in maintaining the form of life in question and in securing the links that bind the peripheral system into the world system. Matters of class, ideology, ethnicity and culture can be discussed around this acknowledged central role of the state.

In contrast to liberal democratic theories, which argue that the state represents the 'common interest' and acts as a mediator in group disputes, the classical marxian view is that the state represents the interests of the dominant economic grouping and that claims to represent the 'common interest' are ideological obfuscations. Marx and Engels saw the capitalist state presiding over formal equality – all citizens are equal before the law – and substantive, real, economic and social inequality. A genuinely democratic society, they argued, would see both formal and substantive equality: it would also see an end to the class nature of the bourgeois state. The various administrative functions of the state would be devolved to local, elected, popular and democratic institutions. Hence the notion of the 'withering away of the state': the vision is thus libertarian.

As for 'bourgeois democracy', both Marx and Engels valued it highly: it was the politically most advanced state form that had yet emerged. But it was far from perfect. In analysing the bourgeois state, Marx distinguished between 'state' and 'civil society', where the latter was the sphere of personal and family economic life. The distinction originally came from Hegel, who had argued that the state ordered the egoism of civil society. So far as Marx is concerned, the relationship is to be reversed: the state is built on the economics of civil society.

This distinction has reappeared, in various ways, in much subsequent marxist work. The distinction aimed at is, in political terms, between the general taken-for-grantedness of a form of life (civil society) and its formal expression (the state). It is this split that allowed the nineteenth-century bourgeoisie to adhere to its notion of liberty under the law to pursue private economic goals. Liberal democratic theory, as noted, accepts the split and allocates the state the role of referee between the competitors. Marx, however, looks to reconnect state and civil society via libertarian democracy – his 'example' was the Paris Commune – where political power is widely dispersed in a society of economic equality. The transition to this preferred situation might well be awkward, and here we meet the notorious notion of the 'dictatorship of the proletariat'. However, in brief, Marx saw the state as expressing the fundamental nature of an economy and society, a form of life. The bourgeois state, built on the economy and society of the nineteenth-century bourgeoisie, was to be seen as both valuable and imperfect: the next step was a libertarian democracy.

However, the point of departure of present relevance is that in contemporary peripheral capitalist societies, the state does not necessarily emerge from and express 'civil society' simply because, typically, it is an implanted state: a state implanted by the colonial powers, usually by force, and subsequently handed on via the process of decolonization to the new rulers. So, generally speaking – for there are multiple variants of state forms in the Third World – the state assumes a considerably more overt economic and social role. What we must do, then, is try to plot the varieties and natures of colonial and post-colonial states. This problem has exercised many marxist theorists over recent years.

It will be appropriate to begin with the colonial state itself. Often, this has been seen as a somewhat monolithic and fixed entity but, like the rest of the social world, it, too, underwent specific patterns of change. The Indian historian Chandra[240] considers India under the rule of the British and makes reference both to A. G. Frank's idea of the 'development of underdevelopment' and to the post-neo-marxian schemes of 'modes of production'. Chandra argues, in sum, that the colonial mode of production was not only created by colonialism, but went through discernible stages. The formally constituted colonial state is that form called forth by the final phase of colonial expansion.

Chandra's argument, in more detail, has three elements: characterization of colonialism; its stages; and the nature of the state. This last is the key element for our purposes, and Chandra remarks both that many nationalist leaders mistook decolonization for the removal of the colonial mode of production and that the legacy of the colonial mode of production is the starting-point for post-colonial statehood.

So Chandra argues, first, that colonial societies were created by colonialism: they are not to be regarded as expressions of pre-colonial days. A. G. Frank is followed on this point – the active underdevelopment of the colonial society. However, Chandra also uses the phrase 'mode of production' and argues that the colonial mode of production was shaped by contact with the metropolis, and that there were stages in this exchange. Chandra, we can note, is mixing two distinct lines of marxian theorizing and then adding in stages! In much of this 'preliminary characterizing' type of marxist writing, considerable tolerance is demanded of the reader. Continuing with Chandra, the next point made is that the colonial mode of production is underdeveloping the territory from the start. This position opposes both the orthodox modernization theorists and the classical marxists who, speaking initially of positive benefits and only later of negative factors, failed adequately to characterize colonialism. According to Chandra:

> many colonial and metropolitan intellectuals, including Marx before 1859, failed to grasp the basic features of colonial societies in the early years of their structuring and came to have a certain positive image of colonialism. Later, as the reality surfaced, they were able to see its essentially negative features. Instead of seeing the change as an aspect of intellectual and political history linked to the early stages of colonialism, they assumed that reality had undergone a drastic reversal.[241]

Thus Chandra insists upon a general process of underdevelopment. Additionally, the colonial mode of production changes as does the manner of surplus appropriation in the metropolis: 'The change from one stage to another was partially the consequence of the changing patterns of metropolis's own social, economic and political development, and of its changing position in the world economy and polity.'[242] This is an argument that we have also met with Catley (see pp. 213–15).

Chandra then spells out these stages. Stage number one is that of 'monopoly trade and revenue appropriation', which is characterized by plunder and seizure of goods and wealth, and by monopoly control of markets. Perhaps surprisingly, Chandra adds that in this period there was little change in the basic structure of society: only the top layer of society changed – a new rapacious elite replaced the old. The peasantry continues its strategies of passive evasion.[243] The ideology of the new colonial rulers was not developmentalist: colonial rule was simply superimposed on existing socio-economic forms.

In stage two, plunder gives way to a longer-term strategy of appropriation through trade. The colony becomes a 'subordinate trading partner'[244] and this arrangement requires the establishment of the full colonial state apparatus. This new relationship required that existing patterns of life be 'shattered and transformed all along the line'.[245] Again, this recalls Catley. Interestingly, Chandra adds that this extensive reworking was actively pursued 'under the slogan of development and modernization'[246] and, moreover, he sees little to choose between these ideologies and the post-Second World War orthodoxies of development theory. So, in sum, the colonialists took themselves to be pursuing development, but what they produced, in the nature of things, was underdevelopment.[247]

In stage three, there is international competition for colonies but the shift to formal empire has an ambiguous impact. Although new capital was made available, it was not widely invested: indeed, capital continued to flow out. Chandra argues that this situation indicates that the underdevelopment of colonial economies was already such that they were unable to absorb the capital. And now, interestingly, the ideology of the colonialists shifts from 'development' to 'looking after the childish natives': 'Geography, "race", climate, history, social organisation, culture and religion of the colonial peoples were cited as factors which made them permanently unfit for self government.'[248] This position was relaxed only under the pressure of post-Second World War circumstances.

The final part of Chandra's argument deals with the nature of the colonial state in general – thus picking up the issue which I raised earlier. Chandra draws a bold contrast: thus where the bourgeois state is an instrument for the oppression of one class by another, the colonial state 'is the instrument for *oppressing entire societies*'.[249] Whatever the real value of this contrast, the last point is useful and it leads Chandra to pursue the matter of the role of the colonial state in maintaining the colonial mode of production: the colonial state does not rest on an economic base; rather, it is the principal means of shaping that economy. These 'means' include using: the law (to regulate the economy to the advantage of the colonialists, to suppress dissent); government functions (to promulgate notions of harmonious development via the institutional apparatus of hegemony, as Scott might put it); informal opinion and the media (to promulgate ideologies of 'childishness' and 'tribalism'); and the usual instruments of organized violence to enforce the state's will.

Chandra concludes by considering the present legacy of this long-drawn-out historical episode: and though he offers no 'list', his views can be assumed to centre upon economic and cultural dependency. In respect of this last-noted element, one major problem he does specify is the mistake made by post-colonial rulers when they mistook the removal of foreign rulers for the destruction of the colonial mode of production. Chandra's point, typical of marxist thinking here, is to stress the continuity of capitalist relations between 'centres' and 'peripheries': formal political decolonization is only one element of the effective abolition of the colonial mode of production. And this is a crucial matter for marxists which we can pursue: the idea that has been advanced which follows on from Chandra's argument is 'neo-colonialism'.

Looking at Southeast Asia in general, and using the Indonesian example in particular, Feith[250] argues that the notion of neo-colonialism is of considerable value in illuminating the post-independence situation of the region. Feith's is an early attempt to present the argument and is thus, perhaps, a little overgeneral; none the less, the essay has the virtue of directness. The strategy adopted is one of asking whether or not the notion 'neo-colonialism' is useful in analysing Southeast Asia. Feith will argue that the term is useful and he characterizes a neo-colonial situation as one where 'Key elements of the structure of dependency and unequal exchange characteristic of a colonial relationship are maintained or restored after colonial rule had been ended.'[251] The notion entails, therefore, the idea of continuity – decolonization is, in some significant sense, not 'real' change at all. Feith reports: 'There are six major trends in the ASEAN states since the mid-1960s which seem to have recreated or strengthened economic, social and political structures characteristic of the colonial period.'[252] And these the author then proceeds to review.

He takes note of the role of outside sources of capital and identifies it as the 'principal determinant of the direction and pace of change in the period since the mid-60s . . . Cheap labour had been a principal factor of attraction.'[253] Feith notes the extent of growth and extent of local participation, but insists on the power of foreign capital.

The second point made involves the 'entrenchment of established classes'[254] after the period of fluidity around the time of decolonization. I think that what he means is that it took a while for new elites to secure their positions – a claim that seems both plausible and not very enlightening. Feith then goes on to observe that elite groups are now looking like new ruling classes: that is, power, wealth and prestige are concentrated in a hierarchical society with channels of social mobility restricted. Internal patterns of elite group formation are noted, as are the linkages of local elites to overseas capital. Feith sees a cultural/political 'dualism', redolent of the colonial days, with a cosmopolitan elite controlling, paternalistically, peasant and urban masses.

Third, Feith notes the 'accelerated destruction of pre-capitalist social formations'[255] as 'commercialization' spreads. A curious point, this – and one that, whether empirically true or not of recent years, fits uneasily with the dependency perspective adopted. These areas have been extensively modified over the period since – on Catley's reading – 1870. This point recalls, clearly, Worsley's work (see pp. 230–1). It seems as if there are two claims, both plausible, which do not sit easily with one another. First, that the period of formal colonialism, with its extensive social, cultural and economic impact, massively changed established forms of life and drew the peasantry into the capitalist system. And, second, that the peasantry is still declining. I think the lacuna is probably going to be filled only by a detailed discussion of just how the peasantry as a group or class was, and is, linked to the world capitalist system.

The fourth element of Feith's analysis concerns the business of politics. Feith remarks:

> In each of the ASEAN countries except Thailand, government is more restrictive and repressive today than it was in 1965. None of these countries has yet reached Brazilian, Iranian, or South Korean levels of oppression and totalitarianism, but the trends in that direction are well established particularly in Indonesia, and to a lesser extent, in Singapore and the Philippines.[256]

This is a claim we have met before and need not pursue further, except to note that Feith underlines this movement as a consequence of the role in the world economy (with consequent internal political arrangements) taken by these states.

Interestingly, in element five, Feith identifies one possible source of progressive change when he speaks of the 'expansion of middle-class groupings'.[257] The middle class is a group that benefits from the economic growth of these nations, without having any interest in the political repression that accompanies elite-group closure – itself not an obvious advantage to the middle class. A similar point, of course, was made by Hamilton and Halliday above. Feith thinks that in periods of upheaval, 'fragments' of the elite, in competition with other 'fragments', might well come to see the middle-class groupings as a source of allies: a constituency to make political appeals to. In passing, we can note a variant on this theme which has been offered by Chua Beng Huat[258] for Singapore: the author's speculation is that the younger generation faces affluence and not, as for the older generation, the climb out of poverty. Here, argues Chua, is a source of tension and, given the present dominance of the long-established elite, the search is on for new legitimating ideological symbols which encompass the experience of comparative material prosperity.

Finally, with his sixth element, Feith looks to 'incipient stirrings of mass protest'[259] and speculates that just so long as the masses – rural and urban – are excluded, then the potential for general disturbance will remain even if, as Feith acknowledges, there is little obvious present sign of such protest and nor is there any easy way of 'predicting' such outbreaks.

Feith concludes that it is with respect to all these areas of concern that evidence can be adduced to establish the plausibility of his claim in relation to the usefulness of the term 'neo-colonial'. So far as Feith is concerned, Southeast Asia provides more than a few 'neo-colonial' regimes.

Thus far, we have the colonial state characterized, in its several varieties, and a first statement of the usefulness of the notion of 'neo-colonial'. To advance matters, we can take note of the way in which marxists subsequently offered more detailed characterizations of the 'post-colonial' state: detailed in the sense of considering the variety of ways in which peripheral-dependent capitalisms could be inserted into the world system. Additionally, the notion of class – noticeably absent from Chandra and only sketched by Feith – is invoked.

Petras[260] argues not for generalizations about state forms, but instead that attention be focused on the particular sets of circumstances that shape them. The primary role of the state in peripheral capitalism is stressed. Civil society is not well formed and nor is the local bourgeoisie – the consequence being that the state plays a very overt role in both establishing an order and in forging links to the outside.

Petras begins the presentation of varieties of peripheral states by acknowledging that there have been some changes, over the last decade, in the world economy and, in particular, we have seen the rise of the NICs. He argues against generalizing from this experience too quickly, as Warren has done in advancing what Hamilton referred to as the 'inevitabilist' argument; instead, Petras advocates specific enquiry. This he then proceeds to illustrate by distinguishing NIC and non-NIC and identifying the varieties of state forms to be found.

In the non-NIC category – that is, primary-product exporters – four state forms are identified. First, neo-colonial states which 'depend heavily upon metropolitan political and military support to sustain their ruling class',[261] instances of which are Zaire, Gabon, Thailand and the Cameroons. Looking at Southeast Asia, one might want to add in both the Philippines and Indonesia. And here we could note both that Feith had Indonesia in mind and that he offered a much wider notion of neo-colonialism than does Petras who is, as we shall see below, strongly concerned with the politics of peripheral states. Second, Petras identifies dependent developmental states whose local rulers are firmly in political control but which are linked closely economically to the capitalist metropoles. Here Kenya, Egypt and Colombia are cited. Third, Petras distinguishes state capitalist countries which are very heavily dependent upon oil exports to support state-organized development work; here Petras cites Algeria, Libya and Iraq. Fourth, there are the revolutionary regimes which are making changes in economic and social arrangement, but which are still fixed in a primary-product exporting role – for example, Cuba.

Similarly in the NIC category Petras finds great diversity. First, there are the colonial regimes (like Hong Kong) and colonial settler regimes (like South Africa). At which point one could think of adding in Israel, with its massive post-war immigration plus apparently limitless US economic and military aid. Second, Petras names dependent development regimes which have seen very high rates of economic growth, and, for some, equally spectacular growth of debt. South Korea, Taiwan, Singapore and Brazil are instanced. As regards the Asian trio, I would further divide them – an argument pursued earlier when I suggested that the four Asian NICs were really 2 + 1 + 1. Third, there are the state capitalist countries such as India. Fourth, we have revolutionary regimes such as China. On a substantive point, pursuing his debate with Warren, Petras reports that many of the NICs base their success on cheap labour and the question inevitably arises of the durability of their success – a point others have raised. Indeed, so far as Petras is concerned, apart from the Asian NICs there has been little real change. However, setting that debate aside, what Petras's essay neatly illustrates is the way marxists have characterized a diversity of post-colonial state forms. That there are a variety of forms is easily granted, but effectively characterizing them is more difficult. I will pursue this business of characterizing state forms, focusing on the idea of authoritarianism and looking at the example of Singapore.

We can begin with a polemical piece by Gook Aik Suan,[262] who characterizes the polity under the PAP as fascist. The PAP is seen as having masterminded the unrelenting delivery of Singaporean (and immigrant Malaysian) labour to the needs of the multinationals. Says Gook, having described the recent pattern of repressive and elitist social and labour measures:

> The fascist rule of the PAP in Singapore is necessitated by nothing other than the creation of 'stable' political conditions to allow Western imperialist exploitation . . . The Singapore 'economic miracle' that is so much lauded in the West consists of nothing more than a pragmatic strategy of prostituting itself to the different factions of foreign capital . . . The entire island is a Free Trade Zone to serve foreign capital.[263]

Gook finishes his discussion in the following way: 'When one muses at the number of fascist regimes that were once considered "to work" e.g. the Shah's and Park's, and which have since collapsed . . . there is abundant cause for optimism.'[264]

Again looking at Singapore, the local scholar Heyzer offers a similar, if considerably less polemical, analysis: Heyzer is interested in the cultural, political and social consequences of Singapore's development strategy. She also states that the idea of 'development' must encompass 'social development for the working poor'[265] and not just economic growth.

She compresses the history of Singapore into a note on the conflict between the 'populist movement' – the Chinese-educated trade union movement – and the PAP elite – who were Western-educated. A temporary alliance secured independence and then the PAP moved away from the populists and adopted the strategy of 'inviting in the MNCs'. In contrast, populist strategies revolved around the idea of moving away from dependent status.

Now the MNCs in the post-war period have gone in for transnational production; Singapore has been one of the overseas bases that have been set up by the MNCs. Singapore has thus, on this analysis, become integrated with the world economy as a subsidiary manufacturing centre. What have been the social, cultural and political consequences?

Heyzer remarks, echoing all our other commentators, that 'Central to the penetration of foreign big business in Singapore is the creation of a government–industrial bureaucratic network'[266] which encourages overseas capital and allocates local capital to a subordinate role. Local capital indeed tends to drift away from manufacturing and into services, property or small-scale industry.

This strategy of development has created a definite pattern of employment and reward. The author notes:

> The nature of foreign industries in Singapore and the

> bureaucratic network that has grown up side by side with industrialization have . . . [seen] the creation of a technocratic elite . . . the formation of a group of middle-level bureaucrats and technicians . . . the growth of a group of skilled workers and a mass of workers employed as cheap labour in labour intensive industries.[267]

She continues: 'In other words . . . the emergence of class polarizations.'[268]

Heyzer concludes that the administration's strategy is the result of three considerations: the Singapore economy was always orientated to the world market and 'independent development' would be difficult; the MNCs offered a readily available 'package'; the local political scene demanded that results be produced quickly. The PAP administration's actions are thus perfectly intelligible, but the 'package' does have a price tag. Thus Heyzer notes:

> The state and its bureaucracy had developed a highly authoritarian character, disallowing actions and programmes that do not fit in with a state or elite-defined social reality . . . [there has been] the creation of a highly stratified system . . . To conclude, if we take development, in the broadest sense of the term to be the banishment of human suffering and the promotion of human creativity, the development strategy followed by Singapore leaves much to be desired . . . cannot a more socially appropriate development model be followed?[269]

Thus far we have focused upon the state and have taken note of the marxist theorists' stress upon both its central role in ordering society, and its key role in establishing linkages to the world capitalist economy. Matters of internal class relationships have been alluded to, but not pursued in any very great detail. However, the business of the way in which dependent economic linkages are expressed within the peripheral society is important: the relationship of dependency is not that of a passive victim having a local agent colluding with foreign economic powers: it is, rather, an active exchange of a broader nature. We can now usefully pay some more careful attention to this business of class within peripheral capitalist states. This can be done by looking at the work of Brennan,[270] whose particular concern here is with class and ethnicity.

The most general point urged by Brennan is that ethnicity in Malaysia is a convenient, if dangerous, source of legitimation for class groups. Thus a Malay–Chinese ruling class controls its lower classes by invoking ethnicity. Brennan thinks that it is an obvious and dangerous strategy, and, moreover, one that is becoming increasingly implausible as the transparency of class divisions grows. To begin, Brennan grants the crucial role of the state and then looks to illuminate class relationships as they revolve around the state. Three main class groupings are identified: the dominant/ruling class, the petit bourgeoisie, and the dominated classes.

The ruling group comprises four elements. First, the Malay aristocracy which wielded political and economic power in the pre-colonial situation. The arrival of the British altered their position: the sultanate retained a significant measure of political and economic power but was simultaneously marginalized as the implanted capitalist mode of production grew. In the post-independence period it has attempted to recover economic power and Brennan argues that the ideology of 'bumiputraism' is an attempt to legitimate this atavistic aspiration. In practice, an alliance has been formed with other groups, including the second element, landlords. Here it was the British who created landlords by introducing private property in land. A landlord class has emerged in the kampungs and, argues Brennan, wields considerable power. The third, and arguably key, element of the ruling class is the new state bureaucracy (civil servants, police and military), or at least its higher echelons. These three elements of the ruling group find expression in the UMNO (United Malay National Organization) – they represent the 'hegemonic fraction'. Attached to this core trio are the comprador capitalists, mainly Chinese and allied to UMNO via their own association, the MCA (Malaysian Chinese Association). Evidently this 'ruling class' is a complex grouping with extensive scope for conflicts.

The second major class grouping identified by Brennan is labelled 'petit bourgeoisie': largely urban and comprising the middle-ranking apparatchiks, professionals, and small-scale capitalists. This group has been loyal to the status quo, notwithstanding some parties of a 'social democratic' type. In passing, we can note that these the sort of people that theorists such as Hamilton, Feith, and so on, saw as becoming disenchanted with repression: there is not much sign of this here, it would seem.

The third grouping Brennan labels the 'dominated classes', which can be seen to comprise three elements: peasantry, plantation and mine workers, and an urban proletariat. The Malay peasantry has its origins back in the semi-feudal mode of production of pre-colonial days, but its circumstances have altered drastically with the extension of the capitalist mode. Private property, cash cropping, wage labour – all give rise to a particular class identity. But this class identity is overlain by the closely linked trio of 'Malayness', Islam and UMNO. In contrast, the largely immigrant plantation and mine workers – Chinese and Indian – have, in the past, discovered and articulated a class identity. But this was suppressed by government; the isolation of workers in mines and, in particular, on plantations makes control that much easier. Finally, there is an increasingly large urban proletariat. The interesting demographic feature of this proletariat is its increasing Malay element as migration from rural to urban areas occurs. This may have significance for the future, but at the present time workers' organizations are tightly controlled.

The strategies of control pursued by the ruling class derive from that class's own internal tensions and its external links to the world capitalist system: the rulers are, notes Brennan in passing, a 'neo-colony'.[271] Thus, internally, we find: 'The articulation of modes of production and uneven development in Malaysia which has given rise to conflict between fractions of the ruling class has in the past led to the burgeoning of a strongly interventionist state'[272] – a point Petras made, in general terms, above. The hegemonic fraction is, as noted, the ethnic Malay trio, with the Chinese comprador capitalists as the junior partner. Externally, argues Brennan, 'this hegemonic fraction is almost totally dependent upon international capital which supports it as a class because it allows the further penetration of imperialism into the formation.'[273] The exchange between the 'senior trio' and 'junior partner' is fraught with difficulty as both must appeal to racial sentiment to help justify themselves (and thus disguise the class nature of the state) and simultaneously must clamp down on ethnic tension lest it erupt in violence. It is a precarious position, and, again, it reinforces the tendency to an authoritarian interventionist state.

UMNO is the political vehicle of the dominant hegemonic fraction; three control strategies, additional to the racial manipulation cited, are used. First, amending the constitution – that is, changing the rules of the game so as to pre-empt or 'dissolve' problems. Thus in 1984 Prime Minister Mahathir had the constitution amended so as to curb the power of the monarch, as the incoming king, the Sultan of Johor, was widely regarded as an unstable figure. If kings can be so treated, other groups are easy targets. The second technique is simple repression; and the third is ideological manipulation via, in particular, the mass media. Brennan comments: 'The official ideology of a benevolent government striving to build a prosperous multi-racial society is hammered home relentlessly.'[274]

Brennan concludes by reaffirming his view that appeals to ethnicity serve to legitimate and obscure power relationships in a class-divided, neo-colonial state. The author observes, finally, that even though this strategy is dangerous – race riots in extreme cases – the ruling group seems either unwilling or unable to tackle the basic inequalities of society.

So, in sum, marxists are concerned under this heading of 'superstructure' to look at the social and cultural consequences of particular economic patterns of activity. Of particular concern are the issues of the nature of class divisions and class activity, patterns of political debate – or ideology – and, in the Third World especially, the nature of the state. In the Third World we confront, so far as marxists are concerned, an implanted state – implanted in the first instance by colonial power, but continuing into the post-independence period. The post-colonial state is, on these examples of argument, the key to understanding patterns of dependent capitalist development.

Summary

I have now presented, with illustrative intent, a series of marxian analyses of Southeast Asia. It is appropriate to recall that it is the intention of such analyses to uncover the possibilities for the future lodged in the present of whatever society is being considered. Marxian analysis thus has a wholly particular style of enquiry: it considers the totality of any set of circumstances as it endeavours to uncover the forces for change contained there. In this illustrative material, I have looked at the world context of the Southeast Asian nations; then, more specifically, at the particular 'economic base' of the area. Matters of state, class and ideology I looked at under the heading of 'superstructure'. It is a fairly simple exegetical strategy – as was the one adopted for modernization theory – but it has the merit of making clear my central claim that social theorizing is concerned with arguing cases and not simply describing the world.

The material reviewed in this section has illustrated the nature of the marxist approach to analysing peripheral capitalist states in general, and Southeast Asia in particular. Thus we have been preoccupied with the nature of the exchanges between peripheral economies and the world economy: how these linkages are secured in practice; how they interact with local class relationships, and at what costs to which groups. Overall, there has been a concern with patterns of change through history and with discernible pressures for change in the present. All this may be contrasted with the basic scheme of stable, harmonious, smooth, evolutionary change presented by orthodox modernization theorists. It should be clear that these two approaches offer very different interpretations of the nature of the Southeast Asian scene.

It must be clear by now that marxists would see Southeast Asia as firmly lodged within the world capitalist economic system. The major exception would be Indochina and the People's Republic of China, areas which are both socialist and lay claim to marxian-based social systems. I have not treated these areas, as to do so would have doubled the length of this illustrative review! However, we may note that in respect of these 'socialist' areas of Southeast Asia there has been considerable debate. For the countries that we have discussed, analysis proceeds in terms of subordinate incorporation within the world capitalist system – Feith introduced, for us, the term 'neo-colonial'. This would be the most general label; thereafter, there would be more detailed debate as to the precise sets of economic and social dynamics operating within any one of these nations.

Indonesia and Thailand have: (i) large military machines which are routinely and extensively involved in government; (ii) largely rural, peasant populations; (iii) very limited and foreign-dominated industrial development (outside of the import-substituting sector); and (iv) close links with the USA. The military machine is very prominent in both countries, and commentators have doubted the commitment to development (however conceived) of these military groups. Even modernization theorists are pessimistic here.

The commitment to development of the ruling groups of Singapore and Malaysia would be granted by most commentators. However, both remain 'neo-colonial' modes of production, although both have, in Hamilton's phrase, created 'economic space' for themselves. Both remain, however, heavily dependent on foreign capital and large parts of the industrial sectors of both economies are foreign-owned. Marxist commentators would also say that the success in ordinary economic terms which both have secured has been gained at a very high social and cultural cost, and, moreover, that the burdens and rewards have been unequally spread. Both are unequal societies and – in Singapore especially – the cultural costs of post-independence changes have been high: Singapore is now actively being Westernized by the PAP. And within each of these countries ethnic tensions are evident. With Malaysia and Singapore the labels marxists would apply, within the general frame of 'neo-colonial', would call attention to Malaysia's primary-product exporting role and to Singapore's trading role. It is with this pair of states that disputes between marxists and modernization theorists would be most acute: for the latter, both states are success stories.

In the case of the Philippines there might well be more of a coincidence of view: the modernizers would see a presently economically moribund system presided over by an erratic dictator plus his oligarchic family clique. Undoubtedly, a 'breakdown' in modernization! The marxists would be similarly unimpressed, but would see the Marcos regime as a singularly inept variant of a steady procession of neo-colonial regimes that have been in power in the Philippines ever since the Americans first arrived in the closing years of last century. At the present time there seems to be no very obvious way forward for the country and, notwithstanding active communist guerilla groups, a shift to a more overtly military regime seems likely.

So much for the comparisons: again, like the sketches of the views of modernization theorists that I offered above, they are not to be taken too seriously. They serve to offer a brief summary of the sorts of argument strategies that we have looked at above. Marxists would talk in these terms about these nations but, as with the modernization summaries, my intention is illustrative only. For a sophisticated grasp of these debates and any substantive discussion, the detailed texts of analysis must be looked at.

In sum, there are, so far as I can see, no neutral theories in social science and thus, inevitably, no neutral social scientific discussions of Southeast Asia's development history and possible future. The earlier discussions of classical and contemporary theory, and the recently concluded illustrative review of ways of making sense of Southeast Asia's development career, carry the incontrovertible message that contemporary theories of development are constructed with reference to disciplinary traditions of enquiry that stretch back to the work of the nineteenth century; that theorizing development is an intellectually complex, problematical and creative exercise; and that current interpretations of the Southeast Asian scene are not and cannot be neutral and technical, but are themselves creative exercises in interpretation. They are ways of making sense. The burden of this position for scholarly enquiry is that theorists must be explicit in respect of the manner of their theory-construction. Other interested groups will proceed according to the pragmatic dictates of those interests: scholarship will have to characterize these various positions as it 'pursues the truth'. All of which reveals a distinctly more awkward task for social science than orthodox empiricists will allow.

Part 4
Making sense of development

Preamble

Thus far this text has been concerned to show: first, that social theorizing is a complex and creative business; second, that theories of development both draw on classical traditions of social theorizing and are themselves creative exercises in theorizing. Having reviewed the major post-Second World War theories of development in the light of these claims, we went on illustratively to review their application to Southeast Asia.

This final part of the text is rather more speculative: it enquires into the 'lessons for the future' that can be drawn from the foregoing material. Two areas of concern are presented – social theorizing *per se* and theorizing development – and a series of concluding remarks is offered. The gist of the latter being that as social theorizing is, in its classic guise, concerned to make practical and political sense of complex 'real world' situations, then so too must current attempts to theorize development be circumstance-sensitive and problem-specific.

15 Lessons for the future?[1]

The lessons of the post-Second World War career of development studies are considered in this final, rather more speculative and essayistic, chapter. I want to suggest that there are two broad sets of lessons: for our ideas about the nature of social theorizing and for our approach to theorizing development.

So, first, in respect of social theorizing, it can be argued that this should be seen as a diversity of loosely related modes of enquiry, each concerned to 'make sense' of the social world, with social scientific, scholarly thought as one of these modes of enquiry. One that is to be seen as centred *not* on the familiar model of the natural sciences, but, instead, formally, upon the 'dispassionate pursuit of the truth' and, substantively, as within the tradition of classical social theory which was established in the nineteenth century in Western Europe.

Turning, second, to development theory, it can be argued that the familiar post-war goal of the provision of technical recipes for ordering change is slowly giving way to a subtler appreciation of the complexity of the business of making sense of development, and the variety of particular interests that can be held in respect of 'development'. The upshot can be taken to entail both an attention to *specificity* of theorizing – to the time- and place-boundedness of attempts to solve problems – and to the broad *historical* scale of the processes of which development theorists speak.

Social theorizing

In the first chapter of this text I remarked that over the years there had been much debate about the precise intellectual status of social science and I went on to offer a brief summation of these very complex debates in terms, taken from philosophy, of a distinction between 'empiricism' and 'rationalism'. This scheme drew upon certain recent debates within the philosophy of social science. Moving on a little from these preliminary remarks, I will sketch in these debates by presenting a three-part characterization of the nature of social theorizing. This characterization draws on the work of Habermas and, intellectually, it can be lodged within both the philosophical rationalist tradition and (though rather less obviously) the humanist marxian school.

The political philosopher Fay[2] is concerned with how ideas about society affect our actions within society. In orthodox social science these matters are divorced as theorists insist upon a distinction, which goes back to the philosopher Hume, between 'matters of fact' and 'matters of value'. On the basis of this split, orthodox theorists report that social science merely describes the facts and has nothing to say about valuation – the basis of action – which business is best left to political philosophers to discuss, and moralists, politicians and private citizens to practise. Fay objects that this view wholly distorts the nature and role of social theory because there are logically necessary relations between social theory and political practice. The realm of the social sciences is then divided into three: positivist, interpretive and critical.[3]

Mainstream social science is characterized as both affirming the familiar model of the natural sciences and as aspiring to produce knowledge of the social world of a kind precisely analogous to that of the natural world produced by natural scientists. The orthodox aspire to the production of causally precise knowledge. In the natural sciences, argues Fay, explanation is understood as the ability to control conditions so as to secure a predicted state of affairs. Thus explanation, prediction and control are linked. So in the social sciences, conceived in this fashion, social theory engages with the world, or is available for use, in a technical, manipulative, expert fashion. Social scientific knowledge is thus *essentially* about controlling the social world: Fay calls this 'policy science'; it is the social theory of the social role of 'planner'. And, clearly, within orthodox development theory, arguing on behalf of the planners is an utterly routine mode of enquiry. Fay thinks that this position is formally incoherent – thus, having insisted on splitting fact and value so as to treat only the facts, it then proceeds in an evidently value-laden way – and issues in a manipulative and restricted politics: that is, a political approach that attempts to reduce (public) politics to (expert) planning.

An alternative is to be found within the tradition of interpretive social science where the idea of understanding comes to the fore as the overall conceptualization of the social is sharply reformulated. No longer is 'the social' to be seen as a realm of causes and effects amongst objects – with human beings as a (peculiar) variety of object – but, instead, as a language-based realm of meanings. The relation of theory and practice implied similarly alters from technical–manipulative to the enhancement of the possibilities for communication. Interpretive social science offers social actors new possibilities for action by offering new interpretations. However, Fay lodges two objections to interpretive social science. In the first place, interpretive social science leaves no space for the conditions which surround and give rise to action. In my terms, it leaves out the real history in which social practices necessarily are embedded. In the second place, argues Fay, the scheme of the relationship of theory and practice affirmed is unsatisfactory: this is for two reasons. First, that interpretive social science does not treat resistance to the 'free communication' which it posits. Thus people might not want to hear what the interpretive theorist says: behaviour in society and self-image are closely linked, so new interpretations may offer unwelcome challenges to established self-images. And, second, interpretive social science is conservative in that it tends to explain conflict in terms of 'breakdowns of communication' and thus rules out consideration of questions of differences of interest – as between, say, First World and Third World where, for example, the failure of the NIEO programme clearly was *not* a simple breakdown in communication.

The critical social sciences endeavour, on Fay's account, to integrate theory and practice in their scheme of social theory. Critical theory acknowledges the usefulness of interpretive categories but, significantly, adds in sets of conditioning circumstances (that is, history) and links theory and practice by having the theorist enter into dialogue with particular social groups. The objective of this dialogue is the fostering within the 'target group' of a clearer understanding of 'how the world works' and, consequently, the establishment of a more effective social practice. Both partners to this exchange are taken to be equal – it is a *mutual* learning process, a dialogue. This notion of dialogue is central to critical theory: it takes active involvement in the world to be a necessary aspect of the pursuit of social science. We can further note here both that critical theory is the, arguably remote, inheritor of the marxian tradition, and that this scheme of 'critique' has itself been criticized as distinctly idealist and – notwithstanding its own claims – rather disengaged from the real world.

However, despite continued discussion of these schemes, this trio of varieties of social science offered by Fay represents a reasonable sketch, from a rationalist and humanist marxist (critical theory) stance, of the debates that have been pursued over recent years. The familiar claims of the orthodox to have settled the *object* of social science and its *method* in the structural functionalist analysis of industrial (and, by extension, industrializing) societies cannot now be accepted. In place of the confidence that First World social science displayed in the 1950s and early 1960s, when the orthodoxy reigned supreme, there is now a routinely expressed doubt as to the precise nature of social science.

This loss of surety has seen a variety of responses and these can usefully be detailed after the style of Giddens.[4] I will then go on to add a note on how, in my view, the issue of the nature of social theorizing looks in the light of the 'lessons' of the post-Second World War career of development theory.

Giddens has identified three responses to the reawakening of debate about the nature of social theorizing consequent upon the attacks made upon the positivistic orthodoxy: the despairing, the dogmatic, and the celebratory. In their place he espouses the programme of a systematic reconstruction of social theory.

The despairing response is a familiar one: the argument goes that if specialists in social theory cannot agree amongst themselves, then 'ordinary practising social scientists' would do well to leave them to it and get on with some useful practical work. This is the 'appeal to usefulness': reasonable men and women, it is claimed, can agree on a whole range of problems that need tackling and it is precisely these problems that ought to be addressed. Further, it has been argued that if social scientists were to resolve to act in this fashion, then many of the strained and peculiar sceptical doubts of those preoccupied with theory will disappear, anyway, and intellectual productivity will be restored: Myrdal has adopted this view. However, tempting as these responses are, they neither settle the issues outstanding and nor are they themselves 'theory-free'.

The dogmatic response is equally familiar. In the face of the confusion there is an appeal to a figure of authority whose work can be taken to have either settled or perspicaciously discussed (or 'anticipated') all the outstanding issues. Appeals are made, rather routinely, to both Marx and Weber; associated with the former case is the cautionary example of the degeneration of marxism into Marxism–Leninism that took place in the USSR after the revolution. Recently, within orthodox economics there has been an appeal made to Hayek (and thence to Adam Smith) as the authority whose work establishes the core of free-market theories. There are dogmas of the 'right', as well as those of the 'left'. However, there must be many ways of dogmatically invoking authority – the orthodox celebration of the natural sciences being an obvious and 'non-political' instance – and, as Giddens says, they avoid rather than confront and solve the issues.

The celebratory response embraces debate as offering both freedom from intellectual dogmas of all varieties and evidence of the inherent creative diversity of human thinking. The pursuit of social theoretic novelties is thus, at least tacitly, encouraged. This is an essentially optimistic response and, as such, Giddens approves. None the less, he wants to curb this enthusiasm and order this diversity, rather than simply acknowledge or enthusiastically add to it. Now Giddens's point about retaining a significant measure of coherence in our severally developed social scientific enquiries is a good one, which he develops in terms of a programme of the systematic reconstruction of social theory.

This systematic reconstruction would be centred – to simplify – on the scheme Fay called 'critical theory'. This is a sophisticated and influential position: in recent years, the elaboration of ideas of critique has been a social scientific 'growth industry'. However, this pursuit of a systematic reconstruction seems to me to be open to the rather obvious objection that it will encourage the construction of a new orthodoxy: it is not at all clear to me that social science needs another orthodoxy.

If we contextualize these debates, it is apparent that Giddens's project is 'theory-driven': that is, Giddens arrives at the requirement for a systematic reconstruction from a consideration of theoretical debates. These debates have, moreover, been conducted at a very high level of philosophical abstraction. However, if we call attention to the post-Second World War career of development studies and ask if this holds any lessons for social theorizing itself, then, it seems to me, we are obliged to grant that social theorizing is both diverse in its styles and (usually) concerned to make sense of problematical 'real world' situations. This seems to me to be the most appropriate starting-point for our post-consensus reflections and the upshot – to recall Giddens's criticized trio – is a position of mitigated celebration.

Thus if we simply look at what has been proposed as 'social theory', then it is clear that we confront no single 'object'; rather, we find – to borrow an overworked metaphor from Wittgenstein[5] – a *family* of activities. This 'insight' is easily gleaned from reviewing either the history of social theorizing generally or the post-war career of development studies. There is, so far as I can presently see, no reason for, or intellectual profit to be gained from, attempting to squash this diversity into a single mould. Social theorizing encompasses a multiplicity of strategies for making sense of the social world: unity and diversity. A general label might be useful – I am affirming a 'disintegrated' view of social theorizing. The substance of such a view can be *sketched* by offering an extended characterization of two views of the nature of social theorizing. Thus I will distinguish, as I did above, between social scientists who adopt some sort of empiricist stance, on the one hand, and, on the other, those who adopt some sort of rationalist stance.

To cast the matter of my interest in social science at a very general level I would say that my concern is with how actors, collectively, make sense of the social world. Now, clearly, orthodox empiricist theorists could also affirm this as their most general interest. It would be understood as the natural-science-referring description of structure: Bauman's 'Durksonian' social science.[6] For the orthodox theorists, the way in which actors make sense – and the way in which this can be appropriated by social science – is conceived in an essentially passive fashion. Thus social science gives a report on how sense has been made, how the world has been patterned: the social world is a reality *sui generis*. Social scientific enquiry is also, itself, cast in passive form: the provision of value-neutral reports on how things are – how the world has been patterned. The alternative approach is to see the business of making sense as essentially an active process and enquiry itself as active. The given is 'the process of structuration'[7] – the (re)creation of the patterned social world in and through patterned human action. This alternative approach also denies the appropriateness of the invocation of natural science made by the orthodox. A passive engagement with the material of enquiry is seen to be unpersuasively and arbitrarily restricted. Thus the alternative seeks reflexively to lodge the community of social scientists, as one group amongst many, within a society which is conceived as an interplay of processes.

It is this second-noted scheme which I find the more convincing. I use this general conception within a restricted context: thus my interest in making sense centres on those (more or less) deliberate or self-conscious efforts at what would ordinarily be recognized as social-science-type theorizing. So the paradigm case of my interest is the production of ideologies: sets of delimited–formal statements designed to interpret and guide action in the social world. Here, we find the matter of the effective contribution to structuration of actively produced ideas about structures. Thus the key term for my own views about the nature of social theorizing – how it is to be characterized, how it embeds in the social world, how it differs from natural science – is ideology.

For the orthodox social scientist, the production of knowledge is – as noted earlier – essentially a matter of reporting how things are, and problems cluster around accuracy of reports. The notions of science and ideology are resolutely divorced and ideology is seen as the repository for all the errors to which social science is prey if ever it becomes embroiled in matters of values. The contrary rationalist approach takes the production of social scientific knowledge to be less a matter of mimicking the supposed procedures of natural science and much more a matter of the construction of argument. And if social science is taken to revolve around argument-construction, then it is not possible to regard the history of social science as involving the production of ever-improving techniques for the description of an external given reality. It is, on the contrary, a history of particularly located efforts of argument-construction. Any progress in theorizing will be revealed in the ways in which arguments, appropriate to their circumstances, are constructed. The social scientific (and thus general) measure of progress must centre upon the skill with which arguments are crafted so as to uncover the truth. The multiplicity of pragmatic concerns which variously located social actors might have are measured internally and, thereafter, to the measure central to social science. The concerns, in respect of propriety of explanation, which are typical of this line of thought centre upon the matters of appropriate premises, theoretical frameworks, the role of valuation and the rational judgment of competing claims: upon, that is, the business of the construction, criticism and comparative ranking of ideological schemes.

The view of social theorizing and social science which I have been adumbrating runs counter to the post-war orthodoxy of social science. We have seen above that this orthodoxy is in decline. However, there are residual elements of that orthodoxy (and the orthodoxy of development studies) which remain powerful. Thus it seems to me that the common-sense image of natural scientific explanation, affirmed as *the* model of a useful and true explanation, occasions, quite routinely, a great deal of confusion in social theorizing.

The notion of 'received model' has been used by Giddens[8] to designate a particular conception of scientific enquiry around which a series of other views cluster as that model is deployed in the context of social scientific concerns. In its narrow sense, it is a (philosophically unsatisfactory) view about natural science; in its wider sense, it becomes an approach to social science. The image of natural scientific explanation and the presumption of the cognitive superiority of that mode of thought can be found both in 'lay' thought, or common sense as ordinarily understood, and in the common sense of social science. Consequently, to cast social theorizing in terms of 'discovering how things are in fact', as the orthodox do, is to run with the cultural grain in both a general and a particular way. It seems to me that this coincidence of disciplinary and 'lay' common sense – in respect of this matter – makes it all too easy for social theoretic enquiry to become intellectually deformed.

Now the gist of my own claims in respect of the nature of what is ordinarily labelled 'social science' rests on the view that social theoretic engagement is about making problem-specific and circumstance-sensitive sense of particular, problematical situations. The specific role for scholarship (social science) seems to be interpretive commentary oriented to the display of the truth. Now this may seem utterly familiar and even banal; but the point is that the business, thus conceived, is *not* reducible to the collection and description of facts. Scholarship is a particular process and it has its own particular embedding within the generality of processes in the social world. The formulations of scholarly social science have (if they are good, or lucky) their own impacts upon the business of structuration: via, in the main, the dissolving of fixed, interest-group-serving, confusions of thought within a society's politico-social culture.

In sum, following the eclipse of the social scientific orthodoxy, and taking on board the 'lessons' drawn from the career of development studies, the present author's favoured response is a mitigated celebration which bases itself firmly within the rationalist and humanist marxian traditions. That there are a variety of modes of social theoretic engagement can be granted and this diversity can be ordered by relating present forms to the established models of classical social theory. Thus, most centrally, social theorizing – which generically is concerned with making sense of problematical social situations – entails the construction, criticism and comparative ranking of ideological schemes designed to interpret the world and guide action within it. This, it seems to me, captures the core of the classical tradition of social theorizing. Against this we can range formal, scholarly, social science as a sub-type oriented to the dispassionate display of the truth. Other modes of social theoretic engagement can be characterized by social scientific study and may be both located and judged in relation to this central historical tradition.

Development theory

Over the past forty years, since the end of the Second World War, students of development have produced a vast amount of material: 'development' has been a major concern for governments, international agencies, social scientists and others. A survey of the outlines of this material was offered above. To propose any general conclusions, or point to any lessons that can be drawn from this experience, requires that we grasp this career in a simplified form. It seems to me that we can do this by pointing to the pursuit, by orthodox theorists most obviously, of an autonomous disciplinary status for the study of development. The failure of this project – and the analogous shift from an activist optimism that naively celebrated revolution to a more sober theoretical reflection on historical processes by marxist theorists – is, it seems to me, thoroughly instructive in that it can serve to shift the study of development out of the technical ghetto it has inhabited and back into the mainstream of classical social theory.

I will first look at the orthodox theorists' 'pursuit of autonomy' and then go on to add a note on the process of the re-establishment of marxian analyses of development. I will finish with a few of the rather more specific 'lessons' for development studies that can be drawn from this post-war career: here, my remarks will centre on the business of planning.

It can be argued that the post-Second World War period has seen the attempt to constitute an autonomous discipline of development studies: autonomous in the intra-social sense of being one distinct social science amongst others; and autonomous in the extra-social sense of the study having its own external object and methods of enquiry appropriate thereto. This, clearly, is a strategy of conceptualization which is informed by the familiar model of the natural sciences. This attempt to constitute an autonomous discipline is identifiable in growth theory and modernization theory, where matters of development were conceived (variously) as an extension of positive economic science. But it is with the neo-institutional work of the 'dissenting economics' tradition (and *some* dependency work, in particular the 'early' Furtado) that claims to autonomous status were most forcefully and persuasively made. This autonomous discipline was to have as its object 'the process of development' and its method was to be a confident, practically oriented, multi-disciplinary and technical social science. The attempt to constitute an autonomous discipline of development studies failed for two general sets of reasons.

The first was the project's own inherent implausibility: it seems to me that failure was intrinsic to the attempt (made by academic theorists, technical experts in government and international agencies, plus a host of miscellaneous commentators) authoritatively to characterize the major elements of the process of transition to the modern world and to lay claim to particular, technical–manipulative expertise in respect of these identified elements. The overall problem area was both too complex and of interest to too many diversely located groups for it to be amenable to the process of reduction of attention and focusing of enquiry which must be necessary to the constitution of a 'discipline'. Failure was built in to the project design.

A second area of explanation for this failure is to be found in the success that repeated enquiry had in occasioning refinement of argument. From the narrowly economics-based work of the 'committee of experts' in 1951[9] there was refinement of argument, in concert with extensive practical experience, along two axes. First, there was a fairly obvious spread of enquiry. The work of a wide range of social sciences was called upon in the effort to theorize development. Second, there was a process of increasing reflective depth of enquiry. And when we put together this dual process of refinement, then we can plausibly argue that the career of development studies entails a progressive shift from a narrowly technical enquiry detached from the concerns of the mainstream of the social scientific tradition back into that mainstream.

The matters which students of development must now typically address are those of widespread and pervasive change and the extent to which it can be comprehended and its direction made subject to human will. The self-consciousness of students of development now coincides with that of other social scientists: it revolves around the continuing effort to render the nature of social theorizing clear. In sum, in roughly four decades the project first enunciated by the 'committee of experts', as a *technical matter*, has reached a point of being poised to crumble back into social philosophy, or *classical social theory*.

Turning to the marxian camp, we find a similar situation. There is within the marxian camp now much debate as to the precise nature of a properly marxian analysis of development. That this question should exercise marxian theorists is not all that surprising: marxism, both generally and in respect of treatments of development, has returned to intellectual respectability only over the last fifteen years or so. As this process of rediscovery progressed, attention was directed not only to substantive issues but also, reflexively, to the very intellectual machineries being used. There is, of course, a simple contrast to be drawn here between orthodox and marxist theorists: the orthodox theorists had by the post-war period an agreed approach – a consensus – and they supposed that the major problems of social science and methods appropriate thereto were known. Theorizing development simply entailed the application of known intellectual tools to novel situations. For the marxists – emerging from the deserts of 'Marxism–Leninism' – there was no such confidence: the marxian revival was self-conscious from the outset. Amusingly, of course, the consensus of the orthodox has now disintegrated and they face analogous problems to those in the marxian line who, having represented their traditions in *neo-marxist* guise (especially A. G. Frank), now, in the wake of much intense debate, are confronted with the task of securing their approach within the intellectual marxian tradition and deploying it persuasively and to practical political effect.

In sum, I would suggest that there is currently within development studies a widespread disquiet, shared by bourgeois and marxist alike, as to the real nature of the enterprise. I think that this impulse to 'rethink' development coincides with a general impulse to 'rethink' ideas of social theorizing itself: both lines converge on the tradition of classical social theory.

Turning, finally, to some of the more specific 'lessons' of this progressive rediscovery by students of development of the mainstream of social science, there are a series of points to be made. The ideas of orthodox theorists have centred upon one notion of how change might be expected to take place – that is, by planning – and this we must consider. Relatedly, there is the business of ethics of change as both liberal democratic and nationalist developmental schemes can be questioned.

The first area of concern centres on the idea of *intervention*. Confidence amongst theorists, especially the orthodox, in the 'planning mode of social theoretic engagement' has suffered in recent years as a result of both intellectual challenge and 'real world' failure. The intellectual challenge both calls into question the actual effectiveness of the skills claimed by planners and asks new questions in respect of the political, social and cultural *costs* of the societal pursuit of expert-designated goals. Relatedly, there has been comparatively little success in securing 'development', notwithstanding all the effort. Instances of success, like the Asian NICs, are seen to offer deeply ambiguous lessons, as we noted above.

However, that the idea of intervention should figure crucially in studies of development is not surprising. The idea was available within the historically recent experience of the First World. In the political–intellectual realm there had been the experience of the USSR – successful and influential, argues Clairmonte[10] – and the work of Keynes. It is with the name of that great economist that in the First World the legitimacy of planning can be associated: Keynes made it respectable and safe. In the economic realm, the requirement of planning was systemic. The nature of the capitalist system had, by the 1930s, clearly entered into a period of change – and whilst the upshot has been variously labelled (monopoly capitalism, advanced capitalism, welfare capitalism), the key to these changes resides in the dual process of economic concentration (private- and public-sector monopolies dominating a residual, if extensive, market sector) and state direction.

Indeed, so extensive has the role of the state become in monopoly capitalism, so pervasive its involvement in the lives of its citizens, so routinized the pressure to a technocratic politics, that the possibilities of a reconstruction of the public sphere – the key to a politics adequate to modern society – have become a principal concern for the inheritor of the mantle of the Frankfurt School, Jurgen Habermas.[11] This realization of the essential ambiguity of the system-sustaining role of the monopoly-capitalist state has not, of course, been restricted to Habermas. However, it seems fair to report that it was with the New Left in Europe and the USA in the late 1960s and early 1970s that consciousness of the manipulative, restricted competence of the technocratic planning state was first fully enunciated.

Within the context of development studies, these doubts in respect of 'intervention' have moved in two related areas. In the first place, doubt has grown about the claims of the planners to possess the expertise necessary to secure elite-directed, manipulative social change. Claims have been modified, sights lowered and expectations brought under control. The related area and, one suspects, the place where doubt first arose, centred on the perceived interference of the First World in the affairs of putatively sovereign nation states – most notoriously, by agencies such as the World Bank and the IMF. In the face of claims to neutral technical status, the suspicion quickly grew that these agencies embodied sets of values and politics inimical to the interests of the Third World.

This immediate political suspicion on behalf of Third World states has a broader counterpart in the scepticism of the neutrality of planning associated with the New Left. The post-war celebration of authoritative intervention seems to be based on an eventually untenable conception of the relationship of social-scientifically-informed experts to their social world. It can also be noted that a belief in the real possibility of a 'science of the social' goes hand in hand – and has been historically illustrated – with a disposition to force recalcitrant social reality into pre-expected forms when schemes go awry. Putatively authoritative planning can quickly take on the guise of authoritarian politics. It is at this point that doubts emerged about the political, social and cultural *costs* of reliance upon ideas of intervention.

To these growing doubts as to the precise nature of interventionist planning we must add that there has been comparatively little success in actually securing planned change in the Third World. There are, of course, exceptions – such as the Asian NICs – but these exceptions are, notwithstanding their interest to theorists, in world terms comparatively insignificant. Indeed, if one pursues this issue of intervention generally by asking just how successful has this strategy been in securing major change, then the answer produced is that major change seems to be systemic–historical, so to say, rather than the result of planning-type initiatives. An obvious example is the process of dissolution of formal colonial empires that created the 'new nation states' of the Third World. This dissolution was not a planned initiative; it was, rather, the unstoppable by-product of the dislocations attendant upon the Second World War. The present-day international network of nation states is most unlikely to have emerged without that disruptive episode.[12]

Theorists of development can now appreciate both the complexity of theorizing development and the unevenness of social advance. Social change is slow – Marx observed, famously, that 'men make their own history, but not as they choose.' To this we might usefully add – 'nor at the pace they might desire.' Thus if the actual effectiveness of planning initiatives is in doubt, and if there are intellectually well-grounded doubts in respect of the possible social, political and cultural costs of state-sponsored interventionism, then there seems to be little reason for scholarly commentators, or active groups (including states) within the Third World, uncritically to embrace these ideas: in the face of the hugely complex business of development, clear areas of effective action and specific restricted expectations need to be indicated.

Within the context of First World social theory, ideas of planning have tended to be associated with ethics of social reform. In the area of development theory, it seems fairly clear that, for the orthodox, an ethic of 'liberal reformism' has been operating. It is probably safe to cite neo-institutionalism as the 'best example' of the use of this ethic. In this tradition, what is to count as development or progress is taken as specifiable in terms of the enlightened role of government. However, this reliance upon an ethic of liberal reformism cannot be sustained. There have been 'practical' objections to it, most notably the 'Islamic revival', and widespread (and justified) charges of paternalistic cultural neo-colonialism. The theory-derived general objection to the orthodox reliance upon liberal reformism flows from my crucial claim that social theorizing must be circumstance-sensitive and problem-specific: what is to count as development in any particular situation will depend precisely upon the future possibilities of that situation identified in part in the light of the judgments of the groups involved. Again, a matter of ideology-making and, again, to be judged first in its own terms and then in terms of scholarly social scientific criteria.

These criticisms of ethics of liberal reformism are familiar. Perhaps less familiar are questions aimed at the coherence and legitimacy of the ideology of nationalist developmentalism. This ideology has been part of the common experience of the new nations of the Third World and it is also an utterly routine element of the common sense of orthodox development studies. The essential claim embodied in the position can be presented by recalling Gellner's work, wherein he observes that a society today is legitimate in the eyes of its citizens if it is nationalist and if it is industrial or industrializing.

The extent of the ideology's coherence/legitimacy can be approached by noting that the position was as much a product of a particular set of circumstances as was the liberal reformist interventionism discussed above. Commentators have noted that the drive for independence depended upon an alliance of elites and masses – the one interested in political power and the other in socio-economic reforms – and that in the post-independence period this alliance has broken down. Political power has more often been used for the division of the spoils than it has for the pursuit of nationalist developmentalist goals.[13] How we actually read the record of any particular regime will be a matter of specific enquiry and judgment: my general point is that if the 'real world' pattern is more complex than familiar ideology allows, then students of development would do well to acknowledge the situation.

Finally, we can observe that the crucial errors of the orthodox were in seeing 'development' as a rather obvious goal and one to be secured via technical–manipulative social science: this viewpoint was widely promulgated amongst the new elites of the new nation states of the Third World. Relatedly, the arguably key error of the resurgent marxist line was its overemphasis on political activism: upon, that is, schemes of revolutionary disengagement followed by the building of socialism. What must now, generally, be granted is the complexity of the business of development, the diversity of particular interests that various groups might have, the difficulty of specifying and securing changes and, finally, the *historical* scale of the processes involved in the whole business.

Concluding summary

The lessons for the future which can be derived tentatively from a review of the post-Second World War career of development studies are, broadly speaking, twofold: there are lessons for our ideas about the nature of social theorizing, and lessons for our ideas about development. My conclusions about 'development' flow from my views about social theorizing and I have noted them immediately above: the familiar search for a general theory or strategy of development must be abandoned as the task is incoherent.

For social theorizing (and thus theorizing development), it must be noted that making sense of the world – in terms which would be recognizable as in some measure 'social scientific' – is a routine part of the life of human social groups. It seems to me that academic social theorists must acknowledge both this multiplicity of modes of social theorizing and the requirement that they be precise about the character of their own modes of engagement. Mapping the field of modes of engagement and locating ourselves within that field seem to me to be prerequisites of coherent scholarly discourse. The attempt to reduce the multiplicity of modes of engagement to a single model, or a narrowly circumscribed set, seems to me to be a gross error. Thus the naturalist positivist orthodoxy of social science must be rejected: 'policy science' is *not* a plausible social analogue to natural science and it does *not* exhaust the range of possible modes of legitimate social theoretic engagement. Equally unfortunate for enquiry are the *political* 'received models' affirmed by more than a few marxists. It seems to me that we have to acknowledge the diversity and specificity of social theorizing: we confront in our academic role (itself context-specific) a series of situation–sensitive and problem-specific efforts of theorizing. They must be judged, in the first place, in terms of how successfully they achieve their own targets; thereafter, on various specifiable grounds, commentators (including scholars) can decide whether the target was clearly seen, or not, and in the end whether or not it was actually worth aiming at. Human beings are, amongst other things, value-bestowing – and this, I think, is the well-spring of all social theorizing.

Notes

Chapter 1 Social theory

1 See P. W. Preston, *New Trends in Development Theory* (1985), especially Chapter 2 which pursues these issues – how to characterize 'modes of social theoretic engagement' and how to relate them to one another. Academic social theorizing is characterized by its 'pursuit of the truth' (science); other modes may be ordered around this scholarly mode.

2 Often over the post-Second World War period this distinction, empiricism/rationalism, has been close to the distinction Anglo-Saxon and European.

3 See, for example, Sidney Pollard, *The Idea of Progress* (1971).

4 Gellner, borrowing Popper's 'critical rationalism', wants to adopt an idea of science which combines, so to say, the two traditions of empiricism and rationalism. Unfortunately, it cannot be done in this fashion and, in the event, Gellner's position ends up close to the empiricist position. His overall argument is thus ambiguous and unpersuasive as his calls for an authoritative planning rest upon this unsatisfactory notion of science.

5 E. Gellner, *Thought and Change* (1964), p. 179.

6 This particular section is loosely based on A. D. Smith's *Social Change* (1976), which is a useful introductory text.

7 Ankie Hoogvelt, *The Third World in Global Development* (1982), pp. 208–9.

8 Smith, *op. cit.*, pp. 34–6.

9 A. D. Smith, *The Concept of Social Change* (1973), pp. 27–8.

10 All this is pursued at greater length in 'The Ethico-Political Notion of Development: A Memorandum on Commitments', in Preston, *op. cit.*

11 The precise nature of 'intervention' is unclear. In principle, these theorists see the 'free market' as needing no intervention from the state beyond minor corrections and rule-setting. In the First World intervention is thus protective and in the Third World it is to initiate a process of economic growth regarded as subsequently semi-auto-

matic. In reality, state intervention is extensive in both First and Third Worlds.
12 S. H. Alatas, *Modernization and Social Change* (1972), Chapter 1.
13 *Ibid.*, p. 4.
14 *Ibid.*, pp. 8–9.
15 *Ibid.*, p. 13.
16 *Ibid.*, p. 17.
17 *Ibid.*
18 *Ibid.*, Chapter 2.
19 A. Giddens, 'Agency, Structure', in Giddens, *Central Problems in Social Theory* (1979).

Chapter 2 Classical social theory and social change

1 For a good discussion of Marx, Weber and Durkheim, see Anthony Giddens, *Capitalism and Modern Social Theory* (1971).
2 P. Worsley, *Marx and Marxism* (1982), pp. 22–34.
3 *Ibid.*, p. 22.
4 *Ibid.*, p. 25.
5 *Ibid.*, p. 26.
6 Giddens, *op. cit.*, p. 4.
7 *Ibid.*, p. 5.
8 See Giddens, *op. cit.*, or S. Lukes, 'Alienation and Anomie' in P. Laslett and W. G. Runciman (eds), *Philosophy, Politics and Society*, 3rd series) (1967).
9 K. Marx and F. Engels, *Selected Works* (1968), p. 181.
10 Worsley, *op. cit.*, pp. 47–56.
11 R. Williams, 'Base and Superstructure in Marxist Cultural Theory', *New Left Review*, no. 82 (1973).
12 Worsley, *op. cit.*, p. 52.
13 Giddens, *op. cit.*
14 See, for example, M. C. Howard and J. E. King, *The Political Economy of Marx* (1975), or G. Kay, *Development and Underdevelopment: A Marxist Analysis* (1975), or Worsley, *op. cit.*
15 For a discussion of the 'labour theory of value', see Joan Robinson, *Economic Philosophy* (1962), Chapter 2. Also R. L. Meek, *Studies in the Labour Theory of Value* (1956) cited by Giddens. *op. cit.*
16 Giddens, *op. cit.*, pp. 50–2.
17 See R. Brenner, 'The Origins of Capitalist Development: A Critique of Neo-Smithian Marxism', *New Left Review*, no. 104 (1977). A shortened version is reprinted in Hamza Alavi and T. Shanin (eds), *Introduction to the Sociology of the 'Developing Societies'* (1982).
18 We can explain this by noting an element of the more technical economics which we set aside above. Surplus value is the basis of profit. Surplus value is generated in productive enterprise and this productive enterprise has two elements: *constant* and *variable* capital. Constant capital includes plant, machines, buildings, etc., whilst variable capital is the human labour employed. Only variable capital creates value – according to tenets of labour theory of value – and the ratio of constant to variable capital is called the *organic composition of*

capital. As profit derives from surplus value, the greater the organic composition (the higher the capital intensiveness) then the lower the average rate of profit. Absolute profit does not fall – the *rate* of return declines.

19 Giddens, *op. cit.*, p. 35.

20 Terrel Carver (*Karl Marx: Texts on Method (1975)*) explains in his Editor's Preface (pp. 3–45) that Marx undertook the *critique* of political economy because it was *the* social science of nineteenth-century bourgeois capitalism *and* it was marked by that society. A critique could dissolve its ideological (pejorative sense) façade and set the enquiry on its feet: such an enquiry would enhance the class–historical understanding (and thus action) of the proletariat. Carver also very usefully characterizes *the style of enquiry of political economy* – catholic in its intellectual scope and self-critical (see pp. 6–9) – *and Marx's idea of scientificity* – interpretive and prospective (see pp. 40–1).

21 K. Marx, *Grundrisse*, translated by M. Nicolans (1973), p. 83.

22 It has become routine within marxian discourse to distinguish (in some way or other) between 'class-in-itself' and 'class-for-itself' so that the element of human consciousness of group membership (and subsequent action in the light of such recognition) can be acknowledged.

23 Although here, in practice, the story is a little more complex. In the UK the landed aristocracy fused with the English industrial bourgeoisie – the one had money the other status (see John Fowles, *The French Lieutenant's Woman* (1969): Charles has status, Ernestina cash) – in a particular fashion and one which has, via ideologies of Englishness had an impact on the subsequent relative decline of the UK. This is argued by Tom Nairn (see 'Britain's Perennial Crisis', *New Left Review, nos 113–14*). Relatedly: the Sultanate in Malaysia (see *Far Eastern Economic Review* 30 June 1983).

24 See, respectively: H. Marcuse, *An Essay on Liberation* (1969); J. K. Galbraith, *The New Industrial State* (1967); Clark Kerr *et al. Industrialism and Industrial Man* (1960); Daniel Bell *The Coming of Post-Industrial Society* (1973).

25 Giddens, *op. cit.*, p. 39.

26 See Barrington Moore, *Social Origins of Dictatorship and Democracy* (1966). In Southeast Asia there are two rather obvious additional complications: (a) colonial and post-colonial 'interference'; (b) communalism and ethnicity.

27 This is close to my own favoured usage: ideologies are thus self-conscious strategies for interpreting the world so as to guide action in it. This is a rather 'idealistic', and indeed left–Hegelian version!

28 See A. Giddens, 'Ideology and Consciousness', in *Central Problems in Social Theory* (1979); G. Larrain, *The Concept of Ideology* (1979).

29 R. Milliband, *Marxism and Politics* (1977).

30 K. Marx and F. Engels, *op. cit.*, p. 37.

31 For a simple summary of Marx's scattered writings on the state, see

Ralph Milliband's 'Marx and the State', in R. Milliband and J. Saville (eds), *The Socialist Register* (1965).

32 His work on this book was interrupted – by the Russian revolution!

33 Gellner, *op. cit.*, p. 34.

34 Irving Zeitlin, *Ideology and the Development of Sociological Theory* (1968).

35 *Ibid.*, p. 109.

36 *Ibid.*, p. 108.

37 Aidan Foster-Carter, 'Neo-marxist Approaches to Development and Underdevelopment', in E. DeKadt and G. Williams (eds), *Sociology and Development* (1964).

38 G. Palma, 'Dependency: A Formal Theory of Underdevelopment or a Methodology for the Analysis of Concrete Situations of Underdevelopment?', *World Development*, vol. 6 (1978).

Chapter 3 Durkheim and the evolution of the division of labour

1 Ian Roxborough, *Theories of Underdevelopment* (1979), p. 3.

2 Subsequent references in parentheses are to the pages of Giddens's reader: *Emile Durkheim: Selected Writings in Social Theory* (1972a). References in Durkheim can be derived therefrom.

3 Durkheim, in Giddens, *ibid.*, p. 101.

4 *Ibid.*, p. 105.

5 A. Giddens, *Capitalism and Modern Social Theory* (1971), p. ix.

6 S. Lukes, *Emile Durkheim* (1973), Chapter 20.

7 Spencer was very popular with the US bourgeoisie around the turn of the century. They saw in his 'social Darwinism' a legitimating theory (excuse) for their own egocentric pursuit of wealth. In respect of Lamarckianism/Darwinism and their (mis)appropriation by social theorists, the relevant difference is this. In Darwin's theory it is the fittest who survive – that they are the fittest is evidenced solely by their survival. 'Fittest' does *not* mean 'best' and when (mis)applied to the social world does not mean 'socially most deserving'. Lamarck, another biologist, suggested that learned behaviour could be passed on in addition to basic genetic characteristics. Presented in a social context, this can be read as meaning that those who acquire social skills can pass them on – and may have inherited them. Thus it is the culturally best who survive in a competitive society because they are the fittest. 'Fittest' now means best.

8 See G. Hawthorn, *Enlightenment and Despair* (1976) for a history of sociology which identifies how *national* sociologies were formed.

9 I. Zeitlin *Ideology and the Development of Sociological Theory* (1968).

10 Giddens, *op. cit.*, (1971), Chapter 2.

11 *Ibid.*, p. 66. See also John Fowles, *The French Lieutenant's Woman* (1969).

12 Zeitlin, *op. cit.*, p. 235.

13 Marx, it is sometimes said, developed the radical elements.

14 As I indicated above, citing Giddens's readings, Durkheim thinks moral rules in society can indeed be studied empirically *and* that normality and pathology in social systems can be distinguished, again

empirically, just as a medical doctor can distinguish normal and pathological states of a human organism. Here we see that particular, and peculiar, fusion of *claims to expertise* with a *dissolution of ethical-based politics* which is so central to *corporatist* approaches to the social world.

15 Giddens, *op. cit.* (1971), p. 74.

16 See Roxborough, *op. cit.*, Chapter 1. See also R. Nisbet, *The Sociological Tradition* (1966), Chapter 3.

17 The new moral code of individualism is seen as a socially integrative ethic. This rather paradoxical claim is made intelligible if we take note that, for Durkheim, this term was *not* that of English political economy (where it meant a political – social ideology predicated upon natural egoism) and *nor* was it that of marxian humanism (where each individual was seen as uniquely creative in his/her socially located work). *Neither* is the term equivalent to Weber's (and Durkheim oddly does not seem to have come across Weber's work) cultured individual. Durkheim's notion designates an ethic of 'recognition of proper social niche', an acknowledgment of *unity in ordered individual diversity*. Zeitlin is rather scathing in his comments on this corporatist ethic: 'By some curious reasoning Durkheim concluded that, since each now has a sphere of action peculiar to him, this develops his individuality and personality . . . If one had thought that specialization had the opposite effects, i.e. that it fragmented the personality and stifled the free play of one's faculties, he would have been wrong' (Zeitlin, *op. cit.*, p. 245).

18 Lukes, *op. cit.*, Chapter 7.

19 A. Smith, *The Concept of Social Change* (1973), Chapter 2.

20 Zeitlin, *op. cit.*, p. 246.

21 *Ibid.*, p. 250.

22 *Ibid.*

23 *Ibid.*

24 *Ibid.*, p. 251.

25 In *The Rules* Durkheim argues that the field and mode of enquiry of sociology must be classified. He attempts to elucidate the notion 'social', using a schema of *externality* and *constraint*. Man is seen as being born into an *established social world* and the web of rules constituting society simply confronts the individual as a 'given'. A lot of *The Rules* is given over to distinguishing between *normality* and *pathology* in given social situations. Durkheim searches for normality/pathology in societies, using the analogy of the same in biology. He ends by regarding the 'normal' as that which is a functional requisite of the type of society in question. In response to the suggestion that this schema looks rather conservative, Durkheim says not – sociologists just see clearly how things are going anyway.

In *Suicide* Durkheim is concerned to investigate what he takes to be a symptom of the moral unsatisfactoriness of society. The issue of suicide was, it seems, often used as a vehicle for moral speculation by thinkers of that period. Durkheim looks to challenge them with his 'positive scientific approach' which looks at 'social facts' – he simultaneously advances the status claims he lodges for sociology by tackling what is ordinarily regarded as a paradigmatically *individual* phenomenon. Suicide he takes to be occasioned by 'upheaval in the organic conditions of society' – so what is the nature of these failures of integrative moral notions? He distinguishes between: (a) suicide *rates*; and (b) the aetiology of particular cases. It is the former he looks at. The suicide rate is seen to be *patterned* – so what is doing the patterning. He considers, and rejects, geographical and biological explanations and looks to *social* reasons. Thus he finds, for example, that there is a correlation between suicide rate and religion (many more Protestants than Catholics) – both prohibit suicide but the two churches have very different social characters. The Catholic church displays greater *integration*. It is this matter of social integration that Durkheim fastens on – thus, for example, unmarried people commit suicide more than married people. Conversely, suicide rates decline at times of national crisis. So there is a basic relationship: integration is inversely related to suicide. He presents a tripartite categorization: *anomic suicide*, which is linked to the loosening of the bonds in division of labour; *egoistic suicide*, which is a spin-off of the modern cult of the individual; and *altruistic suicide*, where the individual submits to the demands of a strong collective conscience, e.g. suttee.

In *The Elementary Forms* Durkheim pursues the matter of the origins of moral authority and the particular character of moral rules. Religion, for Durkheim, presents the source of all abstract thinking. In the area of moral ideas, Durkheim argues that religious precepts are the symbolic representations of the society itself – so by breaking moral rules the deviant is denying the society which, in Durkheim's view, actually created him – hence the use of retributive sanction. Durkheim elucidates the character of moral authority with reference to the (religious) distinction between the sacred and the profane. In this area of work, Durkheim involves himself both in anthropological enquiries into religious forms and in presenting theories of the sociology of knowledge.

26 See G. Rocher, *Talcott Parsons and American Sociology* (1974).

27 For a detailed argument, see B. Fay, *Social Theory and Political Practice* (1975), Chapters 1 and 2.

28 I do not, myself, think that Marx was scientistic. However, his economic work was turned into a rather wooden and implausible scheme by Soviet ideologists and their allies. The 'rediscovery' of the 'early' Marx, made in the 1920s in Europe, was thus set in the context of a prevailing scientistic reading of Marx. Their criticisms are thus understandable but, I think, overstated.

29 See A. Giddens, *Profiles and Critiques in Social Theory* (1982), Chapter 7 for a brief introduction to Habermas.

Chapter 4 Max Weber and the rationalization of the world

1 I. Zeitlin, *Ideology and the Development of Sociological Theory* (1968), p. 111.

2 See, for example, Z. Bauman, *Towards a Critical Sociology* (1976a) – the remark is, however, something of a commonplace.
3 This is precisely the sort of claim that is to be found in textbooks on structural functionalism.
4 Zeitlin, *op. cit.*, p. 112.
5 A. Giddens, for example, has spoken of a 'brittle synthesis' – see note 25, below.
6 S. Hughes, *Consciousness and Society* (1959).
7 See, for example, A. Giddens, *Central Problems in Social Theory* (1979), Chapter 7, or T. Benton *The Philosophical Foundations of the Three Sociologies* (1977), pp. 46–7.
8 Hughes, *op. cit.*, p. 288.
9 C. Antoni, *From History to Sociology* (1959), pp. 132–4.
10 Text cited in A. Giddens, *Capitalism and Modern Social Theory* (1971), p. 122 *et seq*.
11 These matters are discussed at length in A. Giddens, *Politics and Sociology in the Thought of Max Weber* (1972b) and very briefly in A. Giddens, *Capitalism and Modern Social Theory* (1971).
12 That 'process' he characterized in terms of the increasing *rationalization of the world*: and if we recall Zeitlin's comments on Weber's 'rounding out' of Marx's method, then this rationalization of the world' just looks like the dynamic of capitalist development written in an *ideal* and *generalized* fashion.
13 Giddens, in his discussion of Weber (*Capitalism and Modern Social Theory*), concludes his discussion of *The Protestant Ethic* by citing Weber's own view that his work effectively disposed of naive historical materialism. This may well be so; but we can reasonably ask whether or not the ideal-typical, cultural–historical (and, later, *cross*-cultural) enquiry adopted by Weber actually advances beyond the critical 'reconstruction of the real' through the historical materialist method which is the procedure Marx himself used. Weber would clearly hesitate in making such a claim (well advisedly, in my own view); however, as we will see later, Weber's vulgarizers have had no such inhibitions.
14 Recalling my citation of Zeitlin and adjustment to the view expressed – such that German national, and capitalistic, development was stressed – Carlo Antoni, anticipating the exegetical position adopted by Giddens, argues, of Weber, that: 'All of his activities centred around the nature of Bismarck's succession, that is, around life-possibilities of the Bismarckian empire as a modern state. Weber himself could never forgive Bismarck for having refused to allow the formation around him of a group of political talents capable of assuming the burden of his legacy . . . Above all, his sociology is a theory of the politician class, the absence of which in Germany appeared to him to be the gravest menace of all to the future of his fatherland' (C. Antoni, *op. cit.*, pp. 123–4).
15 H. H. Gerth and C. Wright Mills (eds), *From Max Weber* (1948), p. 32.
16 See, for example, J. E. T. Eldridge, *Max Weber: The Interpretation of Social Reality* (1971), 'Introductory Essay' and pp. 69–71.

17 G. Runciman, *Critique of Weber's Philosophy of Social Science* (1972).
18 This is the textbook structural functionalist position: see Alan Dawe, 'The Relevance of Values', in Arun Sahay (ed.), *Max Weber and Modern Sociology* (1971).
19 Antoni, *op. cit.*
20 Giddens, *op. cit.* (1971).
21 Hughes, *op. cit.*
22 See John Rex, 'Typology and Objectivity: A Comment on Weber's Four Sociological Methods', in Arun Sahay (ed.) *op. cit.*
23 There has been much discussion about Weber's methodological ideas. There has also over the years been much discussion about the nature of social science generally. Recent work in the philosophy of social science has rejected the positivist model of explanation in *natural* science. Putting matters very crudely, Weber's problem, so far as I can see it, is that having begun by affirming, individualistically, the methodological priority of 'meanings' and having at the same time affirmed an essentially orthodox descriptive notion of (natural) science, he has to contrive some link between the two. From this point we enter the confusing realm of 'explanations adequate at the levels of meaning and cause' – fortunately, Weber's focus on politics was so central that it imposes coherence upon what otherwise would be an impossible swirl of competing and irreconcilable philosophical/methodological commitments.
24 Antoni, *op. cit.* Cf. also Zeitlin, *op. cit.*, p. 158.
25 A. Giddens, *Politics and Sociology in the Thought of Max Weber* (1972b) – see the concluding remarks.
26 Zeitlin, *op. cit.*, p. 145.
27 R. I. Rhodes, 'The Disguised Conservatism in Evolutionary Development Theory', *Science and Society*, Vol. 32 (1968), p. 389.
28 Talcott Parsons is cited by Rhodes as reworking Weber and presenting him in his functionalist work: Weber contributes *action* (ideas) and Durkheim the evolutionist/functionalist elements. Parsons's 'pattern variables' are used in development studies to characterize traditional and modern. The patterns of intellectual borrowings/distortions are confusing: see Jamil Hilal, *Sociology and Underdevelopment, mimeo* (1970); A. D. Smith, *The Concept of Social Change* (1973), Chapter 1 esp. p. 3.
29 D. C. McClelland, *The Achieving Society* (1961); E. Hagen, *On The Theory of Social Change* (1962); D. Lerner, *The Passing of Traditional Society* (1958): all cited in R. I. Rhodes, *op. cit.*
30 Rhodes, *op. cit.*, p. 392.
31 B. May, *The Third World Calamity* (1981).
32 *Ibid.*, p. 2.
33 *Ibid.*
34 *Ibid.*, Chapter 9.

Bourgeois liberal theories

1 Ankie Hoogvelt, *The Third World in Global Development* (1982).

Chapter 5 Growth theory

1 See P. W. Preston, *Theories of Development* (1982).
2 K. Kurihara, 'The Dynamic Impact of History on Keynesian Theory', in R. V. Eagly (ed.), *Events, Ideology and Economic Theory* (1968), p. 127.
3 C. Napoleoni, *Economic Thought of the Twentieth Century* (1972), p. 64.
4 G. Kolko, *The Politics of War: US Foreign Policy 1943–45* (1968), p. 4.
5 *Ibid.*, p. 254.
6 See Anthony Harrison, *The Framework of Economic Activity* (1967), Chapter 3, pp. 82–6, for a discussion of these Keynesian-inspired institutions. See also, for a more detailed discussion, W. M. Scamell, *The International Economy Since 1945* (1980), Chapter 2.
7 Kolko, *op. cit.*, p. 624.
8 P. Streeten, *The Frontiers of Development Studies* (1972), Chapter 16.
9 M. M. Postan, *An Economic History of Western Europe 1945–1964* (1967), p. 14.
10 Seymour Harris, *The European Recovery Programme* (1948), p. 3.
11 D. F. Fleming, *The Cold War and Its Origins* (1961), p. 447.
12 *Ibid.*, p. 501.
13 G. Zeylstra, *Aid or Development*? (1977), p. 31.
14 Streeten, *op. cit.*
15 This is the fourth element I cited at the outset of this discussion of the backdrop to growth theory: it is a subsidiary 'cause', as must now be clear.
16 The term 'growth' appears in three ways: economic growth theories are those technical discussions conducted around the Keynesian-inspired work of Harrod. Subsequently, they are revised by Solow. Doctrines of economic growth refer to the general First World political position – adopted by the overwhelming majority of the citizens – which holds that steady growth is the responsibility of the government and 'society's right'. Growth theory, in my sense, is the theory of the time which tackled development in Third World.
17 B. Fay, *Social Theory and Political Practice* (1975), p. 19.
18 Kurihara, *op. cit.*, p.137.
19 *Ibid.*
20 H. Brookfield, *Interdependent Development* (1975), p. 30.
21 R. Harrod, 'An Essay in Dynamic Theory', *Economic Journal* (1939).
22 H. Jones, *An Introduction to Modern Theories of Economic Growth* (1975), p. 44.
23 *Ibid.*, p. 53.
24 Jones explains all this as follows. In the notation of the economists, what has to happen for there to be steady growth of the system is that Ga = Gw = Gn. If equation has the determinants of the various elements inserted, then the problem becomes clear. The elements that determine the three growth rates are independently set, only an accident will bring them into the relation demanded by steady growth

at full employment. This is the 'First Harrod Problem' and is a step towards his aim of showing that the system tends to stagnate. Apart from the inherent pessimism, this view clearly places a huge burden upon the planning agencies: when they intervene, they do so in a system that is not disposed to assist them. The 'Second Harrod Problem' might better be called a paradox. It is the problem of stability. If Ga diverges from Gw, then, within limits, it is likely to carry on doing so. Once the growth path is lost, the rational corrective behaviour of the entrepreneur is such that things get worse, not better. This problem is referred to as the 'knife edge': clearly not something to welcome in the basic logic of a development theory predicated upon authoritatively intervening in the system! Jones summarizes thus: 'Three central issues have been noted: (a) The *possibility* of steady growth at full employment. (b) The *improbability* of steady growth at full employment. (c) The *instability* of the warranted rate of growth' (Jones, *op. cit.*, p. 59).

25 See Napoleoni, *op. cit.*

26 Brookfield, *op. cit.*, p. 25.

27 None of this, let us note, went unchallenged. In the USA and in the UK especially (and also in Europe), there was strong opposition to the notions of planning. In 1944 F. Hayek published a critical text entitled *Road to Serfdom*: Hayek and his views have recenly come right back into fashion with 'monetarists'.

28 Zeylstra discusses an 'ideal-type' of aid. See Zeylstra, *op. cit.*, pp. 15–19.

29 R. F. Mikesell, *The Economics of Foreign Aid* (1968), p. 70.

30 J. White, *The Politics of Foreign Aid* (1973), Chapter 4.

31 UN, *Measures for the Economic Development of Underdeveloped Countries* (1951).

32 *Ibid.*, p. 9.

33 *Ibid.*, p. 38.

34 *Ibid.*, p. 50.

35 *Ibid.*, p. 85.

36 E. Gellner, *Thought and Change* (1964), p. 179.

37 Streeten, *op. cit.*

Chapter 6 Modernization theory

1 R. Aron, *The Imperialist Republic: The US and the World 1945–1973* (1973).

2 D. Caute, *The Great Fear: The Anti-Communist-Purges under Truman and Eisenhower* (1978).

3 G. Kolko, *The Politics of War: US Foreign Policy 1943–45* (1968).

4 Caute, *op. cit.*, p. 25.

5 *Ibid.*, p. 21.

6 J. White, *The Politics of Foreign Aid* (1973).

7 H. Jones, *An Introduction to Modern Theories of Economic Growth* (1975), p. 53.

8 H. Brookfield, *Interdependent Development* (1975), p. 30.

9 R. Solow, 'A Contribution to the Theory of Economic Growth', *Quarterly Journal of Economics* (1956).
10 R. F. Mikesell, *The Economics of Foreign Aid* (1968), p. 32.
11 D. C. Tipps, 'Modernization Theory and the Comparative Study of Societies: A Critical Perspective', in C. E. Black (ed.), *Comparative Modernization* (1976), p. 71.
12 *Ibid.*
13 G. Hawthorn, *Enlightenment and Despair* (1976), p. 242.
14 *Ibid.*
15 A. D. Smith, *The Concept of Social Change* (1973).
16 *Ibid.* p. 12.
17 *Ibid.*, p. 15.
18 Smith offers the following summary of his characterization of 'differentiation': '1. it is the chief motor of historical change; 2. it applies to all elements of social structure and culture; 3. it furnishes the basic framework for classifying types and stages of social structure; 4. it is inevitable and irreversible, in the long run; 5. it increases man's autonomy and society's maturity *pari passu* with its capacity for maximizing his control over nature, and therefore is a beneficial process; 6. it arises only within the context of the system, and the structure of its parts, and so is an immanent process' (*ibid.*, p. 18).
19 *Ibid.*, p. 21.
20 *Ibid.*
21 This trio of ideas is presented as the basic logic of neo-evolutionism. Neo-evolutionism is to be distinguished from (classical) evolutionism: the linkages beween the two are many and the changes in emphasis similarly complex – all these are treated by Smith. I will follow Smith in categorizing *types* of modernizaion theory with reference to their various uses of the basic logic of neo-evolutionism. However: (a) Smith writes as, I think, a historian interested in *explaining social change rather than development*, so his concerns and procedures of writing are different to mine; and (b) in modernization theory work, as *I* understand it, neo-evolutionism often gets jumbled up with evolutionism. Thus although I am here relying upon Smith, I am not offering a simple exposition of his work.
22 Smith, *op. cit.*, p. 65. Smith cites: R. Bellah, who has written on *religion and modernization*; and B. Hoselitz, who has written on *modernization,* using the 'pattern variables'.
23 I will pursue this point about dualistic characterizations (traditional–modern) below. For more detailed criticism, see: J. Hilal, *Sociology and Underdevelopment* (1970), pp. 4–10; A. G. Frank, 'Sociology of Development and Underdevelopment of Sociology', in A. G. Frank, *Latin America: Underdevelopment or Revolution* (1969).
24 Smith cites N. Smelser, 'Toward a Theory of Modernization', in *Essays in Sociological Explanation* (1968).
25 Brookfield, *op. cit.*, p. 53.
26 S. P. Huntington, 'The Change to Change: Modernization, Development and Politics', in C. E. Black (ed.) *op. cit.*, p. 30.
27 *Ibid.*

28 These 'pattern variables' are:

1 Universalism	Particularism
2 Performance	Quality
3 Affective neutraliy	Affectivity
4 Role specificity	Role diffuseness

This is the 'basic set': at places in Parsons's work there are five and six 'pattern variables'. In modernization theory, a variation of no. 2 is often used: achieved status/ascribed status.
29 See A. G. Frank, *op. cit.*
30 See Part 1, above: this is an aspect of the debate between rationalists and empiricists.
31 Huntington, *op. cit.*, p. 35.
32 A. G. Frank, *op. cit.* See also R. I. Rhodes, 'The Disguised Conservatism in Evolutionary Development Theory', *Science and Society*, vol. 32 (1968).
33 *Ibid.*, p. 40.
34 Huntington, *op. cit.*, p. 37.
35 *Ibid.*
36 *Ibid.*
37 W. W. Rostow, *The Stages of Economic Growth: A Non-communist Manifesto* (1960), p. 1.
38 *Ibid.*, p. 3.
39 *Ibid.*, pp. 12–13.
40 *Ibid.*, p. 14.
41 Clark analysed societies in terms of sectoral maturation: primary sector, secondary sector, tertiary, quaternary. The shift is from raw-material-producing to knowledge-based economies. (See Brookfield, *op. cit.*, Chapter 2.)
42 B. Higgins, *Economic Development* (2nd edn, 1968), pp. 174–87.
43 E. Hagen, *On the Theory of Social Change* (1962), pp. 514–22.
44 P. Baran and E. Hobsbawm, 'The Stages of Economic Growth', *Kyklos*, vol. 14 (1961).
45 W. W. Rostow, 'The Take-off into Self-sustained Growth', *Economic Journal* (1956).
46 The phrase 'New Frontier' was President Kennedy's and marked the intention of his administration to tackle social reform.
47 Brookfield, *op. cit.*, p. 38.

Chapter 7 Dissenting economics: neo-institutionalism

1 See P. W. Preston, *Theories of Development* (1982).
2 D. Seers, 'The Limitations of the Special Case' (1963), reprinted in K. Martin and J. Knapp (eds), *The Teaching of Development Economics* (1967).
3 P. Streeten, *The Frontiers of Development Studies* (1972).
4 G. Hawthorn, *Enlightenment and Despair* (1976).
5 H. Brookfield, *Interdependent Development* (1975), p. 99.
6 G. Myrdal, *The Challenge of World Poverty* (1970b), p. 268.
7 *Ibid.*, p. 21.
,8 By 'realistic', Myrdal and others seem to mean a model which is

adequate to the fine-grain of the 'real world'. It is to be contrasted to the abstract formal models of growth theory and the somewhat schematic models of modernization theory. The neo-institutionalists made much of this pursuit of realistic models as vehicles for understanding and ordering development. The earlier concern for economics, narrowly understood – that is, as one orthodox discipline of social science amongst others – drops out of sight.

9 Seers, *op. cit.*

10 See P. W. Preston, *Theory and Practice in Development Studies: The Neo-institutionalists in the Late 1950s and 1960s*', Leeds University, Occasional Papers in Sociology no. 11 (1981), for a much fuller version of this discussion.

Chapter 8 After modernization

1 See A. Hoogvelt, *The Third World in Global Development* (1982), Chapter 4.

2 *Ibid.*, p. 128.

3 *Ibid.*, p. 123.

4 The first (1972) report in particular; subsequent reports look more 'second generationist', especially in their approval of NIEO.

5 Hoogvelt, *op. cit.*, p. 79.

6 These points were sketched out in very great detail – but I do not think it would help us to pursue this detail; the history of development studies is littered with planning proposals.

7 In a report prepared at the Barlioche Foundation, Canada, and edited by A. O. Herrera *et al.*, entitled *Catastrophe or a New Society* (1975).

8 Hoogvelt, *op. cit.*, p. 100.

9 See Paul Streeten, *Development Perspectives* (1981), Chapter 19.

10 *Ibid.*, Chapter 18.

11 *Ibid.*, pp. 332–3.

12 See P. W. Preston, *The Common Sense of Development Studies: Elements of Reconsideration*, mimeo (1983), p. 3 *et seq.*

Chapter 9 Monetarism

1 For a discussion of the idea of 'residual common sense', see Part 4.

2 See P. Donaldson, *Economics of the Real World* (1973), Chapter 6.

3 Milton and Rose Friedman, *Free to Choose* (1980), p. 224.

4 Joan Robinson comments: 'The enormous ideological attraction of the Quantity Theory of Money, that kept it going for nearly forty years after its logical content was exploded [by Keynes], is due to the fact that it conceals the problem of political choice under an apparently impersonal mechanism' (J. Robinson, *Economic Philosophy* (1962), p. 93).

5 Jean Robinson, in a discussion of the fierce resistance put up against Keynes by the orthodox, of whom Friedman in this present sense is emphatically one, remarks that: 'There is also a psychological element in the survival of equilibrium theory. There is an irresistible attraction about the concept of equilibrium – the almost silent hum of a perfectly running machine; the apparent stillness of the exact balance of

counteracting pressures; the automatic smooth recovery from a chance disturbance. Is there perhaps something Freudian about it? Does it connect with a longing to return to the womb? We have to look for a psychological explanation to account for the powerful influence of an idea that is intellectually unsatisfactory' (*ibid.*, pp. 77–8).

6 Reagan represents the 'New Right' in the USA and they have extensive interests, direct and indirect, in the prosperity of the arms industry in the USA. See Mike Davis, 'The New Right's Road to Power' and Alan Wolfe, 'Sociology, Liberalism and the Radical Right', *New Left Review,* no. 128 (1981).

7 C. Furtado, *Economic Development in Latin America* (2nd edn, 1976).

8 P. J. O'Brien, 'A Critique of Latin American Theories of Dependency', in I. Oxaal *et al. (eds), Beyond the Sociology of Development* (1975), p. 9.

9 Furtado, *op. cit.*, p. 118.

10 *Ibid.*

11 Furtado speaks of demand–pull and cost–push, and he also criticizes the orthodox for focusing exclusively upon 'propagation mechanisms' within money flows. In terms of my present distinction between Keynesians and monetarists, it rather seems as if Furtado is happy to collapse them into a unitary position: we must bear with this lack of clarity for the present.

12 Furtado, *op. cit.*, p. 126.

13 For an excellent discussion, see *IDS Bulletin*, vol. 13, (1981), on monetarism and Latin American experience.

14 This essay appears in the collection *Essays in Positive Economics* (1953).

15 *Ibid.*, p. 4.

16 *Ibid.*, p. 39.

17 See P. W. Preston,'The Impact of the "Received Model" of Natural Science upon Social Theorizing', in *New Trends in Development Theory* (1985).

18 Robinson, *op. cit.*, p. 71.

19 *Ibid.*, p. 73.

20 See Milton Friedman, *Capitalism and Freedom* (1962), Introduction and Chapters 1 and 2.

21 C. B. Macpherson, *Democratic Theory: Essays in Retrieval* (1973).

22 *Ibid.*, p. 146.

23 At this point I will leave this material before we become too deeply embroiled in political philosophy: however, the matter of the nature of the modern capitalist system's legitimating ideology of liberal democracy is pursued by Macpherson. In his *Democratic Theory*, Chapter 1 addresses the *claims* made by liberal democracy, and Chapter 8 discusses the varieties of democracy. On this last point, see also C. B. Macpherson, *The Real World of Democracy* (2nd edn, 1972).

24 Maria Elena Hurtado, 'Fiesta to Fiasco: Chile's Free Market Hangover', *South* (May 1983).

25 *Ibid.*, p. 25.

26 Richard Gott, 'Pinochet's Last Stand', *Guardian Weekly* (1983).
27 For an angry, polemical, discussion of the work of the 'Chicago Boys' in Chile see A. G. Frank, *Economic Genocide in Chile: Monetarist Theory versus Humanity* (1976). See also Karel Jansen (ed.), *Monetarism, Economic Crisis and the Third World* (1983).

Marxist theories

1 Following the distinction of Ankie Hoogvelt, *The Third World in Global Development* (1982).
2 The distinction between *practical* and *technical* thinking has been a major concern of the German marxist social theorist Jürgen Habermas, who has diagnosed a routine error in orthodox social theorizing, and a crucial problem for modern industrial societies, in the *substitution* of technical (social scientific) thinking for practical (political) thinking. The upshot is a drift, or tendency, towards more or less authoritarian corporatism – and *away* from democracy.
3 Terrel Carver, *Karl Marx: Texts on Method* (1975), pp. 40–1.
4 Thus I pursue these matters from *within* the 'rationalist' or 'social philosophical' approach I detailed in Part 1. To make this declaration more explicit, I would say that it is within this area of marxian enquiry that the more plausible discussions of development are to be found.
5 See G. Palma 'Dependency: A Formal Theory of Underdevelopment or a Methodology for the Analysis of Concrete Situations of Underdevelopment?', *World Development,* vol. 6 (1978)

Chapter 10 Latin American dependency theory

1 A. G. Frank *Lumpenbourgeoisie–Lumpendevelopment* (1972).
2 See F. Clairmonte, *Economic Liberalism and Underdevelopment* (1960).
3 In a book entitled *The Economic Development of Latin America and its Principal Problems* (1949).
4 P. J. O'Brien, 'A Critique of Latin American Theories of Dependency', in I. Oxaal *et al.* (eds), *Beyond the Sociology of Development* (1975), p. 9.
5 Celso Furtado, *Economic Development in Latin American* (2nd edn, 1976), p. 298.
6 Furtado's third period is the late 1960s and early 1970s, when there was something of an economic boom fuelled by enormous inflows of capital. This does not affect Furtado's thinking or, more importantly, this review of the emergence of dependency theory. The recent (i.e. after Furtado's 1976 text) debt crises of Latin American economies would, in any case, support his position.
7 Norman Girvan, 'The Development of Dependency Economics in the Caribbean and Latin America: Review and Comparison', *Social and Economic Studies*, vol. 22 (1973).
8 O'Brien, *op. cit.*, p. 11.
9 *Ibid.*
10 There has been a great deal written on dependency and it simplifies

study if we look at the work of an *eminent* theorist. (See the Preface to Celso Furtado, *Development and Underdevelopment* (1964).)
11 *Ibid.*
12 *Ibid.*
13 *Ibid.*
14 *Ibid.*
15 *Ibid.*
16 See P. W. Preston, *Theories of Development* (1982), pp. 145–56.
17 Furtado, *op. cit.* (1964), p. 127.
18 *Ibid.*, p. 129.
19 *Ibid.*, p. 136.
20 *Ibib.*, p. 139.
21 Girvan, *op. cit.*, p. 12.
22 Furtado, *op. cit.*, (1976), p. 300.
23 Philip Ehrensaft, 'Semi-Industrial Capitalism in the Third World: Implications for Social Research in Africa', *Africa Today* (1971), p. 50.
24 Furtado, *op. cit.* (1976), p. 300.
25 *Ibid.*
26 In a subsequent text, *Accumulation and Development* (1983; original Brazilian edition published in 1978), Furtado tackles a broad-scale discussion of dependency: seeing it as a structural condition bequeathed by history. The themes of earlier work are here pursued in a broad cultural, historical, theoretical style – the author calls his text an 'academic anti-book' (p. i) as the issues will not fit into available social science categories.

Chapter 11 Neo-marxism and Paul Baran

1 See Aidan Foster-Carter, 'Neo-marxist Approaches to Development and Underdevelopment', in E. DeKadt and G. Williams (eds), *Sociology and Development* (1964).
2 See Gabriel Palma, 'Dependency: A Formal Theory of Underdevelopment or a Methodology for the Analysis of Concrete Situations of Underdevelopment?', *World Development*, vol. 6 (1978).
3 G. Kay, *Development and Underdevelopment: A Marxist Analysis* (1975), p. 18.
4 N. Birnbaum, 'The Staggering Colossus', in J. Nagel (ed.), *Student Power* (1969), p. 142.
5 S. Goode, *Affluent Revolutionaries: A Portrait of the New Left* (1974), p. 33.
6 Birnbaum, *op. cit.*, p. 149.
7 G. Statera, *Death of a Utopia* (1975).
8 *Ibid.*, p. 88.
9 *Ibid.*, p. 93.
10 Birnbaum, *op. cit.*, p. 144.
11 B. Davidson, *Africa in Modern History* (1978), p. 178.
12 *Ibid.*, p. 227.
13 *Ibid.*
14 On the situation in Singapore see, for example, Chan Heng Chee,

'The Political System and Political Change', in Riaz Hassan (ed.), *Singapore: Society in Transition* (1976).
15 See C. B. Macpherson, *The Real World of Democracy* (1966).
16 Davidson, *op. cit.*, p. 328.
17 *Ibid.*, p. 358.
18 G. Chaliand, *Revolution in the Third World* (1977).
19 *Ibid.*, p. xiv.
20 *Ibid.*, p. 23.
21 *Ibid.*, p. 184.
22 *Ibid.*
23 Davidson, *op. cit.*, p. 328.
24 P. Baran, *The Political Economy of Growth* (1959); with an Introduction by R. Sutcliffe (1973), p. 29.
25 See C. Napoleoni, *Economic Thought of the Twentieth Century* (1972), or A. Brewer, *Marxist Theories of Imperialism* (1980).
26 See C. Napoleoni. *op. cit.*
27 R. Sutcliffe in Baran, *op. cit.*, pp. 90–1.
28 L. Culley. 'Economic Development in Neo-Marxist Theory', in B. Hindessn (ed.), *Sociological Theories of the Economy* (1978), p. 107.
29 Brewer, *op. cit.*, pp. 13841.
30 See P. W. Preston, *Theories of Development* (1982), pp. 220–1.
31 R. Brenner, 'The Origins of Capitalist Development: A Critique of Neo-Smithian Marxism', *New Left Review*. no. 104 (1977).
32 See Brewer, *op. cit.*, Chapter 6 for a note on Sweezy's position in all this.
33 Brenner, *op. cit.*, p. 48.
34 *Ibid.*, p. 61.
35 *Ibid.*, p. 68.
36 *Ibid.*, p. 27.
37 Culley. *op. cit.*, p. 102.
38 *Ibid.*, p. 103.
39 See Brewer, *op. cit.*, pp. 131–3.
40 See Preston, *op. cit.*, pp. 221–3.
41 C. Leys, 'Underdevelopment and Dependency: Critical Notes', *Journal of Contemporary Asia,* vol. 7 (1977), p. 93.

Chapter 12 A. G. Frank

1 For a brief 'autobiographical' note, see A. G. Frank, *Economic Genocide in Chile* (1976).
2 D. Booth, 'André Gunder Frank: An Introduction and Appreciation', in I. Oxaal *et al.* (eds), *Beyond the Sociology of Development* (1975), p. 61.
3 J. K. Galbraith, *The Affluent Society* (1958), Chapter 2.
4 H. Brookfield, *Interdependent Development* (1975), p. 163.
5 Booth, *op. cit.*, pp. 64–9.
6 *Ibid.*, p. 52. See also P. Ehrensaft, 'Semi-Industrial Capitalism in the Third World', *Africa Today* (1971), who further elucidates this rather unexpected claim by saying that the difference between A. G. Frank and dependency theory is one of political commitment. There is much

truth in this – but I don't think Ehrensaft appreciates this: his remark was rather dismissive of A. G. Frank.

7 A term I associate with C. Leys, 'Underdevelopment and Dependency', *Journal of Contemporary Asia*, vol. 7 (1977), and H. Bernstein, 'Sociology of Underdevelopment versus Sociology of Development', in D. Lehmann (ed.), *Development Theory* (1979).
8 A. G. Frank, *On Capitalist Underdevelopment* (1975), p. 96.
9 A. G. Frank, *Capitalism and Underdevelopment in Latin America* (1967) p. 3.
10 *Ibid.*, p. 9.
11 I suppose that this intriguing notion is taken straight from Marx – see K. Marx and F. Engels, *The Communist Manifesto*.
12 A. G. Frank, *Latin America: Underdevelopment or Revolution* (1969b), p. ix.
13 *Ibid.*, p. x.
14 *Ibid.*, p. 3.
15 *Ibid.*
16 *Ibid.*
17 *Ibid.*, p. 4.
18 *Ibid.*
19 *Ibid.*
20 *Ibid.*
21 *Ibid.*
22 *Ibid.*, p. 5.
23 See P. W. Preston, *New Trends in Development Theory (1985)*, Chapters 2 and 4.
24 Frank, *op. cit.*, (1969b), p. 9.
25 *Ibid.*, p. 15.
26 *Ibid.*
27 *Ibid.*
28 A. G. Frank, *Lumpenbourgeoisie–Lumpendevelopment* (1972), p. 4.
29 *Ibid.*
30 *Ibid.*
31 *Ibid.*, pp. 7–8.
32 See the response of Snowball to setbacks in George Orwell's *Animal Farm* (1945).
33 Frank, *op. cit.* (1972), p. 110.
34 *Ibid.*, p. 145.
35 Ernesto Laclau, 'Feudalism and Capitalism in Latin America', *New Left Review*, no. 67 (1971), p. 22.
36 Robert Brenner, 'The Origins of Capitalist Development: A Critique of neo-Smithian Marxism', *New Left Review*, no. 104 (1977).
37 *Ibid.*, p. 28.
38 *Ibid.*, p. 29.
39 C. Leys, 'Underdevelopment and Dependency: Critical Notes', *Journal of Contemporary Asia*, vol. 7 (1977).
40 *Ibid.*, p. 93.
41 *Ibid.*
42 H. Bernstein, *op. cit.*, p. 94.

43 *Ibid.*
44 A. G. Frank, *Dependent Accumulation and Underdevelopment* (1978), p. xiii.
45 *Ibid.*, p. 1.
46 *Ibid.*
47 *Ibid.*, p. 2.
48 *Ibid.*
49 Indeed, it is debatable that the old Frank ever went away. If the text *Dependent Accumulation and Underdevelopment* (1978a) dealt with theoretical issues then a companion volume, *World Accumulation 1492–1789* (1978b), again dealt extensively with historical material. Frank's preoccupation with a political understanding of these issues – rather than a neutral academic understanding – is further evidenced in a recent two-volume study of the recent economic crisis: *Crisis in the Third World* (1981a) and *Crisis in the World Economy* (1981b).
50 P. Ehrensaft, 'Semi-Industrial Capitalism in the Third World: Implications for Social Research in Africa', *Africa Today* (1971), p. 50.
51 Frank, *op. cit.* (1969b), p. ix.
52 Frank, *op. cit.* (1972), p. 145.
53 See P. W. Preston, *op. cit.*, Chapter 2.

Chapter 13 Post-neo-marxism

1 A. Giddens, *Central Problems in Social Theory* (1979), Chapter 7.
2 See, for example, Alex Callinicos, *Althusser's Marxism* (1976).
3 F. H. Cardoso and E. Faletto, *Dependency and Development in Latin America* (1979).
4 Marx's Preface to *A Contribution to the Critique of Political Economy* (1859).
5 See P. Worsley, *Marx and Marxism* (1982), Chapter 3.
6 See A. Brewer, *Marxist Theories of Imperialism* (1980), Chapter 8, for a review – it is this text which I rely upon in particular.
7 See Aidan Foster-Carter, 'The Modes of Production Controversy', *New Left Review* no. 107 (1978). Also A. Hoogvelt, *The Third World in Global Development* (1982), pp. 174–84.
8 T. Carver, *Karl Marx: Texts on Method* (1975), p. 7.
9 *Ibid.*, pp. 11–17.
10 *Ibid.*, p. 88.
11 Cardoso and Faletto, *op. cit.*, p. ix.
12 *Ibid.*
13 Carver, *op. cit.*, p. 129.
14 *Ibid.*, p. 130.
15 *Ibid.*, p. 132.
16 *Ibid.*, pp. 40–1.
17 The tradition of *critical theory* is that of the Frankfurt School of marxists who focus, especially, on the production and maintenance of ideologies within capitalist society. The dissolution, via critique, of such justificatory ideologies is taken as a prerequisite of further social progress. The job of the theorist is to help people see the world as it 'really is'. Theories are made by the specialists and checking or testing

at this stage is called 'validation', then they are offered to whatever client group the theorist has in mind and if they are accepted and acted on they are said to be 'authenticated'.

18 Cardoso and Faletto, *op. cit.*, p. xiv.

19 *Ibid.*

20 *Ibid.*

21 This book was first published in 1967, a second, translated, edition appeared in 1976. References here are to the 1979 print.

22 *Ibid.*, p. xviii.

23 *Ibid.*, p. 151.

24 See Gabriel Palma, 'Dependency: A Formal Theory of Underdevelopment or a Methodology for the Analysis of Concrete Situations of Underdevelopment?', *World Development,* vol. 6 (1978).

Orthodox and radical views of Southeast Asia

Chapter 14 Analysing Southeast Asia

1 See Harold Brookfield, *Interdependent Development* (1975), Chapter 6.

2 See, for example, Ernest Gellner, *Thought and Change* (1964).

3 This is a very tricky point, but put simply the claim is that the marxian position was: (a) first presented in the West; (b) and has subsequently been exported and widely revised and shaped to local circumstances. Generally, the history of marxism is the history of its occasions/circumstances of deployment.

4 See Ankie Hoogvelt, *The Third World in Global Development* (1982).

5 H. D. Evers (ed.), *Modernization in Southeast Asia* (1973), Introduction, p. xiii.

6 S. P. Huntington, 'The Change to Change: Modernization, Development, and Politics', in C. E. Black (ed.), *Comparative Modernization* (1976), p. 27.

7 See A. D. Smith, *The Concept of Social Change* (1973); R. Nisbet, 'Developmentalism: A Critical Analysis', in J. Mckinney and E. Tiryakian (eds), *Theoretical Sociology* (1970); R. Bendix, 'Tradition and Modernity Reconsidered', *Comparative Studies in Society and History*, vol. 9 (1967).

8 D. A. Rustow and R. E. Ward (eds), *Political Modernization in Japan and Turkey* (1964), Introduction, pp. 6–7; cited in Huntington, *op. cit.*, pp. 29–30.

9 Huntington, *op. cit.*, p. 30.

10 *Ibid.*, p. 39.

11 *Ibid.*, pp. 44–5. We can also note that one of the basic problems which I think Huntington has run up against is the difficulty of separating out political change/political development/political modernization/political Westernization. Within the modernization framework, this is certainly a problem for the simple reason that modernization theory is an ideology centred upon Western, especially US, interests and assumptions, and consequently all

political change tends to be collapsed into one – Westernization, or, more precisely, US-ization. Huntington has realized that this situation is unsatisfactory and he is trying to extricate himself from the problem. His solution is to advance an abstract general scheme of political change. However, whilst he is undoubtedly moving in the right direction, his footsteps are dogged by the nonsense of the original position. The major substantive change is the recognition that social and political change is a complex and uneven process. Huntington says: 'A political system can be thought of as an aggregate of components, all changing, some at rapid rates, some at slower ones . . . The rate, scope, and direction of change in one component may be compared with the rate, scope, and direction of change in other components . . . [with] other elements of the same component . . . Finally . . . [we can look at] changes in power . . . for any one element' (Huntington, *op. cit.*, p. 57). The style and goal are unchanged – it is a policy-scene analysis. For further discussion of political modernization, see Eva Etzioni-Halevy, *Social Change* (1981), where the author restates in a thoughtful manner the orthodox position, and considers the marxian view. See also Wilbur Moore, *World Modernization* (1979), for a restatement of the orthodoxy.

12 S. N. Eisenstadt, 'The Influence of Traditional and Colonial Political Systems on the Development of Post-traditional Social and Political Orders', in H. D. Evers (ed.), *op. cit.* (1973), p. 3.

13 *Ibid.*

14 *Ibid.*, p. 5 (original emphasis).

15 See *ibid.*, pp. 8–10.

16 *Ibid.*, p. 10.

17 *Ibid.*, p. 13.

18 F. C. Darling, *The Westernization of Asia: A Comparative Political Analysis* (1979).

19 J. L. S. Girling, *The Bureaucratic Polity in Modernizing Societies* (1981).

20 F. Rigg, *Thailand: The Modernization of a Bureaucratic Polity* (1966).

21 See Herbert Feith, 'South-East Asian Neo-Colonialism', in E. P. Wolfers (ed.), *Australia's Northern Neighbours* (1976).

22 For the claim, see H. D. Evers (ed.) *op. cit.* (1973), Introduction.

23 M. A. Nawawi, 'Tradition, Mobilization and Development in Indonesia', in Evers (ed.), *op. cit.*, (1973).

24 *Ibid.*, p. 19.

25 *Ibid.*, p. 20.

26 *Ibid.*, p. 28 (original emphasis).

27 *Ibid.*, p. 31.

28 Remigio E. Agpalo, 'Political Modernization in the Philippines', in Evers (ed.), *op. cit.*, (1973).

29 Zakaria Haji Ahmad, 'The Political Structure', in E. K. Fisk and H. Osman-Rani (eds), *The Political Economy of Malaysia* (1982).

30 *Ibid.*, p. 88.

31 B. N. Pandy, *South and South-East Asia 1945–1979: Problems and Policies* (1980).
32 *Ibid.*, p. 26.
33 *Ibid.*, p. 27.
34 *Ibid.*, p. 29.
35 *Ibid.*
36 *Ibid.*
37 P. Chen and H. D. Evers (eds), *Studies in ASEAN Sociology* (1978).
38 H. D. Evers, 'The Role of Professionals in Social and Political Change', in *Ibid.*, p. 8.
39 *Ibid.*, p. 10.
40 J. Habermas and the Frankfurt School are influential within present European social theory. They work within a 'humanist marxian' tradition. For an introduction, see D. Held *Introduction to Critical Theory* (1980).
41 P. Chen, 'The Power Elite in Singapore', in Chen and Evers(eds), *op. cit.*, p. 75.
42 See D. Cruise O'Brien, 'Modernization, Order and the Erosion of a Democratic Ideal', *Journal of Development Studies*, vol. 8 (1972).
43 Chan Heng Chee and H. D. Evers, 'National Identity and Nation Building in Singapore', in Chen and Evers (eds), *op. cit.*
44 Or, indeed, a mix of both: for example, in some varieties of 'African socialism' we have the idea of moving forwards to recapture the primitive communism of the African tribal past. Other examples could be offered from other parts of the world: thus the 'New Right' in the First World – especially Reagan and Thatcher – have argued for a radical programme of reconstructing nineteenth-century-type, laissez-faire-type, societies. Their views can be summarized in the slogan: 'Forward into the Past!'
45 Compare also W. F. Wertheim, 'The Trading Minorities in South-East Asia', in H. D. Evers (ed.), *Sociology of Southeast Asia* (1980).
46 Chan and Evers, *op. cit.*, p. 119.
47 See Chan Heng Chee, 'The Political System and Political Change', in Riaz Hassan (ed.), *Singapore: Society in Transition* (1976).
48 Chan and Evers, *op. cit.*, p. 128.
49 *Ibid.*, p. 129 (emphasis added).
50 Darling, *op. cit.*
51 *Ibid.*, p. 257.
52 *Ibid.*, p. 259.
53 *Ibid.*, p. 293.
54 *Ibid.*, p. 321–2.
55 *Ibid.*, pp. 349–51.
56 *Ibid.*, p. 386.
57 *Ibid.*, p. 414.
58 Joan Robinson, *Economic Philosophy* (1962), p. 93.
59 See the comment in her obituary, *Journal of Contemporary Asia* (1982).
60 See P. Sweezy, 'Discussion', in R. V. Eagly (ed.), *Events, Ideology and Economic Theory* (1968), pp. 147–8.

61 See below where I discuss type-one orthodox and type-two, or dissenting, orthodox.
62 In terms of economists' names: version one – J. R. Hicks, P. Samuelson, M. Friedman, P. T. Bauer, D. Rimmer and W. W. Rostow would be adherents; version two – G. Myrdal, J. Robinson, P. Streeten, J. K. Galbraith and Prebisch. For a more authoritative discussion, see the short review by K. Clements, *From Right to Left in Development Theory*, Institute of Southeast Asian Studies Occasional Paper no. 61 (1980); and J. Cameron, Ken Cole and Chris Edwards, 'Teaching Economic Principles as Part of Development Studies', *Bulletin of the Institute of Development Studies*, vol. 11 (1980).
63 Given the confusions in this area, it will become clear that much economics writing has elements of both type-one and type-two mixed in together. Disentangling the threads is sometimes not at all easy.
64 K. Clements, *op. cit.*, offers a useful, simplified scheme and this suits my purposes here.
65 See C. B. Macpherson, *Democratic Theory: Essays in Retrieval* (1973).
66 Clements, *op. cit.*, pp. 13–14.
67 *Ibid.*, p. 14.
68 *Ibid.*, p. 16.
69 *Ibid.*, p. 12.
70 Lim Chong Yah, 'Singapore's Economic Development: Retrospect and Prospect', in P. Chen (ed.), *Singapore: Development Policies and Trends* (1983).
71 *Ibid.*, p. 89.
72 *Ibid.*
73 *Ibid.*, p. 90.
74 *Ibid.*, p. 91 *et seq.*
75 *Ibid.*, p. 94.
76 *Ibid.*
77 *Ibid.*
78 See P. W. Preston *New Trends in Development Theory* (1985), Chapter 6.
79 Lim, *op. cit.*, p. 96.
80 *Ibid.*, p. 99.
81 See below (pp. 212–51), when I look at marxist approaches to Southeast Asia.
82 Lim, *op. cit.*, p. 99.
83 *Ibid.*
84 *Ibid.*
85 *Far Eastern Economic Review*, 10 January 1985.
86 Lim, *op. cit.*, p. 100.
87 *Ibid.*
88 See B. Hoselitz, 'Theories of Stages of Economic Growth', in Hoselitz (ed.), *Theories of Economic Growth* (1960).
89 John Wong, *ASEAN Economies in Perspective*, (1979).
90 *Ibid.*, p. 9.

91 *Ibid.*, p. 10.
92 *Ibid.*, p. 13.
93 *Ibid.*, p. 53.
94 *Ibid.*, p. 54.
95 See Girling, *op. cit.*, and Hamish McDonald, *Suharto's Indonesia* (1980).
96 Wong, *op. cit.*, p. 64.
97 *Ibid.*, p. 68.
98 *Ibid.*, p. 69.
99 *Ibid.*, p. 72.
100 *Ibid.*, p. 93.
101 *Ibid.*
102 *Ibid.*, p. 95.
103 *Ibid.*, p. 121.
104 *Ibid.*, pp. 122–3.
105 *Ibid.*, p. 123.
106 *Ibid.*
107 *Ibid.*, p. 124.
108 *Ibid.*
109 My remarks here on rural life will be very brief: but see B. A. R. Mokhzani (ed.), *Rural Development in Southeast Asia* (1979), and, generally, R. Chambers, *Rural Development: Putting the Last First* (1983).
110 For illustrative examples, see Chen (ed.), *op. cit*; Chen and Evers (eds), *op. cit.*; Hassan (ed.), *op. cit.*; and Evers (ed.), *op. cit.* (1973). For a general discussion, see D. Conyers, *An Introduction to Social Planning to the Third World* (1982).
111 Wong, *op. cit.*, p. 93 *et seq.*
112 W. F. Wertheim, 'Resistance to Change – From Whom?', in Evers (ed.), *op. cit.*, (1973), p. 97.
113 See Wong, *op. cit.*, p. 101 *et seq.*
114 Wertheim, *Ibid.*, p. 101.
115 Wertheim *Ibid.*, p. 107.
116 See below, pp. 212–25 of this chapter.
117 See R. I. Rhodes, 'The Disguised Conservatism in Evolutionary Development Theory', *Science and Society*, vol. 32 (1968).
118 For an unusual treatment of modern Islam, see V. S. Naipaul, *Among the Believers: An Islamic Journey* (1981).
119 For summary diagrams, see Darling, *op. cit.*, pp. 34, 35, 59, 60.
120 S. H. Alatas, *Modernization and Social Change* (1972).
121 *Ibid.*, p. 21.
122 See note 11, above. Alatas has the same problem as Huntington.
123 Alatas, *op. cit.*, p. 22. See also S. N. Eisenstadt, 'Breakdowns of Modernization', *Economic Development and Cultural Change*, vol. 12 (1964).
124 *Ibid.*
125 *Ibid.*, p. 25.
126 *Ibid.*
127 *Ibid.*

128 *Ibid.*, p. 28.
129 *Ibid.*, p. 29.
130 *Ibid.*, p. 33.
131 *Ibid.*, p. 36.
132 *Ibid.*, p. 39.
133 *Ibid.*, p. 40.
134 See J. Clammer, *Islam and Capitalism in Southeast Asia*, National University of Singapore Sociology Working Paper no. 63. On the related, and rather broader, issue of changes in cultural patterns attendant upon industrialization, see R. Vente and P. Chen (eds), *Culture and Industrialization: an Asian Dilemma* (1980).
135 These judgments represent a fairly casual synthesis of the above-noted theorists; but more especially, Darling, Wong, Jeffrey and Pandy.
136 This phrase is from A. W. McCoy, 'The Philippines: Independence without Decolonization', in R. Jeffrey (ed.), *Asia: The Winning of Independence* (1981).
137 There is a revision to my typification of patterns of withdrawal – peaceful and violent – to be made at this point. There is a sub-category of 'mainly peaceful but with a defeated rebellion': Philippines and Malaysia. In both these cases the new nations had the experience of receiving help from the departing colonial power in defeating internal left-wing revolts. In Indonesia there is a rather different situation, as we will see.
138 Compare with Wong on land reforms attempted in ASEAN.
139 This phrase is from Anthony Reid, in Jeffrey (ed.), *op. cit.*
140 *Ibid.*
141 *Ibid.*, p. 131.
142 *Ibid.*, p. 134.
143 This can be compared with the way in which the French managed to pass off their attempted reconquest of Vietnam as a war against communism, thus gaining the assistance of the USA.
144 Reid, *op. cit.*, pp. 154–5.
145 This phrase is from Lee Kam Hing, 'Malaya: New State and Old Elite', in Jeffrey (ed.), *op. cit.*
146 S. Bedlington, *Malaysia and Singapore: The Building of New States* (1978), p. 37.
147 *Ibid.*
148 *Ibid.*, pp. 61–5.
149 Lee, *op. cit.*, p. 227.
150 This will be a comparatively brief note, as the Singapore example crops up rather often in this text.
151 See Pang Keng Fong, 'The Malay Royals of Singapore', unpublished dissertation (1984).
152 Bedlington, *op. cit.*, p. 210.
153 The example of Hong Kong is an obvious comparison. See Theodore Geiger and Frances Geiger, *The Development Progress of Hong Kong and Singapore* (1975).
154 This label is taken from Girling, *op. cit.*

155 Bob Catley, 'The Development of Underdevelopment in Southeast Asia', *Journal of Contemporary Asia*, vol. 6 (1976), reprinted in H. D. Evers (ed.) *op. cit.* (1980) p. 263.
156 *Ibid.*, p. 264.
157 *Ibid.*, p. 265.
158 *Ibid.*, p. 266.
159 *Ibid.*
160 See Aidan Foster-Carter, 'Neo-marxist Approaches to Development and Underdevelopment', in E. DeKadt and G. Williams (eds), *Sociology and Development* (1964).
161 Sritua Arief and Adi Sasono, *Indonesia: Dependeny and Underdevelopment* (1980).
162 G. Palma, 'Dependency: A Formal Theory of Underdevelopment or a Methodology for the Analysis of Concrete Situations of Underdevelopment?', *World Development,* vol. 6 (1978).
163 M. Bienefeld, 'Dependency and the Newly Industrializing Countries', in D. Seers (ed.), *Dependency Theory: A Critical Reassessment* (1981).
164 This position would seem to be an advance on a 1980 paper, 'Dependency in the Eighties', in which Bienefeld – arguing for a historically and social scientifically integrated approach – observed (correctly, I think) that 'The dependency debate with all its inadequacies represents the major forum in which such an attempt is made' (*IDS Bulletin*, vol. 12 (1980), p. 10). For an unpersuasive counterview, see S. Lall, 'Is Dependence a Useful Concept in Analysing Underdevelopment?', *World Development*, vol. 3 (1975) – the author answers his own question with an unequivocal 'no'.
165 Bienefeld, *op. cit.*, (1981), p. 86.
166 G. Lamb, 'Rapid Capitalist Development Models: A New Politics of Dependence', in Seers (ed.), *op. cit.*
167 John Wong, *op. cit.*, and Lim Chong Yah, in Wolfers (ed.), *op. cit.*
168 M. Bienefeld and M. Godfrey, *The Struggle for Development: National Strategies in an International Context* (1982).
169 For an influential general introduction, see John Taylor, *From Modernization to Modes of Production* (1979), esp. pp. 175–86. See also Peter Worsley, *The Three Worlds* (1984).
170 Umberto Melotti, *Marx and the Third World* (1977).
171 M. Caldwell, Foreword, in *ibid.*
172 Peter Worsley, *Marx and Marxism* (1982).
173 Melotti, *op. cit.*, p. 50.
174 On this claim about 'mental set', see: Ignacy Sachs, *The Discovery of the Third World* (1976); S. H. Alatas, *The Myth of the Lazy Native* (1977); S. H. Alatas, *Thomas Stamford Raffles: Schemer or Reformer* (1971).
175 Alec Gordon, 'Indonesia, Plantations and the "Post Colonial" Mode of Production', *Journal of Contemporary Asia*, vol. 12 (1982).
176 *Ibid.*, p. 169.
177 *Ibid.*, p. 80 (original emphasis).
178 *Ibid.*

179 See Bill Warren, 'Imperialism and Capitalist Industrialization', *New Left Review*, no. 81 (1973); Bill Warren, *Imperialism: Pioneer of Capitalism* (1980).
180 P. Limqueco, 'Contradictions of Development in ASEAN', *Journal of Contemporary Asia*, vol. 13 (1983), p. 283.
181 *Ibid.*
182 *Ibid.*, p. 288.
183 *Ibid.*, p. 297.
184 *Ibid.*, p. 301.
185 Clive Hamilton, 'Capitalist Industrialization in East Asia's Four Little Tigers', *Journal of Contemporary Asia*, vol. 13 (1983).
186 *Ibid.*, p. 35.
187 *Ibid.*
188 *Ibid.*, p. 36.
189 *Ibid.*
190 *Ibid.*
191 *Ibid.*
192 *Ibid.*, p. 38
193 *Ibid.*, p. 40.
194 *Ibid.*, p. 42.
195 *Ibid.*, p. 43.
196 *Ibid.*, p. 47.
197 *Ibid.*
198 *Ibid.*, p. 68.
199 For a further discussion of a 'modest dependency' type see *IDS Bulletin*, vol. 15 (1984). In this the records of the People's Republic of China, South Korea and Taiwan are considered against the claims of neo-classicism and the role of the state is stressed. Indeed, the editors (White and Wade) argue that 'the search for a deeper understanding of the economic role of the state poses a challenge not only to development economics but to development studies as an interdisciplinary endeavour' (*IDS Bulletin*, vol. 15 (1984), p. 3).
200 Robin Lim, 'The Philippines and the Dependency Debate: A Preliminary Case Study', *Journal of Contemporary Asia*, vol. 8 (1978).
201 *Ibid.*, p. 201.
202 Jon Halliday, 'Capitalism and Socialism in East Asia', *New Left Review*, no. 124 (1980), p. 3.
203 *Ibid.*, pp. 4–5.
204 *Ibid.*, p. 5.
205 See *Far Eastern Economic Review*, 13 January 1983.
206 Halliday, *op. cit.*, p. 8.
207 The Frankian syntax generated many curious formulations as it was revised and this is one of them. Many commentators have said that this is rather unhelpful.
208 Hong Kong is the centre of the Asian banking world with Singapore in second position: a continuation for both of their mercantile capitalist histories.

209 I think more has to be said: the 4 NIC's look more like 2 + 1 + 1 when their particular positions are considered.
210 Halliday, *op. cit.*, p. 11.
211 *Ibid.*, p. 12.
212 *Ibid.*, p. 13.
213 *Ibid.*
214 *Ibid.*, p. 14.
215 *Ibid.*, p. 22.
216 *Ibid.*, p. 23.
217 John Wong, *op. cit.*, Chapter 5.
218 P. Worsley, *op. cit.*, (1984).
219 *Ibid.*, pp. 72–3 (original emphasis).
220 *Ibid.*, pp. 145–55.
221 S. B. D. de Silva, *The Political Economy of Underdevelopment* (1982).
222 *Ibid.*, p. 185.
223 *Ibid.*
224 *Ibid.*, p. 188.
225 *Ibid.*, p. 190.
226 *Ibid.*, p. 195.
227 Alec Gordon, 'Indonesia, Plantations and the "Post Colonial" Mode of Production', *Journal of Contemporary Asia*, vol. 12 (1982), p. 179.
228 Alec Gordon, 'Stages in the Development of Java's Socio-economic Formations 700–1979', *Journal of Contemporary Asia*, vol. 9 (1979).
229 *Ibid.*, p. 133.
230 *Ibid.*
231 Shamsul Amri Baharuddin, 'The Development of the Underdevelopment of the Malaysian Peasantry', *Journal of Contemporary Asia*, vol. 9 (1979), p. 434.
232 *Ibid.*, p. 440.
233 *Ibid.*
234 *Ibid.*, p. 441.
235 *Ibid.*, p. 442.
236 What follows is based primarily on James C. Scott, 'Hegemony and the Peasantry', in S. Matsumoto (ed.), *Southeast Asia in a Changing World* (1980). The matters of peasant thought and its possibilities as an 'oppositional meaning system' are pursued in more detail in James C. Scott, 'Protest and Profanation: Revolt and the Little Tradition', *Theory and Society*, vol. 4 (1971).
237 Antonio Gramsci was an Italian communist theorist who paid particular attention to 'cultural' issues.
238 For an interesting, conservative discussion of peasant protest and change in Southeast Asia, see Michael Adas, 'From Avoidance to Confrontation: Peasant Protest in Precolonial and Colonial Southeast Asia', *Comparative Studies in Society and History*, vol. 23 (1981). Adas argues that peasants have always faced rapacious elites and, in pre-colonial days, with loose social control, could rely on a range of avoidance tactics. The coming of efficient bureaucratic colonial states, plus new economic demands, forced more open responses to

the new rapacious elite. Eventually, Adas notes (reluctantly, it seems) that these responses channelled into nationalism and guerilla war: spontaneity is rather read out of Adas's scheme.

239 In particular, Ralph Milliband, *The State in Capitalist Society* (1973) recent debates. See also W. Ziemann and M. Lanzendorfer, 'The State in Peripheral Societies', in R. Milliband and J. Saville (eds), *The Socialist Register* (1977).

240 Bipan Chandra, 'Colonialism, Stages of Colonialism and the Colonial State', *Journal of Contemporary Asia*, vol. 10 (1980).

241 *Ibid.*, p. 274.

242 *Ibid.*

243 See Adas, *op. cit.*

244 Chandra, *op. cit.*, p. 276.

245 *Ibid.*, p. 277.

246 *Ibid.*

247 For an exotic example, see Brian Inglis, *The Opium Wars* (1976).

248 Chandra, *op. cit.*, p. 280.

249 *Ibid.*, p. (original emphasis).

250 *Feith, op. cit.*

251 *Ibid.*, p. 29.

252 *Ibid.*, p. 30.

253 *Ibid.*, p. 31.

254 *Ibid.*, p. 34.

255 *Ibid.*, p. 36.

256 *Ibid.*, p. 37.

257 *Ibid.*, p. 39.

258 Chua Beng Huat, 'Re-opening Ideological Discussion in Singapore: A New Theoretical Direction', *Southeast Asian Journal of Social Science*, vol. 11 (1983).

259 Feith, *op. cit.*, p. 40.

260 James Petras, 'The "Peripheral State": Continuity and Change in the International Division of Labour', *Journal of Contemporary Asia*, vol. 12 (1982).

261 *Ibid.*, p. 426.

262 Gook Aik Suan, 'Singapore: A Third World Fascist State', *Journal of Contemporary Asia*, vol. 11 (1981).

263 *Ibid.*, p. 251.

264 *Ibid.*, p. 253.

265 N. Heyzer, 'International Production and Social Change: An Analysis of the State, Employment, and Trade Unions in Singapore', in Chen (ed.), *op. cit.*

266 *Ibid.*, p. 113.

267 *Ibid.*, p. 116.

268 *Ibid.*

269 *Ibid.*, pp. 125–6.

270 Martin Brennan, 'Class, Politics and Race in Modern Malaysia', *Journal of Contemporary Asia*, vol. 12 (1982). See also: Lin Mah Hui, 'Ethnic and Class Relations in Malaysia', *Journal of Contemporary Asia*, vol. 10 (1980); Fatimah Halim, 'Capital, Labour and

the State: The West Malaysian Case', *Journal of Contemporary Asia*, vol. 12 (1982); Lin Mah Hui and William Canak, 'The Political Economy of State Policies in Malaysia', *Journal of Contemporary Asia*, vol. 11 (1981). For a rather different, anthropological, view, see Judith Nagata, 'The Status of Ethnicity and the Ethnicity of Status', *International Journal of Comparative Sociology*, vol. 27 (1976), in which she argues that class and ethnicity represent different ways of interpreting the social world which may be 'mixed' together in a variety of ways. She rejects modernization-theory schemes which see 'ethnicity' as more 'primitive' than class and liable to disappear as political modernization runs its course. I assume that she would reject orthodox marxist ideas of ethnicity as ideological obfuscation also – on Worsley-type grounds. But Brennan, it seems to me, is mixing both 'cultural' and 'marxian economic' schemes to produce a more sophisticated and tentative marxian analysis.

271 Brennan, *op. cit.*, p. 203.
272 *Ibid.*
273 *Ibid.*, p. 204.
274 *Ibid.*, p. 208.

Chapter 15 Lessons for the future?

1 This chapter is loosely based on P. W. Preston, *New Trends in Development Theory* (1985).
2 B. Fay, *Social Theory and Political Practice* (1975). This text is an early commentary/exposition of the work of Jurgen Habermas. There have been many others published since, but Fay's is a reasonable and concise introduction.
3 This trio of labels is Fay's, but the three types of enquiry he has in mind are taken directly from Habermas's trio of empirical–analytic, historical–hermeneutic, and critical.
4 See A. Giddens, *Central Problems in Social Theory* (1979), esp. Chapter 7.
5 Wittgenstein was a noted philosopher of language who argued that words did not have any finally fixed – and thus clearly definable – meaning; instead, they had a 'meaning in use'. The upshot was that words had as many 'shades of meaning' as there were ways of using the word. His famous example involved the word 'game': lots of activities, he pointed out, count as 'games' and whilst true that they all have some things roughly in common, no *one* activity is *the* game.
6 Z. Bauman, *Towards a Critical Sociology* (1976a). Here, Bauman is pointing to the influence of Durkheim and Talcott Parsons in shaping the structural functionalist orthodoxy of social science.
7 Giddens, *op. cit.*, Chapter 2.
8 *Ibid.*, Chapter 7.
9 UN, *Measures for the Economic Development of Underdeveloped Countries* (1951).
10 F. Clairmonte, *Economic Liberalism and Underdevelopment* (1960).
11 Habermas is an influential social theorist working within the rationalist and humanist marxian traditions: an outline of his earlier work is

given by Fay, *op. cit.* For more exhaustive treatments, see Richard Bernstein, *The Restructuring of Social and Political Theory* (1976), or, for a more specific analysis, T. McCarthy, *The Critical Theory of Jurgen Habermas*, or more generally, D. Held, *Introduction to Critical Theory* (1980).

12 On the matter of war, see, for example, B. Bond, *War and Society in Europe 1870–1970* (1984), and V. G. Kiernan, *European Empires from Conquest to Collapse, 1815–1960* (1982). Also, relatedly, Barrington Moore, *The Social Origins of Dictatorship and Democracy* (1966).

13 See, for example, A. D. Smith, *State and Nation in the Third World* (1983).

Bibliography

Adas, M. (1981), 'From Avoidance to Confrontation: Peasant Protest in Precolonial and Colonial Southeast Asia', *Comparative Studies in Society and History*, vol. 23.

Alatas, S. H. (1971), *Thomas Stamford Raffles: Schemer or Reformer*, Sydney, Angus & Robertson.

Alatas, S. H. (1972), *Modernization and Social Change*, Sydney, Angus & Robertson.

Alatas, S. H. (1977), *The Myth of the Lazy Native*, London, Frank Cass.

Alavi, H. and Shanin, T. (eds) (1982), *Introduction to the Sociology of the 'Developing Societies'*, London, Macmillan.

Allen, V. (1975), *Social Analysis: A Marxist Critique and Alternative*, London, Longman.

Antoni, C. (1959), *From History to Sociology*, Wayne State University Press.

Arief, Sritua and Sasono, Adi (1980), *Indonesia: Dependency and Underdevelopment*, published for the Institute for Development Studies, Jakarta, Indonesia by META.

Aron, R. (1973), *The Imperial Republic: The US and the World 1945–1973*, London, Weidenfeld & Nicolson.

Avineri, S. (1968), *The Social and Political Thought of Karl Marx*, Cambridge University Press.

Baharuddin, S. A. (1979), 'The Development of the Underdevelopment of the Malaysian Peasantry', *Journal of Contemporary Asia*, vol. 9.

Baran, P. (1973), *The Political Economy of Growth*, Harmondsworth, Pelican.

Baran, P. and Hobsbawm, E. (1961), 'The Stages of Economic Growth', *Kyklos*, vol. 14.

Bauer, P. (1971), *Dissent on Development*, London, Weidenfeld & Nicolson.

Bauman, Z. (1976a), *Towards a Critical Sociology*, London, Routledge & Kegan Paul.

Bauman, Z. (1976b), *Socialism: The Active Utopia*, London, George Allen & Unwin.

Bedlington, S. (1978), *Malaysia and Singapore: The Building of New States*,

Bell, D. (1973), *The Coming of Post Industrial Society*, Harmondsworth, Penguin.

Benton, T. (1977), *The Philosophical Foundations of the Three Sociologies*, London, Routledge & Kegan Paul.

Berlin, I. (1969), *Four Essays on Liberty*, Oxford University Press.

Bernstein, H. (1971), 'Modernization Theory and the Sociological Study of Development', *Journal of Development Studies*, no. 7.

Bernstein, H. (1979), 'Sociology of Underdevelopment versus Sociology of Development', in Lehmann, D. (ed.), *Development Theory*, London, Cass.

Bernstein, R. (1976), *The Restructuring of Social and Political Theory*, Oxford, Blackwell.

Bienefeld, M. (1980), 'Dependency in the Eighties', *Bulletin of the Institute of Development Studies*, vol. 12.

Bienefeld, M. and Godfrey, M. (eds) (1982), *The Struggle for Development: National Strategies in an International Context*, Chichester, John Wiley.

Bendix, R. (1967), 'Tradition and Modernity Reconsidered', *Comparative Studies in Society and History*, vol. 9.

Black, C. E. (ed.) (1976), *Comparative Modernization*, London, Collier Macmillan.

Bond, B. (1984), *War and Society in Europe 1870–1970*, London, Fontana.

Brennan, M. (1982), 'Class, Politics and Race in Modern Malaysia', *Journal of Contemporary Asia*, vol. 12.

Brenner, R. (1977), 'The Origins of Capitalist Development: A Critique of Neo-Smithian Marxism', *New Left Review*, no. 104.

Brewer, A. (1980) *Marxist Theories of Imperialism*, London, Routledge & Kegan Paul.

Brookfield, H. (1975), *Interdependent Development*, London, Methuen.

Callinicos, A. (1976), *Althusser's Marxism*, London, Pluto.

Cameron, J., Cole, K., Edwards, C. (1980), 'Teaching Economic Principles as Part of Development Studies', *Bulletin of the Institute of Development Studies*, vol. 11.

Cardoso, F. H. and Faletto, E. (1967; 2nd edn 1979), *Dependency and Development in Latin America*, University of California Press.

Carroll, J. (1980), *Sceptical Sociology*, London, Routledge & Kegan Paul.

Carver, T. (1975), *Karl Marx: Texts on Method*, Oxford, Blackwell.

Catley, B. (1980), 'The Development of Underdevelopment', in Evers., H. D. (ed.), *Sociology of Southeast Asia*, Kuala Lumpur, Oxford University Press.

Caute, D. (1970), *Fanon*, London, Fontana.

Caute, D. (1978), *The Great Fear: The Anti-Communist Purges under Truman and Eisenhower*, London, Secker & Warburg.

Chaliand, G. (1977), *Revolution in the Third World*, Hassocks, Harvester.

Chambers, R. (1983), *Rural Development: Putting the Last First*, London, Longman.

Chandra, B. (1980), 'Colonialism, Stages of Colonialism and the Colonial State', *Journal of Contemporary Asia*, vol. 10.
Chen, P. and Evers, H. D. (eds) (1978), *Studies in ASEAN Sociology*, Singapore, Chopmen.
Chen, P. (ed.) (1983), *Singapore: Development Policies and Trends*, Oxford University Press.
Chua, Beng Huat (1983), 'Re-opening Ideological Discussion in Singapore: A New Theoretical Direction', *Southeast Asian Journal of Science*, vol. 11.
Clairmonte, F. A. (1960), *Economic Liberalism and Underdevelopment*, Bombay, Asia Publishing House.
Clammer, J. (1978), *Islam and Capitalism in Southeast Asia*, Department of Sociology Working Paper, National University, Singapore, Chopmen.
Clark, C. (1957), *The Conditions of Economic Progress*, 3rd edn, London, Macmillan.
Clements, K. P. (1980), *From Right to Left in Development Theory*, Singapore, Institute of Southeast Asian Studies Occasional Paper no. 61.
Conyers, D. (1982), *An Introduction to Social Planning in The Third World*, London, Wiley.
Cranston, M. (ed.) (1970), *The New Left*, London, Bodley Head.
Crick, B. (1980), *Guardian*, 9 October.
Culley, L. (1978), 'Economic Development in Neo-marxist Theory', in Hindess, B. (ed.), *Sociological Theories of the Economy*, London, Macmillan.
Cumper, G. (1974), 'Dependence Development and the Sociology of Economic Thought', *Social and Economic Studies*, vol. 23.
Darling, F. C. (1979), *The Westernization of Asia: A Comparative Political Analysis*, Boston, G. K. Hall.
Davidson, B. (1978), *Africa in Modern History*, London, Allen Lane.
Davis, Mike (1981) 'The New Right's Road to Power', *New Left Review*, 128.
Dawe, A. (1971), 'The Relevance of Values', in Sahay, A. (ed.), *Max Weber and Modern Sociology*, London, Routledge & Kegan Paul.
Debray, R. (1967), *Revolution in the Revolution*, London, Monthly Review Press.
Debray, R. (1970), *Strategy for the Revolution* (ed R. Blackburn), London, Cape.
De Kadt, E. and Williams, G. (eds) (1964), *Sociology and Development*, London, Tavistock.
de Silva, S. B. D. (1982), *The Political Economy of Underdevelopment*, London, Routledge & Kegan Paul.
di Marco, L. E. (ed.) (1972), *International Economics and Development: Essays in Honour of Raul Prebisch*, London, Academic Press.
Dobb, M. (1973), *Theories of Value and Distribution since Adam Smith*, Cambridge University Press.
Donaldson, P. (1973), *Economics of the Real World*, Harmondsworth, Penguin.

Eagly, R. V. (ed.) (1968), *Events, Ideology and Economic Theory*, Wayne State University Press.

Ehrensaft, P. (1971), 'Semi-Industrial Capitalism in the Third World: Implications for Social Research in Africa', *Africa Today*.

Eisenstadt, S. N. (1964), 'Breakdowns of Modernization', *Economic Development and Cultural Change*, vol. 12.

Eldridge, J. E. T. (1971), *Max Weber: The Interpretation of Social Reality*, London, Michael Joseph.

Etzioni-Halevy, Eva (1981), *Social Change*, London, Routledge & Kegan Paul.

Evers, H. D. (ed.) (1973), *Modernization in Southeast Asia*, Kuala Lumpur, Oxford University Press.

Evers, H. D. (ed.) (1980), *Sociology of Southeast Asia*, Kuala Lumpur, Oxford University Press.

Fanon, F. (1967), *The Wretched of the Earth*, Harmondsworth, Penguin.

Far Eastern Economic Review, Hong Kong, Charles H. Stolbach.

Fay, B. (1975), *Social Theory and Political Practice*, London, Allen & Unwin.

Fisk, E. K. and Osman-Rani, H. (eds) (1982), *The Political Economy of Malaysia*, Kuala Lumpur, Oxford UP.

Fleming, D. F. (1961), *The Cold War and its Origins*, New York, Doubleday.

Foster-Carter, A. (1964), 'Neo-marxist Approaches to Development and Underdevelopment', in DeKadt, E. and Williams, G. (eds), *Sociology and Development*, London, Tavistock.

Foster-Carter, A. (1978), 'The Modes of Production Controversy', *New Left Review*, no. 107.

Fowles, John (1969), *The French Lieutenant's Woman*, London, Cape.

Frank, A. G. (1967), *Capitalism and Underdevelopment in Latin America*, New York, Monthly Review Press.

Frank, A. G. (1969a), *Latin America: Underdevelopment or Revolution*, New York, Monthly Review Press.

Frank, A. G. (1972), *Lumpenbourgeoisie–Lumpendevelopment*, New York, Monthly Review Press.

Frank, A. G. (1975), *On Capitalist Underdevelopment*, Bombay, Oxford University Press.

Frank, A. G. (1976), *Economic Genocide in Chile: Monetarist Theory versus Humanity*, Nottingham, Spokesman.

Frank, A. G. (1978a), *Dependent Accumulation and Underdevelopment*, London, Macmillan.

Frank, A. G. (1978b), *World Accumulation 1492–1789*, London, Macmillan.

Frank, A. G. (1981a), *Crisis in the Third World*, London, Macmillan.

Frank, A. G. (1981b), *Crisis in the World Economy*, New York, Holmes & Meier.

Friedman, M. (1953), *Essays in Positive Economics*, University of Chicago Press.

Friedman, M. (1962), *Capitalism and Freedom*, University of Chicago Press.

Friedman, M. and Friedman, R. (1980), *Free to Choose*, London, Secker & Warburg.

Furtado, C. (1964), *Development and Underdevelopment*, University of California Press.

Furtado, C. (1965), *Diagnosis of the Brazilian Crisis*, University of California Press.

Furtado, C. (1969; 2nd edn 1976), *Economic Development in Latin America: A Survey from Colonial Times to the Cuban Revolution*, Cambridge University Press.

Furtado, C. (1983), *Accumulation and Development*, Oxford, Martin Robertson.

Galbraith, J. K. (1967), *The New Industrial State*, Harmondsworth, Pelican.

Galbraith, J. K. (1958), *The Affluent Society*, Harmondsworth, Pelican.

Galbraith, J. K. (1975), *Economics and the Public Purpose*, Harmondsworth, Pelican.

Geiger, T. and Geiger, F. (1975), *The Development Progress of Hong Kong and Singapore*, Hong Kong, Macmillan.

Gellner, E. (1964), *Thought and Change*, London, Weidenfeld & Nicolson.

Gellner, E. (1974), *Legitimation of Belief*, Cambridge University Press.

Gerth, H. H. and Mills, C. W. (eds) (1948), *From Max Weber*, London, Routledge & Kegan Paul.

Giddens, A. (1971), *Capitalism and Modern Social Theory*, Cambridge University Press.

Giddens, A. (1972a), *Emile Durkheim: Selected Writings in Social Theory*, Cambridge University Press.

Giddens, A. (1972b), *Politics and Sociology in the Thought of Max Weber*, London, Macmillan.

Giddens, A. (1976), *New Rules of Sociological Method*, London, Hutchinson.

Giddens, A. (1979), *Central Problems in Social Theory*, London, Macmillan.

Giddens, A. (1982), *Profiles and Critiques in Social Theory*, London, Macmillan.

Girling, J. L. S. (1981), *The Bureaucratic Polity in Modernizing Societies*, Institute of Southeast Asian Studies, Singapore.

Girvan, N. (1973), 'The Development of Dependency Economics in the Caribbean and Latin America: Review and Comparison'. *Social and Economic Studies*, vol. 22.

Goode, S. (1974), *Affluent Revolutionaries: A Portrait of the New Left*, New York, New Viewpoints.

Gook, Aik Suan (1981), 'Singapore: A Third World Fascist State', *Journal of Contemporary Asia*, vol. 11.

Gordon, A. (1979), 'Stages in the Development of Java's Socio-economic Formations 700–1979', *Journal of Contemporary Asia*, vol. 9.

Gordon, A. (1982), 'Indonesia, Plantations and the "Post Colonial" Mode of Production', *Journal of Contemporary Asia*, vol. 12.

Gott, R. (1983), 'Pinochet's Last Stand', *Guardian Weekly*.

Habermas, J. (1971a), *Knowledge and Human Interest*, Boston, Beacon Press.
Habermas, J. (1971b), *Towards a Rational Society*, London, Heinemann.
Habermas, J. (1974), *Theory and Practice*, London, Heinemann.
Hagen, E. (1962), *On the Theory of Social Change*, Homewood, Ill., Dorsey.
Halliday, J. (1980), 'Capitalism and Socialism in East Asia', *New Left Review*, no. 124.
Halim, F. (1982), 'Capital, Labour and the State: The West Malaysian Case' *Journal of Contemporary Asia*, vol. 12.
Hamilton, C. (1983), 'Capitalist Industrialization in East Asia's Four Little Tigers', *Journal of Contemporary Asia*, vol. 13.
Harris, Seymour (1948), *The European Recovery Programme*, London, Harper & Row.
Harrison, Anthony (1967), *The Framework of Economic Activity*, London, Macmillan.
Harrod, R. (1939), 'An Essay in Dynamic Theory', *Economic Journal.*
Hassan, R. (ed.) (1976), *Singapore: Society in Transition*, Kuala Lumpur, Oxford University Press.
Hawthorn, G. (1976), *Enlightenment and Despair*, Cambridge University Press.
Hayek, F. (1944), *The Road to Serfdom*, London, Routledge & Kegan Paul.
Held, D. (1980), *Introduction to Critical Theory*, London, Hutchinson.
Herrera, A. O. *et al.* (1975), *Catastrophe or a New Society*, Ottawa, International Development Research Centre.
Heyzer, N. (1983), 'International Production and Social Change: An Analysis of the State, Employment and Trade Unions in Singapore', in Chen. P. (ed.), *Singapore: Development Policies and Trends*, Oxford University Press.
Higgins, B. (1968), *Economic Development*, 2nd edn, London, Constable.
Hilal, J. (1970), *Sociology and Underdevelopment*, mimeo, Durham University.
Hindess, B. (1977), *Philosophy and Methodology in the Social Sciences*, Hassocks, Harvester.
Hindess, B. (ed.) (1978), *Sociological Theories of the Economy*, London, Macmillan.
Hoogvelt, A. (1982), *The Third World in Global Development*, London, Macmillan.
Hoselitz, B. (ed.) (1960), *Theories of Economic Growth*, New York, Free Press.
Howard, M. C. and King, J. E. (1975), *The Political Economy of Marx*, Harlow, Longman.
Hughes, S. (1959), *Consciousness and Society*, London, MacGibbon & Kee.
Huntington, S. P. (1971), 'The Change to Change: Modernization, Development, and Politics', in Black, C. E. (ed.) (1976), *Comparative Modernization*, London, Collier Macmillan.

Hurtado, M. E. (May 1983), 'Fiesta to Fiasco: Chile's Free Market Hangover', *South*.
Inglis, B. (1976), *The Opium War*, London, Hodder & Stoughton.
Jansen, K. (ed.) (1983), *Monetarism, Economic Crisis and the Third World*, London, Frank Cass.
Jeffrey, R. (ed.) (1981), *Asia: The Winning of Independence*, London, Macmillan.
Jones, H. (1975), *An Introduction to Modern Theories of Economic Growth*, London, Nelson.
Kay, G. (1975), *Development and Underdevelopment: A Marxist Analysis*, London, Macmillan.
Kerr, C. *et al.* (1960), *Industrialism and Industrial Man*, Harmondsworth, Penguin.
Kiernan, V. G. (1982), *European Empires from Conquest to Collapse 1815–1960*, London, Fontana.
Kitching, G. (1982), *Development and Underdevelopment in Historical Perspective*, London, Methuen.
Kolko, G. (1968), *The Politics of War: US Foreign Policy 1943–45*, New York, Vintage.
Kurihara, K. (1968), 'The Dynamic Impact of History on Keynesian Theory', in Eagly (ed.), *Events, Ideology and Economic Theory*, Wayne State University Press.
Laclau, E. (1971), 'Feudalism and Capitalism in Latin America', *New Left Review*, no. 67.
Lall, S. (1975), 'Is Dependence a Useful Concept in Analysing Underdevelopment?', *World Development*, vol. 3
Lamb, G. (1981), 'Rapid Capitalist Development Models: A New Politics of Dependence', in Seers (ed.), *Dependency Theory: A Critical Reassessment*, London, Frances Pinter.
Larrain, G. (1979), *The Concept of Ideology*, London, Hutchinson.
Laslett, P. and Runciman, W. G. (eds) (1967), *Philosophy Politics and Society*, 3rd series, Oxford, Blackwell.
Lehmann, D. (ed.) (1979), *Development Theory*, London, Frank Cass.
Lerner, D. (1958), *The Passing of Traditional Society*, New York, Free Press.
Lewis, W. A. (1955), *The Theory of Economic Growth*, London, Allen Unwin.
Leys, C. (1977), 'Underdevelopment and Dependency: Critical Notes', *Journal of Contemporary Asia*, vol. 7.
Lim, R. (1978), 'The Philippines and the Dependency Debate: A Preliminary Case Study', *Journal of Contemporary Asia*, vol. 8.
Limqueco, P. (1983), 'Contradictions of Development in ASEAN', *Journal of Contemporary Asia*, vol. 13.
Lin, Mah Hui (1980), 'Ethnic and Class Relations in Malaysia', *Journal of Contemporary Asia*, vol. 10.
Lin, Mah Hui and Canak, W. (1981), 'The Political Economy of State Policies in Malaysia', *Journal of Contemporary Asia*, vol. 11.
Lukes, S. (1973), *Emile Durkheim*, London, Macmillan.
McDonald, H. (1980), *Suharto's Indonesia*, London, Fontana.

Macpherson, C. B. (1966), *The Real World of Democracy*, Oxford University Press.
Macpherson, C. B. (1973), *Democratic Theory: Essays in Retrieval*, Oxford University Press.
Magee, B. (1973), *Popper*, London Fontana.
Marcuse, H. (1969), *An Essay on Liberation*, Harmondsworth, Penguin.
Martin, K. and Knapp, J. (eds) (1967), *The Teaching of Development Economics*, London, Frank Cass.
Marx, K. (1859), Preface to a Contribution to the Critique of Political Economy reprinted in K. Marx and F. Engels (1968). Selected Works, London *Lawrence* and Wishart.
Marx, K. (1957), *Economic and Philosophical Manuscripts*, trans. M. Milligan, Moscow.
Marx, K. (1973), *Grundrisse*, Harmondsworth, Pelican.
Marx, K. and Engels, F. (1968), *Selected Works*, London, Lawrence & Wishart.
Marx, K. and Engels, F. (–), *The Communist Manifesto*, Moscow, Progress.
May B. (1981), *The Third World Calamity*, London, Routledge & Kegan Paul.
McCarthy, T. (1978), *The Critical Theory of Jurgen Habermas*, London, MIT Press.
McClelland, D. C. (1961), *The Achieving Society*, New York Van Nostrand.
McKinney, J. and Tiryakian (eds) (1970), *Theoretical Sociology*, New York, Appleton-Century-Crofts.
Meek, R. L. (1956), *Studies in the Labour Theory of Value*, London.
Melotti, Umberto (1977), *Marx and the Third World*, London, Macmillan.
Merton, R. K. (1968), *Social Theory and Social Structure*, New York, Free Press.
Mikesell, R. F. (1968), *The Economics of Foreign Aid*, London, Weidenfeld & Nicolson.
Milliband, R. (1965), 'Marx and the State', in Milliband, R. and Saville, J. (eds), *The Socialist Register*, London, Merlin.
Milliband, R. (1977), *Marxism and Politics*, Oxford University Press.
Milliband, R. (1973). *The State in Capitalist Society*, London, Quartet.
Moore, B. (1966), *The Social Origins of Dictatorship and Democracy*, London, Allen Lane.
Moore, W. (1979), *World Modernization*, New York, Elsevier.
Myrdal, G. (1957), *Economic Theory and Underdeveloped Regions*, London, Duckworth.
Myrdal, G. (1958), *Value in Social Theory* (ed. Paul Streeten), London, Routledge & Kegan Paul.
Myrdal, G. (1970a), *Objectivity in Social Research*, London, Duckworth.
Myrdal, G. (1970b), *The Challenge of World Poverty*, London, Allen Lane.
Nagata, J. (1976), 'The Status of Ethnicity and the Ethnicity of Status', *International Journal of Comparative Sociology*, vol. 27.

Nagel, J. (ed.) (1969), *Student Power*, London, Merlin.
Naipaul, V. S. (1981), *Among the Believers: An Islamic Journey*, London, André Deutsch.
Nairn, T. (1979), 'Britain's Perennial Crisis', *New Left Review*, nos 113–14.
Napoleoni, C. (1972), *Economic Thought of the Twentieth Century*, London, Martin Robertson.
Nisbet, R. (1966), *The Sociological Tradition*, London, Heinemann.
O'Brien, D. C. (1972, 'Modernization, Order and the Erosion of the Democratic Ideal', *Journal of Development Studies*, vol. 8.
Orwell, G. (1945), *Animal Farm*, London, Secker & Warburg.
Oxaal, I., Barnett, T. and Booth, D. (eds) (1975) *Beyond the Sociology of Development*, London, Routledge & Kegan Paul.
Palma, G. (1978), 'Dependency: A Formal Analysis of Underdevelopment or a Methodology for the Analysis of Concrete Situations of Understand?', *World Development*, vol. 6.
Pandy, B. N. (1980), *South and South-East Asia 1945–1979: Problems and Policies*, London, Macmillan.
Pang, Keng Fong (1984), 'The Malay Royals of Singapore', unpublished dissertation, Department of Sociology, National University of Singapore.
Petras, J. (1982), 'The "Peripheral State": Continuity and Change in the International Division of Labour', *Journal of Contemporary Asia*, vol. 12.
Pollard, S. (1971), *The Idea of Progress*, Harmondsworth, Pelican.
Postan, M. M. (1967), *An Economic History of Western Europe 1945–1964*, London, Methuin.
Preston, P. W. (1981), *Theory and Practice in Development Studies: Neo-institutionalism in the Late 1950s and 1960s*, Leeds University, Occasional Papers in Sociology no. 11.
Preston, P. W. (1982), *Theories of Development*, London, Routledge & Kegan Paul.
Preston, P. W. 'The Common Sense of Development Studies: Elements of Reconsideration', mimeo.
Preston, P. W. (1985), *New Trends in Development Theory: Essays in Development and Social Theory*, London, Routledge & Kegan Paul.
Rey, P. P. (1971), *Colonialisme, neo-colonialisme et transition au capitalisme*, Paris, Maspero.
Rhodes, R. I., (1968), 'The Disguised Conservatism in Evolutionary Development Theory', *Science and Society*, vol. 32.
Rigg, F. (1966), *Thailand: The Modernization of a Bureaucratic Polity*, Honolulu, East-West Centre Press.
Robinson, J. (1962), *Economic Philosophy*, Harmondsworth, Pelican.
Rocher, G. (1974), *Talcott Parsons and American Sociology*, London, Nelson.
Rostow, W. W. (1956), 'The Take-off into Self-sustained Growth', *Economic Journal*,
Rostow, W. W. (1960), *The Stages of Economic Growth: A Non-communist Manifesto*, Cambridge University Press.

Roxborough, I. (1979), *Theories of Underdevelopment*, London, Macmillan.

Runciman, G. (1972), *Critique of Weber's Philosophy of Social Science*, Cambridge University Press.

Sachs, I. (1976), *The Discovery of the Third World*, London, MIT Press.

Sahay, A. (ed.) (1971), *Max Weber and Modern Sociology*, London, Routledge & Kegan Paul.

Scamell, W. M. (1980), *The International Economy since 1945*, London, Macmillan.

Scott, J. C. (1971), 'Protest and Profanation: Revolt and the Little Tradition, *Theory and Society*, vol. 4.

Seers, D. (ed.) (1981), *Dependency Theory: A Critical Reassessment*, London, Frances Pinter.

Shanin, T. (ed.) (1972), *The Rules of the Game: Cross Disciplinary Essays on Models in Scholarly Thought*, London, Tavistock.

Shaw, M. (1975), *Marxism and Social Science: The Roots of Social Knowledge*, London, Pluto Press.

Smelser, N. (1968) Essays in Sociological Explanation, Englewood Cliffs, NJ, Prentice-Hall.

Smith, A. D. (1973), *The Concept of Social Change*, London, Routledge & Kegan Paul.

Smith, A. D. (1976), *Social Change: Social Theory and Historical Process*, London, Routledge & Kegan Paul.

Smith, A. D. (1983), *State and Nation in the Third World*, Brighton, Wheatsheaf.

Solow, R. (1956), 'A Contribution to the Theory of Economic Growth', *Quarterly Journal of Economics*.

Statera, G. (1975), *Death of a Utopia*, Oxford University Press.

Streeten, P. (ed.) (1970), *Unfashionable Economics: Essays in Honour of Lord Balogh*, London, Weidenfeld & Nicolson.

Streeten, P. (1972), *The Frontiers of Development Studies*, London, Macmillan.

Streeten, P. (1981), *Development Perspectives*, London, Macmillan.

Sutcliffe, R. (1973), *Introduction to Baran*, Harmondsworth, Penguin.

Taylor, J. (1974), 'Neo-marxism and Underdevelopment: A Sociological Phantasy', *Journal of Contemporary Asia*, vol. 4.

Taylor, J. (1979), *From Modernization to Modes of Production*, London, Macmillan.

United Nations (1951), *Measures for the Economic Development of Underdeveloped Countries,* E/1986ST/ECA/10.

Van Nieuwenhuijze, C. A. O. (1982), *Development Begins at Home*, Oxford, Pergamon.

Vente, R. and Chen, P. (eds) (1980), *Culture and Industrialization: An Asian Dilemma*, Singapore, McGraw Hill.

Warren, B. (1973), 'Imperialism and Capitalist Industrialization', *New Left Review*, no. 81.

Warren, B. (1980), *Imperialism: Pioneer of Capitalism*, London, New Left Books.

Weber, M. (1958), *The Protestant Ethic and the Spirit of Capitalism*, New York.
Weber, M. (1968), *Economy and Society*, New York.
White, J. (1973), *The Politics of Foreign Aid*, London, Bodley Head.
Williams, R. (1973), 'Base and Superstructure in Marxist Cultural Theory', *New Left Review*, no. 82.
Wolfe, A. (1981), 'Sociology, Liberalism and the Radical Right', *New Left Review*, no. 128.
Wolfers, E. P. (1976), *Australia's Northern Neighbours*, The Australian Institute of International Affairs and Hawaii University Press.
Wong, J. (1979), *ASEAN Economies in Perspective*, London, Macmillan.
Worsley, P. (1964), *The Third World*, London, Weidenfeld & Nicolson.
Worsley, P. (1969), 'Revolutionary Theories', *Monthly Review Press*.
Worsley, P. (1982), *Marx and Marxism*, London, Tavistock.
Worsley, P. (1984), *The Three Worlds: Culture and World Development*, London, Weidenfeld & Nicolson.
Zeitlin, Irvine (1968) *Ideology and the Development of Sociological Theory*, Englewood, NJ, Prentice Hall, Cliffs.
Zeylstra, G. (1977), *Aid or Development?*, Leyden, A. W. Sijthoff.

Index